INTRODUCTION

Collecting coins of the world has become more and more popular in recent years. This low-priced volume has served as a convenient reference book through several editions, each of which had included new issues, revisions, corrections and revaluations. The thickness of the book is, we believe, at a maximum. If pages were to be added, the book would become unwieldy and higher priced. A few years ago it was decided to close the book to new type coins issued after approximately 1950 and confine changes in this and succeeding editions to valuations, corrections and refinements.

Another catalog, CURRENT COINS OF THE WORLD, now serves as a reference for coins presently in circulation, to which new issues and new countries are added as they are introduced. Our starting point for this companion catalog is approximately 1950. Existing catalog numbers assigned to coins in this, the original Catalog of Modern World Coins, are duplicated for the overlapping period in the newer catalog. Thus the continuity has been preserved and the books become useful references separately or together.

Although this book has been designed with the American collector in mind, it is hoped that it will prove a world coin book in readership as well as content.

Just a word to the beginner. Perhaps you are consulting this book upon the suggestion of a friend. You may recently have happened upon a small hoard of foreign coins in an attic hideaway. Someone in your family may have returned from overseas service in World War I or II or from a peacetime tour in foreign lands with a pocketful of strange coins. Confronted with this assortment of unfamiliar coins you naturally wonder about the country of their origin and their worth. If there are no gold pieces included, it is doubtful if the coins so discovered are worth enough premium to repay you for the time and effort to sell them. Coin values are generally determined by the condition of the coins, and rarity. With this realization, why not "look them up" elsewhere in this book. Look upon this fact as a sort of challenge, or opportunity to learn about the countries of their origin, the denominations, relative monetary values and other facts of history, government, rulers and geography which they represent. The chances are that you will consider the possibility of starting your own personal coin collection. If you do, you can be assured of a rewarding experience, which may last your lifetime.

Perhaps you are a collector who may have reached a point of waning interest in your present specialty, such as some United States coin series. Bring out those miscellaneous foreign pieces you have put aside from time to time and start a new collection consisting of one or more foreign countries. There are literally thousands of coins of other nations obtainable at little cost— and the whole wide world to choose from.

Possibly one or more of the following series will be of interest to the reader of this book:

Gold coins of the world.
Crowns (dollar size) coins of the world.
Type coins of the world.
Commemorative coins of the world.
One coin of each country of the world.
All types of coins of one country (or of several countries).

Other series may be devised by the collector to suit his own desire.

In any event we hope this volume will make your coin collecting experience more enjoyable.

R. S. Yeoman

PURPOSE

It should be obvious that a single volume such as this covering coins of the world cannot include illustrations of every coin listed. Common coins receive preference in order to accommodate the greatest number of collectors. Scarcer coins are pictured wherever possible. In some countries, particularly in the Orient, only a part of their coinage is represented. With few exceptions medals, bullion coins, patterns and tokens are excluded. There are varieties of coins in many countries too numerous to list. Only the major or popular varieties find space in this crowded volume.

This is essentially an introductory coin book. It is intended as an outline or framework for organizing a collection of world coins. As such it has usefulness for even the advanced collector, as a handy reference to supplement certain specialized books. Such books are fully illustrated and list all mints, all dates, all varieties and their values. The cover jacket of this book lists several specialized works published by Whitman. There are others available, many in English, others in German, French, Spanish, Italian, and so forth. The list of English language reference books, country by country, will gradually increase, and Whitman plans to eventually publish a specialized catalog for each coin-issuing country.

INFORMATION

Arrangement

A simple alphabetical sequence is employed for finding each country in this book, regardless of geographical location or government affiliation. This arrangement was decided upon to reduce the use of the index.

Illustrations in every instance are adjacent to corresponding listings and descriptions for easy identification.

Historical and geographical data and monetary equivalents are placed at the beginning of each country group.

In conformity with other Whitman coin books, minor coinage is listed first in each period or type group, followed by more precious metals, silver and gold.

The abbreviation "Br." is for "Bronze," always. "Brass" is not abbreviated, but always spelled out.

Scope

Approximately a century — from mid-nineteenth century to about 1960 — of coinage of the world is the scope of this book. A logical starting date for each country has been selected. For example, the Great Britain section commences with the beginning of Queen Victoria's reign in 1837, while the coins of Brazil start in 1889 when the republic was established.

Listings of Dates

The first and last known dates of issue of each type are shown (viz. 1898-1911). Coinage during intervening years may not necessarily be continuous. Dates shown are those actually appearing on the coins. For some countries they do not always conform to the year of production. See details of unusual dating systems on pages 6-7.

Valuations

A price is given opposite each catalog number, and in each instance the price refers to the commonest date and mint mark if coined in several years or at several mints. The omission of a price often denotes rarity and no recent sale record, but may also indicate lack of information about a newly-discovered type or variety. As in other Whitman coin reference books, values are approximate and intended only as a guide. Latest prices may be obtained from established coin dealers.

The opinions of many dealers and collectors are combined to arrive at each value. Inasmuch as neither the editor nor the publishers engage in selling coins, the values shown are not offers to buy or sell but are included only as general information.

Unless otherwise stated, the values shown are for conditions as follows:

Fine — Before 1920 approximately, except gold.
Very Fine (V. Fine) — 1920 to 1953 approximately, and earlier gold.
Uncirculated (Unc.) — 1953 and later.

Numbering System

When a coin type is inserted in a previously established sequence, capital letters A, B, etc. are placed before a catalog number to avoid the necessity of renumbering all later issues. A small letter a, b, etc. following a catalog number indicates a minor difference of a re-issued type, such as a change of metal or size only.

There are instances throughout this catalog where numbers and their corresponding listings have been removed. Reasons are numerous but the most likely causes are: combining with earlier types which are identical except for date, coins discovered to be patterns, medals or otherwise unauthorized for circulation as money. We regret that since earlier editions, occasional renumbering or rearranging has been necessary. This is done only to make the continuity more natural and useful, and is kept to a minimum. In cases of complete country renumbering, the old number is included in parentheses.

A star preceding a listing indicates that it is the coin illustrated at the top of the group.

HOW TO DETERMINE THE ORIGIN OF A COIN

First of all, a magnifying glass will prove useful in reading the legends, symbols, dates and other interesting details on your coin specimens.

Sort your coins as best you can, grouping them by countries, or at least by similar types for later checking. Start with the easy ones, which will probably be coins using our own familiar "English" alphabet, with portraits of monarchs familiar to you and languages which you may recognize immediately, such as German, French, Italian. etc. Country names are often similar to the Anglicized spelling such as NEDERLAND for NETHERLANDS, LIBAN for LEBANON, etc. Bear in mind, however, that there are many colonial issues. Thus, a coin with French legends could be issued for such faraway places as French Indo-China (Indo-Chine Française) French West Africa (Afrique Occidentale Française), etc.

Many countries, especially in Asia, have alphabets strange to us. Until characteristics of such coins become familiar to the collector, it is best to page through this volume until you locate illustrations which are similar to the coin. Far from being an arduous task, this phase can be intriguing to a reader with the true collector instinct. If the coin was struck during the past 100 years, the chances are it can be located in this book.

The denomination shown on the coin often is a short cut to identification. SHILLING, CENTAVO, FRANC, etc. are more or less familiar to us and it would be natural to conclude that they belong respectively to Great Britain, Mexico and France. The table of denominations, however, might reveal that this is not necessarily so. A more careful inspection of the coins may show that the **SHILLING** actually was struck for Southern Rhodesia, the **CENTAVO** for St. Thomas and Prince Islands and the **FRANC** for Guadeloupe, where the same coin denominations are or have been used. That is the romance of collecting foreign coins. The quest is the thing.

Millimeter Scale

ERAS AND DATING SYSTEMS

Most countries show the date more or less prominently on their coins. Little difficulty will be encountered with the coins of Europe, parts of Africa and the Americas. In the Arabic countries and countries of the Near East and the Orient, however, strange symbols and letters pose a difficult problem of translation both of legends and dates. The chart below shows some of the date numerals now in use throughout the world, while other less common systems are shown with their respective countries.

NUMERALS

WESTERN	1	2	3	4	5	6	7	8	9	0	10	100	1000
ARABIC	١	٢	٣	٤	٥	٦	٧	٨	٩	٠	١٠	١٠٠	١٠٠٠
ARABIC VARIANTS (Persia, etc.)	١	٢	٣	۴	۵	۶	٧	٨	٩	٠			
CHINESE, JAPANESE, KOREAN (Ordinary)	一	二	三	四	五	六	七	八	九		十	百	千
CHINESE, JAPANESE, KOREAN (Official)	壹	貳	叁	肆	伍	陸	柒	捌	玖		拾	(半=½)	
DEVANAGARI (India, Nepal)	९	२	३	४	५	६	७	८	९	०			

Many countries using Arabic numerals observe the Mohammedan Era, also known as the Era of the Hegira (AH or SH), dating from Mohammed's flight from Mecca to Medina in AD 622. This era has traditionally been based on a lunar year of 354 days, or about 3% fewer days than the 365 in our Gregorian (AD) solar year. Mohammedan lunar dates are indicated by the letters AH in this volume. The following method may be used for an approximate conversion of AH to AD dates:

> *Example:* To convert AH 1330 into AD date.
> 3% of 1330 = 39.90 (closest whole number is 40)
> 1330 − 40 = 1290
> 1290 + 622 = 1912 AD

A few countries such as Afghanistan and Iran have adopted a modification of the Mohammedan calendar based on a solar year of normal length. Such dates are indicated by the letters SH, and the corresponding AD year is found by simply adding 621.

The coins of Siam use the dating systems of three eras:
1. The "Buddhist" era (abbreviated as B.E.) which dates from 543 B.C.; *subtract* 543 for AD dates. Four numerals are found on current issues.
2. The "Bangkok" or Ratanakosind-sok era (abbreviated as R.S.) which dates from 1782; *add* 1781 to convert to an AD date. Dates will have three numerals.
3. The "Little" or Chula-Sakarat era (abbreviated as C.S.) which dates from AD 638; *add* 638 to convert to AD dates. Dates will have four numerals. Example: AD 1910 would be respectively B.E. 2453, R.S. 129 and C.S. 1271.

Several different eras were observed on the coinage of the INDIA NATIVE STATES.

The VIKRAMA Era has its initial point in 57 B.C. and is observed mainly in Northern India. This is also known as the SAMVAT ERA. Their year 1957 is our 1900 AD.

The SAKA ERA originated in the Southwest corner of Northern India, is the dominant era and the great historical reckoning of Southern India. It dates from AD 78 but is based on elapsed years, so that AD equivalents are found by adding 78. Thus, Saka 1822 began in AD 1900.

CHINESE dates are correctly read from right to left. Coins of the Republic, when dated, start with the year 1912 AD. Unlike our own system, coins of the Chinese Empire are dated according to a 60-year (sexagenary) cycle. For the purpose of this book dates have been translated to the AD Era and placed in parentheses.

Coins with NO DATE are indicated by the abbreviation ND, followed by the date of striking in parentheses when known.

AFGHANISTAN

Afghanistan is a mountainous inland country in southwest Asia surrounded by the U.S.S.R., Iran, Pakistan and China. An independent kingdom from 1747 to 1973, it was then proclaimed a republic. Principal exports are hides and agricultural products. Area: 250,000 square miles. Official languages: Persian, Pushtu. Capital: *Kabul.*

The traditional reverse design is the national emblem, a mosque with pulpit, generally over crossed arms. Inscriptions have been mostly in Persian; Pushtu was introduced in 1929 and used exclusively after 1950. Islamic era lunar dating (AH) was used until AH 1337 (1919) and during the period AH 1347-50 (1929-31). In 1919 the solar calendar (SH) was introduced, which was about 40 years earlier than the AH calendar at that time. To obtain AD dates from AH and SH dates, see introduction.

Before AD 1926, 10 Dinar = 1 Paisa; 60 Paisa = 12 Shahi = 6 Sanar = 3 Abbasi = 2 Qiran = 1 Kabuli Rupee. From 1926, with the introduction of a decimal system, 100 Pul = 1 Afghani; 20 Afghani = 1 Amani.

AMIR ABDUR RAHMAN
AH 1297-1319 (1880-1901)

For crude "dump" issues of this reign, which preceded the machine-struck types, see *Craig.*

Note: Because of extensive catalog revisions, new numbers were assigned in the 8th edition.

		Fine
★5	1 Paisa no wreaths 1317 (20mm)	3.00
6	1 Paisa 1317, obv. of No. 5, rev. of No. 2	7.50

Silver

All silver of this reign has a toughra in wreath on the obverse and a mosque in wreath on the reverse, but there are many minor varieties of inscriptions, ornamentation such as stars and weapons, and location of date.

Copper or Brass

		Fine
1	1 Paisa AH 1309 (1891) 24mm	25.00
★2	1 Paisa 1309-17 (20-21mm)	3.50
3	1 Shahi 1309 (31mm)	12.50
4	100 Dinar 1311 (41mm)	100.00

7	100 Dinar 1315 (13mm) 2 vars	7.50
8	1 Abbasi 1313-14 (15-16mm)	4.50
9	½ Rupee 1308-19 (18-20mm)	4.50
★10	1 Rupee 1308-19 (23-26mm)	4.50
11	5 Rupee 1314 (39mm, thick)	25.00

AFGHANISTAN

Fine

16	1 Qiran 1320-21, 25 (19mm)	7.50
★17	1 Rupee 1319-21, 25 (25mm)	4.50
18	5 Rupee 1319 (46mm)	50.00

Gold

V. Fine

19 1 Tilla 1319-20 (21mm)...100.00

Fine

12 5 Rupee 1316 (45mm, thin)..........24.00

Gold

★13 1 Tilla 1313-16 *V. Fine* (19-21mm)..........100.00

14 2 Tilla 1309 (21mm, 9.1 gm).......200.00

Second Coinage

Brass

Design similar to No. 2.

Fine

20 1 Paisa AH 1329 (1911) 20mm...................7.50

Silver

Obv: Inscription in wreath
Rev: Mosque in wreath

21	1 Sanar 1325-29 (13mm)	6.00
22	1 Abbasi 1324-29 (17mm)	7.50
23	1 Qiran 1323-29 (19mm)	4.50
★24	1 Rupee 1321-29 (25mm)	5.00

AMIR HABIBULLAH
AH 1319-1337 (1901-1919)

First Coinage

Designs similar to Nos. 8-10, 12-13.
Obv: Toughra in wreath
Rev: Mosque in wreath

Silver

15 1 Abbasi AH 1320 *Fine* (1902) 16mm..........15.00

AFGHANISTAN

<table>
<tr><td></td><td></td><td>Fine</td></tr>
</table>

*29 1 Qiran 1329-37 (20mm). . .3.00
30 1 Rupee 1329-37 (25mm). . .4.50

Gold
V. Fine

31 1 Tilla 1336-37 (21mm). .125.00

AMIR AMANULLAH

AH 1337, SH 1298-1307
(1919-1929)

Fine

25 5 Rupee 1322-29 (45mm). . .22.50

Third Coinage
Copper or Brass

Obv: Inscription
Rev: Mosque in sunburst

26 1 Paisa AH 1329-37
(1911-19) 19-22mm 2.50

Silver

27 1 Sanar 1329-37 (13mm) 5.00

Obv: Inscription in wreath
Rev: Mosque in sunburst in wreath

28 1 Abbasi 1330-37 (17mm) . . .5.50

First Coinage

Copper or Brass

Obv: Inscription in wreath
Rev: Mosque in sunburst

Fine

32 1 Paisa AH 1337, SH 1298
(1919) 20mm 3.00

Obv: Inscription in stars
Rev: Mosque in sunburst in stars

33 1 Paisa SH 1299-1303
(20mm) 2.50
*34 1 Shahi AH 1337 (25mm) . .6.50
35 1 Sanar AH 1337
(29-30mm) 6.50
36 3 Shahi AH 1337, SH 1298-
1300 (33mm) 3.00

AFGHANISTAN

Billon

V. Fine

★37 1 Abbasi SH 1298
(20mm) 30.00
38 1 Abbasi SH 1299
(25mm) 20.00

Designs similar to Nos. 29-31.

Silver

★39 ½ Rupee AH 1337, SH 1298-
1300 (20mm) 2.50
40 1 Rupee AH 1337, SH 1298-
99 (25mm) 5.00

Gold

★41 1 Tilla AH 1337 (21mm) . . 75.00
42 2 Tilla SH 1298 (23mm) . 100.00

Second Coinage

Obv: Toughra in stars
Rev: Mosque in sunburst in stars

Copper

Fine

43 3 Shahi SH 1300-01
(33mm) 3.00

Copper or Billon

V. Fine

44 1 Abbasi 1299-1303
(25mm) 2.50

Obv: Toughra in wreath
Rev: Mosque in sunburst in wreath

Silver

45 ½ Rupee SH 1300-03
(20mm) 2.00
★46 1 Rupee 1299-1303
(27mm) 3.50
47 2½ Rupee 1298-1303
(34mm) 15.00

AFGHANISTAN

Gold

48 ½ Amani SH 1299 *V. Fine*
(16mm)..............45.00
49 1 Amani 1299 (22mm)...75.00
★50 2 Amani 1299-1303
(24mm).............125.00
51 5 Amani 1299 (34mm)..350.00

Decimal System 1926-
100 Pul = 1 Afghani

Third Coinage

Copper

52 2 Pul SH 1304-05 *Fine*
(1926-27) 18mm........1.50
53 5 Pul 1304-05 (22mm)....2.50
★54 10 Pul 1304-06 (24mm)....3.00

Silver

55 20 Pul 1304 (19mm)......50.00

56 ½ Afghani 1304-07 *V. Fine*
(25mm)..............2.50
★57 1 Afghani 1304-07
(29mm).............3.00
58 2½ Afghani 1305-06
(38mm)............22.50

Gold

59 ½ Amani 1304-06
(18mm)............45.00
★60 1 Amani 1304-06
(23mm).............75.00
61 2½ Amani 1306 (29mm).250.00

HABIBULLAH GHAZI
(BACHA-I-SAQAO)
AH 1347-1348 (1929)
Lunar Dating Resumed

First Coinage
Horizontal Legend

Copper or Brass

62 20 Paisa AH 1347 (1929)
25mm.................5.00

AFGHANISTAN

Silver

V. Fine

63 1 Qiran 1347 (21mm).....8.50
★64 1 Rupee 1347 (25mm)....15.00

Gold

65 1 Habibi 1347 (21mm)....175.00

Second Coinage
Circular Legend

Copper

66 10 Paisa 1348 (22mm).....17.50

Silver

67 1 Qiran 1348 (21mm).....17.50

V. Fine
★68 1 Rupee 1347 (26mm)....30.00

MUHAMMAD NADIR SHAH
AH 1348-50, SH 1310-12
(1929-33)

First Coinage—Lunar Dating
Copper or Brass

Fine
69 1 Pul AH 1349 (1930)
(15mm)................2.00

70 2 Pul 1348 (18mm).......1.25
71 5 Pul 1349-50 (22mm)....4.00
72 10 Pul 1348-49 (25mm)....2.50
★73 20 Pul 1348-49 (25mm)....2.75
74 25 Pul 1349 (25mm).......2.50

Silver

V. Fine
★75 ½ Afghani 1348-50
(24mm)................2.50
76 1 Afghani 1348-50
(30mm)................4.00

AFGHANISTAN

Gold

V. Fine

78 20 Afghani 1349-50
(22mm) 150.00

MUHAMMAD ZAHIR SHAH
SH 1312-1352 (1933-1973)

First Coinage
(Also see Nos. 80-82 above.)

Second Coinage
Solar Dating Resumed

Copper or Brass

V. Fine

85 25 Pul SH 1312-16
(1933-37) 24-25mm 2.50

Brass

80 2 Pul SH 1311-14
(1932-35) 18mm 2.00
81 5 Pul 1311-14 (21mm) 2.50
*82 10 Pul 1311-14 (23mm) 2.50

Nos. 80-82 do not bear the name of the
ruler and were continued into the reign of
Muhammad Zahir.

Silver

86 ½ Afghani 1312-16
(24mm) 2.00

Silver

*83 ½ Afghani 1310-12
(24mm) 2.50
84 1 Afghani 1310 (27mm) . . 50.00

Gold

87 1 Tilla 1313 (6 gm,
22mm) 150.00

88 1 Tilla "4 Grams"
1315, 17 (19mm) 100.00
*89 2 Tilla "8 Grams"
1314-15 (22mm) 175.00

AFGHANISTAN

Second Coinage
Bronze

90 2 Pul SH 1316 (1937) *V. Fine*
  15mm.................... .35
91 3 Pul 1316 (16mm)........ .35
★92 5 Pul 1316 (17mm)........ .35

Copper-Nickel

93 10 Pul 1316 (18mm)........ .50

94 25 Pul 1316 (20mm)........ .75

Later Issues
Bronze

95 25 Pul SH 1330-32   *Unc.*
  (1951-53) 20mm.......... .75

96 50 Pul 1330 (22mm)....... 1.00

Nickel-Clad Steel
Unc.
95a 25 Pul 1331-34 edge
  plain or reeded......... .50
96a 50 Pul 1331-34............ .75

97 50 Pul 1331.............. 1.50

Aluminum

★98 2 Afghani 1337 (1958)..... 2.25
99 5 Afghani 1337........... 3.25

Nickel-Clad Steel

100 1 Afghani 1340 (1961)..... .35

101 2 Afghani 1340............ .50
102 5 Afghani (portrait)
  SH 1340/AH 1381...... 1.00

ALBANIA (Shqipni, Shqipëri)

The smallest of the Balkan states, Albania lies between Greece and Yugoslavia on the Adriatic coast. It declared independence from the Ottoman Empire in 1912, but underwent many political changes before coming under communist control in 1944. Mountainous terrain has hindered both agriculture and industry, making it Europe's poorest nation. Area: 11,097 square miles. Language: Albanian. Capital: *Tiranë*.

100 Qindar Leku = 1 Lek   100 Qindar Ari = 1 Franka Ari = 5 Lek

REPUBLIC 1912-1928

Bronze

V. Fine
1 5 Qindar Leku 1926.......12.50

2 10 Qindar Leku 1926.......17.50

Note: Because of catalog revisions, new numbers from 3 to 17 were assigned in the 9th edition.

Nickel

3 ¼ Leku 1926-27...........4.00

4 ½ Lek 1926...............4.00

V. Fine
5 1 Lek 1926-31..............3.50

Silver

Ex. Fine
6 1 Franka Ari 1927-28.......85.00

7 2 Franka Ari 1926-28......115.00

Obv: President Amet Zogu
8 5 Franka Ari 1925-27......250.00

ALBANIA

Gold

Obv: President Zogu
Rev: Eagle

		Ex. Fine
9	10 Franka Ari 1927	125.00
10	20 Franka Ari 1926-27	150.00

11	100 Franka Ari 1926	300.00
11a	100 Franka Ari 1927, modified rev. die	300.00

Skanderbeg

12	20 Franka Ari 1926-27	160.00

KINGDOM 1928-1939
Amet Zogu as King ZOG I
First Coinage

Nickel

		V. Fine
13	½ Lek 1930-31	3.50

No. 5 was also struck during this period.

Second Coinage
Bronze

		Ex. Fine
14	1 Qindar Ar. 1935	5.00
15	2 Qindar Ar. 1935	5.00

Silver

16	1 Franka Ari 1935-37	7.50
17	2 Franka Ari 1935	20.00

25th Anniversary of Independence
Dated 28 XI (Nov. 28) 1912-1937

Silver

★18	1 Franka Ari 1937	20.00
19	2 Franka Ari 1937	30.00

Gold

20	20 Franka Ari 1937	100.00
21	100 Franka Ari 1937	450.00

Marriage of King Zog
Dated 27 IV (April 27) 1938

Gold

22	20 Franka Ari 1938	100.00
23	100 Franka Ari 1938	300.00

ALBANIA

10th Anniversary of Reign

Dated 1 IX (Sept. 1) 1928-1938

Gold

Ex. Fine

24 20 Franka Ari 1938......100.00
25 50 Franka Ari 1938......200.00
26 100 Franka Ari 1938......375.00

VITTORIO EMANUELE III as King of Albania 1939-43

1 Lek = 1 Lira

Aluminum-Bronze

V. Fine

27 0.05 Lek 1940-41...........2.00

28 0.10 Lek 1940-41...........2.50

Stainless Steel

Two different alloys were used for Nos. 29-32: non-magnetic in 1939 and part of 1940, and magnetic in the balance of 1940 through 1941.

V. Fine

29 0.20 Lek 1939-41...........1.50

30 0.50 Lek 1939-41...........1.75
31 1 Lek 1939-41
(Head right)...........2.00
32 2 Lek 1939-41
(Head left)...........3.00

Dates after 1939 of Nos. 31-32 not for circulation.

Silver

33 5 Lek 1939...............9.00
34 10 Lek 1939 (Head right)..35.00

PEOPLE'S REPUBLIC 1946-

Zinc

Ex. Fine

35 ½ Leku 1947-57...........85
36 1 Lek 1947-57...........1.00
37 2 Lekë 1947-57...........1.40
38 5 Lekë 1947-57...........2.00

Later issues in *Current Coins of the World.*

ALGERIA (Algérie)

An Islamic state on the Mediterranean coast of north Africa, Algeria was nominally part of the Ottoman Empire until being colonized by France in the 19th century. It became an independent republic in 1962. Although much of the country is desert, it has petroleum and other minerals, while the coastal plain is highly agricultural. Area: 919,951 square miles. Languages: Arabic, French, Berber dialects. Capital: *Algiers*.

100 Centimes = 1 Franc

France No. 89 (2 Francs 1944) was also issued in Algeria during World War II.

Postwar Issues

Copper-Nickel

			V. Fine
1	20 Francs 1949-56	..	1.25
2	50 Francs 1949-50	..	1.75
3	100 Francs 1950-53	..	2.25

Later issues in *Current Coins of the World.*

ANGOLA

A large territory on the west coast of Africa, Angola has been under Portuguese control since the 1500's. Having important mineral resources, it exports coffee, petroleum, diamonds and iron ore. Area: 481,351 square miles. Languages: Portuguese, many native tongues. Capital: *Luanda*.

5 Centavos = 1 Macuta   100 Centavos = 1 Escudo

Bronze	**Copper-Nickel**

		V. Fine
12	1 Centavo 1921	15.00
13	2 Centavos 1921	20.00
14	5 Centavos 1921-24	10.00

		V. Fine
15	10 Centavos 1921-23	5.00
16	20 Centavos 1921-22	7.50

Nickel

★17	50 Centavos 1922-23	6.50

ANGOLA

Nickel-Bronze

		V. Fine
18	5 Centavos 1927	2.00
19	10 Centavos 1927-28	3.00
*20	20 Centavos 1927-28	3.00
21	50 Centavos 1927-28	6.00

New Coinage System
Bronze

		Unc.
22	10 Centavos 1948-49	.50
23	20 Centavos 1948-49	.60

24	50 Centavos Nic.-Br.
	1948-50 .... 1.50

Decree of Jan. 21, 1952
COLONIA DE Omitted
Bronze

		Unc.
23a	20 Centavos 1962	.25
25	50 Centavos 1953-61	.35
26	1 Escudo 1953-72	.65

27	2½ Escudos Cop-Nic.	
	1953-69	.75

Silver

28	10 Escudos 1952-55	2.50
29	20 Escudos 1952-55	5.00

Later issues in Current Coins of the World.

ANNAM

Now part of South Viet Nam, formerly one of the states of French Indo-China; located along the coast of the South China Sea. Produces spices, silk, rice, rubber and minerals. Language: Khmer. Capital: *Hue*. Coinage obsolete.

THAN THOI 1889-1907
Cast Coins

		Fine
1	1 Sapeque Brass (Rev. Blank)	3.50
2	10 Sapeque Copper or Brass (Rev. Two Characters)	1.00

ANNAM

DUY TAN 1907-1916

Fine

3 10 Sapeque Brass (Rev. Two
Characters).............. 2.00

KHAI DINH 1916-1926

Copper Alloy

4 1 Sapeque (Cast)...........4.00
★5 1 Sapeque (Struck).........1.00

BAO DAI 1926-45

Brass

6 1 Sapeque (Rev. Blank)   *Fine*
Small Planchet...........4.00

6a 1 Sapeque (Rev. Blank)
Large Planchet...........2.00

7 10 Sapeque................4.00

ARABIAN SULTANATES

(Hadhramaut)

Small semi-independent sultanates under British control in the former East
Aden Protectorate, now part of the Southern Yemen Republic. At one time
these sultanates were sovereign states, extending along the lower coast of
the Arabian Peninsula and into the "Empty Quarter." Languages: Arabic
and English.

QUAITI STATE

Coinage obsolete.

Sultan Monasar Bin Abdullah

Coinage of East Africa, British East India Company, and Maria Theresa
Talers counterstamped in Arabic, both copper and silver (dated 1307).

ARABIAN SULTANATES

c/s = Counterstamp

Copper

Fine

1 ¼ Anna size, small c/s......10.00

2a ½ Anna size, small c/s....15.00
★2 ½ Anna size, large c/s....15.00

Silver

3 ½ Rupee size, small c/s.....22.50
4 ½ Rupee size, large c/s.....35.00
5 1 Rupee size, small c/s.....30.00
6 1 Rupee size, large c/s.....35.00
7 1 Ryal (Crown) small c/s..45.00
7a 1 Ryal, large c/s..........50.00

Sultan Nawaz Bin Omer

Copper

Fine

8 5 Chomsihs A.H. 1315 (1897).16.00

9 5 Chomsihs 1318 (1900).....17.50

SULTANATE OF MUKALLA
Sultan Al Nakib Salah

1 ½ Chomsihs A.H. 1276
   (1859)..................40.00
★2 1 Chomsihs 1276..........30.00

LAHEJ

Small semi-independent Sultanate just north of the city of Aden in the former West Aden Protectorate.

128 Pessa (Pice) = 1 Indian Rupee   Coinage obsolete.

Sultan Ali Mohasan 1849-1863
Copper

V. Fine

1 ½ Pessa ND (1860)........15.00

Sultan Fazal Bin Ali 1874-1898

Fine

2 ½ Pessa ND (1896).......17.50
Date AH 1291 (1874) on coin is accession date.

ARGENTINA

Republic occupying the major portion of southern South America. World's largest exporter of meats and linseed, and ranks high in the production of corn, wool, wheat, hides and skins, most of which are raised on the rich grasslands of the pampas. Language: Spanish. Capital: *Buenos Aires.*

100 Centavos = 1 Peso   5 Pesos = 1 Argentino

Bronze

		Fine
1	1 Centavo 1882-96	.65
2	2 Centavos 1882-96	.75

Silver

		V. Fine
3	10 Centavos 1881-83	2.00
4	20 Centavos 1881-83	3.50
5	50 Centavos 1881-83	6.00
6	1 Peso 1881-83	60.00

Gold

10	½ Argentino 1884	325.00
11	1 Argentino 1881-96	100.00

Copper-Nickel

	V. Fine

7	5 Centavos 1896-1942	.15

		V. Fine
8	10 Centavos 1896-1942	.20
9	20 Centavos 1896-1942	.25
14	50 Centavos Nickel 1941	.50

Bronze

12	1 Centavo 1939-44	.15
13	2 Centavos 1939-47	.20

Copper, Crude

12a	1 Centavo 1945-48	.20
13a	2 Centavos 1947-50	.30

Aluminum-Bronze

15	5 Centavos 1942-50	.15
16	10 Centavos 1942-50	.20
17	20 Centavos 1942-50	.25

Centennial
Death of San Martín

Copper-Nickel

18	5 Centavos 1950	.50
19	10 Centavos 1950	.50
20	20 Centavos 1950	.75

ARGENTINA

Regular Issues

Reeded Edge, Copper-Nickel *V. Fine*
21   5 Centavos 1951-53........ .15
22 10 Centavos 1951-52........ .20
23 20 Centavos 1951-52........ .25

Smooth Edge, Copper-Nickel-Clad Steel
Unc.
21a   5 Centavos 1953-56...... .15
22a 10 Centavos 1952-56...... .20

Unc.
23a 20 Centavos 1952-56...... .25
24 50 Centavos 1952-56...... .60
NOTE: Smaller bust nos. 21a-23a, 1954 and later.

Nickel-Clad Steel

25   5 Centavos 1957-59........ .15
26 10 Centavos 1957-59........ .15
27 20 Centavos 1957-61........ .20
28 50 Centavos 1957-61........ .30
29   1 Peso 1957-62............ .40
Later issues in *Current Coins of the World.*

AUSTRALIA

Dominion of the British Commonwealth; exports wheat, wool, dairy products, meats and minerals; there is heavy industrial development, chiefly engaged in manufacturing for home consumption. Most of the population is concentrated in a few large cities, and much of the arid interior is uninhabited. Language: English. Federal capital: *Canberra.*

12 Pence = 1 Shilling
 2 Shillings = 1 Florin

5 Shillings = 1 Crown
20 Shillings = 1 Pound (Sovereign)

Gold
Australian mints at Melbourne, Perth and Sydney struck Sovereigns and Half Sovereigns starting 1871 until 1931 with mint marks M, P, S. The designs are standard British types.

VICTORIA 1837-1901

Young Head
Types of Great Britain Nos. 13-15
V. Fine
A1 ½ Sovereign 1871-87..... 45.00
 B1 1 Sovereign Rev. Shield
    1871-87.............. 75.00
 C1 1 Sovereign Rev. St. George
    1871-87.............. 65.00

Jubilee Head
Types of Great Britain Nos. 28-29
V. Fine
D1 ½ Sovereign 1887-93..... 35.00
E1 1 Sovereign 1887-93..... 65.00

Old Head
Types of Great Britain Nos. 42-43
F1 ½ Sovereign 1893-1901... 35.00
G1 1 Sovereign 1893-1901... 65.00

AUSTRALIA

EDWARD VII 1901-1910
Silver

		Fine
1	3 Pence 1910	3.50
2	6 Pence 1910	4.50
3	1 Shilling 1910	8.00
4	1 Florin (2 Shillings) 1910	16.00

Gold
Types of Great Britain Nos. 56-57
V. Fine

A5	½ Sovereign 1902-10	30.00
B5	1 Sovereign 1902-10	65.00

GEORGE V 1910-1936
Bronze

5	½ Penny 1911-36	.35
6	1 Penny 1911-36	.50

Silver

9	3 Pence 1911-36	.75
10	6 Pence 1911-36	1.25
11	1 Shilling 1911-36	2.00
12	1 Florin 1911-36	3.50

Gold
Types of Great Britain Nos. 77-78

A13	½ Sovereign 1911-16	30.00
B13	1 Sovereign 1911-31	65.00

COMMEMORATIVE ISSUES
Establishment of Parliament at Canberra
Silver

V. Fine

7	1 Florin 1927	3.00

Centennial of Victoria and Melbourne

Ex. Fine

8	1 Florin, "1934-35" on coin	60.00

GEORGE VI 1936-1952
Bronze

V. F.

13	½ Penny 1938-39	.50

14	½ Penny 1939-48	.20
15	1 Penny 1938-48	.25

AUSTRALIA

Silver

V. Fine

16 3 Pence 1938-48 25

17 6 Pence 1938-48 40

18 1 Shilling 1938-48 80

19 1 Florin 1938-47 . . . . 1.50

20 1 Crown 1937-38 . . . . 10.00

New Legend: without IND: IMP.

Bronze

V. Fine

21 ½ Penny 1949-52 20
22 1 Penny 1949-52 30

Silver

Fifty Year
Jubilee
Florin

23 1 Florin 1951 . . . . 3.00
The following have reverses similar
to Nos. 16-19.
24 3 Pence 1949-52 50
25 6 Pence 1950-52 60
26 1 Shilling 1950-52 . . . . 1.25
27 1 Florin 1951-52 . . . . 2.50

ELIZABETH II 1952-
Rev. designs like Nos. 14-19

	Bronze	*Unc.*
28	½ Penny 1953-55 . .	.75
29	1 Penny 1953	1.00

	Silver	*Ex. Fine*
30	3 Pence 1953-54 . .	1.25
31	6 Pence 1953-54 . . .	1.75
32	1 Shilling 1953-54 . .	2.25
33	1 Florin 1953-54 . . .	3.50

AUSTRALIA

Royal Visit Commemorative

34 1 Florin 1954 . . . . 2.25 *Ex. Fine*

New Legend: letters F:D
added starting 1955

Bronze

		Unc.
35	½ Penny 1959-64	.15
36	1 Penny 1955-64	.20

Silver

37	3 Pence 1955-64	.25
38	6 Pence 1955-63	.40
39	1 Shilling 1955-63	.65
40	1 Florin 1956-63	1.50

Later issues in Current Coins of the World.

AUSTRIA
(Oesterreich)

A republic in central Europe, Austria is noted for both industrial and agricultural production. Tourism is an important industry. Chief exports include metals and metal products, chemicals, textiles, paper, and machinery. Population: 7,500,000. Language: German. Capital: *Vienna.*

100 Kreuzer = 1 Florin (Gulden) 1857-92
1½ Florin = 1 Vereinsthaler
100 Heller = 1 Krone 1892-1923

10,000 Kronen = 1 Schilling 1923-24
100 Groschen = 1 Schilling 1924-

EMPIRE
FRANZ JOSEPH I
1848-1916

I. Vereinsmünzen (1857-68)

"Convention Money" struck for circulation throughout the Austrian and German states observing the monetary agreement of 1857.

Regular Issues

First obv: portrait with light sideburns

Silver

		V. Fine
⋆1	1 Vereinsthaler 1857-65	20.00
2	2 Vereinsthaler 1865	400.00

AUSTRIA

Gold

		V. Fine
4	½ Krone 1858-65	160.00
★5	1 Krone 1858-65	275.00

Second obv: portrait with heavier beard

Silver

1a	1 Vereinsthaler 1866-68	40.00
2a	2 Vereinsthaler 1866-67	300.00

Gold

4a	½ Krone 1866	450.00
5a	1 Krone 1866	650.00

Commemorative Issues

Silver

Opening of Vienna-Trieste Railway

		Ex. Fine
3	2 Vereinsthaler 1857	1200.00

3rd German Shooting Fest

		Ex. Fine
A16	1 Thaler 1868	100.00

Opening of Mt. Raxalpe Inn

A20	1 Thaler 1877	——

No. A20 was issued strictly for presentation, and was struck long after the formal end of the Vereinsthaler system.

II. Landesmünzen (1857-92)

Subsidiary coinage for circulation within the Austro-Hungarian Empire alone. Note that after 1868 Hungary had a separate coinage, but that the money of the two countries continued interchangeable.

Regular Issues
Copper

		Fine
6	⁵⁄₁₀ Kreuzer 1858-91	.50
7	1 Kreuzer 1858-91	.15
8	4 Kreuzer 1860-64	1.50

AUSTRIA

First obv: portrait with light sideburns

Billon

		Fine
9	5 Kreuzer 1858-64	1.75
10	10 Kreuzer 1858-65	3.25

Silver

		V. Fine
★13	¼ Florin 1857-59, large eagle	5.00
14	¼ Florin 1859-65, small eagle	3.50
15	1 Florin 1857-65	3.00
16	2 Florin 1858-66	40.00

Gold

		Ex. Fine
★23	1 Dukat 1860-65	35.00
25	4 Dukaten 1860-65	275.00

Similar gold types dated 1852-59 with a younger portrait were issued both before and after the Monetary Convention of 1857. These pieces will be listed in the 3rd edition of *Craig*.

Second obv: portrait with heavier beard (as No. 11)

Billon

		Fine
9a	5 Kreuzer 1867	35.00
10a	10 Kreuzer 1867	35.00

Silver

		V. Fine
14a	¼ Florin 1866	60.00
15a	1 Florin 1866	35.00
16a	2 Florin 1866	50.00

Gold

		Ex. Fine
23a	1 Dukat 1866	60.00
25a	4 Dukaten 1866	400.00

New Reverse Legend: LOMB. ET VEN. omitted

Billon

		V. Fine
11	10 Kreuzer 1868-72	.75
12	20 Kreuzer 1868-72	1.50

Designs similar to Nos. 14a-25a

Silver

		V. Fine
14b	¼ Florin 1867-71	35.00
15b	1 Florin 1867-72	15.00
16b	2 Florin 1867-72	50.00

Gold

		Ex. Fine
23b	1 Dukat 1867-72	40.00
25b	4 Dukaten 1867-72	275.00

AUSTRIA

Silver

		V. Fine
14c	¼ Florin 1872-75	40.00
15c	1 Florin 1872-92	3.00
16c	2 Florin 1872-92	40.00

Gold

		Ex. Fine
23c	1 Dukat 1872-1915	30.00
25c	4 Dukaten 1872-1915	110.00

Nos. 23c and 25c dated 1915 have been officially restruck in recent years. These restrikes are valued at about $20.00 and $90.00 respectively.

Trade Coinage

Gold

21	4 Florin-10 Francs 1870-92	35.00
22	8 Florin-20 Francs 1870-92	50.00

Nos. 21-22 were struck on the standard of the Latin Monetary Union to facilitate foreign trade. Coins dated 1892 have been officially restruck in recent years.

Commemorative Series

Silver

Pribram Mine

		Ex. Fine
17	1 Florin 1875	225.00

Vienna Shooting Fest

		Ex. Fine
18	2 Florin 1873	325.00
A18	4 Dukaten gold 1873	——

Silver Wedding Anniversary

19	2 Florin 1879	27.50

AUSTRIA

Reopening of Kuttenberg Mines

Ex. Fine

20 2 Florin 1887.............—

50th Anniversary of Reign

Gold

24 1 Dukat 1848-51, with
1898 below eagle.......175.00

KRONE STANDARD
Regular Issues

Bronze

V. Fine
26 1 Heller 1892-1916......... .10
28 2 Heller 1892-1915......... .10

Nickel

*29 10 Heller 1892-1911....... .25
30 20 Heller 1892-1914....... .25

Silver

Obv: laureate head

V. Fine
35 1 Krone 1892-1907......... 1.50
39 5 Kronen 1900, 07......... 8.50

Gold

42 10 Kronen 1896-1906...... 25.00
43 20 Kronen 1892-1905...... 45.00

Silver

Obv: small plain bust (as No. 36)

Fine
41 5 Kronen 1909............ 11.00

Gold

V. Fine
47 10 Kronen 1909........... 35.00
48 20 Kronen 1909.......... 175.00

Silver

Obv: large plain head by Schwartz

37 1 Krone 1912-16......... 1.00
38 2 Kronen 1912-13........ 2.25
A41 5 Kronen 1909......*Fine* 9.00

AUSTRIA

Gold

V. Fine

49 10 Kronen 1909-12 . . . . . . 25.00
50 20 Kronen 1909-16 . . . . . . 55.00
51 100 Kronen 1909-15 . . . . . . 225.00

No. 49 dated 1912 and Nos. 50-51 dated 1915 have been officially restruck in recent years.

60th Anniversary of Reign

Silver

36 1 Krone 1908 . . . . 2.00
40 5 Kronen 1908, rev.
　　running figure 12.50

Gold

44 10 Kronen 1908 . . . . 27.50
45 20 Kronen 1908 . . . . 100.00
46 100 Kronen 1908 . . . . 350.00

World War I Issues

Copper-Nickel-Zinc

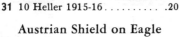

31 10 Heller 1915-16 20

Austrian Shield on Eagle

27 1 Heller 1916, Br. 7.50
32 10 Heller 1916, Cop.-
　　Nic.-Zinc 40

Iron

V. Fine

33 2 Heller 1916-18 25
34 20 Heller 1916-18 35

Gold

52 20 Kronen 1916 . . . . 125.00

Trade Coin

Silver

55 1 Taler 1780 . . . . *Unc.* 6.00

An unofficial "trade dollar," the final date of the famous Maria Theresia thaler has been struck intermittently to modern times at many world mints. It has been used in many areas that lacked a firm local coinage, particularly in north and east Africa and the Near East.

AUSTRIA

REPUBLIC (Republik Oesterreich 1918-38)

Monetary Law of Dec. 21, 1923

Bronze

V. Fine
56 100 Kronen 1923-24........ .75

57 200 Kronen 1924.......... 1.00

58 1000 Kronen Cop.-Nic. 1924. 1.50

Coinage Reform of Dec. 20, 1924

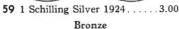

59 1 Schilling Silver 1924...... 3.00

Bronze

60 1 Groschen 1925-38......... .20

V. Fine
61 2 Groschen 1925-38........ .25

Copper-Nickel

62 5 Groschen 1931-38......... .40

63 10 Groschen 1925-29........ .40

64 50 Groschen 1934.... *Ex. F.* 45.00

65 50 Groschen 1935-36........ 2.00

AUSTRIA

66 1 Schilling 1934-35 . . . . *V. Fine* 1.50

Silver

67 ½ Schilling 1925-26 . . . . 1.50

68 1 Schilling 1925-32 . . . . 2.00

COMMEMORATIVE SERIES
1928-1937
Franz Schubert

69 2 Schilling 1928 . . . . *Ex. Fine* 5.00

Dr. Theodor Billroth

70 2 Schilling 1929 . . . . *Ex. Fine* 7.50

von der Vogelweide

71 2 Schilling 1930 . . . . 7.50

Mozart

72 2 Schilling 1931 . . . . 15.00

Haydn

73 2 Schilling 1932 . . . . 30.00

AUSTRIA

Dr. Seipel

Ex. Fine
74 2 Schilling 1932..........12.50

Prince Eugen

Ex. Fine
77 2 Schilling 1936............8.50

Dr. Dollfuss

75 2 Schilling 1934..........10.00

Karlskirche in Vienna

78 2 Schilling 1937............8.50

Dr. Lueger

76 2 Schilling 1935..........10.00

Madonna of Maria Zell
79 5 Schilling 1934-36........18.00

Gold

80 20 Kronen
1923-24.....350.00
81 100 Kronen
1923-24. ...650.00

AUSTRIA

Ex. Fine
82 25 Schilling 1926-34......75.00

Unc.
87 5 Groschen 1948-........10

Ex. Fine
88 10 Groschen 1947-49.....75

83 100 Schilling 1926-34....250.00

Aluminum

84 25 Schilling St. Leopold
1935-38..............225.00

Unc.
89 2 Groschen 1950-.......10

85
100 Schilling
Madonna of
Maria Zell
1935-38
......500.00

90 10 Groschen 1951-..........10

REPUBLIC
RE-ESTABLISHED 1945-

Zinc

Ex. Fine
86 1 Groschen 1947............35

91 50 Groschen 1946-55........50

AUSTRIA

Unc.
103 50 Groschen 1959-. 15

Ex. Fine
92 1 Schilling 1946-57. 75

104 1 Schilling 1959-. 20
Silver

93 2 Schilling 1946-52. . . . . .1.00

106 5 Schilling 1960-68. . . . . . . .1.00

99 10 Schilling 1957-73. . . . . . . .1.50

COMMEMORATIVE ISSUES
Silver
Reopening of Bundestheater

94 5 Schilling 1952-57. . . . . . . .2.00

Aluminum-Bronze

Unc.
95 20 Groschen 1950-54. 65

Ex. Fine
96 25 Schilling 1955. . . . . .17.50

AUSTRIA

Bicentennial Birth of Mozart

97 25 Schilling 1956...........4.50

Ex. F.

8th Centennial Maria Zell Cathedral

98 25 Schilling 1957...........4.50

Centennial Birth of Von Welsbach

100 25 Schilling 1958..........4.00

Tirol Sesquicentennial

101
50 Schilling
1959..10.00

Andreas Hofer

Centennial Death of Archduke Johann

102 *Ex. Fine*
25 Schilling
1959....4.00

40th Anniversary Carinthian Plebiscite

105 25 Schilling 1960..........4.00

40th Anniversary–Burgenland

107 25 Schilling 1961..........5.50

Anton Bruckner

108 25 Schilling 1962..........6.00
Later issues in Current Coins of the World.

AZORES

Group of islands, part of the Republic of Portugal, lying in the North Atlantic about 1,000 miles west of Lisbon. Chief products are fruits, wines and other agricultural crops. The chief export item is pineapple. There is an extensive tourist trade. Language: Portuguese. Chief city: *Ponta Delgada*.
Coinage obsolete.

LOUIS I 1861-89

Copper

		Fine
1	5 Reis 1865-80	3.00
2	10 Reis 1865-66	3.50
3	20 Reis 1865-66	4.50

CARLOS I 1889-1908

Copper

		Fine
4	5 Reis 1901	3.50
5	10 Reis 1901	5.00

About 1887 foreign coins were counterstamped with crown and G.P. to authorize circulation locally in the islands. These carry approximate valuations as follows:

C1	Counterstamp on copper or bronze coin	22.50
C2	Counterstamp on small silver coin	20.00
C3	Counterstamp on ¼ dollar size coin	25.00
C4	Counterstamp on ½ dollar size coin	37.50
C5	Counterstamp on dollar size coin	75.00

The counterstamp is most often found on Brazilian coins. Older coins (1750 or earlier) with the counterstamp are somewhat scarcer.

BELGIUM (Belgique, België)

One of the Low Countries, lying on the North Sea between France and the Netherlands. Chiefly a manufacturing nation, producing iron and steel, food and beverages, textiles and chemicals; agriculture is intensive, with every useful acre under cultivation. With a population of 9,700,000, it is one of the most densely populated countries in Europe. Languages: Flemish and French. Capital: *Brussels*.
100 Centimes = 1 Franc, Frank

French and Flemish Inscriptions

The population of Belgium is divided into well-defined groups, the Flemings and the Walloons (French). Since 1886 all coins have either been minted in equal numbers of French and Flemish specimens, or where not, the coin is inscribed with both languages.

BELGIUM

LEOPOLD II 1865-1909
Copper

		Fine
1	1 Centime 1869-1907	.25
2	2 Centimes 1869-1909	.25

Copper-Nickel

3	5 Centimes 1894-1901	.25
4	10 Centimes 1894-1901	.35

Silver

5	50 Centimes 1866-99	1.75
6	1 Franc 1866-87	2.25
7	2 Francs 1866-87	4.00
8	5 Francs 1865-76	8.00

50th Anniversary of Independence

		V. Fine
9	1 Franc 1880	12.50
10	2 Francs 1880	25.00

Copper-Nickel

		Fine
12	5 Centimes 1901-07	.10
13	10 Centimes 1901-06	.10
14	25 Centimes 1908-09	.20

NOTE: Nos. 12-14 French var. one star CES. Flemish var. two stars CEN.

Silver

15	50 Centimes 1901	1.75

16	50 Centimes 1907-09	1.50

17	1 Franc 1904-09	2.75
18	2 Francs 1904-09	3.75

BELGIUM

Gold

V. Fine
19 20 Francs 1867-82........ 65.00

Nickel-Brass

V. Fine
24a 5 Centimes 1930-32.......1.50
25a 10 Centimes 1930-32.......1.25
Star over value denotes change of alloy.

ALBERT I 1909-1934

Copper

Fine
22 1 Centime 1912-14......... .25
23 2 Centimes 1910-19........ .20

Nickel

27 50 Centimes 1922-34........ .20
28 1 Franc 1922-35........... .25
29 2 Francs 1923-30..........1.25

Copper-Nickel

V. Fine
24 5 Centimes 1910-28.. ..... .10
25 10 Centimes 1910-29....... .15
26 25 Centimes 1910-29....... .20

30 5 Francs/1 Belga 1930-34 . . .2.00

BELGIUM

Centennial of Independence
1830-1930

Nickel

V. Fine
31 10 Francs/2 Belgas 1930 ... 25.00

32 20 Francs/4 Belgas 1931-32. 20.00

Silver

V. Fine
33 50 Centimes 1910-14....... 1.25
34 1 Franc 1910-14.......... 1.75
35 2 Francs 1910-12......... 2.75

36 20 Francs 1933-34......... 3.50

Gold

37 20 Francs 1914......... 100.00

COINS OF THE
GERMAN OCCUPATION
(World War I, 1914-1918)

Zinc

Fine
38 5 Centimes 1915-16........ .25
39 10 Centimes 1915-17....... .35
40 25 Centimes 1915-18........ .40

BELGIUM

Nickel

Fine

41 50 Centimes 1918...........2.50

V. F.

45 1 Franc 1939-40........... .25
46 5 Francs 1938-39.......... .60

LEOPOLD III 1934-1950

All Leopold III coins minted in both Flemish and French varieties (except Nos. 49 and 56.)

Legend: BELGIË-BELGIQUE or BELGIQUE-BELGIË
Nickel-Brass

V. Fine

42 5 Centimes 1938-40........ .25
43 10 Centimes 1938-39........ .15
44 25 Centimes 1938-39........ .25

Example of Two Languages
47 5 Francs 1936-37..........1.50

**Brussels
Exposition
and
Railway
Centennial**

Silver

Ex. Fine

48 50 Francs
1935....100.00

49 20 Francs 1934-35....3.00

BELGIUM

V. Fine

50 50 Francs 1939-40 . . . . 6.00

ALLIED ISSUE

Zinc-Coated Steel
(U. S. 1943 Cent Planchet)
Struck at Philadelphia

56 2 Francs 1944 50

WORLD WAR II GERMAN OCCUPATION (1940-1945)

		Zinc	V. Fine
51	5 Centimes 1941-43		.35
←**52**	10 Centimes 1941-46		.20
53	25 Centimes 1942-46		.25
54	1 Franc 1941-47		.25
55	5 Francs 1941-47		.40

  →

POSTWAR ISSUES
Copper-Nickel

Unc.

57 1 Franc 1950- 15
58 5 Francs 1948- 40

Silver

59 20 Francs 1949-55 . . . . .2.50
60 50 Francs 1948-54 . . . . .4.00

Unc.

61 100 Francs 1948-54 . . . . . . .7.00

BAUDOUIN I 1951-
Bronze

62 20 Centimes 1953-63 15
63 50 Centimes 1952- 15

BELGIUM

Brussels Fair

Marriage Commemorative

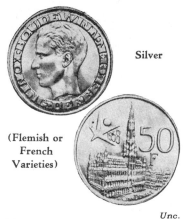

Silver

(Legend
Only In
Latin)

(Flemish or
French
Varieties)

Unc.

65 50 Francs 1960 . . . . 8.50

Unc.

64 50 Francs 1958 . . . . 9.00

66 25 Centimes Cop.-Nic. 1964- .10

Later issues in *Current Coins of the World.*

BELGIAN CONGO (Belgisch Congo, Congo Belge)

Former Belgian colony in equatorial Africa; became independent in 1960;
short coastline where the Congo River empties into the Atlantic. Languages:
Bantu, French. Capital: *Leopoldville* (renamed Kinshasa).

100 Centimes = 1 Franc   Coinage obsolete.

LEOPOLD II 1865-1909 Free State Founded 1885

Copper

V. Fine

1 1 Centime 1887-
88 . . . . 2.00
2 2 Centimes 1887-
88 . . . . 2.50
3 5 Centimes 1887-
94 . . . . 3.00
4 10 Centimes
1887-94 . . 4.00

Silver *V. Fine*

5 50 Centimes 1887-96 . . . . 10.00
6 1 Franc 1887-96 . . . . 18.00
7 2 Francs 1887-96 . . . . . . 30.00
8 5 Francs 1887-96 . . . . . . 125.00

BELGIAN CONGO

Copper-Nickel
V. Fine

9   5 Centimes 1906-08 . . . . 1.75
10 10 Centimes 1906-08 . . . . 2.00
11 20 Centimes 1906-08 . . . . 2.50

As Belgian Colony, Treaty of 1908
New Legend: CONGO BELGE — BELGISCH CONGO

12   5 Centimes 1909 . . . . 5.00
13 10 Centimes 1909 . . . . 6.50
14 20 Centimes 1909 . . . . 8.00

Copper-Nickel

ALBERT I 1909-1934
Copper

V. Fine

17   5 Centimes 1910-28 40
18 10 Centimes 1910-28 60
19 20 Centimes 1910-11 85

15 1 Centime 1910-19 . . . . 3.00
16 2 Centimes 1910-19 . . . . 3.00

(French or Flemish in some years)

20 50 Centimes 1921-29 . . . . . . 1.25
21   1 Franc 1920-30 . . . . 1.75

LEOPOLD III 1934-1950

Brass

22 1 Franc 1944-49 . . . . 1.00
23 2 Francs 1946-47 . . . . 1.25

24 2 Francs 1943 . . . . 5.00
    (Philadelphia mint)

BELGIAN CONGO

(Nos. 22, 23, 25 and 27 struck at Pretoria, South Africa mint due to World War II.)

V. Fine

25 5 Francs 1947-48...... 3.50

Nickel-Bronze

26 5 Francs 1936-37.........15.00

Silver

27 50 Francs 1944..........45.00

BELGIAN CONGO AND RUANDA-URUNDI
BAUDOUIN I 1951-1960

Aluminum-Bronze   **Aluminum**

Unc.

29 50 Centimes 1954-55..... .75
30 1 Franc 1957-60........1.00
31 5 Francs 1956-59.......1.50

Unc.

28 5 Francs 1952............5.00

For later issues see Katanga and Rwanda & Burundi.

BERMUDA

This group of islands, 677 miles southeast of New York City, is the oldest self-governing British Colony. Settled by Sir George Somers who was shipwrecked there in 1609. Population: 54,000. Capital: *Hamilton.*

British monetary system.

ELIZABETH II 1952-
Commemorating 350th Anniversary of Founding

Silver

1 1 Crown 1959

Unc.

20.00

Later issues in *Current Coins of the World.*

BHUTAN

A semi-independent kingdom in the eastern Himalayas. India controls its external relations. Area: 19,305 square miles. Population: 1,100,000. Capital: *Thimbu.*

Some modern Bhutanese coins use cyclical dates, which appear as the top line in the reverse square as shown below:

ঝ৷ ম'৭ব্রুশ (1928) Yr. of Earth-Dragon

৪ঞ্জ'ঝৰ্ষণ (1950) Yr. of Iron-Tiger

MAHARAJAH JIGME WANGCHUK 1926-1952

DORJI WANGCHUK 1952-

Copper Alloy

V. Fine

5 1 Pice ND (ca. 1800-1930)....1.00

Bronze *Ex. Fine*

1 1 Pice CD 1928 (as No. 4)...40.00

Silver

Ex. Fine

4 ½ Rupee CD 1928.........20.00

Second Coinage
Bronze

3 1 Pice ND (1951-55).........1.50

Nickel

4a ½ Rupee CD 1928, 50 (24.1mm)..............1.50

No. 4a was struck until 1955.

Later issues in *Current Coins of the World.*

BOLIVIA
(Republica de Bolivia, Republica Boliviana)

A landlocked country in central South America containing the highest heavily populated areas in the world, over half the inhabitants living at altitudes above 10,000 feet. Chief industry is mining, much of which must be carried on by native-born citizens, since outsiders can't work in the rarefied air of the Andes. Population: 5,200,000; over 50% are Indians. Languages: Spanish, Indian. Capitals: *La Paz* and *Sucre*.

8 Soles (Sueldos, Reales) = 1 Peso
2 Pesos (Silver) = 1 Scudo (Gold)
100 Centavos = 1 Boliviano(to 1962)

Silver

		V. Fine
13	¼ Sol 1852	7.50

		Fine
A13	¼ Sol 1853	27.50

Laureated Head Facing Left
Name Below Neck

14	½ Sol 1853-56 (16mm)	2.00
15	1 Sol 1853-54 (20mm)	3.00
16	2 Soles 1853	10.00
17	4 Soles 1853 (32mm)	8.50
18	8 Soles 1852-56	35.00

Value Indicated

14a	½ Sol 1856-58	2.00
15a	1 Sol 1855-58	2.50
16a	2 Soles 1854-58	5.00
17a	4 Soles 1853-58	3.50
18a	8 Soles 1854-55	17.50

		Fine
19	½ Sol 1859	10.00
20	1 Sol 1859	20.00
21	2 Soles 1859	15.00
★22	4 Soles 1859	6.00
23	8 Soles 1859	——

PESO and Weight Below Bust
Design Similar to Nos. 19-23

24	1/16 Peso 1859 25 Gs	7.50
A24	1/8 Peso 1859 50 Gs	15.00
25	¼ Peso 1859 100 Gs	40.00
26	1 Peso 1859 400 Gs	17.50

PESO Omitted from Legend

27	1/16 Peso 1860-63 25 G	2.50
28	1/8 Peso 1859-63 50 Gs	2.50
29	¼ Peso 1859-63 100 Gs	2.50
30	½ Peso 1860 200 Gs	32.50
31	1 Peso 1859-63 400 Gs	8.00

Gold
Name on Neck

		Ex. Fine
50	½ Scudo 1852-56	75.00
★51	1 Scudo 1852-56	150.00
52	8 Scudos 1852-56	600.00

BOLIVIA

LA PAZ MINT

Silver

Obv: bare head of Bolívar

Fine
A43   2 Soles 1853 . . . . ——
 43   4 Soles 1853 . . . . 75.00

Obv: laureate head of Bolívar

39   ½ Sol 1853-59 . . . . 12.00
40   1 Sol 1853-58 . . . . 10.00
41   2 Soles 1854-56 . . . . 50.00
42   4 Soles 1853-59 . . . . 9.00

Nos. 39-42 have several minor varieties in style of bust.

DECIMAL SYSTEM 1864-

Copper

44   1 Centecimo 1864 . . . . 45.00
45   2 Centecimos 1864 . . . . . . 37.50

Silver

46   1⁄20 Boliviano 1864-65 . . . . . . 7.00
47   1⁄10 Boliviano 1864-67 . . . . . . 4.50
48   1⁄5 Boliviano 1864-66 . . . . . . 3.00
49   1 Boliviano 1864-67
     (9 stars) 9.00
49a   1 Boliviano 1867-69
     (11 stars) 8.50

MELGAREJO ISSUES

Fine
★A49   ¼ Melgarejo 1865 . . . . . . 5.00
 B49   ½ Melgarejo 1865, 68 . . . . 3.75

C49   1 Melgarejo 1865-66
     (400 Granos) 14.00

Gold

Bolivian National Arms
Rev. Laurel and Oak Wreath

Ex. Fine
53   ½ Escudo 1868 . . . . 275.00
54   1 Escudo 1868 . . . . 300.00
55   1 Onza 1868 . . . . ——

Silver

Legend:
LA UNION HACE LA FUERZA
Obv: 11 stars at bottom
Rev: with weight in grams

Fine
56   5 Centavos 1871 . . . . 8.00
57   10 Centavos 1870-71 . . . . . . 3.00
58   20 Centavos 1870-71 . . . . . . 35.00
59   1 Boliviano 1870-71 . . . . . . 8.00

BOLIVIA

Fine

56a	5 Centavos 1871-72	......	4.00
57a	10 Centavos 1871	....	8.00
58a	20 Centavos 1871	....	20.00

Obv: 9 stars at bottom

56b	5 Centavos 1872	....	6.00
57b	10 Centavos 1872	....	4.00
★58b	20 Centavos 1871-72	.....	9.00
59a	1 Boliviano 1871-72	.....	9.00

Legend:
LA UNION ES LA FUERZA

Lettering Larger on Issues
Before 1885

60	5 Centavos 1872-84	......	1.00
61	10 Centavos 1872-84	......	1.25
62	20 Centavos 1872-85	......	1.25
63	½ Boliviano/50 Centavos 1873	....	8.00
A63	½ Boliviano 1879	....	—
64	1 Boliviano 1872-79	.....	9.00

Different Dies

60a	5 Centavos 1885-1900	...	1.50
61a	10 Centavos 1885-1900	...	5.00
62a	20 Centavos 1885-1907	...	1.25
63a	½ Boliviano/50 Centavos 1891, weight below value	....	50.00
A63a	½ Boliviano/50 Centavos 1891-1900, weight omitted	....	2.50

Nos. 60a-63a dated 1884 are patterns, as are probably all 1884-93 dates of the 1 Boliviano.

Daza Commemorative

Fine

A64	20 Centavos 1879	......	15.00

Copper

65	1 Centavo 1878	....	47.50
66	2 Centavos 1878	....	35.00

Ex. Fine

67	1 Centavo 1883	....	3.50
68	2 Centavos 1883	....	5.00

Copper-Nickel

69	5 Centavos 1883	....	6.00
70	10 Centavos 1883	....	4.50

BOLIVIA

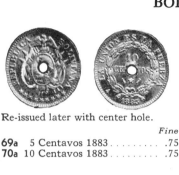

Re-issued later with center hole.

		Fine
69a	5 Centavos 1883	.75
70a	10 Centavos 1883	.75

73	5 Centavos 1892	.75
74	10 Centavos 1892	.75

75	5 Centavos 1893-1919	.50
76	10 Centavos 1893-1919	.50

Nos. 75 and 76 were issued until about 1935 with old dates.

Silver

Obv: stars above arms
Rev: fineness "9 Ds"

80	50 Centavos 1900-08	3.50

No. 80 now includes former No. 80a.

Obv: stars below arms
Rev: fineness "10/12"

		V. Fine
81	20 Centavos 1909	1.25
82	50 Centavos 1909	2.50

Copper-Nickel

Similar to Nos. 75-76 but
Reduced Size

		V. Fine
83	5 Centavos 1935	.40
84	10 Centavos 1935-39	.30
88	50 Centavos 1939 .... Ex. F.	.60

85	10 Centavos 1937	.50
86	50 Centavos 1937	42.50

Zinc

		Ex. Fine
89	10 Centavos 1942 (17mm.)	.75
90	20 Centavos 1942 (21mm.)	1.00

Bronze

91	50 Centavos 1942	.50
91a	50 Centavos Restrike — Poor Detail 1942	.25

		Unc.
92	1 Boliviano 1951	.35
93	5 Bolivianos 1951	.75

94	10 Bolivianos 1951	1.50

Later issues in Current Coins of the World.

BRAZIL
(Estados Unidos do Brasil)

The largest country in South America, covering over one-half of the continent. Produces a wealth of tropical products including timber, rubber, fruits, cocoa, wax, and three-quarters of the world's coffee. Vast mineral resources are being increasingly developed and industry is growing rapidly, with manufacturing comprising over 60% of the total production. Population: 95,000,000. Language: Portuguese. Capital: *Brasilia*.

1000 Reis = 1 Milreis   100 Centavos = 1 Cruzeiro

REPUBLIC 1889-

Bronze

V. Fine
1   20 Reis 1889-1912 75

2   40 Reis 1889-1912 75

Copper-Nickel

3   100 Reis 1889-1900 75
4   200 Reis 1889-1900 . . . . .1.00

Silver

Fine
5   500 Reis 1889 . . . . .2.00
6   1000 Reis 1889 . . . . .5.00
7   2000 Reis 1891-97 . . . . *V. F.* 250.00

400th Anniversary of Discovery

Ex. Fine
8   400 Reis 1900 . . . . 30.00
9   1000 Reis 1900 (Liberty
       Head-Plow) 50.00
10   2000 Reis 1900 (Ship) 85.00
11   4000 Reis 1900 (Cabral) . . .350.00

Copper-Nickel

Fine
12   100 Reis 1901 25
13   200 Reis 1901 50
14   400 Reis 1901 75

Liberty Holding Tablet
Inscribed LEX   *Ex. Fine*
A14   400 Reis 1914 . . . . .75.00

BRAZIL

Silver

		Fine
15	500 Reis 1906-12	1.25
16	1000 Reis 1906-12	2.00
17	2000 Reis 1906-12	4.25

18	500 Reis 1912	3.00
19	1000 Reis 1912-13	3.00
20	2000 Reis 1912-13	7.00

21	500 Reis 1913	1.25
22	1000 Reis 1913	2.00
23	2000 Reis 1913	5.00

Silver

V. Fine

24 2000 Reis 1924-34 .... 3.00

Gold
Design Similar to Nos. 5-7

25 10,000 Reis 1889-1922 ..... 750.00
26 20,000 Reis 1889-1922 ..... 850.00

Copper-Nickel

V. Fine

27 20 Reis 1918-27 .... .35

28	50 Reis 1918-31	.25
29	100 Reis 1918-35	.30
30	200 Reis 1918-35	.40
31	400 Reis 1918-35	.60

Aluminum-Bronze

32	500 Reis 1924-30	.50
33	1000 Reis 1924-31	.75

COMMEMORATIVE ISSUES
Independence Centennial
1822-1922

Dom Pedro and Pres. Pessoa

34	500 Reis 1922	1.00
35	1000 Reis 1922	1.00
34a	500 Reis 1922 (BBASIL error)	35.00
35a	1000 Reis 1922 (BBASIL error)	7.50

BRAZIL

Silver

Aluminum-Bronze

		V. Fine
38	2 Milreis 1922	.............2.50

400th Anniversary of Colonization — 1932

Ramalho

		Ex. Fine
42	500 Reis 1932	.............6.00

Copper-Nickel

Cazique Tiberica

		Ex. Fine
39	100 Reis 1932	.............1.25

Da Sousa

43	1000 Reis 1932	.............5.00

40	200 Reis 1932	.............2.00

Silver

John III

44	2000 Reis 1932	.............4.00

41	400 Reis 1932	.............3.00

BRAZIL

NATIONAL HEROES SERIES 1935-1938

Copper-Nickel

Tamandare

Ex. Fine
45 100 Reis 1936-38. 40

Maua
46 200 Reis 1936-38. 60

Gomes
47 300 Reis 1936-38. . . . . .1.00

Cruz
48 400 Reis 1936-38. . . . . .1.00

Aluminum-Bronze

Feijo

Ex. Fine
49 500 Reis 1935 (4 gr.). 8.00
50 500 Reis 1936-38 (5 gr.). 1.00

Anchieta
51 1000 Reis 1935 (26mm.). 4.50
52 1000 Reis 1936-38 (24mm.). .1.00

Caxias
53 2000 Reis 1936-38. . . . . .2.00
54 2000 Reis (Polygonal) 1938. .4.50

Silver

Caxias
55 2000 Reis 1935. . . . . .3.00

BRAZIL

Santos Dumont *Ex. Fine*
56 5,000 Reis 1936-38.........3.00

Peixoto *Ex. Fine*
63 2000 Reis 1939............2.25

NEW GOVERNMENT
Copper-Nickel

Pres. Getulio Vargas
57 100 Reis 1938-42............25
58 200 Reis 1938-42............30
59 300 Reis 1938-42............40
60 400 Reis 1938-42............50
The 1942 issues have a yellow color due to higher copper content.

FAMOUS MEN SERIES 1939
Aluminum-Bronze

Assis
61 500 Reis 1939.............1.50

Barreto
62 1000 Reis 1939............ 2.00

CURRENCY REFORM 1942
100 Centavos = 1 Cruzeiro
Copper-Nickel

V. Fine
64 10 Centavos 1942-43........ .40
65 20 Centavos 1942-43........ .50
66 50 Centavos 1942-43........ .75

Aluminum-Bronze *Ex. Fine*
64a 10 Centavos 1943-47....... .25
65a 20 Centavos 1943-48....... .30
66a 50 Centavos 1943-47....... .40

67 1 Cruzeiro 1942-56.......... .40
68 2 Cruzeiros 1942-56......... .60
69 5 Cruzeiros 1942-43.........1.75

Bonifacio *Unc.*
73 10 Centavos 1947-55........ .35

BRAZIL

Barbosa

Pres.
Dutra

Unc.

Unc.

74 20 Centavos 1948-56........ .50   **75** 50 Centavos 1948-56........ .65

Later issues in *Current Coins of the World.*

BRITISH CARIBBEAN TERRITORIES
— see *Current Coins of the World*

BRITISH GUIANA

A former crown colony on the north shore of South America which gained independence as the Republic of Guyana in May, 1966. The agricultural area along the coast produces sugar, rum, rice, molasses and copra. Interior jungle produces timber. Exports mineral products including gold, diamonds, manganese and bauxite. The escarpment rising behind the coastal plain is the site of many famous waterfalls. Language: English. Capital: *Georgetown.*

50 Pence = 1 British Guiana Dollar
Coinage obsolete.

VICTORIA 1837-1901
Silver
Fine

A1 4 Pence (Same as Gr. Brit.
No. 4) 1838-55......... 2.50
B2 Four Pence Silver 1888
(Struck for B.G. & W.I.
only)................. 15.00

Legend: BRITISH GUIANA and WEST INDIES

1 4 Pence 1891-1901.......... 4.00

EDWARD VII 1901-1910

2 4 Pence 1903-1910.......... 5.00

GEORGE V 1910-1936

Fine
3 4 Pence 1911-1916.......... 5.00

Legend: BRITISH GUIANA Only

4 4 Pence 1917-1936.......... 2.50

GEORGE VI 1936-1952

V. Fine
5 4 Pence 1938-45............. 1.75
For later issues see GUYANA in *Current Coins of the World.*

BRITISH HONDURAS

British Honduras, on the Caribbean coast of Central America, was settled in the 1600's and prospered despite Spanish opposition. It was administered as part of Jamaica from 1862 to 1884, when it became a separate Crown colony. Upon independence in 1973, it took the name Belize. Until recent years forestry was the most important industry. Area: 8,866 square miles. Languages: English, Spanish. Capital: *Belize City* (to 1970).

100 Cents = 1 Dollar

VICTORIA 1837-1901
Bronze

Fine
1 1 Cent 1885-94.............8.50

Silver

2 5 Cents 1894...............7.50
3 10 Cents 1894..............5.00
4 25 Cents 1894-1901.........6.00
5 50 Cents 1894-1901........12.00

EDWARD VII 1901-1910
Bronze

6 1 Cent 1904-09 ..10.00

Copper-Nickel

Fine
7 5 Cents 1907-09.........20.00

Silver

8 25 Cents 1906-07...........7.50
9 50 Cents 1906-07..........10.00

GEORGE V 1910-1936
Bronze

10 1 Cent 1911-13...........50.00

11 1 Cent 1914-36.............3.00

BRITISH HONDURAS

Copper-Nickel

Fine

12 5 Cents 1911-36. . . . . .2.75

Silver

13 10 Cents 1918-36. . . . . .3.00
14 25 Cents 1911-19. . . . . .4.00
15 50 Cents 1911-19. . . . . .8.50

GEORGE VI 1936-1952

16 1 Cent Bronze 1937-47. 75

17 5 Cents Cop.-Nic. 1939. . . .3.50
17a 5 Cents Nic.-Brass 1942-47 .1.00

Silver

18 10 Cents 1939-46. . . . . .2.00

New Legend:
KING GEORGE THE SIXTH

V. Fine

19 1 Cent Br. 1949-51. 85
20 5 Cents Nic.-Brass 1949-52 .1.00
21 25 Cents Cop.-Nic. 1952. . . .1.50

ELIZABETH II 1952-

Bronze

22 1 Cent 1954 75

Unc.

23 1 Cent 1956-73. 20

Nickel-Brass
24 5 Cents
      1956-73. . . .35

Copper-Nickel

25 10 Cents 1956-70. 50
26 25 Cents 1955-73. 90
27 50 Cents 1954-71. . . . . .2.00

BRITISH NORTH BORNEO

A former colony on the northern tip of the island of Borneo, now known as
Sabah. It is part of the Federation of Malaysia. Languages: Various. Capital:
Jesselton.

100 Cents = 1 Straits Dollar
Coinage obsolete.

Legend:
BRITISH NORTH BORNEO CO.

New Legend:
STATE OF NORTH BORNEO

Bronze

Copper-Nickel

Fine
1 ½ Cent 1885-1907 . . . . 3.00

V. Fine
3 1 Cent 1904-41 . . . . 1.25
4 2½ Cents 1903-20 . . . . 3.00
5 5 Cents 1903-41 . . . . 2.50

Silver

2 1 Cent 1882-1907 . . . . 2.00

6 25 Cents 1929 . . . . 10.00

BRITISH WEST AFRICA

An administrative grouping of four separate British colonies on the west
coast of Africa: The Gambia, Sierra Leone, Gold Coast (now Ghana), and
Nigeria. They gained independence between 1957 and 1965, and each now
has its own coinage.

12 Pence = 1 Shilling
Coinage obsolete.

Copper-Nickel

EDWARD VII 1901-1910

Legend: NIGERIA —
BRITISH WEST AFRICA

Aluminum

Ex. Fine
3 ⅒ Penny 1907-08 . . . . 5.00

Fine
1 ⅒ Penny 1908-10 . . . . 1.50
2 1 Penny 1907-10 . . . . 2.00

BRITISH WEST AFRICA

GEORGE V 1910-1936

Copper-Nickel

Similar to Nos. 1-3

			V. Fine
4	1/10 Penny 1911		3.50
5	1/2 Penny 1911		8.00
6	1 Penny 1911		20.00

New Legend: BRITISH WEST AFRICA

Copper-Nickel

7	1/10 Penny 1912-36		.60
8	1/2 Penny 1912-36		.85
9	1 Penny 1912-36		1.00

Silver

Value and Wreath

			Fine
14	3 Pence 1913-20		2.50
15	6 Pence 1913-20		3.50

16	1 Shilling 1913-20		3.75
17	2 Shillings 1913-20		6.50

Nickel-Brass

			V. Fine
14a	3 Pence 1920-36		2.00
15a	6 Pence 1920-36		2.50
16a	1 Shilling 1920-36		3.00
17a	2 Shillings 1920-36		3.50

EDWARD VIII 1936

Copper-Nickel

			Ex. Fine
18	1/10 Penny 1936		1.00
19	1/2 Penny 1936		1.00
20	1 Penny 1936		1.50
21	10 Cents 1936, obv. of East Africa No. 26 (error)		150.00

GEORGE VI 1936-1952

Copper-Nickel

			V. Fine
22	1/10 Penny 1938-47		.20
23	1/2 Penny 1937-47		.50
24	1 Penny 1937-47		.75

25	3 Pence 1938-47		.40

Brass

26	6 Pence 1938-47		.50

BRITISH WEST AFRICA

Bronze

		V. Fine
29a	1/10 Penny 1952	1.25
30a	1/2 Penny 1952	.50
31a	1 Penny 1952	.75

Nickel-Brass

32	6 Pence 1952	7.50
33	1 Shilling 1949-52	1.50
34	2 Shillings 1949-52	3.00

		V. Fine
27	1 Shilling 1938-47	1.00
28	2 Shillings 1938-47	1.50

ELIZABETH II 1952-

New Legend: without IND · IMP
Designs similar to Nos. 22-28.

Copper-Nickel

29	1/10 Penny 1949-50	3.00
30	1/2 Penny 1949-51	4.00
31	1 Penny 1951	14.00

Bronze

		Unc.
38	1/10 Penny 1954-57	1.00
39	1 Penny 1956-58	2.00
A39	1 Penny 1956, George VI obv. legend (error)	*Ex. Fine* 135.00

Copper-Nickel

40	3 Pence 1957	25.00

For later issues see each of the four former colonies in *Current Coins of the World*.

BRUNEI

A British protected Sultanate since 1888 on the island of Borneo. Capital: *Brunei*. Coinage obsolete.
100 Cents = 1 Straits Dollar

Sultan HASHIM JELAL
1885-1906

Bronze

		Fine
1	1 Cent AH 1304 (1887)	7.50

Later issues in *Current Coins of the World*.

BUKHARA — see Russian Turkestan

BULGARIA (Blgariya)

Bulgaria, on the Balkan peninsula of Europe, gained partial independence
from the Ottoman Empire as a principality in 1878 and was proclaimed a
kingdom in 1908. After coming under communist control during World War
II, it became a republic in 1946. It was primarily agricultural in earlier years,
but more recently has had rapid industrial growth. Area: 42,785 square miles.
Language: Bulgarian. Capital: *Sofia*.

100 Stotinki = 1 Lev

ALEXANDER I
Prince 1879-1886
Bronze

		Fine
1	2 Stotinki 1881	3.50
2	5 Stotinki 1881	2.50
3	10 Stotinki 1881	2.00

Silver

		V. Fine
4	50 Stotinki 1883	2.00
5	1 Lev 1882	2.00
6	2 Leva 1882	4.00
7	5 Leva 1884-85	10.00

FERDINAND I
Prince 1887-1908
Copper-Nickel

		Fine
8	2½ Stotinki 1888	2.50

		Fine
9	5 Stotinki 1888	.50
10	10 Stotinki 1888	.50
11	20 Stotinki 1888	.75

Silver

12	50 Stotinki 1891	1.75
13	1 Lev 1891	2.50
14	2 Leva 1891	3.50
15	5 Leva 1892	10.00

Different Legend

13a	1 Lev 1894	2.00
14a	2 Leva 1894	3.00
15a	5 Leva 1894	10.00

Gold

		V. Fine
21	10 Leva 1894	35.00
22	20 Leva 1894	65.00
23	100 Leva 1894	250.00

BULGARIA

Minor Issues

Bronze

V. Fine

16 1 Stotinka 1901-12 . . . . 1.50
17 2 Stotinki 1901-12 . . . . 1.25

Copper-Nickel

18 5 Stotinki 1906-13 20
19 10 Stotinki 1906-13 25
20 20 Stotinki 1906-13 35

World War I Issues

Zinc

18a 5 Stotinki 1917 75
19a 10 Stotinki 1917 75
20a 20 Stotinki 1917 . . . . 1.00

As King 1908-1918

Silver

24 50 Stotinki 1910 . . . . 1.50
25 1 Lev 1910 . . . . 2.00
26 2 Leva 1910 . . . . 3.00

27 50 Stotinki 1912-16 . . . . 1.50
28 1 Lev 1912-16 . . . . 2.00
29 2 Leva 1912-16 . . . . 3.00

Establishment of Kingdom and 25th Year of Reign

Gold

V. Fine

30 20 Leva 1912 . . . . 85.00
31 100 Leva 1912 . . . . 400.00

BORIS III 1918-1943

Aluminum

Designs like Nos. 34-35

32 1 Lev 1923 . . . . 4.00
33 2 Leva 1923 . . . . 5.00

Copper-Nickel

34 1 Lev 1925 25
35 2 Leva 1925 35

36 5 Leva 1930 . . . . 1.00
37 10 Leva 1930 . . . . 1.50

BULGARIA

Aluminum-Bronze

Copper-Nickel

V. Fine

41 50 Stotinki 1937 35

V. Fine

42 20 Leva 1940 . . . . 1.00
43 50 Leva 1940 . . . . 1.50

Silver

38 20 Leva 1930 . . . . 1.25
39 50 Leva 1930 . . . . 2.50
40 100 Leva 1930 . . . . . *Ex. Fine* 6.00

WORLD WAR II ISSUES

Iron

34a 1 Lev 1941 . . . . 5.00
35a 2 Leva 1941 . . . . 1.00
36a 5 Leva 1941 . . . . 4.00
37a 10 Leva 1941 . . . . 15.00
★A45   2 Leva diff. arms 1943 . 1.25

Nickel-Clad Steel

36b 5 Leva 1943 . . . . 1.00
37b 10 Leva 1943 . . . . 1.75
43a 50 Leva 1943 . . . . 1.50

44 50 Leva 1934 . . . . 3.00
45 100 Leva 1934-37 . . . *Ex. Fine* 5.00

Later issues in Current Coins of the World.

BURMA

Located on the Bay of Bengal between India and Thailand, modern Burma was unified in the 1700's. This kingdom ended in 1886 with annexation to British India. It became a separate British colony in 1937, was occupied by Japan in World War II, and gained independence as a republic in 1948. An agricultural nation, it exports rice, lumber, rubber and ores. Area: 261,789 square miles. Languages: Burmese, English, many others. Capital: *Mandalay* (1857-1885), *Rangoon* (from 1886).

BURMA

	1	2	3	4	5	6	7	8	9	0
Burmese Numerals	၁	၂	၃	၄	၅	၆	၇	၈	၉	၀

Like Siam, early coins are dated in the Chula-Sakarat system (seepage 7).
16 Annas = 1 Kyat (Rupee)
16 Kyat = 1 Mohur

MINDON
CS 1214-1240 (1853-1878)

Lead

Obv: hare to left
Rev: similar to No. 1

V. Good
C1 ⅟₃₂ Anna CS 1231 (1869)
20-21mm............25.00
D1 ⅟₁₆ Anna 1231 (21-22mm) .20.00

Copper

Fine
1 ¼ Anna CS 1227 (1865) 6.50
1a ¼ Anna 1227, Iron ...V.G. 35.00

The existence of former Nos. A1 and B1 cannot be confirmed.

2 ½ Anna CS 1231 (1869) 40.00

Silver

Accession date CS 1214 on coins

Fine
3 1 Anna ND (12mm)......14.00
4 ⅛ Kyat ND (15mm).....12.00
5 ¼ Kyat ND (20mm).....11.00
6 ½ Kyat ND (25mm).....10.00
★7 1 Kyat ND (30mm)......12.50

Gold

V. Fine
★10 1 Kyat ND (12mm)......80.00
11 2 Kyat ND (16mm).....140.00

A8 1 Kyat CS 1228 (1866)
12mm................80.00
★8 ¼ Mohur 1228
(18-19mm)..........175.00
B8 1 Mohur 1228 (25mm)..475.00

BURMA

THIBAW
CS 1240-1248 (1880-1885)

Accession date CS 1240 on coins

Copper

		Fine
9	¼ Anna ND	7.50

Gold

		V. Fine
C8	½ Mohur ND (21mm)	175.00

REPUBLIC 1948-
Copper-Nickel

		Ex. Fine
★13	½ Anna 1949	.75
14	1 Anna 1949-51 (scalloped)	1.00
15	2 Annas 1949-51 (square)	1.50

Nickel

★16	4 Annas 1949-50	3.00
17	8 Annas 1949-50	5.50

Later issues in *Current Coins of the World.*

CAMBODIA (Cambodge)

The kingdom of Cambodia, on the southeast Asian peninsula, became a French protectorate in 1863, and in 1887 was federated with Annam, Tonkin and Laos to form French Indochina. Independence was restored between 1949 and 1953. With an economy based largely on subsistence agriculture, it exports rice and rubber. Area: 66,000 square miles. Languages: Khmer, French. Capital: *Phnom Penh.*

100 Centimes = 1 Franc
5 Francs = 1 Piastre

NORODOM I 1859-1904
Brass

Bronze

		Fine
1	1 Centime ND (1897)	8.50
2	5 Centimes 1860	6.00
3	10 Centimes 1860	6.00

CAMBODIA

Nos. 2-9 were struck in Phnom Penh ca. 1875-87. The date 1860 on coins is (incorrect) accession date. Pieces with E or ESSAI on obverse are collectors' samples struck in Europe. No. 9 was issued for presentation only, as were strikings in gold of this and other denominations.

NORODOM SIHANOUK
1941-1955

100 Centimes = 1 Franc

Aluminum

		Unc.
11	10 Centimes 1953	.75

Silver

		V. Fine
4	25 Centimes 1860	10.00
5	50 Centimes 1860	10.00
6	1 Franc 1860	15.00
*7	2 Francs 1860	20.00
8	4 Francs 1860	125.00
9	1 Piastre 1860 .... *Ex. F.*	1000.00

| 12 | 20 Centimes 1953 | 1.00 |
| 13 | 50 Centimes 1953 | 2.00 |

Later issues in Current Coins of the World.

CAMEROUN (Cameroon)

Cameroun became a French territory in 1919 when the former German colony of Kamerun in west central Africa was divided between Britain and France. It attained independence as a republic in 1960. Primarily an agricultural nation, its major exports are food crops, cotton, timber and aluminum. Area: 183,381 square miles. Languages: French, native dialects. Capital: *Yaounde.*

100 Centimes = 1 Franc

Issues Under French Mandate

Aluminum-Bronze

		Fine
1	50 Centimes 1924-26	1.00
2	1 Franc 1924-26	1.25
3	2 Francs 1924-25	1.75

CAMEROUN

Bronze

Aluminum

		V. Fine
4	50 Centimes 1943	4.00
5	1 Franc 1943	5.00

New Legend: with LIBRE

		Unc.
8	1 Franc 1948	.40
9	2 Francs 1948	.60

Later issues in *Current Coins of the World.*

		V. Fine
6	50 Centimes 1943	4.00
7	1 Franc 1943	5.00

CANADA

A member of the British Commonwealth of Nations occupying most of northern North America. Population: 21,600,000. Products of her industrial, agricultural and mineral resources make her the third richest trading nation. Languages: English and French. Nearly a third of the nation is of French origin. Capital: *Ottawa.*

100 Cents = 1 Dollar

VICTORIA 1837-1901

Bronze

Obv: laureate head

Silver

		Fine
1	1 Cent 1858-59	1.00

		Fine
2	5 Cents 1858-1901	1.75
3	10 Cents 1858-1901	3.25
4	20 Cents 1858	50.00

CANADA

Bronze

Obv: head with coronet

		Fine
5	1 Cent 1876-1901	1.00

Silver

		Fine
8	25 Cents 1870-1901	3.00
9	50 Cents 1870-1901	15.00

EDWARD VII 1901-1910

Bronze

10	1 Cent 1902-10	.80

Silver

11a	5 Cents 1902, Royal crown on rev.	1.00

		Fine
11	5 Cents 1903-10 (Imperial crown)	.80
12	10 Cents 1902-10	2.00
13	25 Cents 1902-10	3.25
14	50 Cents 1902-10	9.00

Gold

Type of Great Britain No. 57
with Mint Mark C (Ottawa)

		V. Fine
A14	1 Sovereign 1908-10	85.00

GEORGE V 1910-1936

Bronze

		Fine
15a	1 Cent 1911	1.00

Silver

17a	5 Cents 1911	2.50
18a	10 Cents 1911	10.00
19a	25 Cents 1911	15.00
20a	50 Cents 1911	50.00

DEI GRA: added to Obv. Legend

Bronze

		V. Fine
15	1 Cent 1912-20	.80

CANADA

Silver

V. Fine

17	5 Cents 1912-21	1.00
18	10 Cents 1912-36	1.50
19	25 Cents 1912-36	3.25
20	50 Cents 1912-36	6.50
A22	1 Dollar 1936 (Rev. like No. 22)	12.50

Gold

23	5 Dollars 1912-14	175.00
24	10 Dollars 1912-14	275.00

Type of Great Britain No. 78 with Mint Mark C

25	1 Sovereign 1911-19	70.00

Bronze

16	1 Cent 1920-36	.30

Nickel

21	5 Cents 1922-36	1.25

25th Anniversary of Reign

Silver

V. Fine

22	1 Dollar 1935	13.50

GEORGE VI 1936-1952
Various Metals

26	1 Cent Br. 1937-47	.15

27	5 Cents Nic. 1937-42	.80

CANADA

V. Fine

28 5 Cents Brass (12 Sided)
  1942..................1.25
28a 5 Cents Nic. 1946-47...... .50

29 5 Cents Brass 1943........ .75
29a 5 Cents Chromium Plated
  Steel 1944-45............ .40

Silver

30 10 Cents 1937-47........... .60

31 25 Cents 1937-47..........1.25

32 50 Cents 1937-47..........2.00

V. Fine

33 1 Dollar 1937-47......... 12.50

Royal Visit Commemorative

Parliament Buildings

34 1 Dollar 1939.............6.50

**New Legend: without IND: IMP:
Designs Sim. to Nos. 26, 28, 30-33**

Various Metals

35 1 Cent Bronze 1948-52..... .10
36 5 Cents Nic. (12 Sided)
  1948-50................ .30
36a 5 Cents Chromium Plated
  Steel 1951-52............ .20

Silver

38 10 Cents 1948-52............ .45
39 25 Cents 1948-52........... .90
40 50 Cents 1948-52...........2.00
41 1 Dollar 1948-52..........5.00

CANADA

Commemorating Entry of Newfoundland into Canada as a Province

Ship of Discoverer John Cabot

V. Fine

42 1 Dollar 1949 . . . . 14.00

200th Anniversary Isolation of Nickel

37 5 Cents Nic. 1951 45

ELIZABETH II 1952-
Various Metals

Unc.

43 1 Cent Br. 1953-64 10

V. Fine

44 5 Cents Chromium Plated
Steel 1953-54 30

Unc.

45 5 Cents Nic. 1955-62 20
45a 5 Cents Nic. (Round)
1963-64 15

Silver
Rev. Designs Like Nos. 30-33

46 10 Cents 1953-64 40
47 25 Cents 1953-64
(2 Vars. in 1953) 90
48 50 Cents 1953-58 . . . . 3.00
49 1 Dollar 1953-63 . . . . 4.00

Later issues in *Current Coins of the World.*

CANADA—NEW BRUNSWICK

Separated from Nova Scotia in 1784, it joined the Canadian federation in 1867. Capital: *Fredericton.*

Coinage obsolete.

VICTORIA 1837-1901

Copper

Fine

1 ½ Penny 1843 . . . . 2.50
2 1 Penny 1843 . . . . 3.50

Fine

3 ½ Penny 1854 . . . . 3.00
4 1 Penny 1854 . . . . 4.00

CANADA—NEW BRUNSWICK

Bronze   **Silver**

Famp;iamp;
Fine
5 ½ Cent 1861........ *V. F.* 55.00
6 1 Cent 1861-64............ 1.75

Fine
7 5 Cents 1862-64...........30.00
8 10 Cents 1862-64...........20.00
9 20 Cents 1862-64...........12.50

CANADA—NEWFOUNDLAND

With its dependency, Labrador, it was independently administered by the British government. In 1949 by referendum vote, it united with Canada to become the tenth province. Exports: fish (especially cod), iron, and paper. Capital: *St. John's.*

Coinage obsolete.

VICTORIA 1837-1901
Bronze

Fine
1 1 Cent 1865-96..............2.00

Silver

2 5 Cents 1865-96............6.00
3 10 Cents 1865-96............5.50
4 20 Cents 1865-1900..........1.50
5 50 Cents 1870-1900..........3.00

Gold

V. Fine
6 2 Dollars 1865-88..........125.00

EDWARD VII 1901-1910

Bronze

Fine
7 1 Cent 1904-09..............2.50

Silver

8 5 Cents 1903-08...........3.00
9 10 Cents 1903-04...........4.00
10 20 Cents 1904.............12.50
11 50 Cents 1904-09...........2.50

CANADA — NEWFOUNDLAND

GEORGE V 1910-1936
Bronze

GEORGE VI 1936-1952
Bronze

V. Fine

12 1 Cent 1913-36............1.50

V. Fine

18 1 Cent 1938-47.............50

Silver

Silver

19 5 Cents 1938-47............50

13 5 Cents 1912-29...........2.00
14 10 Cents 1912-19..........4.50
15 20 Cents 1912.............3.00
16 25 Cents 1917-19..........1.75
17 50 Cents 1911-19..........3.00

20 10 Cents 1938-47...........90

CANADA — NOVA SCOTIA

First settled by the French. Passed to England in 1621, its possession being contested by both nations until ceded to Britain by Treaty of Utrecht in 1713. Joined the Dominion in 1867. Capital: *Halifax*.

Coinage obsolete.

VICTORIA 1837-1901
Copper

Fine

3 ½ Penny 1840-43...........3.00
4 1 Penny 1840-43...........4.00

Fine

5 ½ Penny 1856..............4.00
6 1 Penny 1856..............5.00

CANADA — NOVA SCOTIA

Bronze

Fine

7 ½ Cent 1861-64............5.00
8 1 Cent 1861-64............2.00

CANADA — PRINCE EDWARD ISLAND

Colonized by the French about 1720, it became a British possession in 1763, and was united with Canada in 1873. It is the smallest Canadian Province with an area of only 2184 square miles. Capital: *Charlottetown*.
Coinage obsolete.

Bronze *Fine*

1 1 Cent 1871..............1.25

CAPE VERDE ISLANDS
(Cabo Verde)

An overseas province of Portugal lying in the North Atlantic about 600 miles off the West African Coast. Chief products are coffee and other agricultural products. Language: Portuguese. Population: 275,000. Capital: *Praia*.

100 Centavos = 1 Escudo

Bronze

Nickel-Bronze

Fine

1 5 Centavos 1930............1.50
2 10 Centavos 1930............1.75
3 20 Centavos 1930............2.00

Ex. Fine

6 50 Centavos 1949............2.00
7 1 Escudo 1949..............2.50

Decree of Jan. 21, 1952

New Legend:
COLONIA DE omitted

Various Metals

Nickel-Bronze

4 50 Centavos 1930............4.00
5 1 Escudo 1930...........10.00

Unc

A8 50 Centavos Bronze
1968 ....1.25
8 1 Escudo Bronze
1953-68 ....1.25
9 2½ Escudos Cop.-Nic.
1953-67.............1.50
10 10 Escudos Silver
1953................5.00

Later issues in Current Coins of the World.

CEYLON

A large island off the southern tip of India, Ceylon came under British control around 1800. Gaining independence within the Commonwealth in 1948, it changed its name to Sri Lanka in 1972. Primarily agricultural, it exports tea, rubber and coconut. Area: 25,332 square miles. Languages: Sinhala, Tamil, English. Capital: *Colombo.*

4 Farthings = 1 Penny
100 Cents = 1 Rupee

VICTORIA 1837-1901

Copper

1839-42 for Ceylon

		Fine
1	¼ Farthing 1839-53	12.50
2	½ Farthing 1839-56	2.00

In 1842 No. 2 was changed at bottom reverse to conform to English coinage and was declared current in the United Kingdom starting in that year. For more on Nos. 1-3, see Great Britain introduction.

		V. Fine
3	1½ Pence Silv. 1838-62	4.00

(Also used in Jamaica)

Decimal System

Copper

		Fine
4	¼ Cent 1870-1901	1.25
5	½ Cent 1870-1901	1.00
6	1 Cent 1870-1901	.75
7	5 Cents 1870-92	2.50

Silver

		Fine
8	10 Cents 1892-1900	1.25
9	25 Cents 1892-1900	2.00
10	50 Cents 1892-1900	3.00

EDWARD VII 1901-1910

Copper

		Fine
11	¼ Cent 1904	4.50
12	½ Cent 1904-09	1.00
13	1 Cent 1904-10	.60

Copper-Nickel

14	5 Cents 1909-10	1.50

CEYLON

Silver

		Fine
15	10 Cents 1902-10	1.50
16	25 Cents 1902-10	2.25
17	50 Cents 1902-10	4.50

GEORGE V 1910-1936

Copper

		V. Fine
18	½ Cent 1912-26	.40
19	1 Cent 1912-29	.60

Copper-Nickel

20	5 Cents 1912-26	.75

Silver

21	10 Cents 1911-28	1.25

		V. Fine
22	25 Cents 1911-26	1.50
23	50 Cents 1913-29	3.00

GEORGE VI 1936-1952

Copper

		Ex. Fine
24	½ Cent 1937-40	.35
25	1 Cent 1937-42	.50

Larger Head

Bronze

26	1 Cent 1942-45 Thin	.25

Nickel-Brass

		V. Fine
27	2 Cents 1944	.25

28	5 Cents 1942-43 (Thick)	.50
28a	5 Cents 1944-45 (Thin)	.25

29	10 Cents 1944	.25

CEYLON

                                    V. Fine
30 25 Cents 1943.............. .35
31 50 Cents 1943.............. .50

                                    Unc.
39 2 Cents 1955-57............ .35

Silver

                                    Ex. Fine
32 10 Cents 1941...........2.00
33 50 Cents 1942...........4.50

2500 Years of Buddhism

Copper-Nickel

New Legend:
KING GEORGE THE SIXTH

Nickel-Brass

40 1 Rupee 1957 ....2.50

Silver

                                    Unc.
34 2 Cents 1951.............. .15
35 5 Cents 1951 (Square)
         (Proofs Only).........12.50
36 10 Cents 1951 (Scalloped)... .35

37 25 Cents 1951.............. .65
38 50 Cents 1951..............1.00

41 5 Rupees 1957............12.50
         1957 Proof set (2 each 40
         and 41)...............110.00

Later issues in Current Coins of the World.

CHILE

A republic on the Western coastline of South America lying between the Andes and the Pacific. Principal resources are mining and agriculture, mineral exports running about 70% of the total. Also ranks high among the wine producing countries. Population: 9,000,000. Languages: Spanish and Indian. Capital: *Santiago.*

8 Reales = 1 Peso
16 Reales = 1 Escudo (Gold)
10 Centavos = 1 Decimo
100 Centavos = 1 Peso
10 Pesos = 1 Condor

Copper

Obv: Small flat star, large letters

Rev: Different wreath

Fine

7 (½) MEDIO CENTAVO
1835 . . . . 1.75
8 (1) UN CENTAVO 1835 . . . 1.75

Fine

13 (½) MEDIO CENTAVO
1853 . . . . 1.25
14 (1) UN CENTAVO 1853 . . . 1.25

Obv: Large flat star, date between stars

9 (½) MEDIO CENTAVO
1851 . . . . 1.75
10 (1) UN CENTAVO 1851 . . . 1.50

Silver

19 ½ R(eal) 17mm. 1838-42 . . . 12.50
20 1 R(eal) 21.5mm.
1838-42 . . . . 8.00
21 2 R(eales) 24.5mm. 1839 . . . ——
22 8 R(eales) 39mm. 1839 . . . . 40.00

Obv: Star in relief, date between dots

11 (½) MEDIO CENTAVO
1851 . . . . 2.00
12 (1) UN CENTAVO 1851 . . . 2.50

19a ½ R(eal) 15.5mm.
1844-51 . . . . 6.00
20a 1 R(eal) 19mm. 1843-50 . . 3.50
★21a 2 R(eales) 23mm.
1843-52 . . . . 3.00
22a 8 R(eales) 38.5mm.
1848-49 . . . . 40.00

CHILE

Gold

			V. Fine
23	1 E(scudo) 1838		60.00
24	2 E(scudos) 1837-38		75.00
★25	4 E(scudos) 1836-37		300.00
26	8 E(scudos) 1835-38		200.00

Like Nos. 31-33 but different dies

27	1 E(scudo) 1839-45		50.00
28	2 E(scudos) 1839-45		75.00
29	4 E(scudos) 1839-41		550.00
30	8 E(scudos) 1839-43 (36mm)		200.00
30a	8 E(scudos 1844-45 (35.5mm)		200.00

31	1 E(scudo) 1847-51		50.00
32	2 E(scudos) 1846-51		75.00
33	8 E(scudos) 1846-51		200.00

Silver

35	(½) MEDIO DECIMO	*Fine*	
	1.25 gr. 1851-59		2.50

		Fine
36	(1) UN DECIMO 2.5 gr. 1852-59	2.50
37	20 C(entavos) 5 gr. 1852-59	2.50
38	50 C(entavos) 1853-62	5.00

A38 (1) UN PESO 1853-62...32.50

Reduced Weight Silver

35a	(½) MEDIO DECIMO 1.15 gr. 1860-62	7.50
36a	(1) UN DECIMO 2.3 gr. 1860-62	5.00
37a	20 C(entavos) 4.6 gr. 1860-62	2.50

Like Nos. 44-48 but slightly different dies

39	(½) MEDIO DECIMO 1865-66	10.00
40	(1) UN DECIMO 1864-66	6.00
41	20 Centavos 1863-67	2.00
42	50 Centavos 1862-67	10.00
43	1 PESO 1867.....*V. F.*	400.00

CHILE

Fine

44 (½) MEDIO DECIMO
    1867-81 . . . . 1.50
★**45** (1) UN DECIMO 1867-80 1.25
46   20 Centavos 1867-78 . . . . . 1.50
47   50 Centavos 1867-72 . . . . 7.50
48 (1) UN PESO 1867-91 . . . 10.00

Same in .500 Silver

49 (½) MEDIO DECIMO
    1879-94 . . . . : 75
50 (1) UN DECIMO 2.5 gr.
    1879-94 . . . . 1.50
50a (1) UN DECIMO 2.0 gr.
    1891 . . . . 3.00
★**51**   20 Centavos 5 gr. 1879-93. 1.50
51a   20 Centavos 4 gr.
    1891 . . . . 4.00
52   20 Centavos .200 Silver
    4.9 gr. 1891 . . . . 50.00

Copper-Nickel

53 (½) MEDIO CENTAVO
    1871-73 . . . . 2.75
★**54** (1) UN CENTAVO
    1871-77 . . . . 2.25
55 (2) DOS CENTAVOS
    1871-77 . . . . 2.25

Copper

Fine

56 (½) MEDIO CENTAVO
    1883-94 . . . . 2.00
57 (1) UN CENTAVO
    1878-98 . . . . 1.25
58 (2) DOS CENTAVOS
    1878-94 . . . . 2.00
★**59** 2½ CENTAVOS
    1886-98 . . . . 2.00

Gold

V. Fine

60 1 Peso as No. 62 but value in
    wreath on rev.
    1860-73 . . . . 25.00
61 2 P(eso)s as No. 62
    1856-75 . . . . 35.00
★**62** 5 P(eso)s 1851-77 . . . . . . 50.00
63 10 P(eso)s Sim. 1851-92 . . . 75.00

64 (5) CINco PESOS
    1895-96 . . . . 50.00
★**65** (10) DIEZ PESOS
    1895 . . . . 60.00

CHILE

.835 Silver

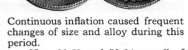

66 (5) CINCO CENTAVOS *Fine*
1896 . . . . 5.00
67 (10) DIEZ CENTAVOS
1896 . . . . 2.50
68 (20) VEINTE CENTAVOS
1895 . . . . 20.00
69 (1) UN PESO 1895-97 . . . . 10.00

Copper

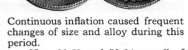

70 (1) UN CENTAVO
1904-19 . . . . 1.00
★71 (2) DOS CENTAVOS
1919 . . . . 2.00
72 2½ CENTAVOS
1904-08 . . . . 1.50

Silver

Continuous inflation caused frequent changes of size and alloy during this period.

Nos. 66-69 and 73-94 are all of the same design.

.500 Silver
Fine
73 (5) CINCO CENTAVOS
1899-1907 75
74 (10) DIEZ CENTAVOS
1899-1907 50
75 (20) VEINTE CENTAVOS
1899-1907 75

.700 Silver
★76 50 CENTAVOS 1902-06 2.50
77 (1) UN PESO 1902-05 . . 8.50
78 (5) CINCO CENTAVOS
1908-19 50
79 (10) DIEZ CENTAVOS
1908-20 50
80 (20) VEINTE CENTAVOS
1907-20 75
81 40 CENTAVOS 1907-08 . . 1.75

0.9 Silver
82 (1) UN PESO 31.5 mm.
1910 . . . . 5.00

0.45 Silver
83 (5) CINCO CENTAVOS
1915-19 50
84 (10) DIEZ CENTAVOS
1915-18 50
85 (20) VEINTE CENTAVOS
1916 . . . . 1.25

0.72 Silver
86 (1) UN PESO 1915-17 . . . 3.50

0.5 Silver
V. Fine
87 (1) UN PESO 1921-25 . . . 2.50
87a 1/UN/PESO 1927 . . . . . 2.00

Copper-Nickel

88 5 Centavos 1920-38 20
89 10 Centavos 1920-41 25
90 20 Centavos 1920-41 35
★91 1 Peso 1933-40 60

CHILE

Silver

V. Fine
*92 (1) UN PESO 1932........1.50

0.5 Silver

93 2/DOS/PESOS 1927.....4.00

0.9 Silver

94 5/CINCO/PESOS 1927.10.00

Gold

95 (5) CINCO PESOS
    1898-1925....,......20.00

*96 (10) DIEZ PESOS
    1896-1925...........35.00

97 (20) VEINTE PESOS
    1896-1925...........60.00

Unc.
*98 20 Pesos 1926..........35.00

99 50 Pesos 1926...........70.00

100 100 Pesos 1926.........100.00

Unc.
*101 100 Pesos 1932.........100.00

Bronze

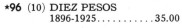

V. Fine
102 20 Centavos 1942-53....... .15
103 50 Centavos 1942......... .75
104 1 Peso 1942-54........... .35

Aluminum   Unc.

105 1 Peso 1954-58........... .25

106 5 Pesos (Medio Condor)
    1956...................1.00

107 10 Pesos (Un Condor)
    1956-59...............1.25

Later issues in Current Coins of the World.

CHINA

A country in eastern Asia (about one-third larger than continental U.S.) which contains about one-fourth of the world's population. Despite efforts of the last two governments, China remains largely the agricultural nation it was at the beginning of its recorded history over 4,000 years ago. Vast mineral resource, particularly coal, iron, tin and tungsten. Population: 775,000,000 (1966 Govt. estimate). Capital: *Peking.*

Coins not listed are probably either fantasies or patterns. Beware of (often clever) forgeries of the rarer coins, including rare dates.

10 Li = 1 Fen (Candareen)
10 Fen = 1 Ch'ien (Mace)
10 Ch'ien = 1 Liang (Tael)
7 Mace and 2 Candareens = 1 Dollar
10 Cash, Wen, Li = 1 Cent, Fen, Hsien
10 Cents = 1 Chio, Hao
100 Cents = 1 Dollar, Yuan

Note: Because of extensive catalog revisions to China, new numbers were assigned in the 9th edition.

Cyclical Dates

Many dated coins use the Chinese sexagenary system as shown below. Coins bearing these cyclical dates are indicated in this catalog by the abbreviation CD preceding the date.

戌戊	1898	末丁	1907
亥己	1899	申戊	1908
子庚	1900	酉己	1909
丑辛	1901	戌庚	1910
寅壬	1902	亥辛	1911
卯癸	1903	子壬	1912
辰甲	1904	亥癸	1923
巳乙	1905	子甲	1924
午丙	1906		

Mint Names

The first column below shows the abbreviated name used in the center of Tai-Ch'ing-Ti-Kuo coppers. The second column shows the full name as used on most other provincial coins.

皖	Huan for Anhwei	安徽
浙	Che for Chekiang	浙江
直	Chi for Chili	直隸
淮	Huai for Ching-Kiang	清江
閩	Ming for Fukien	福建
奉	Fung for Fengtien	奉天
汴	Bien for Honan	河南
湘	Shiang for Hunan	湖南
鄂	Ngau for Hupeh	湖北
贛	Kung for Kiangsi	江西
寧	Ning for Kiangnan	江南
蘇	Su for Kiangsu	江蘇
吉	Chi for Kirin	吉林
桂	Kuei for Kwangsi	廣西
粵	Yueh for Kwantung	廣東
黔	Ch'ien for Kweichow	貴州
山	Shan for Shansi	山西
陝	Shen for Shensi	陝西
東	Tung for Shantung	山東
川	Ch'uan for Szechuan	四川
雲	Yun for Yunnan	雲南
滇	Dien for Yunnan	雲南
川滇	Dien/Ch'uan for Yunnan/Szechuan	雲南四川

CHINA

EMPIRE
KUANG HSU 1875-1908

Reign Symbols 光緒 on coins
Legend: HU POO

The Hu Poo (National Board of Revenue) coins were issued about 1903-05 for general circulation. No. 5 was also struck during the early Republican period. Similar silver coins are patterns.

Copper or Brass

Fine

3	5 Cash dragon circled	10.00
*4	10 Cash dragon uncircled	1.00
5a	20 Cash dragon circled	40.00
5	20 Cash dragon uncircled	1.00

Legend: TAI-CH'ING-TI-KUO

Typical coin of
Tai-Ch'ing-Ti-Kuo series

Note: The 2 date characters appear at the top as shown below for all coins dated 1905-06, but for some varieties of later dates they appear at the sides in place of the "Hu Pu" characters (see No. 11e).

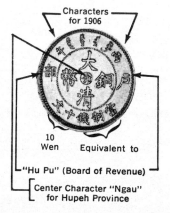

Characters for 1906

10 Wen   Equivalent to

"Hu Pu" (Board of Revenue)

Center Character "Ngau"
for Hupeh Province

Brass

Fine

*7	1 Wen (Cash) 1908 general	4.00
7c	1 Wen 1908 Chihli	7.00
7g	1 Wen 1908 Honan	27.50
7j	1 Wen 1908 Hupeh	7.50
7k	1 Wen 1908 Kiangnan	6.00

Copper

Unless otherwise stated, nos. 8-11 and 19-21 in brass rather than copper are generally contemporary counterfeits, usually cast.

8	2 Wen (Cash) 1905-07 general (blank center)	5.00
*8b	2 Wen 1906 Chekiang	12.00
8f	2 Wen 1906 Fukien brass	6.00
8j	2 Wen 1906 Hupeh	50.00
8n	2 Wen 1906 Kiangsu brass	65.00
8s	2 Wen 1906 Shantung	37.50

9	5 Wen (Cash) 1905-07 general (blank center)	6.00
9b	5 Wen 1906 Chekiang	10.00
9c	5 Wen 1906 Chihli	6.00
*9j	5 Wen 1906 Hupeh	7.50
9k	5 Wen 1906 Kiangnan (vars.)	50.00
9n	5 Wen 1906 Kiangsu brass	40.00

CHINA—EMPIRE

Fine

10	10 Wen (Cash) 1905-07 general (blank center)	.35
10a	10 Wen 1906 Anhwei	2.00
10b	10 Wen 1906 Chekiang	1.50
10c	10 Wen 1906 Chihli	1.00
10d	10 Wen 1906 Chingkiang	1.50
10e	10 Wen 1905-07 Fengtien	2.50
10f	10 Wen 1906 Fukien	1.00
10g	10 Wen 1906 Honan	1.50
10h	10 Wen 1906 Hunan	1.00
★10j	10 Wen 1906 Hupeh	.50
10k	10 Wen 1906-08 Kiangnan (vars.)	.50
10m	10 Wen 1906 Kiangsi	2.00
10n	10 Wen 1906 Kiangsu	2.00
10r	10 Wen 1906-08 Kwangtung	.50
10s	10 Wen 1906 Shantung	2.50
10t	10 Wen 1906 Szechuan	1.50
10u	10 Wen 1906 Yunnan "Yun" center	25.00
10v	10 Wen 1906 Yunnan "Tien" center	35.00
10w	10 Wen 1906 Yunnan-Szechuan	40.00

11	20 Wen (Cash) 1905-07 general (blank center)	2.50
11a	20 Wen 1906 Anhwei	100.00
11b	20 Wen 1906 Chekiang	35.00

Fine

11c	20 Wen 1906 Chihli	35.00
★11e	20 Wen 1905-07 Fengtien	7.50
11j	20 Wen 1906 Hupeh	75.00
11n	20 Wen 1906 Kiangsu	25.50
11t	20 Wen 1906 Szechuan	10.00
11u	20 Wen 1906 Yunnan "Yun" center	75.00
11v	20 Wen 1906 Yunnan "Tien" center	75.00
11w	20 Wen 1906 Yunnan-Szechuan	75.00

Silver

12	10 Cents ND (1908)	15.00
★13	20 Cents ND	20.00
14	1 Dollar ND	20.00

Gold

15	1 Liang (Tael) ND (1906)	——

HSUAN T'UNG 1908-1911
Reign Symbols 宣統 on coins

Designs like Nos. 7-11

Brass

18	1 Wen 1909 general	30.00

Copper

19	5 Wen 1909 general (blank center)	65.00
19e	5 Wen 1909 Fengtien	50.00
20	10 Wen 1909 general (blank center)	.75
20a	10 Wen 1909 Anhwei	40.00
20e	10 Wen 1909 Fengtien	6.50
20f	10 Wen 1909 Fukien	25.00
20g	10 Wen 1909-11 Honan	3.50
20j	10 Wen 1909 Hupeh	2.00
20p	10 Wen 1909 Kirin	10.00
20r	10 Wen 1909 Kwangtung	1.00
20t	10 Wen 1909 Szechuan	1.50
20x	10 Wen 1909 rosette center (Kirin style dragon)	17.50

CHINA—EMPIRE

Fine

21	20 Wen 1909 general (blank center)	2.00
21e	20 Wen 1909 Fengtien	50.00
21p	20 Wen 1909 Kirin	35.00
21t	20 Wen 1909 Szechuan	20.00

Silver

22 20 Cents 1909 Kirin.....35.00

23 5 Chio/½ Dollar ND (1910).............35.00

Other denominations similar to No. 23 are patterns.

Second Coinage

Brass

25 1 Wen ND.................2.00

The origin and date of No. 25 are unknown. Some authorities claim it is not a regular issue; others have assigned it to the series of 1905 or 1909.

Bronze

V. Fine

26	5 Wen Yr. 3 (1911)	100.00
*27	10 Wen Yr. 3	6.00

Some authorities claim No. 26 is a pattern, as are a similar 20 wen and coins denominated in fen or li.

Silver

*28	1 Chio Yr. 3	6.00
29	2 Chio Yr. 3	12.50
30	5 Chio Yr. 3	120.00

31 1 Dollar Yr. 3...........10.00

CHINA—EMPIRE

PROVINCIAL COINAGE

Provincial coins, especially the copper 10 Cash pieces, exist in many varieties; only the major types can be listed in this catalog.

Anhwei

Side view dragon

		Fine
34	1 "Cen" (10 Cash) ND	25.00
34a	1 "Sen" ND	35.00
35	5 Cash ND	100.00
36	10 Cash ND	2.00
★36a	(10 Cash) ND, no English value	2.00
37	20 Cash ND	175.00

Front view dragon

★38a	"ToENCASH" (ND)	7.50
38b	(10 Cash) ND, no English value	6.00

Flying dragon (as No. 78)

39	10 Cash ND, AN-HUI	——

Silver

41	5 Cents	15.00

42	10 Cents	10.00
★43	20 Cents	15.00
44	50 Cents	35.00
45	1 Dollar	50.00

Two major varieties of nos. 41-45: with or without small letters A-S-T-C in obv. field. Coins are undated (1897) or variously dated yrs. 23-25 (1897-99) and CD 1898.

Chekiang
Copper or Brass

★49	(10 Cash) ND	1.00
50	(20 Cash) ND	45.00

Silver

51	5 Cents ND (1902)	5.00
52	10 Cents Yrs. 22-23 (1896-97), ND	6.00
★53	20 Cents Yrs. 22-23, ND	10.00
54	50 Cents ND	150.00
55	1 Dollar ND	——

Chihli
Legend: PEKING

Silver

58	10 Cents CD 1900	——
59	20 Cents CD 1900	——

Some authorities claim nos. 58-59 are patterns. Other denominations are strikings made later from unused dies.

CHINA—EMPIRE

Chihli (cont.)

Legend: PEI YANG ARSENAL

Fine

61 ½ Chio Yrs. 22-24
    (1896-98) 8.00
62 1 Chio Yrs. 22-24 .... 7.00
63 2 Chio Yrs. 22-24 ...... 10.00
★64 5 Chio Yrs. 22-24 ...... 25.00
65 1 Yuan Yrs. 22-24 ...... 20.00

The year 22 issue is a major variety without the words "Ta Tsing" in legend.

Brass

66 1 Wen ND 4.00

Legend: PEI YANG

Copper or Brass

★67 10 Cash ND 1.00
68 20 Cash ND 12.50

Silver

Fine

69 5 Cents Yrs. 25-26
    (1899-1900) 10.00
70 10 Cents Yr. 25 .... 12.50
★71 20 Cents Yrs. 25-26 ..... 15.00
71a 20 Cents Yr. 31 dragon
    circled 40.00
72 50 Cents Yr. 25 .... 30.00
73 1 Dollar Yrs. 25-34 ..... 15.00
74 1 Liang (Tael) Yr. 33 ... ——

Chingkiang or Tsingkiang
Legend: CHING/KIANG
Copper or Brass

77 (10 Cash) ND 2.00

Legend: TSING-KIANG
Copper or Brass

78 10 Cash ND 1.25

CHINA—EMPIRE

Fengtien (Fung-Tien)

Despite inscriptions on the following coins, Fengtien was not a province but the capital city of Shengking province.

First Coinage
Copper

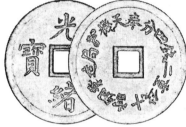

Fine

81 10 Ch'ien (Cash) ND......35.00

Silver

83 ½ Chio Yr. 25 (1899)......10.00
84 1 Chio Yr. 24...........12.50
★85 2 Chio Yr. 24...........15.00
86 5 Chio Yrs. 24-25.......40.00
87 1 Yuan Yrs. 24-25.......40.00

Second Coinage
Legend: FEN-TIEN PROVINCE
Brass

88 10 Cash CD 1903........75.00

Legend: FUNG-TIEN PROVINCE

Fine

89 10 Cash CD 1903-06.......2.00
90 20 Cash CD 1903-05.......7.50

Nos. 88-90 struck in copper are patterns or trial strikes.

Silver

★91 20 Cents CD 1904
    (2 var.)...............8.50
92 1 Dollar CD 1903
    (2 var.)..............40.00

For later Fengtien issues
see Manchurian Provinces

Formosa — see Taiwan

Fukien
Brass

95 1 Wen ND..............40.00

No. 95 is attributed to Fukien by the Manchu character at right on the reverse. Do not confuse with Nos. 191, 204.

CHINA—EMPIRE

Fukien (cont.)

Copper or Brass

Legend: F. K. CUSTOM-HOUSE

Fine

97 10 Cash ND.............. 2.00

Legend: FOO-KIEN CUSTOM

98 10 Cash ND............. 100.00

Legend: FOO-KIEN

 99 5 Cash ND........... 15.00
★100 10 Cash ND............. 1.25
 101 20 Cash ND........... 20.00

Silver

 102 5 Cents ND (1898-1902) . 5.00
 103 10 Cents ND............ 3.00
★104 20 Cents ND............ 5.00
 105 1 Dollar ND (1898)..... ——

The 1898 coins have 5 characters at top of obverse (illustrated), while the 1902 issues have only 4.

Hsuan T'ung Reign

Brass

*Different characters in obv. center
(see page 88)*

V. Fine

106 1 Wen ND............. 90.00
See note with No. 95.

Honan

Copper or Brass

108 10 Cash ND,
dragon circled........ 1.50
108a 10 Cash ND,
dragon uncircled...... 1.50

Hunan

Copper or Brass

Side view dragon

112 10 Cash ND (vars.)....... 1.50

CHINA—EMPIRE

Hunan (cont.)

Flying dragon

Fine

113 10 Cash ND (vars.).......1.50

Silver

115 10 Cents CD 1898-99,
ND (1902).........12.50
★116 20 Cents ND..........12.50

Hupeh

Copper

Side view dragon

120 10 Cash ND,
dragon circled........5.00
120a 10 Cash ND, dragon
uncircled (vars.)....... .75

Front view dragon

121 1 Cash ND..............5.00

Fine

122 10 Cash ND (vars)........ .75

Extremely rare patterns exist in brass; these are very heavy, unlike the cast brass counterfeits.

Silver

123 5 Cents ND (1896).....75.00
124 10 Cents ND (1895-96)...3.00
★125 20 Cents ND (1895-96)...2.50
126 50 Cents ND (1896).....10.00
127 1 Dollar ND (1895-96)..12.50

The 1895 date (extremely rare) is an experimental issue with 2 Chinese characters added to side of dragon.

128 1 Tael Yr. 30 (1904).....100.00

Hsuan T'ung Reign

*Different characters in obv. center
(see page 88)*

129 10 Cents ND (1909)......17.50
130 20 Cents ND..........200.00
131 1 Dollar ND..........15.00

CHINA—EMPIRE

Kiangnan

(A region consisting of Kiangsu, Anhwei and Kiangsi provinces.)

Copper or Brass

Flying dragon

135 10 Cash ND,
CD 1902-05 . . . . .75 *Fine*

Front view dragon

138 10 Cash CD 1905 (2 vars.) . 1.25
140 10 Cash CD 1906, obv. of
no. 10k, rev. of no. 138 . . . 2.00
Other mules of Kiangnan coppers exist.

Silver
Dragon circled

141 5 Cents ND (1897) 20.00
142 10 Cents ND, CD 1898 . . . . 7.50
143 20 Cents ND, CD 1898 . . . 17.50
144 50 Cents ND 120.00
145 1 Dollar ND 40.00

Dragon not circled

141a 5 Cents ND,
CD 1899-1901 . . . . 8.50

Fine
142a 10 Cents CD 1898-1905 . . 2.50
★143a 20 Cents CD 1898-1905 . . 3.50
144a 50 Cents CD 1899-1900 90.00
145a 1 Dollar CD 1898-
1905 . . . . 15.00

The 20¢ and dollar have a different dragon starting in 1899. Most coins dated 1901-05 have small English initials on the obverse.

Hsuan T'ung Reign

*Different characters in obv. center
(see page 88)*

146 10 Cents ND (1909) 7.50
147 20 Cents ND 14.00

Kiangsi

Copper or Brass

Side view dragon

★149 10 Cash KIANG-see, dragon
circled or uncircled 7.00
150 10 Cash KIANG-SI 1.25

Front view dragon

152 10 Cash KIANG-SI 4.00
153 10 Cash KIANG-SEE
PROVINCE 1.25
Flying dragon

154 10 Cash KIANG-SI 75.00

CHINA—EMPIRE

Kiangsu
Copper or Brass

Side view dragon

Fine
158 EIVE (=5) CASH ND 35.00

Front view dragon
160 10 Cash ND..............1.50

Flying dragon

159   2 Cash ND 125.00
161   5 Cash ND 150.00
162 10 Cash ND,
    CD 1902-03, 05........1.00
163 20 Cash ND.............25.00

Kirin
First Coinage
Silver

169 1 Ch'ien (Mace)
    Yr. 10 (1885)..........——
170 3 Ch'ien Yr. 10..........——
★171 5 Ch'ien Yr. 10..........——

Fine
172 7 Ch'ien Yr. 10..........——
173 1 Liang (Tael) Yr. 10....——

Second Coinage
Copper

★175   2 Wen ND...........40.00
174 10 Wen ND.............——

Copper or Brass
Side view dragon

176 10 Cashes ND.........40.00
A176 20 Cashes ND.........——
B176 50 Cashes CD 1901.....——

Flying Dragon

177 10 Cashes ND...........5.00
178 20 Cashes ND..........35.00

Silver

Obv. center: flower vase

179   5 Cents ND (1896-98),
    CD 1899-1908.........6.00
180 10 Cents ND, 1899-1907...6.00
181 20 Cents ND, 1899-1908...7.00
182 50 Cents ND, 1899-1908..14.00
183   1 Dollar ND, 1899-
    1908................30.00

Kirin (cont.)

Obv. center: Yang-Yin

Fine

179a 5 Cents CD 1900-05 .... 7.50
180a 10 Cents CD 1900-05 .... 7.00
★181a 20 Cents CD 1900-05 .... 8.00
182a 50 Cents CD 1900-05 ... 15.00
183a 1 Dollar CD 1900-05 ... 30.00

Obv. center: 2 Manchu characters

181b 20 Cents CD 1908 ...... 50.00
182b 50 Cents CD 1908 ...... 75.00
183b 1 Dollar CD 1908 ..... 200.00

Obv. center: Arabic number

180c 10 Cents CD 1908
"1" in center 35.00
181c 20 Cents CD 1908
"2" in center 35.00
183c 1 Dollar CD 1908
"11" in center 200.00

Kwangtung

Nos. 189-191 and 204 are attributed to Kwangtung by the Manchu character on reverse — at left on 189, at right on 190-191.

Brass

V. Fine

189 1 Ch'ien ND (1889-90) .... .50

V. Fine

190 (1 Ch'ien) ND (1892-94) .... .25

191 1 Wen ND .... .25

Copper

192 1 Cent ND (1900) .... .75
193 10 Cash ND .... .50

Silver

Obv. with English legend

194 5 Cents ND (1889) 200.00
195 10 Cents ND 150.00
★196 20 Cents ND 125.00
197 50 Cents ND 250.00
198 1 Dollar ND 700.00

Two varieties of nos. 194-198: the first slightly heavier and inscribed with higher weights, the second (illus.) of normal weight for provincial silver.

CHINA—EMPIRE

Rev. with English legend
(regular provincial type)

		V. Fine
199	5 Cents ND (1890)	3.00
200	10 Cents ND	1.50
★**201**	20 Cents ND	1.50
202	50 Cents ND	10.00
203	1 Dollar ND	15.00

Hsuan T'ung Reign
Different characters in obv. center
(see page 88)

Brass
204 1 Wen ND (as no. 191)..... .35

Silver
205 20 Cents ND (1909).......2.00
206 1 Dollar ND 15.00

Manchurian Provinces
(Fengtien, Heilungkiang, Kirin)

Silver
		Fine
209	10 Cents Yr. 33 (1907)	12.50
210	20 Cents Yr. 33	5.00
211	50 Cents Yr. 33	100.00
212	1 Dollar Yr. 33	90.00

Hsuan T'ung Reign
Different characters in obv. center
(see page 88)

213 20 Cents Yr. 1 (1909)....4.00
★**213a** 20 Cents ND (1909-10) ..4.00

No. 213 is inscribed either "1st Year" or
"First Year." Do not confuse 213a with 217.

Peiyang — see Chihli

Shansi
Silver

Fine

217 20 Cents ND 100.00

The obverse of no. 217 bears Chinese characters for Shansi, but the reverse is a crude
copy of no. 213a. Several varieties exist,
all struck in the early years of the Republic.

Shantung
Copper
Side view dragon

220 10 Cash ND 10.00

Flying dragon

221 10 Cash ND SHANTUNG....5.50
221a 10 Cash ND SHANG-TUNG .4.00

Sinkiang — see
Chinese Turkestan

Szechuan
Copper or Brass
Side view dragon

225 5 Cash ND.............50.00
226 10 Cash ND............20.00
227 20 Cash ND............40.00

CHINA—EMPIRE

Szechuan (cont.)

Flying dragon

		Fine
228	5 Cash ND	——
*229	10 Cash ND	1.50
230	20 Cash ND	10.00

Front view dragon

| **231** | 10 Cash ND | —— |
| **233** | 30 Cash ND | —— |

Some authorities believe Nos. 231-233 are patterns.

Silver

234	5 Cents ND (1897)	12.50
235	10 Cents ND	10.00
236	20 Cents ND	7.50
*237	50 Cents ND	15.00
238	1 Dollar ND	12.50

Hsuan T'ung Reign

Different characters in obv. center
(see page 88)

239	5 Cents ND (1909)	25.00
240	10 Cents ND	17.50
242	50 Cents ND	60.00
243	1 Dollar ND	17.50

Taiwan (Formosa)
Silver

		Fine
246	5 Cents ND (ca. 1890)	85.00
*247	10 Cents ND (2 var.)	20.00
248	20 Cents ND (2 var.)	200.00

Tsingkiang — see Chingkiang
Turkestan — see
Chinese Turkestan

Yunnan
Silver

Regular provincial type

252	20 Cents ND (1907)	12.50
*253	50 Cents ND	5.00
254	1 Dollar ND	15.00

No English legends

255	10 Cents ND (1908)	17.50
256	20 Cents ND	15.00
*257	50 Cents ND	3.00
258	1 Dollar ND	15.00

Yunnan (cont.)

Hsuan T'ung Reign
Different characters in obv. center
(see page 88)
Regular provincial type

                                          Fine
259 50 Cents ND (1909)......6.50
260 1 Dollar ND, CD 1910...17.50

REPUBLIC 1911-1949
General Coinage 1911-26

Copper or Brass

301 10 Cash ND (vars.)....... .35

302 10 Wen (Cash) ND
(vars.) 40

★303 10 Cash ND. 30
304 10 Wen ND, obv. of 303,
rev. of 302. . . . . .12.50

No. 304 is listed by Woodward as No. 1086.

                                          Fine
305 10 Cash ND. 15.00

★306 10 Cash ND, 4 chars.
at bottom (3 vars.) 35
306a 10 Cash ND, 5 chars.
at bottom 7.00

★307 1 Mei (10 Cash) ND 40
308 20 Wen (20 Cash)
Yr. 8 (1919) 1.25

★307a 1 Mei ND, as 307
but ornate flag. 75
308a 20 Wen Yr. 10 sim. 3.00

CHINA—REPUBLIC

Fine

★309 10 Cash ND............15.00
310 20 Cash ND, English at
      bottom both sides....25.00

311 10 Wen Yr. 13 (1924)....——
★312 2 Mei (Cents) Yr. 13....8.00

Some authorities believe No. 311 is a pattern.

V. Fine

318 1 Yuan ND (1912).......65.00

No. 318 has stars on rev. (see arrows). Do not confuse with the common 1927 issue, no. 318a.

Silver

Obv: Sun Yat-sen

V. Fine

317 (20 Cents) ND (1912).....8.50

319 1 Dollar ND, obv. as
     no. 318................50.00

CHINA—REPUBLIC

Obv: Li Yuan Hung

V. Fine

320 1 Dollar ND (1912) 125.00

321 1 Dollar ND (1912) 40.00

Obv: Yuan Shih-kai

322 1 Dollar ND (1914) 100.00

Bronze

V. Fine

323 5 Li Yr. 5 (1916) 15.00
★324 1 Fen Yr. 5 . . . . 2.50

Also see similar 1933 issues, nos. 324a and 325a below. The 2 Fen Yr. 5 is a pattern.

Silver

326 1 Chio Yrs. 3-5
    (1914-16) 2.00
327 2 Chio Yrs. 3-9 . . . . 3.00
★328 ½ Yuan Yr. 3 . . . . 6.00
329 1 Yuan Yrs. 3-10 . . . . 7.00

Gold

330 10 Yuan Yr. 8 (1919) . . . . ——
★331 20 Yuan Yr. 8 . . . . ——

HUNG HSIEN Reign 1915-16
Title assumed by Yuan Shih-kai
(Also see no. 401)

Silver
332 (1 Yuan) Yr. 1, obv. as
    322, rev. as 333 . . . . 100.00

CHINA—REPUBLIC

Gold

V. Fine

333 10 Yuan Yr. 1 . . . .——

Republican Issues Resumed

Silver

334 1 Chio Yr. 15 (1926) 3.50
★335 2 Chio Yr. 15. . . . . .5.00
336 1 Yuan Yr. 12. . . . . . . .150.00

Nationalist Coinage 1927-49

Brass "Ration" Coins

Obv: Value in center
Rev: Nationalist sun

337 1 Fen Yr. 17 (1928) 100.00
338 2 Fen Yr. 17 . . . .——

Nos. 337-338 always have a small incuse
punch mark on both sides.

Silver

Sun Yat-sen

339 1 Chio Yr. 16 (1927) 17.50
★340 2 Chio Yr. 16. . . . . .12.50

As 318, but rosettes on rev.

V. Fine

318a 1 Yuan ND (1927-32) 6.00

Bronze

324a 1 Fen Yr. 22 (1933) 35.00
325a 2 Fen Yr. 22 . . . . .100.00

Silver

Rev: Birds over junk, sun at right

Ex. Fine

344 1 Yuan Yr. 21 (1932) 125.00

CHINA—REPUBLIC

Rev: No birds or sun

Ex. Fine

345 1 Yuan Yrs. 22-23 . . . . 7.00

Other coins of various denominations similar to no. 345 are patterns.

Currency Reform Nov. 1935

First Coinage

Bronze

V. Fine

346 ½ Fen Yr. 25 (1936) 1.75
★**347** 1 Fen Yrs. 25-28 75

Nickel, Plain Edge

348 5 Fen Yrs. 25-28
    (1936-39) 50
★**349** 10 Fen Yrs. 25-28 35
350 20 Fen Yrs. 25-28 65

World War II
Provisional Issues
Brass

V. Fine

★**353** 1 Hsien (Cent)
    Yr. 28 (1939) 60.00
354 2 Hsien Yr. 28 . . . . 4.00

Aluminum

355 1 Fen Yr. 29 (1940) 50

356 5 Fen Yr. 29 50

Second Coinage
Brass

★**357** 1 Fen Yr. 29 50
358 2 Fen Yr. 29 50

Copper-Nickel, Reeded Edge

359 5 Fen Yrs. 29-30 50

CHINA—REPUBLIC

★360 10 Fen Yrs. 29-31........ .40
361 20 Fen Yr. 31 (1942)..... .50
362 ½ Yuan Yrs. 31-32......1.50

Third Coinage
Bronze

363 1 Fen Yr. 37 (1948)......25.00

For Nationalist Issues on
Taiwan (Formosa), see nos. 531-536

Provincial and Regional
Issues

Chekiang
Silver

Fine
★371 10 Cents Yr. 13 (1924)....4.00
372 20 Cents Yr. 13 sim.....200.00
373 20 Cents Yr. 13 (lg. 20).200.00

Fukien
Cast Brass

374 1 Wen ND (1911)....... ——
★375 2 Wen ND (2 vars).....15.00

Silver

V. Fine
377 20 Cents CD 1911.......16.50

Copper

379 10 Cash ND (1912)......15.00

Silver

380 10 Cents ND (1912),
CD 1924............10.00
★381 20 Cents ND,
CD 1923-24..........7.50

382 10 Cents ND (1913).....7.00
★383 20 Cents ND..........4.00
383a 20 Cents Yr. 13 (1924) .40.00

CHINA—REPUBLIC

Fukien (cont.)

Northern Expedition Commemoratives

★384 2 Hao (20 Cents)   *V. Fine*
    Yr. 16 (1927) 275.00
385 2 Hao Yr. 16, obv.
    center 4 chars. 350.00

Canton Martyrs Commemoratives

388 10 Cents Yrs. 17, 20
    (1928, 31) 10.00
★389 20 Cents Yrs. 17, 20 . . . . . 9.00
390 10 Cents Yr. 21 (1932)
    obv. flags 100.00
391 20 Cents Yr. 21 sim. 40.00

Honan

Copper or Brass

Obv: value in center

A392 10 Cash ND 1.00

Obv: flower in center

                              Fine
★392 10 Cash ND (1912) 2 vars. .60
393 20 Cash ND (2 vars.) . . . 2.00
394 50 Cash ND (38mm) 4.50
395 100 Cash ND (40mm) 5.00
396 200 Cash ND (42mm) 5.00

New Legend: CHINA replaces HO-NAN

393a 20 Cash ND 50.00
394a 50 Cash ND 20.00

Obv: Nationalist sun
Rev: Value in wreath

                             V. Fine
397 50 Wen Yr. 20 (1931) . . 70.00
★398 100 Wen Yr. 20 . . . . 12.50

CHINA—REPUBLIC

Hunan

Copper

V. Fine

399 10 Cash ND (2 vars.) 1.50

Copper or Brass

400 20 Cash ND, value
 TWENTY spelled out
 (many vars.).......... .75
400a 20 Cash ND, value
 "20" in numerals..... ——

Hung Hsien Reign

401 10 Cash Yr. 1 (1915) 15.00
Also see nos. 332-333 for this reign.

Provincial Constitution
Commemoratives

Copper

V. Fine

402 10 Cash Yr. 11 (1922)
 2 vars. 10.00
403 20 Cash Yr. 11 ....20.00

Silver

404 1 Dollar Yr. 11 ....100.00

Hupeh

Copper or Brass

A405 20 Wen ND..........100.00
Attribution to Hupeh is uncertain.

Design similar to No. 449

405 50 Wen Yrs. 3, 7
 (1914, 18) 100.00

Silver

406 2 Chio Yr. 9 (1920) 75.00
As no. 327 but two characters for Hupeh
added at sides of head.

CHINA—REPUBLIC

Kansu

Silver

Obv: Yuan Shih-kai

V. Fine

407 1 Yuan Yr. 3 (1914).....450.00

As no. 329 but two characters for Kansu added at sides of head.

Silver

Obv: Sun Yat-sen

V. Fine

410 1 Yuan Yr. 17 (1928)....200.00

Copper

Fine

★408 50 Wen Yr. 15 (1926)...——
409 100 Wen Yr. 15........100.00

Kiangsi

Copper

Obv: Sim. to no. 10m
Rev: Stylized Republican star (design of balls and arcs)

411 10 Wen CD 1911.........——

Fine

412 10 Cash CD 1912......——
★412a 10 Cash CD 1912,
diff. obv. legends.....3.00

CHINA—REPUBLIC

Kwangsi

Legend: KWANG SEA

Brass

V. Fine

★413 1 Cent Yr. 8 (1919) 150.00

Silver

415 20 Cents Yrs. 8-13 . . . . . 50.00

Legend: KWANG-SI
Brass

413a 1 Cent Yr. 8 . . . . 40.00

Silver

414 10 Cents Yr. 9 (1920) . . . 100.00
415a 20 Cents Yrs. 8-14 . . . . . . 35.00

Wreath added on rev.

415b 20 Cents Yrs. 15-16
(1926-27) 5.00

V. Fine

416 2 Chio Yr. 38 (1949) 100.00

Kwangtung

Brass or Copper

417 1 Cent Yrs. 1-7 (1912-18) . 1.00
418 2 Cents Yr. 7 . . . . 40.00

Copper-Nickel

★420 5 Hsien/5 Cents
Yr. 8 (1919) 1.00
420a ½ Hao/5 Cents Yr. 12 . . . 1.00

421 5 Cents Yr. 10 . . . . 3.00

Kwangtung (cont.)
Silver

Fine

422 10 Cents Yrs. 2-11
(1913-22)............2.00
423 20 Cents Yrs. 1-13........1.00

V. Fine

424 2 Hao Yr. 13 (1924)......12.00

V. Fine

425 1 Hao Yr. 18 (1929)......1.50
★**426** 2 Hao Yrs. 17-18........1.50

Copper

427 1 Hsien (Cent)   *Ex. Fine*
Yr. 25 (1936)........350.00

Some authorities claim No. 427 is a pattern.

Kweichow
Commemorating
First Road in Kweichow
Silver

V. Fine

428 1 Yuan Yr. 17 (1928)....300.00

Antimony

Fine

429 10 Fen Yr. 20 (1931)......——

Silver

Some authorities consider Nos. 430-433 to be patterns.

Obv: Similar to 429, ornate border

Ex. Fine

430 20 Fen Yr. 38 (1949), rev.
3 seal characters.......——

CHINA—REPUBLIC

Kweichow (cont.)

Ex. Fine

431 20 Fen Yr. 38, rev. "20"... ——
432 ½ Yuan Yr. 38, rev. "50". ——

Obv: Pagoda

433 1 Yuan Yr. 38, rev.
3 bamboo stems .... ——

Manchurian Provinces
Copper

V. Fine

434 1 Fen Yr. 18 (1929) 3.00

Shansi
Copper

A435 1 Mei (10 Cash) ND .. 100.00

As No. 307 but two characters for Shansi
replace stars on obverse. Some authorities
consider No. A435 a pattern, but most
known pieces are well circulated.

Shensi
Copper

Fine

★435 1 Fen ND (ca. 1924)
IMTYPIF 125.00
436 2 Fen ND, IMTYPEF
(vars.) 70.00

Szechuan
Copper or Brass

441 (5 Wen) Yr. 1 (1912) 90.00

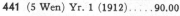

443 5 Wen Yr. 1 .... 90.00

446 5 Wen Yr. 1 .... ——
★447 10 Wen Yrs. 1-2 .... 1.50

CHINA—REPUBLIC

Szechuan (cont.)

		Fine
448	20 Wen Yrs. 1-3 (32mm)	.1.75
449	50 Wen Yrs. 1-3 (36mm)	.2.75
450	100 Wen Yr. 2 (39mm) . . .	2.50

Silver

453	1 Chio Yr. 1	20.00
★454	2 Chio Yr. 1	40.00
455	5 Chio Yrs. 1-2	10.00
456	1 Yuan Yrs. 1, 3	12.50

Copper or Brass

★459 200 Cash Yr. 2 (vars.) . . . 12.00

Copper or Brass

		Fine
462	50 Wen Yr. 15 (1926) . . .	40.00
463	100 Wen Yr. 15	.8.00
464	200 Wen Yr. 15	10.00

466 100 Wen Yrs. 15, 19
(1926, 30) 100.00

Various Metals

468 1 Chio ND (ca. 1926) 70.00

No. 468 exists in silver, brass and several other minor metals. See Kann No. 825.

Silver

Obv: Sun Yat-sen facing
Rev: Value in wreath

473	5 Chio Yr. 17 (1928)	——
474	1 Yuan Yr. 17	——

Many other legitimate coins in silver and minor metals were circulated widely; often these coins lack provincial designation. Warlords (or Chinese communists) copied Yuan Shih-kai and Sun Yat-sen dollars, the latter with spelling errors in the English inscription ($15.00 each). Crudely struck or cast copies of nos. 446-450 are not necessarily counterfeits but often warlord issues.

CHINA—REPUBLIC

Copper or Brass

Silver

V. Fine

476 2 Cents Yr. 19 (1930). . . . .——

V. Fine

479 50 Cents ND (1916). 7.50

Yunnan

Obv: Governor T'ang Chi-yao

Copper or Brass

480 50 Cents ND (1917). 25.00

Gold

481 5 Dollars ND (1919) . .350.00
★482 10 Dollars ND (2 vars.). .450.00

There are two other sets of Yunnan gold
$5 and $10 (struck about 1917 and 1925),
bearing Chinese inscriptions only, but their
authenticity is uncertain.

478 50 Wen ND (ca. 1916). . . .15.00

CHINA—REPUBLIC

Yunnan (cont.)

Copper-Nickel

V. Fine

485 5 Cents Yr. 12 (1923)...50.00
★486 10 Cents Yr. 12.........3.50

Brass

V. Fine

493 2 Chio Yr. 38 (1949).....65.00

World War II Issues

Silver

488 1 Hsien (Cent)
         Yr. 21 (1932).......... ——
489 2 Hsien Yr. 21.......... ——
490 5 Hsien Yr. 21.........175.00

Silver

★491 2 Chio Yr. 21..........7.50
492 ½ Yuan Yr. 21..........4.00

Ex. Fine

★495 ½ Liang (Tael) ND
         (ca. 1942-43)........15.00
496 1 Liang ND..........17.50

CHINA—REPUBLIC

Yunnan (cont.)

Ex. Fine
497 1 Liang ND..........30.00

The exact origin of these so-called "Yunnan-Burma Taels" is uncertain. They are said to have been paid to Chinese troops in southern Yunnan, eastern Burma or the Laotian area of northern Indo-China.

Communist Army
Issues 1930-34

Note: All dated Communist coins bear western dates, usually expressed in Chinese numerals. Dates are written either right-to-left or left-to-right.

Hunan

Silver

Obv: Bust of Lenin to right
Rev: Value above hammer and sickle

Fine
501 1 Yuan ND (ca. 1930) ——

Obv: Hammer and sickle in star
Rev: Value in wreath

502 1 Yuan 1931........——

Nos. 501-502 are controversial. Some authorities consider them bogus.

Hupeh, Anhwei and Honan

Obv: As no. 504
Rev: Sim. to 504, garbled Russian legend

Fine
503 1 Yuan 1932.............——

504 1 Yuan 1932..........175.00

CHINA—REPUBLIC

Communist Army (cont.)

Chinese Soviet Republic (Kiangsi)

Modern copies exist of Nos. 506, 507, 511 and 512.

Copper

V. Fine
506 1 Fen ND (1932) 5.50

507 5 Fen ND (vars.) 12.50

Silver

508 2 Chio 1932-33 . . . . 40.00

Szechuan and Shensi

Copper

510 200 Wen 1933
     (many vars., crude) . . . 40.00

V. Fine
511 200 Wen 1934 . . . . 25.00

512 500 Wen 1934 (vars.) 47.50

→

CHINA—REPUBLIC

Communist Army (cont.)

Silver

V. Fine

*519 1 Chio Yr. 26...........6.00
520 2 Chio Yr. 26...........6.00

V. Fine
513 1 Yuan 1934..........135.00

Meng-Chiang (Inner Mongolia)

Copper-Nickel

"Puppet State" Issues

Japanese-controlled
regional governments

(also see Manchukuo)

521 5 Chio Yr. 27 (1938)......9.00

Chi-Tung (Eastern Hopei)

Bronze

516 5 Li (½ Cent)
    Yr. 26 (1937).........20.00
517 1 Fen Yr. 26.............5.00

Hua Hsing Bank (Shanghai)

Copper-Nickel

Copper-Nickel

Ex. Fine
522 10 Fen Yr. 29 (1940)......2.00

This coin supposedly was not released for
circulation. Other denominations (with different reverse designs) are patterns.

518 5 Fen Yr. 26.............5.00

CHINA—REPUBLIC

Puppet States (cont.)

Federal Reserve Bank of China
(North China district — Peking)

Aluminum

V. Fine

523 1 Fen Yrs. 30-32
(1941-43)..............1.00
524 5 Fen Yrs. 30-32........1.50
★525 1 Chio Yrs. 30-32.......1.00

NATIONALIST ISSUES 1949-
on Taiwan (Formosa)

First Coinage
Bronze

Unc.

★531 1 Chio Yr. 38 (1949)..... .50

Silver

532 5 Chio Yr. 38............2.50

Second Coinage

Aluminum

Unc.

533 1 Chio Yr. 44 (1955)..... .15
★534 2 Chio Yr. 39............ .50

Brass

535 5 Chio Yr. 43............. .50

Nickel-Silver

536 1 Yuan Yr. 49 (1960)...... .40

Many patterns of all Republican coins
exist, including portrait coins.

Later issues in *Current Coins of the World.*

CHINA, PEOPLE'S REPUBLIC
100 Fen = 1 Yuan

Aluminum
Unc.

1 1 Fen 1955-................. .50
2 2 Fen 1956-................1.00
3 5 Fen 1955-57.............1.50

CHINESE TURKESTAN
(Sinkiang)

Claimed by China for 2,000 years and under sporadic control for 500. Though declared autonomous in 1953, it is under Soviet influence. It is China's richest mineral region and is located in central Asia. Population (largely nomadic): 4,047,450. Principal cities: Tihwa (Urumchi) and Kuldja.

10 Miscals = 1 Tael
Coinage obsolete.

CHINESE EMPIRE

KUANG HSU 1875-1908
and
HSUAN T'UNG 1908-1912

Coins Struck in China for General Use in Turkestan

Copper

Modern copies of Nos. 1 and 2 are known.

Fine

1 1 Fen 5 Li ND, Kuang
Hsu Legend (2 Var.)......50.00

2 10 Wen ND, CD 1910-11,
Hsuan T'ung legend
(varieties).............65.00

Silver

Fine
3 1 Miscal (No Date).......125.00
★4 2 Miscals (No Date)......40.00
5 4 Miscals (No Date)......40.00
6 5 Miscals (No Date)......25.00
7 1 Tael (No Date).........75.00

Many varieties, including circled and uncircled dragon, with or without Turkic script, etc.

A7 5 Fen ND, AH 1295
(1878)................12.50
B7 1 Miscal 1292-95......... ——

Revenue Gold

8 1 Miscal (No Date)........——
9 2 Miscals (No Date).......——

Silver

With Title SUNGAREI

★10 1 Mace..................——
11 2 Mace..................——
12 1 Dollar...............——

CHINESE TURKESTAN

Coins Struck at Various Mints in Turkestan
Aksu Mint
Silver

Kuang Hsu Legends

Fine

A13 1 Miscal AH 1311 (1894)
18mm...............——
13 2 Miscal 1311-12 (23mm).——
14 3 Miscal 1311, 13 (26mm) ——
★15 5 Miscal 1310-12 (31mm).——

Kashgar Mint
Silver

Kuang Hsu Legends

16 1 Miscal ND, 1309-10.....——
17 2 Miscal 1310-22
(1892-1904) 23mm......30.00
★18 3 Miscal 1310-22........12.50
19 5 Miscal 1310-22........20.00

A20 1 Miscal AH 1323 (1905).——
B20 2 Miscal 1323 (23mm)....——
★20 3 Miscal 1323 (27mm)....——
21 5 Miscal 1323 (32mm)...35.00

Dragon and Ta Ch'ing Legends

Fine

★23 2 Miscal AH 1325-26
(1907-08) 24mm.......——
25 5 Miscal ND, 1325-28....20.00
26 1 Liang 1325 (40mm).....——

Dragon and Hsuan T'ung Legend

27 5 Miscal AH 1327-29
(1909-11)..............40.00

Dragon and Silver Coin Legend

· **29** 2 Miscal AH 1329 (2 vars.)——
★30 3 Miscal 1329............——

CHINESE TURKESTAN

Silver

Dragon and Revenue Silver Legend

Fine

31 5 Miscal AH 1329-31
(1911-13)............40.00

Urumchi Mint

Silver

Kuang Hsu Legends

33 2 Miscal AH 1321-25
(1903-07) 24mm........25.00
★34 3 Miscal 1321-25........30.00
35 5 Miscal 1321-25........22.50

REPUBLIC OF CHINA

I. Coins Without Mint Name

Copper

Crossed Five-Striped Flags

Fine

41 5 Miscals 1912 (2 stripes
with Arabesques)......40.00
★42 1 Tael 1912, similar.....175.00
41a 5 Miscals 1912 (4 stripes
with Arabesques)......40.00
42a 1 Tael 1912, similar.....175.00

Copper

A39 10 Wen CD 1912
(2 vars.)............——

★B39 10 Wen ND............——
39 20 Wen ND, sim........——

CHINESE TURKESTAN

Obv: similar to No. B38
Rev: Nationalist flags

Silver

Fine

40 10 Wen CD 1929-30 . . . . . . —

II. Aksu Mint

Cast Copper

Fine

43 5 Miscal 1331-34 . . . . 35.00

HUNG HSIEN Reign 1915-16

Copper

37 10 Wen ND . . . . —

III. Kashghar Mint

Copper

A38 10 Wen AH 1334 (1916) . . —

Republican Issues Resumed
Design Similar to No. 38

38a 10 Wen Yrs. 10-11
(1921-22), rearranged
obv. legend . . . . —

A36 5 Wen ND . . . . —
★B36 10 Wen ND . . . . —

★36 5 Wen AH 1331 (1913) . . . —
38 10 Wen ND, 1331-32 . . . . . . —

★B38 10 Wen CD 1928, rev.
Chinese legend . . . . . . —
B38a 10 Wen CD 1929, rev.
Uighur legend . . . . —

CHINESE TURKESTAN

*Design similar to No. A38
but Nationalist flags*

Fine

C38 20 Wen ND (42mm)......——

Uighuristan Republic 1933-34

IV. Tihwa (Urumchi) Mint

Silver

Fine

★D38 10 Wen AH 1352 (1933) .——
E38 20 Wen 1352............——

45 1 Liang (Tael) Yrs. 6-7
(1917-18).............100.00

COLOMBIA

Mountainous republic, northernmost of the South American countries. Products are agricultural and mineral; coffee comprises 80% of Colombian exports. Population: 21,800,000. Language: Spanish. Capital: *Bogotá.*

10 Décimos or Reales = 1 Peso
100 Centavos = 1 Peso

Note: Most silver and gold coins 1862-1908 bear mint names BOGOTA, POPAYAN or MEDELLIN. The many minor variations in size and style of portraits, lettering, dates, etc., are beyond the scope of this catalog.

ESTADOS UNIDOS DE
(= United States of)
COLOMBIA 1862-1886

I. 10 Reales = 1 Peso

Silver

Fine

A4 2 Reales 1880............85.00

II. 10 Décimos = 1 Peso

Silver

Fine

1 ¼ Décimo 1863-81..........3.50

★2 ½ Décimo 1863-65
(.900 fine).............6.00
2a ½ Décimo 1867
(.666 fine)............15.00
3 1 Décimo 1863-66
(.900 fine)............4.50
3a 1 Décimo 1866
(.835 fine).............4.50

COLOMBIA

III. 100 Centavos = 1 Peso

Copper-Nickel

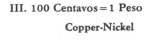

Fine

4 2 Décimos 1865 (.900 fine).50.00
★4a 2 Décimos 1866-67
   (.835 fine)..............4.00

V. Fine

18 1¼ Centavos 1874.........4.00

19 2½ Centavos 1881 (14mm). .25
20 2½ Centavos 1881 (18mm). .40
★21 2½ Centavos 1886 (15mm). .35

Copper

Fine

22 2½ Centavos 1885.........8.50

Silver

12 2½ Centavos 1872-81.......3.00

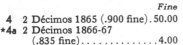

V. Fine

5 1 Peso 1862-68.............32.50

Fine

6 ½ Décimo 1868-76
   (.666 fine)............4.00
6a ½ Décimo 1871-75
   (.835 fine)............4.00
7 1 Décimo 1868-74......3.50
★8 2 Décimos 1870-74......3.00
A9 ½ Peso 1868............——
9 5 Décimos 1868-86
   (.835 fine)............5.00
9a 5 Décimos 1886
   (.500 fine)...........60.00
10 1 Peso 1868-71.... *V.F.* 70.00

No. 9 now includes former No. 11.

Obv: Liberty head
Rev: National arms

★A12 5 Centavos 1872-74.....4.50
B12 10 Centavos 1872-74.....4.00
16 50 Centavos 1872-74
   "50" in numerals.....7.00

COLOMBIA

Obv: Liberty head
Rev: National arms

Fine

13 5 Centavos 1874
(.835 fine)............20.00
13a 5 Centavos 1875-85
(.666 fine)............1.75
14 10 Centavos 1874-85......1.75
15 20 Centavos 1874-82
weight GRAM. 5.........2.50
15b 20 Centavos 1882-85
weight GRAMOS 5. ......2.50

V. Fine

37 1 Peso 1872-73.........40.00
38 2 Pesos 1871-76.........65.00
40 10 Pesos 1862-76..`.......150.00
★41 20 Pesos 1862-78........250.00
Nos. 40-41 include former Nos. 33-34 and
35-36.

.666 Gold
39 5 Pesos 1885.............——

17 50 Centavos 1874-85, value
CINCUENTA spelled
out...................5.00

.500 Silver

14a 10 Centavos 1885-86......25.00
15a 20 Centavos 1886........60.00
17a 50 Centavos 1885-86.......8.00

.900 Gold

Obv: Liberty head
Rev: Value in wreath

V. Fine

A37 1 Peso 1863-64..........65.00
B37 2 Pesos 1863..........120.00
C37 5 Pesos 1862-64........250.00

Obv: Liberty head
Rev: Condor

32 1 Peso 1872-75............35.00

REPUBLICA DE COLOMBIA
1886-

Copper-Nickel
23 2½ Centavos 1902........75.00
No. 23 dated 1900 is now thought to be a
pattern. Nos. 23 and 25 dated 1902 probably
were not released to circulation.

24 5 Centavos 1886, 88
(2 vars).................25

25 5 Centavos 1886, 1902
(Value between branches). .35

COLOMBIA

Silver

Fine

26 5 Décimos 1887-88, head
    sim. to No. 46........40.00

★26a 5 Décimos 1888-89,
    large "ugly" head.....40.00

V. Fine

29 50 Centavos 1892..........4.50
    (Columbus)

Fine

30 10 Centavos 1897..........1.25
31 20 Centavos 1897..........1.50

SANTANDER

Revolutionary Issues by General Ramon Gonzales Valencia.

Struck in thin brass on one side only. Impression shows through on reverse (incuse).

27 50 Centavos 1887........22.50

28 50 Centavos 1888
    (.500 fine)..........50.00
28a 50 Centavos 1889-99,
    1906-08 (.835 fine).....7.50

S1 10 Centavos 1902.........17.50
S2 20 Centavos 1902.........15.00
S3 50 Centavos 1902......... 5.00

COLOMBIA

Copper-Nickel

Fine

42 1 Peso p/m (paper money)
1907-16 75
43 2 Pesos p/m 1907-14 . . . . . . 1.50
44 5 Pesos p/m 1907-14 . . . . . . 1.00

Silver

V. Fine

45 5 Centavos 1902 . . . . 1.25

46 50 Centavos 1902 . . . . 10.00

Bolivar

47 10 Centavos 1911-42 60
★48 20 Centavos 1911-42 90
49 50 Centavos 1912-33
(Narrow Head) 2.75
49a 50 Centavos 1916-34
(Round Head) 2.50

Gold

Stone Cutter

Ex. Fine

50 2½ Pesos 1913 . . . . 65.00
★51 5 Pesos 1913-19 . . . . 60.00

Bolivar

52 2½ Pesos 1919-20 . . . . 35.00
53 5 Pesos 1919-24 . . . . 60.00
54 10 Pesos 1919-24 . . . . 115.00

Bolivar (Smaller Head)

55 2½ Pesos 1924-28 . . . . 40.00
★56 5 Pesos 1924-30 . . . . 60.00

Copper-Nickel

57 1 Centavo 1918-48 10
58 1 Centavo Nickel-clad
steel 1952-58 . . . . *Unc.* .20
59 2 Centavos 1918-47 25
60 5 Centavos 1918-50 20

Bronze

Unc.

61 1 Centavo 1942-66 15

V. Fine

62 2 Centavos 1948-50 50

Unc.

63 5 Centavos 1942-66 25

COLOMBIA

Silver

Billon

Santander   *V. Fine*

64 10 Centavos 1945-52 . . . . 1.00
65 20 Centavos 1945-52 . . . . 1.35

Bolivar
Unc.

69 20 Centavos 1953 . . . . 1.00

Copper-Nickel

Bolivar

66 50 Centavos 1947-48 . . . . 5.00

70 20 Centavos 1956-66 30
71 50 Centavos 1958-66 60

Aluminum-Bronze

Unc.

67 2 Centavos Divided legend
1952,65 20
67a 2 Centavos Continuous
legend 1955-59 20

200th Anniversary of Milled Coinage

Copper-Nickel

68 10 Centavos 1952-53 18mm . .75
68a 10 Centavos 1954-66 18.5mm .25

72 1 Peso Silver 1956 . . . . 15.00

Later issues in *Current Coins of the World.*

COMORO ISLANDS (Grand Comore)

A French overseas territory, located in Mozambique Channel off the coast of Africa. It is a prosperous archipelago of about 850 square miles with a population of 250,000. Capital: *Dzaoudzi.*
100 Centimes = 1 Franc   Coinage obsolete.

COMORO ISLANDS

Bronze

Fine

*1 5 Centimes AH 1308
(1890)................6.00
2 10 Centimes 1308.........8.00

Silver

Ex. Fine
3 5 Francs 1308...........550.00 →

Later issues in *Current Coins of the World.*

COSTA RICA

Republic in southern Central America. Chief products: coffee, bananas, cocoa and abaca. Some mineral export and local manufacturing. Population: 1,800,000. Language: Spanish. Capital: *San José.*

8 Reales = 1 Peso
2 Pesos = 1 Escudo
8 Escudos = 1 Onza (to 1864)

100 Centavos = 1 Peso (1865-96)
100 Centimos = 1 Colon (1896-)

Silver

Fine
5 1/16 Peso 1850-55............15.00
6 1/8 Peso 1850-55.............8.00
7 1/4 Peso 1850-55.............5.00

Gold

V. Fine
22 1/2 Escudo 1850-64.........50.00

V. Fine
*23 1 Escudo 1850-55.......80.00
24 2 Escudos 1850-63......125.00
25 1/2 Onza 1850...........225.00

DECIMAL COINAGE
1864-1896

Copper-Nickel

32 1/4 Centavo ND (1865) 65.00
There are many counterfeits of No. 32.

COSTA RICA

Fine
30 1 Centavo 1865-68........4.00

31 1 Centavo 1874...........3.75

Silver

9 5 Centavos 1865-75.......2.00
10 10 Centavos 1865-72
19.5mm..............4.00
10a 10 Centavos 1875 18mm....3.25
11 25 Centavos Small "25C^S"
1864.................9.00
11a 25 Centavos Large "25C^S"
1864-75..............4.50
12 50 Centavos 1865-75.......9.00

Gold

V. Fine
26 1 Peso 1864-72...........35.00
27 2 Pesos 1866-76..........75.00

28 5 Pesos 1867-76.........100.00
29 10 Pesos 1870-76.........175.00

*Same Type as 1864-76 Gold Series,
but LEI 0.900 G.W. on Reverse*

V. Fine
33 5 Pesos 1873............350.00
34 20 Pesos 1873.............——

Silver

Fine
13 5 Centavos 1885-87.......1.25
14 10 Centavos 1886-87.......2.00
15 25 Centavos 1886-87.......3.00
16 50 Centavos 1880-90.......5.50

HEATON BIRM^M on Reverse

17 5 Centavos 1889-92........ .75
18 10 Centavos 1889-92.......1.00
19 25 Centavos 1889-93.......1.75

20 50 Centavos of Colombia
countermarked on both
sides (1889)............20.00

NEW COINAGE SYSTEM
1896-

Copper-Nickel

Ex. Fine
46 2 Centimos 1903...........1.50

COSTA RICA

Silver

.900 Fine

		Fine
39	5 Centimos 1905-14	1.00
40	10 Centimos 1905-14	1.00
41	50 Centimos 1902-14	22.50

.500 Fine

42	10 Centavos 1917	1.50
A42	50 Centimos 1917-18	——

(All No. A42 were counter-stamped as No. 44 except for 10 presentation pieces.)

.650 Fine

45	25 Centimos 1924	1.25

New Values Stamped on Previous Issues

43	50 Centimos Stamped on various 25c pieces 1923	1.75
44	1 Colon Stamped on 50c Pieces of various dates 1923	3.50

Gold

Columbus

		V. Fine
35	2 Colones 1900-28	25.00
36	5 Colones 1899-1900	45.00
37	10 Colones 1897-1900	80.00
38	20 Colones 1897-1900	225.00

Brass

47	5 Centavos 1917-19	2.50

48	10 Centavos 1917-19	1.00
49	5 Centimos 1920-41	.75
50	10 Centimos 1920-22	.75
51	5 Centimos Bronze 1929	.75
52	10 Centimos Bronze 1929	.75
54	10 Centimos 1936-41	.50

Copper-Nickel

Reverse: B.I.C.R.
(Banco Internacional de Costa Rica)

55	25 Centimos 1935	.50
56	50 Centimos 1935	1.00
57	1 Colon 1935	1.25

COSTA RICA

Reverse: B.N.C.R.
(Banco Nacional de Costa Rica)

Brass

V. Fine
63 25 Centimos 1944-46....... .75

Reverse: B.C.C.R.
(Banco Central de Costa Rica)

Copper-Nickel

V. Fine

58 5 Centimos 1942 Struck
over 2c (No. 46).......1.75

A64 5 Centimos 1951
(BC/CR Divided)..... .50

Unc.

Brass

A58 5 Centimos 1942-47..... .20
B58 10 Centimos 1942-47..... .30

64 5 Centimos 1951, 69-72.. .10
65 10 Centimos 1951, 69-72.. .15

Copper-Nickel

Stainless Steel

59 25 Centimos 1937-48..... .25
60 50 Centimos 1937........ .75
60a 50 Centimos 1948
(Larger).............. .35
61 1 Colon 1937-48......... .50
62 2 Colones 1948..........1.00

66 5 Centimos 1953-67..... .10
67 10 Centimos 1953-67..... .15
68 1 Colon 1954...........1.50
69 2 Colones 1954..........3.00

Later issues in Current Coins of the World.

CRETE
Under Greek Administration 1898-1906

Largest of the Greek Islands, its area is 3,234 square miles. Its history, government and coinage are closely identified with that of Greece from earliest times. Capital: *Canea.*

100 Lepta = 1 Drachma

Coinage obsolete.

Bronze

V. Fine

1 1 Lepton 1900-01...........4.00
2 2 Lepta 1900-01...........4.00

CRETE

Copper-Nickel

Fine

3 5 Lepta 1900..............3.50
4 10 Lepta 1900..............3.50
5 20 Lepta 1900..............4.00

For similar coins dated 1894-95 see Greece Nos. 16-18.

Silver

*Obv: Prince George of Greece
(High Commissioner 1898-1906)*

Fine

6 50 Lepta 1901..............6.00
7 1 Drachma 1901............7.00
8 2 Drachmai 1901...........8.00
9 5 Drachmai 1901..........16.50

CUBA (Republica de Cuba)

Republic occupying the largest of the Caribbean Islands. Sugar cane and its products, including rum, were the principal industry before the Castro regime, with tobacco-growing and its manufacture into cigars and cigarettes ranking second. Other agricultural products are also important, as well as mining. Population: 8,600,000. Language: Spanish. Capital: *La Habana* (Havana).

100 Centavos = 1 Peso

Silver

Ex. Fine

1 Souvenir Peso 1897 (3 vars.) . 85.00

Ex. Fine

2 1 Peso 1898...............450.00

CUBA

Copper-Nickel

Brass

Copper-Nickel

Silver

Gold

Silver

50th Anniversary of Republic

Marti Centennial—1953

Brass

Silver

Later issues in Current Coins of the World.

CURAÇAO

An island in the Netherlands Antilles group in the West Indies (Leeward Islands) near the coast of Venezuela. Now a part of the autonomous government of Netherlands Antilles. Capital: *Willemstad.*

100 Cents = 1 Gulden

WILLIAM I 1813-1840

Silver

Fine

A1 1 Stuiver 1822 . . . . 25.00

B1 1 Reaal 1821 . . . . 30.00

WILHELMINA 1890-1948

First Coinage

Silver

1 ⅒ Gulden 1901 . . . . 4.00
2 ¼ Gulden 1900 . . . . 2.50

Second Coinage

Bronze

V. Fine

3 1 Cent 1944-47 25
4 2½ Cent 1944-48 30

Silver

V. Fine

5 ⅒ Gulden 1944-47 35
6 ¼ Gulden 1944-47 65

7 1 Gulden 1944 . . . . 3.50
10 2½ Gulden 1944 . . . *Ex. Fine* 6.00

For other World War II issues, see Netherlands.

Third Coinage

8 ⅒ Gulden 1948 60

9 5 Cent Cop.-Nic. 1948 40
For issues since 1952, see Netherlands Antilles.

CYPRUS

Island located in the eastern Mediterranean Sea. Four-fifths of the population is of Greek ancestry, the rest of Turkish. The principal activity is agriculture. Until August, 1960, it was a British Crown Colony. On that date it became an independent republic within the British Commonwealth. Population: 659,000. Capital: *Nicosia*.

9 Piastres = 1 Shilling

VICTORIA 1878-1901

Bronze

Fine

5	4½ Piastres 1901	5.00
6	9 Piastres 1901	7.00
7	18 Piastres 1901	12.00

Fine

1	¼ Piastre 1879-1901	5.00
2	½ Piastre 1879-1900	5.00

EDWARD VII 1901-1910

Bronze

8	¼ Piastre 1902-08	5.00
9	½ Piastre 1908	27.50
10	1 Piastre 1908	30.00

Silver

3	1 Piastre 1879-1900	6.00

Silver

4	3 Piastres 1901	7.50
11	9 Piastres 1907	12.50
12	18 Piastres 1907	17.50

CYPRUS

GEORGE V 1910-1936
Bronze
Reverse Same as Nos. 8-10

V. Fine

13 ¼ Piastre 1922-26.........2.50
14 ½ Piastre 1922-31..........4.50
15 1 Piastre 1922-31..........6.00

Copper-Nickel

16 ½ Piastre 1934..............50
17 1 Piastre 1934..............65

Silver
Reverse Design Like Nos. 5-7

18 4½ Piastres 1921..........3.00
19 9 Piastres 1913-21........3.50
20 18 Piastres 1913-21........6.00

50th Anniversary of British Rule

21 45 Piastres 1928..........20.00

GEORGE VI 1936-1952
Copper-Nickel

V. Fine

22 ½ Piastre 1938............35
23 1 Piastre 1938............50

Bronze
22a (24) ½ Piastre 1942-45.....20
23a (25) 1 Piastre 1942-46.....30

Silver

28 4½ Piastres 1938..........2.50
29 9 Piastres 1938-40........2.25
30 18 Piastres 1938-40........3.50

Copper-Nickel

26 1 Shilling 1947...........1.00
27 2 Shillings 1947..........1.50

New Legend:
GEORGIUS SEXTUS DEI GRATIA REX
Bronze

31 ½ Piastre 1949.............20
32 1 Piastre 1949.............30

CYPRUS

Copper-Nickel

Unc.
36 5 Mils 1955-56 30

Copper-Nickel

V. Fine
33 1 Shilling 1949 . . . . 1.00
34 2 Shillings 1949 . . . . 1.50

ELIZABETH II 1952-1960
Decimal Currency 1955-

100 Mils = 2 Shillings
1000 Mils = 1 Pound

37 25 Mils 1955 50
38 50 Mils 1955 . . . . 1.00

Bronze

39 100 Mils 1955-57 . . . . 2.00

Unc.
35 3 Mils 1955 15

Later issues in *Current Coins of the World.*

CZECHOSLOVAKIA
(Republika Ceskoslovenska)

Republic of central Europe created in 1918 through the dissolution of the old Austro-Hungarian Empire. A country of great mineral and agricultural wealth, it is also famous for precision manufacture of a variety of products, among them munitions, glass, textiles, furniture and ceramics. Population: 14,200,000. Languages: Czech and Slovak. Capital: *Praha* (Prague).

100 Haleru = 1 Koruna

Zinc

Bronze

V. Fine
1 2 Halere 1923-25 . . . . 5.00

V. Fine
2 5 Haleru 1923-38 20
3 10 Haleru 1922-38 35

CZECHOSLOVAKIA

Copper-Nickel

V. Fine
4 20 Haleru 1921-38 20

5 25 Haleru 1933 . . . . .1.25

6 50 Haleru 1921-31 30

7 1 Koruna 1922-38 50

Various Metals

8 5 Korun Cop.-Nic.
30 mm. 1925-27 . . . . . . .3.50
9 5 Korun Silv.
27 mm. 1928-32 . . . . . . .1.75
★10 5 Korun Nic. 27 mm.
1937-38 . . . . .4.00

10th Anniversary of Independence
Silver

Ex. Fine
11 10 Korun 1928 . . . . .3.50

Regular Issues

12 10 Korun 1930-33 . . . . .3.50

13 20 Korun 1933-34 . . . . .7.00

CZECHOSLOVAKIA

Death of President Masaryk

Ex. Fine

14 20 Korun 1937............7.00

Fifth Anniversary of Republic

Gold

Obv: as No. 15, dated "1918-1923"
Rev: as No. 15

A15 1 Dukat 1923...........——

All pieces of No. A15 were serially numbered
(from 1 to 1000) below the figure on reverse.

Regular Issues

Gold

Rev: Saint Wenceslas

★15 1 Dukat 1923-39, 51......35.00
16 2 Dukaty 1923-38, 51.....75.00

★17 5 Dukatu 1929-38, 51...150.00
18 10 Dukatu 1929-38, 51...250.00

WORLD WAR II ISSUES
SLOVAKIA — German
Protectorate 1939-1945
100 Halierov = 1 Koruna

Various Metals

V. Fine

S19b 5 Halierov Zinc 1942....4.50

S20 10 Halierov Br. 1939, 42..2.00

S21 20 Halierov Br. 1940-42...2.00
S21a 20 Halierov Alum.
1942-43.............1.00

S22 50 Halierov Cop.-Nic.
1940-41...........2.00
S22b 50 Halierov Alum.
1943-44...........1.50

S23 1 Koruna Cop.-Nic.
1940-45............1.50

CZECHOSLOVAKIA

Father Hlinka *V. Fine*
S24 5 Korun Nickel 1939......2.25

Silver

Pribina-3 Figures *Ex. Fine*
S25 10 Korun 1944............4.50

Election of President Tiso
Commemorative

S26 20 Korun 1939..........10.00

St. Cyril and Methodius
S27 20 Korun 1941...........5.50

5th Anniversary of Slovakia
Commemorative

Ex. Fine
S28 50 Korun 1944...........5.00

BOHEMIA-MORAVIA
German Protectorate 1939-45

Zinc

V. Fine
B29 10 Haleru 1940-44......... .50

B30 20 Haleru 1940-44......... .50
B31 50 Haleru (Like No. 6)
1940-44 ....1.00

B32 1 Koruna 1941-44..........1.00

CZECHOSLOVAKIA

RESTORATION OF REPUBLIC

Various Metals

Unc.

33 20 Haleru Bronze 1947-50
(18mm.) 40

34 20 Haleru Alum. 1951-52
(16mm.) 40

35 50 Haleru Bronze 1947-50 50
36 50 Haleru Alum. (18mm.)
1951-53 50

37 1 Koruna Cop.-Nic.
1946-47 65
38 1 Koruna Alum. 1947-53 50

Unc.

39 2 Koruny Cop.-Nic.
1947-48 75

A39 5 Korun Alum.
1952 . . . . .35.00

No. A39 was not released for circulation because of 1953 currency reform.

Third Anniversary Slovak National Uprising

Silver

40 50 Korun 1947 . . . . .3.00

Third Anniversary Prague Uprising

41 50 Korun 1948 . . . . .3.50

CZECHOSLOVAKIA

6th Centennial
Charles University at Prague

70th Birthday of Stalin

Unc.
45 50 Korun
1949 . . . 4.00
46 100 Korun
1949 . . . 7.50

Unc.
42 100 Korun 1948 . . . . 6.00

30th Anniversary of Communist Party

47 100 Korun
1951 . . . 6.00

30th Anniversary
Separation from Austria

43 100 Korun 1948 . . . . 6.00

CURRENCY REFORM 1953

Aluminum

48 1 Haler 1953-60 15
49 3 Halere 1953-54 15
50 5 Haleru 1953-55 20
51 10 Haleru 1953-58 25
52 25 Haleru 1953-54 40

7th Centennial
Mining Privileges of Jihlava

Aluminum-Bronze

44 100 Korun 1949 . . . . 6.00

61 1 Koruna 1957-60 75

CZECHOSLOVAKIA

10th Anniversary Slovak Uprising 1944-1954

Silver

Unc

53 10 Korun 1954 . . . . 5.00
54 25 Korun 1954 . . . . 8.00

10th Anniversary Liberation From Nazis, May 9, 1945

Silver

55 10 Korun 1955 . . . . 4.00
56 25 Korun 1955 (Soldier,
      woman and child) 6.00

		Unc.
57	50 Korun 1955 (Soldier with rifle aloft)	9.50
58	100 Korun 1955 (Four figures)	17.50

250th Anniversary Technical High School

59
10 Korun
1957 . . . . . 4.50

Bust of
Willenberg

Komensky Commemorative

60 10 Korun 1957 . . . . 4.50

Later issues in *Current Coins of the World.*

DANISH WEST INDIES

A group of about fifty islands lying southeast of Puerto Rico in the Caribbean. They were purchased by the U.S. in 1917 and became the U.S. Virgin Islands. Chief products are rum and bay rum. Principal town: *Charlotte Amalie.*

5 Bit = 1 Cent   20 Cents = 1 Franc   5 Francs = 1 Daler   Coinage obsolete.

CHRISTIAN IX 1863-1906

Bronze

Fine

1 1 Cent 1868-83 . . . . 5.00

DANISH WEST INDIES

Silver

Fine

2 5 Cents 1878-79. . . . . .10.00
3 10 Cents 1878-79. . . . . .7.50

Fine

10 20 Cents-1 Franc 1905. . . . . 15.00
11 40 Cents-2 Francs 1905. . . . 25.00

Gold

4 20 Cents 1878-79. . . . . .17.50

Bronze

12 4 Daler-20 Francs *Ex. Fine*
     1904-05. . . . . 225.00
13 10 Daler-50 Francs 1904 1000.00

FREDERIK VIII 1906-1912
Silver

5 ½ Cent-2½ Bit 1905. . . . . 4.00
6 1 Cent-5 Bit 1905. . . . . 4.50
7 2 Cents-10 Bit 1905. . . . . 5.00

Nickel

Fine

14 20 Cents-1 Franc 1907. . . . . .20.00
15 40 Cents-2 Francs 1907. . . .40.00

CHRISTIAN X 1912-1917

8 5 Cents-25 Bit 1905. . . . . .4.00

Silver

Bronze

9 10 Cents-50 Bit 1905. . . . . . . .5.00

16 1 Cent-5 Bit 1913. . . . . .6.50

DANZIG (Freie Stadt Danzig)

A port on the Baltic Sea, it was created a free city by the Treaty of Versailles in 1919, and brought within the Polish Customs Frontier in 1922. Danzig struck its own coinage until it was proclaimed part of the German Reich in 1939. It is now under Polish administration.

100 Pfennig = 1 Mark (until 1923)
100 Pfennig = 1 Gulden (1923-39)

Coinage obsolete.

Note: New catalog numbers have been assigned in the 10th edition. The original numbers are given in parentheses.

Emergency Issues (Notgeld)
Zinc

V. Fine
*1 **(A1)** 10 Pfennig 1920......10.00
2 **(B1)** 10 Pfennig 1920
      Rev. large "10"...50.00

Regular Issues
First Coinage
Bronze

3 **(1)** 1 Pfennig 1923-37.......2.00
4 **(2)** 2 Pfennig 1923-37.......2.50
Copper-Nickel

5   5 Pfennig 1923-28.........2.00

6 10 Pfennig 1923.............2.50

Silver

Ex. Fine
7 **(11)** ½ Gulden 1923-27.....10.00

8 **(12)** 1 Gulden 1923........15.00
9 **(13)** 2 Gulden 1923........22.50

10 **(14)** 5 Gulden 1923-27.....85.00

DANZIG

Gold

Unc.

11 (18) 25 Gulden 1923......475.00
12 (19) 25 Gulden 1930
(Diff. rev. arms).......——

Second Coinage

Aluminum-Bronze

V. Fine

13 (3) 5 Pfennig 1932..........2.00

14 (4) 10 Pfennig 1932.........2.25

Nickel

15 (7) ½ Gulden 1932.........9.00

16 (8) 1 Gulden 1932.........14.00

Silver

Ex. Fine

17 (15) 2 Gulden 1932........50.00

18 (16) 5 Gulden 1932.......160.00

19 (17) 5 Gulden 1932.......175.00

DANZIG

Third Coinage
Nickel

Ex. Fine

Ex. Fine

20 (9) 5 Gulden 1935. . . . . 85.00   **21 (10)** 10 Gulden 1935. . . . . . 225.00

DENMARK

(Kongeriget Danmark)

A constitutional monarchy occupying the Jutland peninsula and about 500 islands between the Baltic and the North Seas. Exports large quantities of agricultural produce, especially dairy products. Fisheries are also important. Population: 5,000,000. Language: Danish. Capital: *Copenhagen.*

1854   96 Skilling = 1 Rigsdaler
10 Rigsdaler = 1 Christian d'Or
1873 100 Øre = 1 Krone (Crown)

CHRISTIAN IX 1863-1906

Commemorating
Death of Frederik VII and
Accession of Christian IX

Silver

V. Fine

3 2 Rigsdaler 1863. . . . . 150.00 →

Regular Issues

Bronze

Fine

1 ½ Skilling 1868. . . . . .1.50
2 1 Skilling 1867-72 75

DENMARK

Silver

Fine

4 4 Skilling 1867-74 . . . . 5.00

5 2 Rigsdaler 1864-72 . . . . 100.00

Gold   *V. Fine*
6 1 Christian d'Or 1869 . . . . 500.00
7 2 Christian d'Or 1866-70 . 300.00

DECIMAL SYSTEM 1874-

Bronze

Fine

8 1 Øre 1874-1904 50
9 2 Øre 1874-1906 65
10 5 Øre 1874-1906 . . . . 1.00

Silver

11 10 Øre 1874-1905 . . . . 2.00
12 25 Øre 1874-1905 . . . . 3.00

Fine

13 1 Krone 1875-98 . . . . 4.50
14 2 Kroner 1875-99 . . . . 7.50

Gold

V. Fine

18 10 Kroner 1873-1900 . . . . . 50.00
19 20 Kroner 1873-1900 . . . . . . 65.00

Commemorating
25th Year of Reign

Silver

15 2 Kroner 1888 . . . . 22.50

Commemorating
Golden Wedding

16 2 Kroner 1892 . . . . 20.00

DENMARK

40 Years' Reign
Silver

Silver

		Fine
23	10 Øre 1907-12	1.00
24	25 Øre 1907-11	1.50

V. Fine

17 2 Kroner 1903 . . . . 20.00

FREDERIK VIII 1906-1912

Commemorating Death of Christian IX and Accession of Frederik VIII

Gold

V. Fine

26	10 Kroner 1908-09	40.00
27	20 Kroner 1908-12	75.00

Silver

CHRISTIAN X 1912-1947

Bronze

		Fine
28	1 Øre 1913-23	.25
29	2 Øre 1913-23	.30
30	5 Øre 1913-23	.45

25 2 Kroner 1906 . . . . 17.50

Regular Issues
Bronze

Iron

28a	1 Øre 1918-19	1.75
29a	2 Øre 1918-19	1.75
30a	5 Øre 1918-19	2.50

Copper-Nickel

		Fine
20	1 Øre 1907-12	.40
21	2 Øre 1907-12	.50
22	5 Øre 1907-12	.75

31	10 Øre 1920-23	.50
32	25 Øre 1920-22	.75

DENMARK

Aluminum-Bronze

		V. Fine
33	½ Krone 1924-40	1.00
34	1 Krone 1924-41	.75
35	2 Kroner 1924-41	1.25

Commemorating Silver Wedding

Christian X and Alexandrine

		V. Fine
41	2 Kroner 1923	15.00

Silver

Smooth Edges, Type of Nos. 31-32

36	10 Øre 1914-19	.85
37	25 Øre 1913-19	1.25

Commemorating 60th Birthday

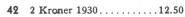

38	1 Krone 1915-16	4.00
39	2 Kroner 1915-16	8.50

42	2 Kroner 1930	12.50

Commemorating Death of Frederik VIII and Accession → of Christian X

40	2 Kroner 1912	15.00

DENMARK

Commemorating 25 Years of Reign

47	2 Øre 1926-40	.15
48	5 Øre 1927-40	.20

Various Metals

49	10 Øre Cop.-Nic. 1924-47	.20
49a	10 Øre Zinc 1941-45	.50
50	25 Øre Cop.-Nic. 1924-47	.25
50a	25 Øre Zinc 1941-45	.60

For similar coins dated 1941, see Faeroe Islands.

43	2 Kroner 1937	12.50

Gold

51	1 Øre Zinc 1941-46	.20
52	2 Øre Alum. 1941	.25
52a	2 Øre Zinc 1942-47	.25

44	10 Kroner 1913-17	65.00
45	20 Kroner 1913-31	75.00

Bronze

53	5 Øre Alum. 1941	.50
53a	5 Øre Zinc 1942-45	.35

46	1 Øre 1926-40	.15
54	1 Krone Al.-Br. 1942-47	.75

DENMARK

Commemorating 75th Birthday

18th Birthday of Princess Margrethe

Unc.
64 2 Kroner 1958 . 12.50

55 2 Kroner Silver 1945 . . *V. F.* 20.00

FREDERIK IX 1947-1972
Zinc

Unc.
56 1 Øre 1948-72 10
57 2 Øre 1948-72 15
58 5 Øre 1950-64 20

Copper-Nickel
59 10 Øre 1948-60 35
60 25 Øre 1948-60 40

Aluminum-Bronze

61 1 Krone 1947-59 . . . . .1.00
62 2 Kroner 1947-59 . . . . .1.50

Greenland Commemorative
Silver

63 2 Kroner 1953 . . . . .30.00

Silver Wedding Commemorative

65 5 Kroner 1960 . . . . .10.00

Bronze
68 5 Øre 1960-72 20

Copper-Nickel

69 10 Øre 1960-72 20
70 25 Øre 1960-67 35

71 1 Krone 1960-72 60
72 5 Kroner 1960-72 . . . . .1.85

Later issues in Current Coins of the World.

DOMINICAN REPUBLIC
(Republica Dominicana)

Occupies the eastern two-thirds of the island of Hispaniola, which lies between Cuba and Puerto Rico. The land is extremely fertile and supports a variety of tropical agricultural crops. Mining and cattle raising are also important. Population: 3,900,000. Language: Spanish. Capital: *Santo Domingo.*

100 Centesimos = 1 Franco
100 Centavos = 1 Peso

Brass or Bronze

Fine
A1 ¼ Real 1844-48 . . . . 4.00

Brass

1 1 Centavo 1877 . . . . 3.50

Copper-Nickel

4 2½ Centavos 1877 . . . . 8.50

Fine
5 5 Centavos 1877 . . . . 7.50

6 1¼ Centavos 1882, 88 . . . . . . 5.00
7 2½ Centavos 1882, 88 . . . . . . 1.00

Bronze

2 5 Centesimos 1891 . . . . 3.00
3 10 Centesimos 1891 . . . . 4.00

Silver

8 50 Centesimos
1891 . . . . 10.00
9 1 Franco 1891 . . . 12.50
10 5 Francos 1891 . . 75.00

DOMINICAN REPUBLIC

Base Silver

		Fine
11	10 Centavos 1897	..........2.00
12	20 Centavos 1897	.........2.50
13	½ Peso 1897	..............4.50
14	1 Peso 1897	......*V. Good* 10.00

Bronze

		Unc.
15	1 Centavo 1937-61	.... .35

Copper-Nickel

16	5 Centavos 1937-72	.... .75
16a	5 Centavos Silver alloy 1944	.............*V. Fine* 1.50

Silver

		Ex. Fine
20	1 Peso 1939-52	..........20.00

Commemorating 25th Year of Trujillo Regime

		Unc.
21	1 Peso 1955	..............25.00

Gold

		Unc.
17	10 Centavos 1937-61	.... .65
18	25 Centavos 1937-61	.......1.50
19	½ Peso 1937-61	...........3.00

22	30 Pesos 1955	...........200.00

Later issues in *Current Coins of the World.*

EAST AFRICA

An administrative grouping of five separate British territories: Kenya (achieved independence 1963), Capital: *Nairobi;* the former Trust Territory of Tanganyika (1961), Capital: *Dar-es-Salaam;* Uganda (1962), Capital: *Entebbe;* former British Somaliland (1960), Capital: *Hargeisa;* and the Sultanate of Zanzibar and Pemba (1963). Tanganyika and Zanzibar joined in 1964 to form Tanzania. This coinage was also legal tender in Ethiopia, and Aden (see South Arabia). All these countries now have their own coinages.

```
 64 Pice = 1 India Rupee to 1905
100 Cents = 1 Rupee 1905-20
100 Cents = 1 Florin 1920-21
100 Cents = 1 Shilling 1921-63
```

VICTORIA 1837-1901

Legend:
EAST AFRICA PROTECTORATE

Bronze

		Fine
1	1 Pice 1897-99	3.50

Copper-Nickel
		Fine
4	½ Cent 1909	7.50
★5	1 Cent 1909-10	1.00
6	10 Cents 1907-10	5.00

The similar 5 cents 1908 is a pattern.

Silver

		Fine
7	25 Cents 1906-10	7.00
8	50 Cents 1906-10	8.50

EDWARD VII 1901-1910

Legend:
EAST AFRICA & UGANDA PROTECTORATE

Aluminum

2	½ Cent 1908	20.00
3	1 Cent 1907-08	3.50

GEORGE V 1910-1936

Copper-Nickel

9	1 Cent 1911-18	1.50
10	5 Cents 1913-19	2.50
11	10 Cents 1911-18	4.50

EAST AFRICA

Silver

Fine

12 25 Cents 1912-18 . . . . 4.50
13 50 Cents 1911-19 . . . . 7.00

New Legend:
EAST AFRICA only
Copper-Nickel

Ex. Fine

14 1 Cent 1920-21 . . . . 60.00
15 5 Cents 1920 . . . . 75.00
16 10 Cents 1920 . . . . 100.00

Silver

17 25 Cents 1920 . . . . 32.50
18 50 Cents/1 Shilling 1920 . . . . ——
19 1 Florin 1920-21 . . . . 35.00

No. 18 probably was not issued to circulation.

Reduced Size Coinage
Bronze

V. Fine

20 1 Cent 1922-35 35
21 5 Cents 1921-36 50
22 10 Cents 1921-36 75

Billon

V. Fine

23 50 Cents/½ Shilling
1921-24 . . . . .1.50
24 1 Shilling 1921-25 . . . . .2.50

EDWARD VIII 1936
Bronze

25 5 Cents 1936 . . . . .1.00
26 10 Cents 1936 . . . . .1.75

GEORGE VI 1936-1952
Bronze

27 1 Cent 1942 15
28 5 Cents 1937-41, thick 30
28a 5 Cents 1942-43, thin 30
29 10 Cents 1937-41, thick 50
29a 10 Cents 1942-45, thin 50

EAST AFRICA

Billon

		V. Fine
30	50 Cents 1937-44	1.00
31	1 Shilling 1937-46	1.75

New Legend:
GEORGIUS SEXTUS REX

Bronze

32	1 Cent 1949-52	.25
33	5 Cents 1949-52	.35
34	10 Cents 1949-52	.50

Copper-Nickel

35	50 Cents 1948-52	.50
36	1 Shilling 1948-52	1.00

ELIZABETH II 1952-1963

Bronze

		Unc.
37	1 Cent 1954-62	.15

38	5 Cents 1955-63	.25
39	10 Cents 1956	.75

Copper-Nickel

40	50 Cents 1954-63	.50

Later issues in *Current Coins of the World.*

ECUADOR

(Republica del Ecuador)

A republic on the northwest coast of South America. The country is divided into three distinct areas, coastal, plateau and eastern, by two chains of the Andes Mountains. Rich mineral resources are beginning to be exploited, and Ecuador exports many agricultural products, especially coffee, cacao and balsa wood. Population: 6,500,000. Language: Spanish. Capital: *Quito.*

16 Reales = 1 Escudo	10 Decimos = 1 Sucre
10 Centavos = 1 Decimo	25 Sucres = 1 Condor

ECUADOR

Silver

Fine

1 ¼ Real 1842-43 . . . . 60.00

*Obv: draped bust of Liberty,
fineness "8 Ds"*

Legend varieties exist for Nos. 3-4.

		Fine
2	½ Real 1838, 40	8.50
3	1 Real 1836-41	5.00
4	2 Reales 1836-41	6.00
5	4 Reales 1841-43	10.00

		Fine
8	¼ Real 1849-62	10.00
9	½ Real 1848-49	8.00
★10	2 Reales 1847-57	7.00
11	4 Reales 1855-57	10.00
12	8 Reales 1846 . . . . . *E. F.* 475.00

Obv: fineness ".666"

| 10a | 2 Reales 1862 . . . . | —— |
| 11a | 4 Reales 1862 . . . . | —— |

Gold

V. Fine

★16 4 Escudos 1836-41 . . . . . . 275.00
17   8 Escudos 1838-43 . . . . . . 750.00

Ex. Fine

13 5 Francs 1858 . . . . 225.00

Silver

Fine

6   4 Reales 1844 . . . . 45.00
★7   4 Reales 1845 (Different
     Head) 75.00

Fine

14 2 Reales 1862 . . . . ——
★15 4 Reales 1862 . . . . 35.00

ECUADOR

Gold

Obv: Simón Bolívar

V. Fine

18 8 Escudos 1845,
name on neck.........1500.00
19 8 Escudos 1847-56,
name below neck.......400.00

Decimal System

Copper

Fine

20 ½ Centavo 1890...........2.50
21 1 Centavo 1872, 90........3.50
23 2 Centavos 1872.........10.00

Copper-Nickel

Fine

24 ½ Centavo 1884...........2.25
25 1 Centavo 1884, 86........2.00
26 ½ Decimo 1884, 86........2.50

Silver

27 ½ Decimo 1893-1915......1.00
28 1 Decimo 1884-1916.......1.00
★29 2 Decimos 1884-1916......1.50
30 ½ Sucre 1884............20.00
31 1 Sucre 1884-97..........10.00

Gold
V. Fine
32 10 Sucres 1899-1900.......75.00

Copper-Nickel

Fine

33 ½ Centavo 1909...........2.75
34 1 Centavo 1909...........2 25
35 2 Centavos 1909..........2.50
37 5 Centavos 1909..........2.25

Rev: values spelled out

36 2½ Centavos 1917.........8.00
37a 5 Centavos (thinner)
1917-18...............1.00
39 10 Centavos 1918........6.50
Rev: values in numerals
38 5 Centavos 1919..........1.00
40 10 Centavos 1919.........1.25

ECUADOR

Bolivar

		V. Fine
41	5 Centavos 1924	1.00
42	10 Centavos 1924	1.00

NEW COINAGE LAW
March 4, 1927
Gold

43 1 Condor 1928 . . . . 125.00

Bronze

44 1 Centavo 1928 50

Nickel

45 2½ Centavos 1928 . . . . 2.25

46	5 Centavos 1928	.35
47	10 Centavos 1928	.50

Silver

48 50 Centavos 1928, 30 . . . . 1.00

		V. Fine
49	1 Sucre 1928-34	1.00
50	2 Sucres 1928, 30	2.00

Nickel

51	5 Centavos 1937	.30
52	10 Centavos 1937	.35
53	20 Centavos 1937	.40

54 1 Sucre 1937 75

Brass

51a	5 Centavos 1942, 44	.60
52a	10 Centavos 1942	.75
53a	20 Centavos 1942, 44	.75

Silver

		Ex. Fine
55	2 Sucres 1944	1.50
56	5 Sucres 1943-44	4.50

Copper-Nickel

		Unc.
51b	5 Centavos 1946	.10
52b	10 Centavos 1946	.15
53b	20 Centavos 1946	.25
54a	1 Sucre 1946, Nickel (Bust)	.50

Later issues in *Current Coins of the World.*

EGYPT (Jamhuryat Misr)

A republic (since 1953) occupying the northeast corner of the African Continent. Products are largely agricultural, dependent on the waters of the Nile River; cotton is the most important export. Population: 34,800,000. Capital: *Cairo.*

40 Para = 1 Guerche (Piastre)
10 Milliemes = 1 Piastre

100 Piastres = 1 Egyptian Pound

Coinage Under Turkish Rule

Most coins issued before 1916 are similar to Turkish types but are distinguished by the Arabic word *Misr* (Egypt) on the reverse.

MISR
(In Arabic)

ABDUL AZIZ 1861-1876
(Accession Date A.H. 1277 on Coins)

Obv: Without flower at R. of toughra

Bronze

		Fine
1	4 Para Yr. 4	1.50
*2	10 Para Yrs. 4-10 (29mm)	.50
3	20 Para Yrs. 3-10 (32mm)	.75
3b	20 Para Yr. 7 (29mm, thick)	
4	40 Para Yr. 10	2.00

Silver

8	2½ Guerche Yr. 4	7.50
*9	5 Guerche Yr. 4	12.50
10	10 Guerche Yr. 4	22.50

Similar gold coins dated Year 4 without flower are thought to be patterns only.

Obv: Flower at right of toughra

Copper

		Fine
2a	10 Para Yrs. 8-9	7.50
3a	20 Para Yrs. 8-10	2.50
4a	40 Para Yr. 10	——

Silver

5	10 Para Yrs. 2-16	2.50
*6	20 Para Yrs. 1-15	2.50
7	1 Guerche Yrs. 1-16	2.00
8a	2½ Guerche Yrs. 8-15	12.50
9a	5 Guerche Yrs. 2-10	20.00
10a	10 Guerche Yrs. 2-4	35.00
11	20 Guerche Yrs. 1-2	

Gold

		V. Fine
A11	5 Guerche Yrs. 2-16	30.00
B11	10 Guerche Yrs. 10-14	15.00
C11	25 Guerche Yrs. 4-10	25.00
D11	50 Guerche Yrs. 1-15	40.00
E11	100 Guerche Yrs. 2-16	75.00
F11	500 Guerche Yr. 15	500.00

MURAD V 1876
(Accession Date A.H. 1293 on Coins)

Gold

H11	100 Guerche Yr. 1	

ABDUL HAMID II
1876-1909
(Accession Date A.H. 1293 on Coins)
First Coinage
Designs similar to Nos. 5-11

Silver

		Fine
A17	10 Para Yr. 3	15.00
B17	20 Para Yrs. 1-3	20.00
18a	1 Guerche Yrs. 1-5	3.00
22a	20 Guerche Yrs. 1, 5	

EGYPT

Gold

		V. Fine
A22	5 Guerche Yrs. 2-34	17.50
B22	10 Guerche Yr. 17	17.50
C22	50 Guerche Yrs. 1-2	40.00
D22	100 Guerche Yrs. 1, 8	75.00
E22	500 Guerche Yrs. 1, 6	500.00

Second Coinage

Bronze

		Fine
12	1/40 Guerche Yrs. 10-35	.50
*13	1/20 Guerche Yrs. 10-35	.50

Copper-Nickel

14	1/10 Guerche Yrs. 10-35	.35
*15	2/10 Guerche Yrs. 10-35	.50
16	5/10 Guerche Yrs. 10-33	.35

17	1 Guerche Yrs. 22-33	.75

Silver

18	1 Guerche Yrs. 10-33	1.00

		Fine
19	2 Guerche Yrs. 10-33	1.25
*20	5 Guerche Yrs. 10-33	1.65
21	10 Guerche Yrs. 10-33	3.25
22	20 Guerche Yrs. 10-33	7.50

Gold
Floral borders both sides

		V. Fine
F22	100 Guerche Yr. 12	125.00

MOHAMMED V 1909-1914

(Accession Date A.H. 1327 on Coins)

Designs similar to Nos. 12-22

Bronze

		Fine
23	1/40 Guerche Yrs. 2-6	1.00
24	1/20 Guerche Yrs. 2-6	1.00

Copper-Nickel

25	1/10 Guerche Yrs. 2-6	.85
26	2/10 Guerche Yrs. 2-6	1.25
27	5/10 Guerche Yrs. 2-6	1.50
28	1 Guerche Yrs. 2-6	1.50

Silver

29	1 Guerche Yrs. 2-3	2.50
30	2 Guerche Yrs. 2-3	3.00
31	5 Guerche Yrs. 2-6	2.50
32	10 Guerche Yrs. 2-6	3.50
33	20 Guerche Yrs. 2-6	8.50

BRITISH PROTECTORATE
1914-1922

Sultan HUSSEIN KAMIL
1915-1917

Bronze

34	1/2 Millieme 1917	6.50

EGYPT

Copper-Nickel

Fine

35 1 Millieme 1917.........2.00
36 2 Milliemes 1916-17......1.00
37 5 Milliemes 1916-17...... .75
38 10 Milliemes 1916-17...... .85

Silver

39 2 Piastres 1916-17........1.00
★40 5 Piastres 1916-17.......1.50
41 10 Piastres 1916-17.......4.00
42 20 Piastres 1916-17.......10.00

Gold

V. Fine

43 100 Piastres 1916.........100.00

FUAD I, Sultan 1917-1922

Silver

Fine

44 2 Piastres 1920...........45.00
45 5 Piastres 1920...........30.00
46 10 Piastres 1920...........20.00

INDEPENDENT KINGDOM 1922-1952
FUAD I, King 1922-1936
First Coinage
Bronze

V. Fine

★47 ½ Millieme 1924..........2.00
48 1 Millieme 1924..........1.00

Copper-Nickel

49 2 Milliemes 1924.........1.00
50 5 Milliemes 1924.........1.25
51 10 Milliemes 1924.........1.25

Silver

52 2 Piastres 1923..........2.00
★53 5 Piastres 1923..........3.00
54 10 Piastres 1923.........6.50
55 20 Piastres 1923.........17.50

Gold

56 20 Piastres 1923-29......50.00
57 50 Piastres 1923-29......60.00
58 100 Piastres 1922........80.00
★59 500 Piastres 1922.......450.00

EGYPT

Second Coinage

Bronze

V. Fine

60 ½ Millieme 1929, 32...... .75
★61 1 Millieme 1929-35...... .35

Copper-Nickel

62 2 Milliemes 1929 (round). .75
★63 2½ Milliemes (octagonal)
    1933................. 1.00
64 5 Milliemes 1929-35
    (round).............. .40
65 10 Milliemes 1929-35
    (round).............. .50

Silver

66 2 Piastres 1929 ....1.00
★67 5 Piastres 1929, 33......2.25
68 10 Piastres 1929, 33......5.00
69 20 Piastres 1929, 33......17.50

Gold

70 20 Piastres 1930 ....30.00
71 50 Piastres 1930 ....40.00
72 100 Piastres 1929-30......70.00
73 500 Piastres 1929-30.....400.00

FAROUK I 1936-1952

Bronze

V. Fine

74 ½ Millieme 1938 (round).. .60
75 1 Millieme 1938-50
    (round)................ .35
77 5 Milliemes 1938, 43..... .35
★78 10 Milliemes 1938, 43...... .40

Copper-Nickel

79 1 Millieme 1938.......... 1.00

80 2 Milliemes 1938......... .50
81 5 Milliemes 1938, 41...... .35
★82 10 Milliemes 1938, 41...... .60

Silver

83 2 Piastres 1937-42........1.00
★84 5 Piastres 1937, 39........1.50
85 10 Piastres 1937, 39........3.50
86 20 Piastres 1937, 39.......15.00

EGYPT

V. Fine
87 2 Piastres 1944 . . . . 1.25

Gold

Commemorating Royal Wedding

Type Same as Silver

88 20 Piastres 1938 . . . . 30.00
89 50 Piastres 1938 . . . . 45.00
90 100 Piastres 1938 . . . . 85.00
91 500 Piastres 1938 . . . . 400.00

REPUBLIC 1953-1958

Aluminum-Bronze

Obv: small bust of Sphinx

92 1 Millieme 1954-56 10
*93 5 Milliemes 1954-56 25
94 10 Milliemes 1954-55 40

Obv: large bust of Sphinx

Unc.
92a 1 Millieme 1957-58 15
93a 5 Milliemes 1957-58 30
94a 10 Milliemes 1956-58 50

Silver

V. Fine
*95 5 Piastres 1955-57 90
96 10 Piastres 1955-57 . . . . 1.50
97 20 Piastres 1956 . . . . 5.00

Commemorating Suez Canal Nationalization

98 25 Piastres 1956 . . . . 6.50

Evacuation of the British

99 50 Piastres 1956 . . . . 9.00

Inauguration of National Assembly

Ex. Fine
102 25 Piastres 1957 Silver 6.50

Later issues in *Current Coins of the World.*

EL SALVADOR — See Salvador

ERITREA

A former Italian colony on the Red Sea, Eritrea became federated with Ethiopia in 1952 by an act of her parliament. Products are chiefly agricultural. Languages: Amharic, various. Capital: *Asmara.*

100 Centesimi = 1 Lira   5 Lire = 1 Tallero   Coinage obsolete.

UMBERTO I 1878-1900

Silver

V. Fine
1 50 Centesimi 1890 . . . . 37.50
2 1 Lira 1890-96 . . . . 35.00
3 2 Lire 1890, 96 . . . . 42.50
4 5 Lire (1 Tallero)
   1891, 96 . . . . 175.00

ERITREA

VICTOR EMANUEL III 1900-46

V. Fine
5 1 Tallero
1918..25.00

(Average diameter 40mm. Diameter varies because coins were struck without a collar.)

ESTONIA (Eesti)

Now part of the U.S.S.R., Estonia was a short-lived republic which existed between the two World Wars. Products are chiefly those of farm and forest. Furniture manufacture and precision industries are also important. Language: Estonian. Capital: *Tallinn*.

100 Penni = 1 Mark 1918-23
100 Marka = 1 Kroon 1923-27

100 Senti = 1 Kroon 1928-41
Coinage obsolete.

Copper-Nickel

		V. Fine
4	1 Mark 1922	3.50
5	3 Marka 1922	4.00
6	5 Marka 1922	4.50

Nickel-Bronze

4a	1 Mark 1924	4.50
5a	3 Marka 1925	6.00
6a	5 Marka 1924	6.50
7	10 Marka 1925	10.00

8	1 Mark 1926	7.50
9	3 Marka 1926	11.00
10	5 Marka 1926	30.00
A10	10 Marka 1926	——

NEW COINAGE

Bronze

		V. Fine
1	1 Sent 1929	2.00

1a	1 Sent 1939	15.00
2	2 Senti 1934	2.50
3	5 Senti 1931	3.00

Nickel-Bronze

11	10 Senti 1931	2.50
12	20 Senti 1935	3.00

ESTONIA

Tercentenary University of Tartu

V. Fine
13 25 Senti 1928 . . . . 8.50
14 50 Senti 1936 . . . . 10.00

Aluminum-Bronze

Ex. Fine
17 2 Krooni 1932 . . . . 27.50

15 1 Kroon 1934 . . . . 10.00

Silver

Tenth Singing Festival

Tallinn Castle
Ex. Fine
16 2 Krooni 1930 . . . . 15.00   **18** 1 Kroon 1933 . . . . 35.00

ETHIOPIA

A volcanic mountain country in northeast Africa, Ethiopia is one of the world's oldest Christian nations (since 330 A.D.). Abundant rainfall and the rich soil of the valleys produce two excellent diversified crops a year. Vast mineral resources are being increasingly developed. Population: 24,800,000. Language: Amharic. Capital: *Addis Ababa*.

2 Besa = 1 Gersh (Piastre)   16 Gersh = 1 Talari (Later) Local Issue
20 Gersh = 1 Talari (1st Issue)   100 Cents (Matonas) = 1 Talari (Dollar)

ETHIOPIA

1	2	3	4	5	6	7	8	9	0
፩	፪	፫	፬	፭	፮	፯	፰	፱	◆
፲	፳	፴	፵	፶	፷	፸	፹	፺	፻
10	20	30	40	50	60	70	80	90	100

Ethiopian Era + 7 Years, 8 Mo.=A.D.

MENELIK II 1889-1913

Copper

Fine

*1 ¹⁄₁₀₀ Talari EE 1889 (1897)...4.00
2 ¼ Gersh EE 1888 (1896)...——
3 ½ Gersh EE 1888.........——
4 1 Gersh EE 1888.........——

Lion's left leg raised

Silver

5 1 Gersh EE 1889-95
(1897-1903) 16mm......1.25
6 ⅛ Talari EE 1887 (20mm).30.00
*7 ¼ Talari EE 1887-95.......6.50
8 ½ Talari EE 1887-89
(30mm)..............13.50
9 1 Talari EE 1887-89
(40mm)..............22.50

Lion's right leg raised

V. Fine

10 1 Talari EE 1892-95
(1899-1903).............35.00

Addis Ababa Mint

Though dies were made in Paris, coins were struck without change of date in Addis Ababa from about 1903 to about 1933. They do not have Paris mint mark or symbols.

Lion's right leg raised

Copper

17 (¹⁄₃₂ Talari) EE 1889.......3.00

• 169 •

ETHIOPIA

Fine

17a ½₂ Talari EE 1889........2.50

No. 17 was struck from dies intended for a silver ⅛ Talari as nos. 18-20, and the incorrect value below the lion was defaced or removed. No. 17a is identical in design but the correct value appears at the bottom.

Silver

18 1 Gersh EE 1889 (1897)..90.00
★19 ¼ Talari EE 1889......22.50
20 ½ Talari EE 1889......60.00

Gold

V. Fine

11 ¼ Wark EE 1889........50.00
12 ½ Wark EE 1889........75.00
★13 1 Wark EE 1889......100.00

EMPRESS ZAUDITU
1916-1930
Gold

★21 1 Wark.............175.00
A21 2 Wark 1917.........325.00
22 3½ Wark (Similar)....... —

HAILE SELASSIE I 1930-
Copper

23 1 Matona (Cent) *V. Fine*
    EE 1923 (1931)..........1.50
24 5 Matonas EE 1923.......1.50

Nickel

25 10 Matonas EE 1923......2.00
★26 25 Matonas EE 1923......1.50
27 50 Matonas EE 1923......2.00

Gold

28 ½ Wark 1931...........125.00
★29 1 Wark 1931...........200.00

Bronze

Unc.

30 1 Cent EE 1936 (1944)
    17mm................ .15
31 5 Cents EE 1936
    (20mm)............... .20
★32 10 Cents EE 1936
    (22.5mm)............. .30
33 25 Cents EE 1936
    (25.5mm) ...... *Ex. F.* 35.00

Silver

34 50 Cents EE 1936.... *Ex. F.* 3.50

Bronze

35 25 Cents EE 1936 scalloped
    (Issued 1952-) .... .75

FAEROE ISLANDS (Faerøerne)

Located about 300 miles northwest of the Shetlands in the North Atlantic. Though they are a Danish possession they have extensive home rule. Principal town: *Thorshavn.*

100 Øre = 1 Krone   Coins struck in London in World War II.

CHRISTIAN X 1912-1947
Regular Danish types, initials and mint marks omitted

Bronze   **Copper-Nickel**

		V. Fine
1	1 Øre 1941	6.50
2	2 Øre 1941	4.50
3	5 Øre 1941	4.50

		V. Fine
4	10 Øre 1941	5.00
5	25 Øre 1941	5.00

FIJI

A group of some 320 islands in the South Pacific Ocean. Fiji was a British colony from 1874 to 1970, when it became an independent nation within the British Commonwealth. Its forests furnish valuable woods. The islands are very fertile. Area: 7,073 square miles. Population: 540,000. Capital: *Suva.*

12 Pence = 1 Shilling   2 Shillings = 1 Florin   20 Shillings = 1 Pound

GEORGE V 1910-1936
Copper-Nickel

		V. Fine
1	½ Penny 1934	2.25
2	1 Penny 1934-36	1.00

4	1 Shilling 1934-36	V. Fine 2.50

Silver

3	6 Pence 1934-36	2.50

5	1 Florin (2 Shillings) 1934-36	4.00

FIJI

EDWARD VIII 1936
Copper-Nickel

Ex. Fine
6 1 Penny 1936.............2.50

GEORGE VI 1936-1952

7 ½ Penny 1940-41..........3.50
8 1 Penny 1937-41, 45.......1.50

Brass
7a ½ Penny 1942-43.........1.50
8a 1 Penny 1942-43.........2.00

EMPEROR to right of head
Reverse designs like Nos. 3-5
Silver

Fine
11 6 Pence 1937.............5.50
12 1 Shilling 1937............7.00
13 1 Florin 1937...........10.00

KING EMPEROR to right of head
V. Fine
11a 6 Pence 1938-43..........1.00
12a 1 Shilling 1938-43........1.25
13a 1 Florin 1938-45.........2.50

Nickel-Brass

V. Fine
17 3 Pence 1947.............1.50

New Legend:
KING GEORGE THE SIXTH
Copper-Nickel

18 ½ Penny 1949-52.......... .50
19 1 Penny 1949-52.......... .75

Nickel-Brass
20 3 Pence
1950, 52 (12 Sided)....... .75

ELIZABETH II 1952-
Copper-Nickel
Unc.
21 ½ Penny 1954............. .65
22 1 Penny 1954-68.......... .35

Nickel-Brass

23 3 Pence 1955-67............ .40

Copper-Nickel
Reverse designs like Nos. 3-5
24 6 Pence 1953-67............ .60
25 1 Shilling 1957-65......... 1.00
26 1 Florin 1957-65...........2.00
Later issues in *Current Coins of the World.*

FINLAND (Suomen Tasavalta)

A republic at the northeastern end of the Baltic Sea. Forests cover much of the country and the principal industry is lumbering and paper manufacture; other important exports include iron and steel, furs, chemicals and textiles. Area: 130,165 square miles. Population: 4,700,000. The Finns are a progressive people with the world's highest literacy rate, 99%. Languages: Finnish, Swedish. Capital: *Helsinki.* 100 Penniä = 1 Markka

ALEXANDER II 1855-1881

Nos. 1 to 7 Issued in 2 Varieties,
Coarse (1864-71) and Fine

Copper

		Fine
1	1 Penni 1864-76	2.50
2	5 Penniä 1865-75	2.50
3	10 Penniä 1865-76	3.50

Silver

Nos. 4 through 9 are similar for Alexander II, Alexander III, and Nicholas II.

4	25 Penniä 1865-1917	1.75
5	50 Penniä 1864-1917	3.00

6	1 Markka 1864-1915	3.50
7	2 Markkaa 1865-1908	7.50

Gold

		Ex. Fine
8	10 Markkaa 1878-1913	125.00
9	20 Markkaa 1878-1913	150.00

ALEXANDER III 1881-1894

Copper

		Fine
10	1 Penni 1881-94	2.00
11	5 Penniä 1888-92	3.50
12	10 Penniä 1889-91	6.00

Silver and Gold, See Nos. 4-9 under Alexander II.

NICHOLAS II 1894-1917

Copper

18	1 Penni 1895-1916	.50
19	5 Penniä 1896-1917	.50
20	10 Penniä 1895-1917	1.25

Silver and Gold, See Nos. 4-9 under Alexander II.

FINLAND

CIVIL WAR 1917-1918
Issued by the White (Official) Government
No Crown over Eagle

Copper

		V. Fine
27	1 Penni 1917	2.50
28	5 Penniä 1917	3.50
29	10 Penniä 1917	5.00

Silver

30	25 Penniä 1917	2.50
31	50 Penniä 1917	3.00

Issued by the Reds (Communist Government)
Copper

32	5 Penniä 1918	25.00

REPUBLIC 1918-
Bronze

33	1 Penni 1919-24	.50
34	5 Penniä 1918-40	.30
35	10 Penniä 1919-40	.40

Copper-Nickel

		V. Fine
36	25 Penniä 1921-40	.30
37	50 Penniä 1921-40	.40
38	1 Markka 1921-24 (24mm.)	1.25

39	1 Markka 1928-40 (21mm.)	.25

Aluminum-Bronze

42	5 Markkaa 1928-52	1.00
43	10 Markkaa 1928-39	1.50
44	20 Markkaa 1931-39	2.50

Dates after 1946 of no. 42 vary in composition.

Gold

		Ex. Fine
45	100 Markkaa 1926	250.00
46	200 Markkaa 1926	300.00

Designs Like Nos. 36-42

Bronze

36a	25 Penniä 1940-43	.60
37a	50 Penniä 1940-43	.45
39a	1 Markka 1940-51	.40

Iron

36b	25 Penniä 1943-45	1.00
37b	50 Penniä 1943-48	.75
39b	1 Markka 1943-52	.50

FINLAND

Bronze

V. Fine

40 5 Penniä 1941-43 . . . . 1.25
41 10 Penniä 1941-43 . . . . 1.25

Iron

41a 10 Penniä 1943-45 . . . . 3.00

Unc.

47 1 Markka 1952-53 25
48 5 Markkaa 1952-53 . . . . 1.00

Nickel-Plated Iron

47a 1 Markka 1953-62 15
48a 5 Markkaa 1953-62 20

Aluminum-Bronze

49 10 Markkaa 1952-62 40
50 20 Markkaa 1952-62 60
51 50 Markkaa 1952-62 . . . . 1.00

Commemorating
1952 Olympic Games

52 500 Markkaa Silver   *Ex. Fine*
    1951-52 . . . . 30.00

Silver

Unc.

53 100 Markkaa 1956-60 . . . . . . 4.00
54 200 Markkaa 1956-59 . . . . . . 5.50

Commemorating
Markka Currency System
1860-1960

55 1000 Markkaa 1960 . . . . . . 20.00
Later issues in Current Coins of the World.

FORMOSA—See China

FRANCE (République Française)

France is located in Western Europe and has widely diversified resources of industry and agriculture. The Second Empire under Napoleon III succeeded the Second Republic in 1852 and lasted until 1870 when the Franco-Prussian War caused Napoleon III to flee to England. The Third Republic was formed Sept. 4, 1870 which lasted until World War II. A four-year period of Nazi occupation followed. After the Allied victory in 1945, a new constitution was framed which established the Fourth Republic. Population: 51,700,000. Capital: *Paris*.

100 Centimes = 1 Franc

THE SECOND REPUBLIC
1848-1852
First Coinage
Copper

Gold

V. Fine
8 20 Francs 1848-49 . . . . 65.00

Second Coinage
Silver

Fine
1 1 Centime 1848-51 . . . . 1.50

Silver

		Fine
2	20 Centimes 1849-51	3.00
3	50 Centimes 1849-51	7.50
4	1 Franc 1849-51	15.00
5	2 Francs 1849-51	40.00
6	5 Francs 1849-51	12.50

Gold

		V. Fine
9	10 Francs 1850-51	40.00
10	20 Francs 1849-51	70.00

7 5 Francs 1848-49 . . . . 10.00

FRANCE

Third Coinage
Silver

Obv: President Bonaparte (1851-52)

			Fine
11	50 Centimes 1852		10.00
12	1 Franc 1852		10.00
13	5 Francs 1852		35.00

Gold

			V. Fine
A13	20 Francs 1852		90.00

THE SECOND EMPIRE
EMPEROR NAPOLEON III
1852-1870
First Coinage
Bare Head of Emperor
Bronze

			Fine
14	1 Centime 1853-57		1.50
15	2 Centimes 1853-57		1.25
16	5 Centimes 1853-57		.45
17	10 Centimes 1852-57		.65

Silver

			Fine
22	20 Centimes 1853-63		3.00
23	50 Centimes 1853-63		5.00
24	1 Franc 1853-64		8.50
25	2 Francs 1853-59		60.00
26	5 Francs 1854-59		15.00

Gold

Enlarged

			V. Fine
33	5 Francs 1854-60		45.00
34	10 Francs 1854-60		37.50
35	20 Francs 1853-60		65.00
36	50 Francs 1855-60		175.00
37	100 Francs 1855-60		350.00

Second Coinage
Laureate Head of Emperor
Bronze

			Fine
18	1 Centime 1861-70		1.25
19	2 Centimes 1861-62		1.00
20	5 Centimes 1861-65		.45
21	10 Centimes 1861-65		.60

FRANCE

Silver

43 5 Centimes 1871-98........ .35
44 10 Centimes 1870-98........ .50

	Fine
27 20 Centimes 1864-66........	2.00
28 20 Centimes (increased size) 1867-69.................	1.25
29 50 Centimes 1864-69........	1.50

30 1 Franc 1866-70............2.50
31 2 Francs 1866-70..........4.50
32 5 Francs 1861-70..........10.00

Gold
Laureate Head,
Rev. Value and Date in Wreath

	V. Fine
38 5 Francs 1862-69........	25.00
39 10 Francs 1861-69........	37.50

Laureate Head, Rev. Arms

40 20 Francs 1861-70......70.00
A40 50 Francs 1862-69....200.00
B40 100 Francs 1862-70....375.00

THE THIRD REPUBLIC
1870-1940

Bronze

	Fine
41 1 Centime 1872-97........	1.00
42 2 Centimes 1877-97........	1.00

Silver

45 2 Francs 1870-71..........20.00
46 5 Francs 1870-71..........35.00

With Motto:
LIBERTE, EGALITE, FRATERNITE

Silver

48 50 Centimes 1871-95........1.25
49 1 Franc 1871-95...........1.75
50 2 Francs 1870-95..........4.50
51 5 Francs 1870 ....12.50

	V. Fine
52 5 Francs 1870-78...........	8.50
53 5 Francs (Trident symbol issued by Commune) 1871	85.00

FRANCE

Gold

Design like No. 9

V. Fine

A54 5 Francs 1889 . . . . ——
54 10 Francs 1895-99 . . . . . . 40.00

No. A54 was not issued to circulation.

Gold

55 20 Francs 1871-98 . . . . 65.00
56 50 Francs 1878-1904 . . . . . 325.00
57 100 Francs 1878-1914 . . . . 300.00

Second Coinage

Bronze

58 1 Centime 1898-1920 65
59 2 Centimes 1898-1920 . . . . . 1.00
60 5 Centimes 1898-1920 20
61 10 Centimes 1898-1921 30

Nickel

69 25 Centimes 1903 50

V. Fine

70 25 Centimes Polygonal
1904-05 60

Silver

62 50 Centimes 1897-1920 65
63 1 Franc 1898-1920 . . . . 1.00
64 2 Francs 1898-1920 . . . . 1.75

Gold

65 10 Francs 1899-1914 . . . . 40.00
66 20 Francs 1899-1914 . . . . 65.00

Types With Hole in Center

Nickel

73 10 Centimes 1914 . . . . 250.00
76 25 Centimes 1914-17 . . . . 3.50

FRANCE

V. Fine

71	5 Centimes 1917-20	.15
72	5 Centimes reduced size 1920-38	.10
73a	10 Centimes 1917-38	.10
76a	25 Centimes 1917-37	.25

Nickel- Bronze

72a	5 Centimes 1938-39	.25
73c	10 Centimes 1938-39	.25
76b	25 Centimes 1938-40	.35

Zinc

73b	10 Centimes 1941	.25
74	10 Centimes reduced size 1945-46	3.00
75	20 Centimes 1945-46	10.00

Tokens Issued by French Chamber of Commerce

Aluminum-Bronze

77	50 Centimes 1921-29	.10
78	1 Franc 1920-28	.15
79	2 Francs 1920-27	.20

Aluminum -Bronze

80	50 Centimes 1931-47	.10
81	1 Franc 1931-41	.15
82	2 Francs 1931-41	.20

Aluminum

80a	50 Centimcs 1941-47	.10
81a	1 Franc 1941-59	.10
82a	2 Francs 1941-59	.15

Nickel

V. Fine

83 5 Francs 1933 . . . . 2.50

84	5 Francs Nic. 1933-38	1.25
84a	5 Francs Al.-Br. 1938-47	2.50
84b	5 Francs Alum. 1945-52	.15

Silver

86	10 Francs 1929-39	1.75
87	20 Francs 1929-38	5.00

Copper-Nickel

86a	10 Francs 1945-47 (Large Head)	1.00
86b	10 Francs 1947-49 (Small Head)	.50

Gold

88 100 Francs 1929-36 . . . . 200.00

FRANCE

Allied Occupation Money
Also used in Algeria
Brass

89 2 Francs 1944 . . . . 3.00

V. Fine

Marshal Petain
Unc.

V97 5 Francs Nic.-Br. 1941 . . . 30.00
Not released into circulation.

VICHY FRENCH STATE
Zinc

V. Fine

V90 20 Centimes VINGT 1941 .65
Values in Numerals
V91 10 Centimes 1941-43 20
V92 20 Centimes 1941-44 25
V92a 20 Centimes Iron 1944 . . . 40.00
V93 10 Centimes Zinc 1943-44
(Reduced Size) 50

Aluminum

V94 50 Centimes 1942-44 15
V95 1 Franc 1942-44 20
V96 2 Francs 1943-44 35

FOURTH REPUBLIC
1946-1958
Aluminum-Bronze

Ex. Fine

98 10 Francs 1950-58 30
99 20 Francs 1950 Designer
"Georges Guiraud" 50
99a 20 Francs 1950-53
Designer "G. Guiraud" . .30
100 50 Francs 1950-58 60

Copper-Nickel

101 100 Francs 1954-58 75

Later issues in Current Coins of the World.

FRENCH EQUATORIAL AFRICA
(Afrique Equatoriale Française)

This area consisted of the four territories of Gabon, Middle Congo, Tchad and Ubangi-Shari (now Central African Republic). It was held by France from the mid-19th century until 1960, when each territory was given independence. Area: 970,000 square miles. Languages: French, native tongues. Capital: *Brazzaville.*

100 Centimes = 1 Franc

FRENCH EQUATORIAL AFRICA

Brass

Aluminum

V. Fine

1 50 Centimes 1942...........3.00
2 1 Franc 1942..............3.00

Bronze

1a 50 Centimes 1943..........3.00
2a 1 Franc 1943............3.00

Unc.

3 (6) 1 Franc 1948............ .25
4 (7) 2 Francs 1948........... .35

Later issues in *Current Coins of the World.*

FRENCH COCHIN CHINA
(Cochinchine Française)

Southernmost of the Indo-China states, now a part of South Vietnam. Saigon, the major port of Vietnam, was also the administrative seat. Leading exports were rice, fish, and timber.

5 Sapeque (Cash)=1 Centime
100 Centimes=1 Piastre

Coinage obsolete.

Bronze   *Fine*

A1 (1 Sapeque) 1875..........3.00

This is a France 1 Centime 1875-K (no. 41) punched with a center hole.

Silver

V. Fine

1 2 Sapeque 1879, 85..........6.00

V. Fine

3 10 Centimes 1879-85.......15.00
4 20 Centimes 1879-85.......17.50
*5 50 Centimes 1879-85.......27.50
6 1 Piastre 1879, 85 (Pattern)..

Except for No. 2, coins dated 1885 were issued only in sets for the Antwerp Exposition.

2 1 Centime 1879-85..........6.00

FRENCH INDO-CHINA
(Indo-Chine Française)

Group of states bounded by China, Siam, the Gulf of Siam and the China Sea, which, until 1952-54, were French colonies. Included Annam, Cambodia, Cochin China, Laos and Tonkin. When the Japanese occupying forces departed at the close of World War II, the Communists under Ho Chi Minh came to control much of this area. They were thereafter ousted by the returning French, but commenced guerrilla activity which eventually led to departure of the French. By the Geneva Conference, Indo China was partitioned in 1953 into North Vietnam (Communist), Cambodia, Laos and South Vietnam.

500 Sapeque (cash) = 100 Centimes = 1 Piastre

Bronze

Fine
1 2 Sapeque 1887-1902........3.00

3 1 Centime 1896-1906   *V. Fine*
   (27.5mm)................1.00
4 1 Centime 1908-39 (26mm)... .35

Copper-Nickel

2 1 Centime 1885-94 ....1.50

5 5 Centimes 1923-37......... .30
5a 5 Centimes Nic.-Br.
   (Thin) 1938-39........... .30

Silver

2a 1 Centieme 1895.........15.00

.900 Fine, 27.215 Gr. to Piastre
6 10 Centimes 1885-1895.......3.00

FRENCH INDO-CHINA

Fine

7 20 Centimes 1885-1895.......4.00
8 50 Centimes 1885-1895.......7.00
9 1 Piastre 1885-1895........13.50

.900 Fine, 27 Gr. to Piastre

10 10 Centimes 1895-96........6.50
11 20 Centimes 1895-96........3.50

V. Fine

12 50 Centimes 1896-1936......2.00
13 1 Piastre 1895-1928.......6.00

.835 Fine

14 10 Centimes 1898-1919.....1.50
15 20 Centimes 1898-1916.....2.00

No Fineness Indicated

Fine

14a 10 Centimes 1920.........3.50
15a 20 Centimes 1920.........5.00

.680 Fine

V. Fine

16 10 Centimes 1921-37.......1.00
17 20 Centimes 1921-37.......1.25

Various Metals

Ex. Fine

20 ½ Centime Br. 1935-40.... .25
20a ½ Centime Zinc 1940.....15.00

21 10 Centimes Nic. 1939-40.. .25
21a 10 Centimes Cop.-Nic.
1939, 41................ .25
22 20 Centimes Nic. 1939
Security Edge..........7.50
22a 20 Centimes Cop.-Nic.
1939, 41 Reeded Edge... .40

VICHY GOVERNMENT

Zinc

V. Fine

V30 1 Centime 1940-41........1.00

18 1 Piastre 1931.............7.50   **V31** ¼ Centime 1941-43.......6.00

FRENCH INDO-CHINA

Aluminum

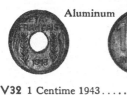

Copper-Nickel

Ex. Fine

V32 1 Centime 1943 35
V33 5 Centimes 1943 50

POSTWAR ISSUES

Aluminum

Ex. Fine
23 50 Centimes 1946 . . . . .2.00

26 5 Centimes 1946 20
27 10 Centimes 1945 25

24 1 Piastre 1946-47
    Security Edge 6.00
25 1 Piastre 1947
    Reeded Edge 2.00

28 20 Centimes 1945 35

For later issues see Cambodia, Laos, North Vietnam and South Vietnam.

FRENCH OCEANIA

(Etablissements Français de l'Océanie)

Made up of a widely scattered group of islands in the South Pacific. Government headquarters are at Papeete, Tahiti. Entire population for the islands is about 132,000. Products: coconuts, copra, pearls, bananas.

100 Centimes = 1 Franc

Aluminum

Unc.

1 50 Centimes 1949 25
2 1 Franc 1949 40
3 2 Francs 1949 75
4 5 Francs 1952 . . . . .1.50

For later issues see French Polynesia, in *Current Coins of the World.*

FRENCH SOMALILAND
(Côte Française des Somalis)

Territory in Northeast Africa covering an area of 8,880 square miles. Capital and also main port is *Djibouti,* which also serves as the main port for Ethiopia on the Gulf of Aden. Products: fish, sheep, salt. Languages: Hamitic, Arabic, French.

100 Centimes = 1 Franc

Aluminum

UNION FRANCAISE Omitted

Aluminum

		V. Fine
1	1 Franc 1949	.60
2	2 Francs 1949	.85
3	5 Francs 1948	1.25

Aluminum-Bronze

		Unc.
5	1 Franc 1959-65	.35
6	2 Francs 1959-65	.50
7	5 Francs 1959-65	.75

Later issues in Current Coins of the World.

4 20 Francs 1952 . . . . 2.00

FRENCH WEST AFRICA
(Afrique Occidentale Française)

Northwest coast of Africa extending eastward to the Sudan. Composed of eight constituent territories with a total population of about 16,000,000. It is now broken up into a number of independent states. Capital: *Dakar.* Languages: Sudanese, Hamitic, Arabic and French.

100 Centimes = 1 Franc

Brass tokens dated 1883 (1, 5 and 10 Centimes) circulated for a time.

FRENCH WEST AFRICA

Aluminum-Bronze

Aluminum-Bronze

V. Fine

1 50 Centimes 1944............5.00
2 1 Franc 1944..............3.50

Unc.

5 5 Francs 1956.............. .50
6 10 Francs 1956.............1.00
7 25 Francs 1956.............1.50

Aluminum

Integrated Coinage
French West Africa — Togo (1957)

Unc.

3 1 Franc 1948-55.............. .25
4 2 Francs 1948-55............ .35

8 10 Francs 1957.............. .75
9 25 Francs 1957.............1.25

For later coinage see West African States.

GERMANY (Deutschland)
COINAGE OF THE INDIVIDUAL STATES
UNDER THE EMPIRE

Capital: *Berlin*.

At the foundation of the Empire in 1871 a new decimal system of coinage was established, based on the mark of 100 pfennig. Coins of 1 mark and under were to be general issues, while coinage of higher values in silver and gold were to be left to the states. The first gold appeared in 1871. Coinage of other metals began in 1873.

The coins of the states, in values of 2, 3, 5, 10 and 20 mark, may be described generally as:

Obverse: head of ruler with name, title and state. Reverse: DEUTSCHES REICH, eagle, value and date. The 5 mark piece of Friedrich of Waldeck 1903 which follows is typical:

GERMANY

Three reverses were used
on coins of the States.

A.
On Gold
1871-73

B. Gold and Silver 1874-89

C. On Coins 1890 onward

GERMAN EMPIRE (States)

ANHALT (Duchy)
Friedrich I 1871-1904
Silver
		V. Fine
S-12	2 Mark 1876	50.00
S-13	2 Mark 1896	80.00
S-14	5 Mark 1896	350.00

Gold
S-15	20 Mark 1875	175.00
S-16	10 Mark 1896-1901	210.00
S-17	20 Mark 1896-1901	155.00

Friedrich II 1904-1918
Silver
S-18	2 Mark 1904	90.00
S-19	3 Mark 1909-11	18.00

Silver Wedding
S-20	3 Mark 1914	19.00
S-21	5 Mark Similar 1914	65.00

Gold
		V. Fine
S-22	20 Mark 1904	140.00

BADEN (Grand Duchy)
Friedrich I 1852-1907
Silver
S-18	2 Mark 1876-88	10.00
S-19	5 Mark 1875-88	12.50
S-20	2 Mark 1892-1902	17.50
S-21	5 Mark 1891-1902	12.00

50th Year of Reign
S-22	2 Mark 1902	6.00
S-23	5 Mark (Similar) 1902	28.00
S-24	2 Mark 1902-07	7.00
S-25	5 Mark 1902-07	10.00

GERMAN EMPIRE (States)

Golden Wedding

		V. Fine
S-26	2 Mark 1906	7.50
S-27	5 Mark (Similar) 1906	38.00

Death of Friedrich

S-28	2 Mark 1907	10.00
S-29	5 Mark (Similar) 1907	50.00

Gold

S-30	10 Mark 1872-73	42.50
S-31	20 Mark 1872-73	60.00
S-32	5 Mark 1877	90.00
S-33	10 Mark 1875-88	30.00
S-34	20 Mark 1874	60.00
S-35	10 Mark 1890-1901	43.00
S-36	20 Mark 1894-95	60.00
S-37	10 Mark 1902-07	45.00

Friedrich II 1907-1918

Silver

S-38	2 Mark 1911-13	50.00
S-39	3 Mark 1908-15	5.00
S-40	5 Mark 1908-13	15.00

Gold

S-41	10 Mark 1909-13	75.00
S-42	20 Mark 1911-14	60.00

BAVARIA (Bayern) (Kingdom)
Ludwig II 1864-1886

Silver

S-26	2 Mark 1876-83	7.50
S-27	5 Mark 1874-76	8.50

Gold

S-28	10 Mark 1872-73	43.00
S-29	20 Mark 1872-73	60.00
S-30	5 Mark 1877-78	90.00
S-31	10 Mark 1874-81	40.00
S-32	20 Mark 1874-78	60.00

Otto III 1886-1913
Under Regency of Prince Luitpold

Silver

S-33	2 Mark 1888	80.00
S-34	5 Mark 1888	125.00
S-35	2 Mark 1891-1913	4.00
S-36	3 Mark 1908-13	3.50
S-37	5 Mark 1891-1913	7.00

Birthday of Regent

		V. Fine
S-38	2 Mark 1911	5.50
S-39	3 Mark (Similar) 1911	6.50
S-40	5 Mark (Similar) 1911	35.00

Gold

S-41	10 Mark 1888	55.00
S-42	10 Mark 1890-1900	37.50
S-43	20 Mark 1895-1913	60.00
S-44	10 Mark 1900-12	33.00

Ludwig III 1913-1918

Silver

S-45	2 Mark 1914	18.00
S-46	3 Mark 1914	9.00
S-47	5 Mark 1914	45.00

Golden Wedding
(100 Struck)

S-48	3 Mark 1918 (Rare)	——

Gold

S-49	20 Mark 1914	245.00

BREMEN (Free City)

Silver

S-10	2 Mark 1904	25.00
S-11	5 Mark 1906	75.00

Gold

S-12	10 Mark 1907	175.00
S-13	20 Mark 1906	175.00

BRUNSWICK (Braunschweig Lüneburg) (Duchy)
Wilhelm 1831-1884
Gold

S-7	20 Mark 1875-76	125.00

Ernst August 1913-1918
Silver
Wedding and Accession

S-8	3 Mark 1915	400.00
S-9	5 Mark (Similar) 1915	600.00

U. LÜNEB Added

S-10	3 Mark 1915	50.00
S-11	5 Mark 1915	150.00

GERMAN EMPIRE (States)

HAMBURG (Free City)
Silver
		V. Fine
S-2	2 Mark 1876-88	11.00
S-3	5 Mark 1875-88	13.00
S-4	2 Mark 1892-1914	5.00
S-5	3 Mark 1908-14	5.00
S-6	5 Mark 1891-1913	8.00

Gold
S-7	10 Mark 1873	280.00
S-8	10 Mark 1874	230.00
S-9	5 Mark 1877	90.00
S-10	10 Mark 1875-88	40.00
S-11	10 Mark 1875-89	60.00
S-12	10 Mark 1890-1913	43.00
S-13	20 Mark 1893-1913	40.00

HESSE-DARMSTADT
(Hessen) (Grand Duchy)
Ludwig III 1848-1877
Silver
S-6	2 Mark 1876-77	20.00
S-7	5 Mark 1875-76	15.00

Gold
S-8	10 Mark 1872-73	55.00
S-9	20 Mark 1872-73	60.00
S-10	5 Mark 1877	175.00
S-11	10 Mark 1875-77	50.00
S-12	20 Mark 1874	80.00

Ludwig IV 1877-1892
Silver
S-13	2 Mark 1888	300.00
S-14	5 Mark 1888	500.00
S-15	2 Mark 1891	100.00
S-16	5 Mark 1891	150.00

Gold
S-17	5 Mark 1877	200.00
S-18	10 Mark 1878-88	65.00
S-19	10 Mark 1890	105.00
S-20	20 Mark 1892	210.00

Ernst Ludwig 1892-1918
Silver
S-21	2 Mark 1895-1900	60.00
S-22	5 Mark 1895-1900	45.00

400th Anniversary Philipp
S-23	2 Mark 1904	16.00
S-24	5 Mark (Similar) 1904	42.50
S-25	3 Mark 1910	30.00

25th Anniversary of Reign
S-26	3 Mark 1917 (Proofs only)	1200.00

Gold
		V. Fine
S-27	10 Mark 1893	130.00
S-28	20 Mark 1893	140.00
S-29	10 Mark 1896-98	130.00
S-30	20 Mark 1896-1903	70.00
S-31	20 Mark 1905-1911	65.00

LIPPE-DETMOLD
(Principality)
Leopold IV 1905-1918
Silver
S-6	2 Mark 1906	90.00
S-7	3 Mark 1913	100.00

LÜBECK (Free City)
Silver
S-1	2 Mark 1901	40.00
S-2	2 Mark 1904-12	25.00
S-3	3 Mark 1908-14	17.00
S-4	5 Mark 1904-13	70.00

Gold
S-5	10 Mark 1901-04	175.00
S-6	10 Mark 1905-10	200.00

MECKLENBURG-SCHWERIN
Friedrich Franz II 1842-1883
Silver
S-8	2 Mark 1876	60.00

Gold
S-9	10 Mark 1872	280.00
S-10	20 Mark 1872	200.00
S-11	10 Mark 1878	210.00

Friedrich Franz III 1883-1897
Gold
S-12	10 Mark 1890	115.00

GERMAN EMPIRE (States)

Friedrich Franz IV 1897-1918

Silver
V. Fine
S-13 2 Mark 1901............65.00

Wedding

S-14 2 Mark 1904............17.50
S-15 5 Mark (Similar) 1904....52.50

Centenary of Grand Duchy

S-16 3 Mark 1915............52.50
S-17 5 Mark (Similar) 1915...155.00

Gold

S-18 10 Mark 1901..........200.00
S-19 20 Mark 1901..........500.00

MECKLENBURG-STRELITZ
(Grand Duchy)
Friedrich Wilhelm 1860-1904
Silver

S-9 2 Mark 1877.............75.00

Gold

S-10 10 Mark 1873 ....1200.00
S-11 20 Mark 1873 ....1200.00
S-12 10 Mark 1874-80.......875.00
S-13 20 Mark 1874 ....1000.00

Adolf Friedrich V 1904-1914
Silver

S-14 2 Mark 1905............95.00
S-15 3 Mark 1913...........140.00

Gold

S-16 10 Mark 1905 ....1000.00
S-17 20 Mark 1905 ....1300.00

OLDENBURG
(Grand Duchy)
Nicolaus Friedrich Peter
1853-1900
Silver

S-8 2 Mark 1891.............70.00

Gold

S-9 10 Mark 1874..........750.00

Friedrich August 1900-1918

Silver
V. Fine
S-10 2 Mark 1900-01........60.00
S-11 5 Mark 1900-01.......130.00

PRUSSIA (Preussen)
(Kingdom)
Wilhelm I 1861-1888
Silver

S-30 2 Mark 1876-84...........5.00
S-31 5 Mark 1874-76..........8.00

Gold

S-32 10 Mark 1872-73........35.00
S-33 20 Mark 1871-73.........60.00
S-34 5 Mark 1877-78........85.00
S-35 10 Mark 1874-88.......32.50
S-36 20 Mark 1874-88........60.00

Friedrich III 1888
Silver

S-37 2 Mark 1888............11.00
S-38 5 Mark 1888............19.00

Gold

S-39 10 Mark 1888...........35.00
S-40 20 Mark 1888...........60.00

Wilhelm II 1888-1918
Silver

S-41 2 Mark 1888............70.00
S-42 5 Mark 1888...........175.00
S-43 2 Mark 1891-1912....... 2.50
S-44 3 Mark 1908-12......... 2.00
S-45 5 Mark 1891-1908....... 4.00

2nd Centenary of Kingdom

S-46 2 Mark 1901.............3.50
S-47 5 Mark (Similar) 1901....11.00

Berlin University

S-48 3 Mark 1910............24.00

Breslau University

S-49 3 Mark 1911............15.00

War of Liberation
*(Eagle Killing Serpent,
Rev. King and Soldiers)*

S-50 2 Mark 1913.............3.75
S-51 3 Mark (Similar) 1913.....3.50

25th Year of Reign

S-52 2 Mark 1913.............3.75

GERMAN EMPIRE (States)

V. Fine

S-53 3 Mark (Similar) 1913.....3.75

Bust of Wilhelm II
S-54 3 Mark 1914.............6.00
S-55 5 Mark 1913-14..........7.00

Centenary of Absorption of Mansfeld
S-56 3 Mark 1915............80.00

Gold
S-57 10 Mark 1889.........400.00
S-58 20 Mark 1888-89.......60.00
S-59 10 Mark 1890-1912......32.00
S-60 20 Mark 1890-1913......60.00
S-61 20 Mark 1913-15........60.00

REUSS-GREIZ
Alterer Linie (Principality)
Heinrich XXII 1859-1902
Silver
S-6 2 Mark 1877...........105.00
S-7 2 Mark 1892.............85.00
S-8 2 Mark 1899-1901........70.00

Gold
S-9 20 Mark 1875.........1500.00

Heinrich XXIV 1902-1918
Silver
S-10 3 Mark 1909...........75.00

REUSS-SCHLEIZ
Jüngerer Linie (Principality)
Heinrich XIV 1867-1913
Silver
S-7 2 Mark 1884.............70.00

Gold
S-8 10 Mark 1882..........800.00
S-9 20 Mark 1881..........475.00

SAXE ALTENBURG
(Sachsen-Altenburg) (Duchy)
Ernst 1853-1908
Silver
S-4 2 Mark 1901...........95.00
S-5 5 Mark 1901...........145.00

50th Year of Reign
S-6 5 Mark 1903............80.00

Gold
S-7 20 Mark 1887...........250.00

SAXE-COBURG-GOTHA
(Duchy)
Ernst II 1844-1893
Gold   **V. Fine**
S-13 20 Mark 1872 ....1400.00
S-14 20 Mark 1886.........275.00

Alfred 1893-1900
Silver
S-15 2 Mark 1895...........105.00
S-16 5 Mark 1895...........525.00
Gold
S-17 20 Mark 1895.........250.00

Carl Eduard 1900-1918
Silver
S-18 2 Mark 1905-11.......140.00
S-19 5 Mark 1907..........350.00
Gold
S-20 10 Mark 1905.........225.00
S-21 20 Mark 1905.........225.00

SAXE-MEININGEN
(Duchy)
Georg II 1866-1914
Silver
S-8 2 Mark 1901...........95.00
S-9 5 Mark 1901..........105.00
S-10 2 Mark 1902-13........75.00
S-11 3 Mark 1908-13........35.00
S-12 5 Mark 1902-08........55.00

Death of Georg
S-13 2 Mark 1915............35.00
S-14 3 Mark (Similar) 1915....45.00
Gold
S-15 20 Mark 1872 ....1900.00
S-16 20 Mark 1882 (ZU).....875.00
S-17 20 Mark 1889 (VON)...700.00
S-18 10 Mark 1890-98.......700.00
S-19 20 Mark 1900-05......1200.00
S-20 10 Mark 1902-14......525.00
S-21 20 Mark 1910-14......1500.00

SAXE-WEIMAR
(Grand Duchy)
Carl Alexander 1853-1901
Silver
S-6 2 Mark 1892-98..........42.50
Gold
S-7 20 Mark 1892-96.......280.00

GERMAN EMPIRE (States)

Wilhelm Ernst 1901-1918
Silver
		V. Fine
S-8	2 Mark 1901	70.00

First Marriage
S-9	2 Mark 1903	21.00
S-10	5 Mark (Similar) 1903	60.00

Jena University
S-11	2 Mark 1908	21.00
S-12	5 Mark (Similar) 1908	60.00

Second Marriage
S-13	3 Mark 1910	15.00

Centenary of Grand Duchy
S-14	3 Mark 1915	45.00

Gold
S-15	20 Mark 1901	575.00

SAXONY (Sachsen) (Kingdom)
Johann 1854-1873
Gold
S-26	10 Mark 1872-73	42.00
S-27	20 Mark 1872-73 (2 Var.)	40.00

Albert 1873-1902
Silver
S-28	2 Mark 1876-88	15.00
S-29	5 Mark 1875-89	13.00
S-30	2 Mark 1891-1902	7.00
S-31	5 Mark 1891-1902	8.00

Death of Albert
S-33	2 Mark 1902	15.00
S-34	5 Mark 1902	40.00

Gold
S-35	5 Mark 1877	90.00
S-36	10 Mark 1874-88	40.00
S-37	20 Mark 1874-78	60.00
S-38	10 Mark 1891-1902	40.00
S-39	20 Mark 1894-95	60.00

Georg 1902-1904
Silver
S-40	2 Mark 1903-04	9.00
S-41	5 Mark 1903-04	12.00

Death of Georg
		V. Fine
S-43	2 Mark 1904	15.00
S-44	5 Mark (Similar) 1904	48.00

Gold
S-45	10 Mark 1903-04	50.00
S-46	20 Mark 1903	60.00

Friedrich August III 1904-1918
Silver
S-47	2 Mark 1905-14	7.00
S-48	3 Mark 1908-13	3.50
S-49	5 Mark 1907-14	7.50

Leipzig University
S-51	2 Mark 1909	21.00
S-52	5 Mark (Similar) 1909	17.50

Battle Monument
S-53	3 Mark 1913	5.25

Reformation Jubilee (100 Struck)
S-54	3 Mark 1917 (V. Rare)	——

Gold
S-55	10 Mark 1905-12	40.00
S-56	20 Mark 1905-14	60.00

SCHAUMBURG-LIPPE (Principality)
Adolf Georg 1860-1893
Gold
S-11	20 Mark 1874	1200.00

Albrecht Georg 1893-1911
Silver
S-12	2 Mark 1898-1904	110.00
S-13	5 Mark 1898-1904	280.00

Death of Georg
S-14	3 Mark 1911	25.00

Gold
S-15	20 Mark 1898-1904	375.00

GERMAN EMPIRE (States)

SCHWARZBURG-RUDOLSTADT
(Principality)
Günther 1890-1918

Silver *V. Fine*
S-10 2 Mark 1898 . . . . 65.00

Gold
11 10 Mark 1898 . . . . 350.00

SCHWARZBURG-SONDERSHAUSEN
(Principality)
Karl Günther 1880-1909

Silver
S-5 2 Mark 1896 . . . . 75.00

25th Year of Reign
S-6 2 Mark 1905 (2 Var.) 20.00

Death of Karl Günther
S-7 3 Mark 1909 . . . . 25.00

Gold
S-8 20 Mark 1896 . . . . 475.00

WALDECK-PYRMONT
(Principality)
Friedrich 1893-1918

Silver
S-5 5 Mark 1903 . . . . 700.00

Gold *V. Fine*
S-6 20 Mark 1903 . . . . 600.00

WÜRTTEMBERG
(Kingdom)
Karl 1864-1891

Silver
S-13 2 Mark 1876-88 . . . . 16.00
S-14 5 Mark 1874-88 . . . . 12.50

Gold
S-15 10 Mark 1872-73 . . . . 42.00
S-16 20 Mark 1872-73 . . . . 60.00
S-17   5 Mark 1877-78 . . . . . . 105.00
S-18 10 Mark 1874-88 . . . . 35.00
S-19 20 Mark 1874-76 . . . . 60.00
S-20 10 Mark 1890-91 . . . . 55.00

Wilhelm II 1891-1918

Silver
S-21 2 Mark 1892-1914 . . . . 4.50
S-22 3 Mark 1908-14 . . . . 3.50
S-23 5 Mark 1892-1913 . . . . 6.00

Silver Wedding
S-24 3 Mark 1911 . . . . 7.50

25th Year of Reign
S-25 3 Mark 1916 . . . . 1200.00

Gold
S-26 10 Mark 1893-1913 . . . . . . 36.00
S-27 20 Mark 1894-1914 . . . . . . 60.00

GERMAN EMPIRE

Coins in General Circulation Throughout the Empire

Copper

V. Fine
1 1 Pfennig 1873-89 40
2 2 Pfennig 1873-77 40

V. Fine
3 1 Pfennig 1890-1916 25
4 2 Pfennig 1904-1916 30

GERMAN EMPIRE

Copper-Nickel

V. Fine

5   5 Pfennig 1874-89 50
6 10 Pfennig 1873-89 55

7 20 Pfennig 1887-88 . . . . .8.50

 8   5 Pfennig 1890-1915 20
 9 10 Pfennig 1890-1916 25
10 20 Pfennig 1890-92 . . . . . . .12.50

Nickel

11 25 Pfennig 1909-12 . . . . .3.00

Silver

12 20 Pfennig 1873-77 . . . . .1.75
13 50 Pfennig 1875-77 (Eagle
        in Plain Field) 3.50

V. Fine

14 50 Pfennig 1877-78 (Small
        Eagle in Wreath) 10.00
17   1 Mark 1873-87 . . . . .1.50

15 50 Pfennig 1896-1901
        (Large Eagle) 85.00
16 ½ Mark 1905-19 50
Last year of No. 16 was struck under
the Republic; ½ marks of 1919 were
blackened to prevent hoarding.
18   1 Mark 1891-1916 75

WORLD WAR I and INFLATION 1915-1923

This period marks the end of the German Empire and the rise of the Weimar Republic in 1919. Silver coins were retained unchanged until stopped, while the lower denominations were made in aluminum, zinc and iron.

OCCUPATION MONEY

**By Authority of German Military
Commander of the East
(Baltic States, Poland and
Northwest Russia)**

Iron

Fine

A18 1 Kopek 1916 . . . . .2.00
B18 2 Kopeks 1916 . . . . .2.00
C18 3 Kopeks 1916 . . . . .2.00

GERMANY (Republic)

Various Metals

V. Fine

19 1 Pfennig Alum. 1917-18.... .25

Fine

21 5 Pfennig Iron 1915-22.... .10
22 10 Pfennig Iron 1916-22
(Small Eagle).......... .10
22a 10 Pfennig Zinc 1917
(Small Eagle).. *V. Fine* 60.00
25 10 Pfennig Zinc 1917-22
(Large Eagle).......... .10

WEIMAR REPUBLIC
1919-1933

Aluminum

V. Fine

26 50 Pfennig 1919-22......... .15

28 3 Mark 1922-23 (3rd Anniversary of Weimar Constit.) .35
29 3 Mark 1922 (No Obverse
Legend)................3.00

V. Fine

30 200 Mark 1923............ .30
31 500 Mark 1923............ .50

Coinage Law of Nov. 8, 1923

Bronze

32 1 Rentenpfennig 1923-29... .20
33 2 Rentenpfennig 1923-24... .20

Aluminum-Bronze

34 5 Rentenpfennig 1923-24... .25
35 10 Rentenpfennig 1923-25... .35
36 50 Rentenpfennig 1923-24...5.00

Coinage Reform of 1924

Bronze

37 1 Reichspfennig 1924-36..... .20
38 2 Reichspfennig 1924-36..... .25

Aluminum-Bronze

40 5 Reichspfennig 1924-36.... .25
41 10 Reichspfennig 1924-36.... .30
42 50 Reichspfennig 1924-25..400.00

39 4 Reichspfennig Br. 1932....3.50

Nickel

43 50 Reichspfennig 1927-38....1.00

GERMANY

Silver

		V. Fine
44	1 Mark 1924-25	4.00
45	1 Reichsmark 1925-27	
	(Value in Oak Wreath)	5.00
46	2 Reichsmark 1925-31	5.00
47	3 Mark 1924-25	10.00
48	3 Reichsmark 1931-33	80.00

V. Fine

49 5 Reichsmark 1927-33 . . . . . . 35.00

COMMEMORATIVE ISSUES

Silver
1925
Thousandth
Year of the
Rhineland

Ex. Fine
50 3 Reichsmark . . 18.00
51 5 Reichsmark . . 60.00

1926
700th Year
Freedom of Lübeck

52 3 Reichsmark . . . 70.00

1927
Hundredth
Anniversary
Bremerhaven

53 3 Reichsmark
. . . . 80.00
54 5 Reichsmark
. . . . 300.00

GERMANY

1927
Thousandth
Anniversary
Founding of
Nordhausen

Ex. Fine

55 3 Reichsmark.....85.00

1927
400th Anniversary
University of
Marburg

56 3 Reichsmark...42.50

1927
450th
Anniversary
University of
Tübingen

57 3 Reichsmark
.........150.00
58 5 Reichsmark
.........200.00

1928
400th Anniversary
Death of Dürer

59 3 Reichsmark...165.00

GERMANY

1928
900th Anniversary
Founding of
Naumburg

Ex. Fine
60 3 Reichsmark.... 70.00

1928
Thousandth
Anniversary
Founding of
Dinkelsbühl

61 3 Reichsmark... 225.00

1929
200th Anniversary
Birth of Lessing

62 3 Reichsmark.... 18.00
63 5 Reichsmark.... 50.00

1929
Waldeck-Prussia
Union

64 3 Reichsmark... 52.50

1929
10th Year
of Constitution

65 3 Reichsmark... 15.00
66 5 Reichsmark... 50.00

GERMANY

1929
Thousandth
Anniversary
of Meissen

Ex. Fine

67 3 Reichsmark. . . 27.50
68 5 Reichsmark. . . 2C0.00

1930
World Flight
of
Graf Zeppelin

69 3 Reichsmark
. . . . 30.00
70 5 Reichsmark
. . . . 70.00

1930
700th Anniversary
Death of
von der Vogelweide

71 3 Reichsmark. . . . 32.50

1930
Evacuation of
Rhineland

72 3 Reichsmark. . . . 15.00
73 5 Reichsmark . . . 70.00

GERMANY

1931
300th Anniversary
Rebuilding
Magdeburg

Ex. Fine
74 3 Reichsmark...100.00

1931
Centenary of Death
of von Stein

75 3 Reichsmark....65.00

1932
Centenary
Death of Goethe

76 3 Reichsmark...35.00
77 5 Reichsmark..700.00

THIRD REICH 1933-1945 — NAZI TOTALITARIAN STATE

Coinage Law of March 18, 1933

Silver

1933
450th Anniversary of
Martin Luther

Ex. Fine
78 2 Reichsmark.......7.50
79 5 Reichsmark......36.00

GERMANY

First Anniversary of Nazi Rule
(Potsdam Military Church)

With Date 21 MARZ 1933

V. Fine
83 2 Reichsmark 1934........ 5.00
84 5 Reichsmark 1934........10.00

Without Date 21 MARZ 1933

85 5 Reichsmark 1934-35...... 2.00

175th Anniversary
Birth of Schiller

86 2 Reichsmark 1934........20.00
87 5 Reichsmark 1934........70.00

Proof coins exist of all German Commemorative coins of Republic and Nazi State.

Regular Issues
Aluminum

V. Fine
80 50 Reichspfennig 1935...... .50
Coined in 1935, but held from circulation until 1939.

Nickel

81 1 Reichsmark 1933-39..... 1.25

Silver

82 5 Reichsmark
1935-36................ 3.50

Bronze

88 1 Reichspfennig 1936-40.... .25
89 2 Reichspfennig 1936-40.... .35

Aluminum-Bronze

90 5 Reichspfennig 1936-39.... .35
91 10 Reichspfennig 1936-39.... .50

GERMANY
Regular Issues

Zinc

V. Fine

A92 1 Reichspfennig 1940-45.. .20
B92 5 Reichspfennig 1940-44.. .25
C92 10 Reichspfennig 1940-45.. .30

Silver   V. Fine
96 2 Reichsmark 1936-39......1.75
97 5 Reichsmark 1936-39......3.25

ALLIED OCCUP. 1945-50
Swastika Omitted
Zinc

92 50 Reichspfennig Alum.
1939-44................ .50

98 1 Reichspfennig 1944-46.10.00
99 5 Reichspfennig 1947-48..8.50
100 10 Reichspfennig 1945-48..5.50

Currency Reform of June 20, 1948
Legend:
BANK DEUTSCHER LÄNDER
Bronze-Clad Steel

93 50 Reichspfennig Nickel
1938-39..............20.00

101 1 Pfennig 1948-49........ .20
Brass-Clad Steel
102 5 Pfennig 1949........... .25
103 10 Pfennig 1949........... .35

German Army Issues

Zinc

94 5 Reichspfennig 1940-41...12.50
95 10 Reichspfennig 1940-41...12.50

104 50 Pfennig Cop.-Nic.
1949-50................ .75

GERMANY-FEDERAL REPUBLIC (West Germany)

West Germany became independent in 1949. Capital: *Bonn*.
100 Pfennig = 1 Deutsche Mark

New Legend:
BUNDESREPUBLIK DEUTSCHLAND

Designs Similar to Nos. 101-104

Bronze-Clad Steel

Unc.

110 1 Deutsche Mark 1950-..... .70

Ex. Fine

111 2 Deutsche Mark 1951....17.50

Unc.

105 1 Pfennig 1950-........... .10
106 2 Pfennig Bronze 1950-68.. .20

Brass-Clad Steel

107 5 Pfennig 1950-........... .10
108 10 Pfennig 1950-........... .15

Copper-Nickel

Silver

Unc.

112 5 Deutsche Mark 1951-.... 5.00

Later issues in Current Coins of the World.

109 50 Pfennig 1950-.......... .35

GERMAN DEMOCRATIC REPUBLIC
— see *Current Coins of the World*

GERMAN EAST AFRICA (Deutsch Ostafrika)

After World War I this German colony was split between Britain and Belgium, who administered for the League of Nations respectively Tanganyika (see East Africa) and Ruanda-Urundi (see Belgian Congo and Ruanda-Urundi) and Portugal. Principal products include sisal, cotton, hides, and ivory. Capital: *Dar-es-Salaam*.

Before 1902, 64 Pesa (Pice)=1 Rupie
After 1902, 100 Heller = 1 Rupie
Coinage obsolete.

WILHELM II 1888-1918
Authority of
German East Africa Co.

Copper

V. Fine

1 1 Pesa 1890-92...............2.50

GERMAN EAST AFRICA

Silver

		V. Fine
2	¼ Rupie 1891-1901	8.50
3	½ Rupie 1891-1901	10.00
4	1 Rupie 1890-1902	9.00
5	2 Rupien 1893-94	175.00

New Legend:
DEUTSCH OSTAFRIKA only

Bronze

6	½ Heller 1904-06	1.00
7	1 Heller 1904-13	1.00
8	5 Heller 1908-09	12.50

Copper-Nickel

11	5 Heller 1913-14	5.00
12	10 Heller 1908-14	6.00

Silver

13	¼ Rupie 1904-14	8.50
14	½ Rupie 1904-14	12.50
15	1 Rupie 1904-14	8.00

Provisional Issues

			Fine
9 (9a)	5 Heller Brass 1916		4.00
10	20 Heller Copper 1916		3.50
10a	20 Heller Brass 1916		2.00

4 varieties each of nos. 10 and 10a (differences in size and shape of lettering and crown).

Gold

		V. Fine
16	15 Rupien 1916	250.00

World War I issues were struck at Tabora (9, 10, 10a and 16).

GERMAN NEW GUINEA (Neu-Guinea)

After World War I under the League of Nations mandate; it is now the Territory of New Guinea, under the U. N. Trusteeship system. Total area for the islands making up this territory is approximately 93,000 square miles. Capital: *Herbertshoehe.*

100 Pfennig = 1 Mark
Coinage obsolete.

Copper

Copper

		Ex. Fine
1	1 Pfennig 1894	22.50
2	2 Pfennig 1894	30.00

Silver
(Same type as 10 pf. copper)   *V. Fine*

4	½ Mark 1894	45.00
5	1 Mark 1894	45.00
6	2 Mark 1894	80.00
7	5 Mark 1894 ..... *Ex. Fine*	350.00

Ex. Fine

3	10 Pfennig 1894	25.00

Gold
(Similar type)

8	10 Mark 1895	——
9	20 Mark 1895	——

GHANA

Situated in West Africa on the Gulf of Guinea, this was the former British colony taken over in 1821 from the British merchant company which had developed the Gold Coast. Ghana was given its independence on March 6, 1957, and became a Republic within the British Commonwealth on July 1, 1960. Population: 8,900,000. Capital: *Accra.*

12 Pence = 1 Shilling

For earlier issues see BRITISH WEST AFRICA.

Bronze

		Unc.
1	½ Penny 1958	.15
2	1 Penny 1958	.20

Copper-Nickel

		Unc.
4	6 Pence 1958	.40
5	1 Shilling 1958	.60
6	2 Shillings 1958 .... *Ex. F.*	1.00

Silver
Proof

7	10 Shillings 1958	15.00

Proof Set Nos. 1 to 7 in case...27.50

Later issues in Current Coins of the World.

3	3 Pence 1958	.30

GREAT BRITAIN

The United Kingdom of Great Britain and Northern Ireland, separated from the European mainland by the North Sea and the English Channel. Population: 56,100,000. Total area: 94,511 square miles. *London,* capital of Great Britain, is the hub of the British Commonwealth of Nations which includes more than one fourth of the world's population. It is also the world's second largest seaport, being surpassed only by New York. Among its exports are iron and steel, woolens, textiles, and machinery.

4 Farthings = 1 Penny	5 Shillings = 1 Crown
12 Pence = 1 Shilling	20 Shillings = 1 Pound
2 Shillings = 1 Florin	20 Shillings = 1 Sovereign (Gold)

HYBRID DENOMINATIONS
FOR USE IN CERTAIN COLONIES

In the 19th century Britain commenced the task of imposing its monetary system upon various colonies which hitherto had used the other systems. In order to make the change palatable to the inhabitants, certain special denominations were coined as bridges between the old and new systems. These coins are indistinguishable from regular British issues except by denomination, hence they are here cross-referenced so that they may be more easily found under the countries where they were chiefly used.

BRITISH GUIANA: 4 pence silver (Britannia groat) 1838-55, 1888. Substitute for old ¼ guilder. (see Great Britain No. 4.)

CEYLON: ¼ farthing 1839-53, ½ farthing 1839-56, 1½ pence 1838-62. (see Ceylon Nos. 1, 2 and 3). The first two were the rough equivalents of the ½ and 1 duit or the ½ and 1 Indian pie, the latter was roughly the Indian anna.

JAMAICA: 1½ pence 1838-62. Substitute for Spanish-American ¼ real. (see Jamaica No. A3).

MALTA: ⅓ farthing 1844-1913. Substitute for 1 grano copper. (see Malta Nos. 1, 2, 3 and 4).

MAURITIUS: 1½ pence 1837-76.

To aid in identification of gold coins the following diameters should be helpful: ½ Sovereign – 19mm., 1 Sovereign – 22mm., 2 Pounds – 29mm., 5 Pounds – 36mm.

VICTORIA 1837-1901

	Copper	Fine
1	1 Farthing 1838-60	1.50
2	½ Penny 1838-59	1.25
3	1 Penny 1841-60	1.25→

	Silver	Fine
A3	3 Pence 1838-87	1.50
← **4**	4 Pence (Groat) 1838-55	2.50

GREAT BRITAIN

Silver

Fine

5 6 Pence 1838-87............2.00
6 1 Shilling 1838-87..........1.75

"Godless" Florin
DEI GRATIA omitted

7 1 Florin 1849.............12.50

8 1 Florin 1851-87............4.00

Gothic Type   *Ex. Fine*
11 1 Crown 1847, 53.......350.00

Maundy Money

Maundy Money is a term for a specially struck set of British silver coins which are distributed to certain poor persons on Maundy Thursday. They consist of one, two, three and four pence coins.

The Threepence was also issued regularly until 1944 and cannot be distinguished until 1927.

9 ½ Crown 1839-87........5.00
*10 1 Crown 1839-47.......27.50

12 Maundy Set 1838-87......40.00

GREAT BRITAIN

Gold

V. Fine

13 ½ Sovereign (10 Shillings)
    (Crowned Shield) 1838-85.45.00
*14 1 Sovereign (Shield in
    wreath) 1838-74......65.00
15 1 Sovereign (St. George
    and Dragon) 1871-85..65.00

Fine

23 1 Florin 1887-92...........3.00

Bronze

Fine

16 1 Farthing 1860-95....... .60
17 ½ Penny 1860-94.........1.00
*18 1 Penny 1860-94.........1.25

*24 ½ Crown 1887-92.........3.50
25 2 Florin 1887-90
    (Same Type as Florin)..10.00

Golden Jubilee Type
Silver

A18 3 Pence 1887-93
    (Wreath Reverse).......1.00
19 6 Pence 1887 (Arms).....1.00
20 1 Shilling (Small Bust)
    1887-89................1.25
*21 1 Shilling(Lg.Bust)1889-92 2.00

V.Fine

26 1 Crown 1887-92.........17.50
22 6 Pence 1887-93 (Value)..1.00
27 Maundy Set 1888-92.*Ex. F.* 50.00

GREAT BRITAIN

Gold

V. Fine

28 ½ Sovereign 1887-93......35.00
★29 1 Sovereign 1887-92......65.00
30 2 Pounds 1887.........225.00
31 5 Pounds 1887.........400.00

Old Bust 1893-1901
Veil over Crown

Bronze

Fine

32 1 Farthing 1895-1901...... .50
33 ½ Penny 1895-1901........ .35
34 1 Penny 1895-1901........ .60

Silver

35 3 Pence (Value in Wreath)
1893-1901............... .50
36 6 Pence 1893-1901.......... .75

37 1 Shilling 1893-1901.......1.50
38 1 Florin 1893-1901.........3.00

Fine

39 ½ Crown 1893-1901 ....3.50
40 1 Crown (St. George and
Dragon) 1893-1900.....10.00

Ex. Fine

41 Maundy Set 1893-1901...35.00

Gold

V. Fine

42 ½ Sovereign 1893-1901....35.00
★43 1 Sovereign 1893-1901....60.00
44 2 Pounds 1893.........250.00
45 5 Pounds 1893.........450.00

EDWARD VII 1901-1910

Bronze   Fine

46 1 Farthing 1902-10........ .50
47 ½ Penny 1902-10.......... .50
48 1 Penny 1902-10........... .50

Silver

49 3 Pence 1902-10 (Value in
Wreath).................. .75
50 6 Pence 1902-10 (Value in
Wreath)..................1.50
51 1 Shilling 1902-10 (Lion)....2.25
52 1 Florin 1902-10 (Britannia).4.00
53 ½ Crown 1902-10 (Crowned
Shield).................6.50

GREAT BRITAIN

V. Fine
66 6 Pence 1911-27............ .65

V. Fine
54 1 Crown 1902............60.00

Unc.
55 Maundy Set 1902-10.......40.00

Gold

67 1 Shilling 1911-27.........1.00

56 ½ Sovereign 1902-10.... 30.00
★57 1 Sovereign 1902-10.... 60.00
58 2 Pounds 1902.........200.00
59 5 Pounds 1902.........425.00

68 1 Florin 1911-26............1.50

GEORGE V 1910-1936

During the period 1925-27 the effigy was
reduced in size. The difference is greatest
on nos. 62 and 64.

Bronze

69 ½ Crown 1911-27.........2.50

Second Coinage

60 1 Farthing 1911-36....... .50
61 ½ Penny 1911-27.......... .65
62 ½ Penny 1928-36.......... .50
63 1 Penny 1911-27.......... .65
64 1 Penny 1928-36.......... .60

The silver coins 1920 onward were
debased to .500 fine.

70 3 Pence 1927-36............ .40
71 6 Pence 1927-36............ .60

Silver

72 1 Shilling
1927-36....1.20

65 3 Pence 1911-26............ .35

GREAT BRITAIN

V. Fine
73 1 Florin
1927-36
...1.50

74
½ Crown
1927-36
1.50

Gold

V. Fine
77 ½ Sovereign 1911-15....30.00
★78 1 Sovereign 1911-25....60.00
79 2 Pounds 1911 Proofs..400.00
80 5 Pounds 1911 Proofs..850.00

Silver
Unc.
81 Maundy Set 1911-20..45.00
A81 Same 1921-36........45.00

GEORGE VI 1936-1952

Bronze

V. Fine
82 1 Farthing 1937-48......... .20

Ex. Fine
75 1 Crown 1927-36........100.00

83 ½ Penny 1937-48.......... .15
84 1 Penny 1937-48
(Britannia)............. .15

Silver Jubilee

Nickel-Brass

76 1 Crown 1935............15.00 **85** 3 Pence 1937-48............ .25

GREAT BRITAIN

Silver

V. Fine

86 3 Pence 1937-44............ .30
87 6 Pence 1937-46............ .40

A. English Crest   B. Scottish Crest

88 1 Shilling (A) 1937-46....... .60
89 1 Shilling (B) 1937-46....... .60

90 2 Shillings 1937-46......... 1.00

91 ½ Crown 1937-46.......... 1.50

V. Fine
92 1 Crown 1937............ 14.00

Unc.
93 Maundy Set 1937-48...... 45.00

Coronation Proof Set in Case
(No. 82 to 92) 1937. Includes
Maundy Set............ 165.00

Copper-Nickel

Designs Same as Nos. 87-91
V. Fine
95 6 Pence 1947-48.......... .15
96 1 Shilling (English) 1947-48 .40
97 1 Shilling (Scottish) 1947-48 .40
98 2 Shillings 1947-48........ .90
99 ½ Crown 1947-48......... 1.00

Gold

Proof
100 ½ Sovereign 1937....... 160.00

• 213 •

GREAT BRITAIN

<table>
<tr><td></td><td></td><td>Proof</td></tr>
<tr><td>*101</td><td>1 Sovereign 1937</td><td>250.00</td></tr>
<tr><td>102</td><td>2 Pounds 1937</td><td>400.00</td></tr>
<tr><td>103</td><td>5 Pounds 1937</td><td>1000.00</td></tr>
</table>

IND. IMP. omitted

Designs similar to Nos. 82-91

Bronze   *V. Fine*

104	1 Farthing 1949-52	.15
105	½ Penny 1949-52	.20
106	1 Penny 1949-51	.30

Nickel-Brass

107	3 Pence (12 Sided) 1949-52	.25

Copper-Nickel

108	6 Pence 1949-52	.25
109	1 Shilling (English) 1949-51	.40
110	1 Shilling (Scottish) 1949-51	.40
111	2 Shillings 1949-51	1.00
112	½ Crown 1949-51	1.00
113	Maundy Set Fine Silver *Unc.* 1949-52	85.00

Proof Set of Nine
(Nos. 104-112) 1950 . . . . . 95.00

114	1 Crown 1951	12.50

Festival of Britain Proof Set 1951

Proof

Set of 10 (Farthing to Crown) in Case 120.00

ELIZABETH II 1952-
1953 Coronation Coins

No. 122
Reduced
Size:

Bronze   *V. Fine*

116	1 Farthing 1953	.20
117	½ Penny 1953	.25
118	1 Penny 1953	1.40

GREAT BRITAIN

V. Fine

119 3 Pence Nic.-Brass 1953 .20

Copper-Nickel

120 6 Pence 1953 25
121 1 Shilling (English) 1953 .25
122 1 Shilling (Scottish) 1953 .30
123 2 Shillings 1953 70
124 ½ Crown 1953 85

Unc.

125 1 Crown 1953 . . . . .7.50
126 Maundy Set Fine Silver
1953 . . . . .175.00

**Without BRITT: OMN:
(Same Metals as 1953)**

127 1 Farthing 1954-56 . . . . . . .1.00

128 ½ Penny 1954-70 15
A128 1 Penny 1961-70 25

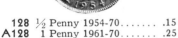

129 3 Pence 1954-70 25
130 6 Pence 1954-70 25
★131 1 Shilling (English) 1954-
70 50
132 1 Shilling (Scottish)1954-
70 50

Unc.

133 2 Shillings 1954-70 85
134 ½ Crown 1954-70 . . . . .1.25
135 Maundy Set 1954-70 . . 60.00
136 5 Shillings 1960 . . . . .13.00

Gold

**Issued Only for
Overseas Distribution**

137 1 Sovereign 1957-68 . . . . . .60.00

Later issues in Current Coins of the World.

British Trade Dollar

Silver

Issued to facilitate British trade in
the Orient. Denomination ONE DOLLAR
appears in Malay, Chinese, English.
Often chopmarked with Chinese
characters.

V. Fine

T-1 1 Dollar 1895 - 1935 . . . . .7.50

GREECE
(Vasilon Tis Ellados—Kingdom of Hellas)

Southernmost of the Balkan states in Eastern Europe, extending down into the Mediterranean Sea. An agricultural nation, it exports tobacco, currants, olives, citrus fruits, leather, and hides. Capital: *Athens*. Area: 51,246 square miles. Population: 8,800,000.   100 Lepta = 1 Drachma

GEORGE I 1863-1913
Young Head
Copper

		Fine
1	1 Lepton 1869-70	2.50
2	2 Lepta 1869	2.50
3	5 Lepta 1869-70	1.50
4	10 Lepta 1869-70	1.25

Silver

5	20 Lepta 1869-83	1.75
6	50 Lepta 1868-83	2.25
7	1 Drachma 1868-83	3.00
8	2 Drachmai 1868-83	6.00

Older Head
Copper

10	1 Lepton 1878-79	2.00

		Fine
11	2 Lepta 1878	2.00
12	5 Lepta 1878-82	.75
13	10 Lepta 1878-82	1.00

Silver

14	5 Drachmai 1875-76	20.00

Copper-Nickel

16	5 Lepta 1894-95	.35
17	10 Lepta 1894-95	.40
18	20 Lepta 1893-95	.50

For similar coins dated 1900, see Crete.

Nickel

19	5 Lepta 1912	.35
20	10 Lepta 1912	.40

GREECE

Fine
21 20 Lepta 1912 50

Silver

22 1 Drachma 1910-11 . . . . .2.50
23 2 Drachmai 1911 . . . . .3.50

Gold
Young Head

V. Fine
24   5 Drachmai 1876 . . . . . .325.00
25 10 Drachmai 1876 . . . . . .225.00
A25 20 Drachmai 1876 . . . . . .200.00

Older Head

26   20 Drachmai 1884 . . . . . . .100.00
27   50 Drachmai 1876 . . . . . .1750.00
28 100 Drachmai 1876 . . . . . .3500.00

GEORGE II
First Reign 1922-23
Aluminum

V. Fine
29 10 Lepta 1922 50

Nickel-Bronze

30 50 Lepta 1921 . . . .——
No. 30 was not issued to circulation.

REPUBLIC 1924-1935
Copper-Nickel

31 20 Lepta 1926 35
32 50 Lepta 1926 35
★33 1 Drachma 1926 50
34 2 Drachmai 1926 75

Nickel

35 5 Drachmai 1930 75

GREECE

Silver

V. Fine
36 10 Drachmai 1930.........4.00

37 20 Drachmai 1930.........5.00

RESTORATION OF MONARCHY
GEORGE II 1922-23, 1935-47
Restoration Commemoratives

A37 100 Drachmai Silver 1935
Proof.............450.00

Gold

B37 20 Drachmai 1935.....800.00
C37 100 Drachmai 1935....2500.00
Nos. A37, B37 and C37 not issued to circulation.

PAUL I 1947-1964

Aluminum

Unc.
38 5 Lepta 1954-71.............15

39 10 Lepta 1954-71............15
40 20 Lepta 1954-71............20

Copper-Nickel

41 50 Lepta 1954-65............20
42 1 Drachma 1954-65.........30
43 2 Drachmai 1954-65........40
44 5 Drachmai 1954-65........75

Nickel
45 10 Drachmai 1959-65.......1.50

Silver

46 20 Drachmai 1960-65.......2.50
Later issues in Current Coins of the World.

GREENLAND (Grønland)

An integral part of Denmark; a large island between the North Atlantic and the Polar Sea. About four-fifths of the island is ice-capped. Capital: *Godthaab*. Area: 840,000 square miles. Population: about 50,000. Exports: cryolite, fish, and fur.

100 Øre = 1 Krone
Coinage obsolete.

	Copper-Nickel	*V. Fine*
5	25 Øre 1926	1.50
6	25 Øre (Center Hole) 1926	4.50
	Aluminum-Bronze	
7	50 Øre 1926	1.25
8	1 Krone 1926	2.50
	Brass	→
9	5 Kroner 1944	6.00

		Unc.
10	1 Krone Alum.-Bronze 1957	3.00
10a	1 Krone Cop.-Nic. ← 1960-64	2.00

GUADELOUPE

Two large islands in the Caribbean near Antigua. They have been French possessions since 1634. Capital: *Basse-Terre*. Population: about 306,000. Area: 583 square miles. Exports: sugar, coffee, rum, cacao, vanilla, and bananas.

100 Centimes = 1 Franc
Coinage obsolete.

	Copper-Nickel	*V. Fine*
1	50 Centimes 1903, 21	3.75
2	1 Franc 1903, 21	4.50

GUATEMALA (Republica de Guatemala)

North Central America, with Mexico bounding it on the north. The main port is Puerto Barrios on the Atlantic. Four fifths of all exports is coffee. Capital: *Guatemala City*. Population: 5,400,000. Area: 42,042 square miles.

8 Reales = 1 Peso
100 Centavos = 1 Peso
100 Centavos = 1 Quetzal

RAFAEL CARRERA
President 1851-1865
First Coinage
Silver

Note: Because of extensive catalog revisions, new numbers were assigned in the 7th edition.

		Fine
1	¼ Real 1859-69	1.75

GUATEMALA

		Fine
2	½ Real 1859-61	2.00
3	1 Real 1859-60	2.50
4	2 Reales 1859 (Thick letters)	100.00
5	2 Reales 1860-61 (Thin letters)	3.50
6	4 Reales 1860-61	5.00
7	1 Peso 1859	100.00

Second Coinage

		Fine
8	½ Real 1862-65	1.25
9	1 Real 1861-65	1.25
*10	2 Reales 1862-65	2.25
11	4 Reales 1863-65	4.50
12	1 Peso 1862-65	8.00

Gold

		V. Fine
13	4 Reales 1860-64	15.00
14	1 Peso 1859-60	30.00

15	2 Pesos 1859	85.00
16	4 Pesos 1861-62	300.00
17	8 Pesos 1864	600.00
18	16 Pesos 1863 (36mm)	——
19	16 Pesos 1865 (33mm)	——

POSTHUMOUS ISSUES
New Legend:
R. CARRERA FUNDADOR
Designs Similar to Nos. 8-19

	Silver	Fine
20	½ Real 1867-69	1.25

		Fine
21	1 Real 1866-67	1.25
22	1 Real 1868-69 (Modified arms on rev.)	1.75
23	2 Reales 1866-69	2.50
24	4 Reales 1867-68	5.00
25	1 Peso 1866-69 (Fineness "10D 20G")	8.00

	Gold	V. Fine
26	4 Pesos 1866-69	150.00
27	8 Pesos 1869	——
28	16 Pesos 1869	500.00

First Decimal System
1869-1870

Designs similar to Nos. 23-28

	Silver	Fine
29	25 Centimos 1869-70	5.00
30	1 Peso 1869-71 (Fineness "0.900")	8.00

	Gold	V. Fine
31	5 Pesos 1869	100.00
32	10 Pesos 1869	160.00
33	20 Pesos 1869	400.00

Second Decimal System
1870-1871

Bronze

34	1 Centavo 1871	4.50

Silver

35	50 Centavos 1870	5.50

After 1871 the silver coinage returned to the *Real* system, while gold was struck in the decimal system.

GUATEMALA

.900 Fine Silver

Fine

36 ¼ Real 1872-78............1.25

37 ½ Real 1872-73............2.50
38 1 Real 1872-78............3.50
39 2 Reales 1872-73..........2.50

.835 Fine Silver

40 ¼ Real 1878 (Wreath of
No. 36)................2.50
41 ¼ Real 1878-79 (Wreath of
No. 42)................2.00
42 ¼ Real 1879-86
Long-rayed sun.........1.00

43 ½ Real 1878-79............1.75

No Fineness Indicated

*44 ¼ Real 1878 G on Rev.
(3 var. - sm., med., or
lg. G)................1.25
45 ¼ Real 1887-88 Short-
rayed sun, rev. lion.....1.00

Fine

46 ¼ Real 1889 (G below
mountains).............1.50
47 ¼ Real 1889-91 (5 stars
below wreath)...........75
48 ¼ Real 1892-93 Long-rayed
sun, rev. lion...........1.00
49 ¼ Real 1893-94 (3 stars
below wreath)...........75
50 ½ Real 1878-93
Like No. 43............2.00
51 1 Real 1878 similar........3.50

Seated Liberty Design
.900 Fine Silver

52 1 Real 1879.............12.50
53 2 Reales 1879.............6.50
54 4 Reales 1873-79
Small wreath..........20.00

V. Fine

56 1 Peso 1872-73 Date below
sm. wreath.............22.50

*57 1 Peso 1878-79 Date
above sm. wreath.....275.00
58 1 Peso 1879 Lg. wreath.250.00
58a 1 Peso 1888-93 Lg. wreath,
obv. modified Liberty.400.00

GUATEMALA

.835 Fine Silver

		Fine
59	½ Real 1879-80 (½ R^L)	1.25
60	½ Real 1880-90 (MEDIO REAL)	1.00
61	1 Real 1883-93	1.00
62	2 Reales 1881, 92-93	7.50
63	4 Reales 1892	200.00

No Fineness Indicated

| ★64 | ½ Real 1893 Sm. wreath | 30.00 |
| 65 | ½ Real 1893 Lg. wreath | 1.50 |

Gold

		V. Fine
★66	5 Pesos 1872-78	250.00
67	20 Pesos 1877-78	——

Third Decimal System 1881-1882

Bronze

| 68 | 1 Centavo 1881 (All struck over No. 34) | 5.00 |

Silver
Design similar to No. 62

		Fine
69	25 Centavos 1881-91	1.25
69a	25 Centavos 1890-93 Larger rev. letters	1.25

| 70 | 5 Centavos 1881 | 15.00 |
| 71 | 10 Centavos 1881 | 15.00 |

| 72 | 25 Centavos 1882 | 125.00 |

| 73 | 1 Peso 1882-89 | 25.00 |

Real System Continued
New Dies 1894
Silver

		V. Fine
74	¼ Real 1894-99	.50

GUATEMALA

PROVISIONAL ISSUES

Bronze

		V. Fine
75	½ Real 1894-97 .835 fine	.50
76	½ Real 1899 .600 fine	1.00
77	1 Real 1894-98 .835 fine	.75
78	1 Real 1899 (No fineness)	2.50
79	1 Real 1899 .750 fine	75.00
80	1 Real 1899 .600 fine	2.00
81	1 Real 1899-1900 .500 fine	.60
82	2 Reales 1894-99 .835 fine	.75
83	4 Reales 1894 .900 fine	3.50
84	1 Peso 1894-97 .900 fine	6.00

V. Fine

89 12½ Centavos 1915 .... 1.50
90 25 Centavos 1915 .... 1.50

Aluminum-Bronze

91 50 Centavos 1922 .... 1.50

92 1 Peso 1923 .... 1.75

Copper-Nickel

Designs similar to Nos. 74, 75, 77

85	¼ Real 1900-01 (Mountains)	.40
86	½ Real 1900-01	.40
87	1 Real 1900-12	.50

93 5 Pesos 1923 .... 2.50

Counterstamped Issues

Silver

Half Real dies of 1894 stamped on Pesos of Chile, Soles of Peru, and others.

88 1 Peso 1894 (on →
     Peru Sol) 10.00
88a 1 Peso 1894 (on
     Chile Peso) 12.50

GUATEMALA

COINAGE REFORM
November 26, 1924

Various Metals

		V. Fine
94	½ Centavo Brass 1932-46...	.35
95	1 Centavo Bronze 1925....	3.50
96	1 Centavo Bronze 1929 Larger arms............	1.75
97	1 Centavo Brass 1932-49...	.25
98	2 Centavos Brass 1932.....	.40

Silver
Long-tailed Quetzal on Scroll

99	5 Centavos 1925, 1944-49..	.35
100	10 Centavos 1925, 1944-49..	.50

Short-tailed Quetzal on Scroll

99a	5 Centavos 1928-43......	.40
100a	10 Centavos 1928-47......	.60
101	¼ Quetzal 1925 Lettered edge.........	2.00
102	¼ Quetzal 1926-29 Different dies.........	1.25
102a	¼ Quetzal 1946-49 Reeded edge..........	1.50
103	½ Quetzal 1925........	12.50
104	1 Quetzal 1925........	450.00

Gold

		V. Fine
105	5 Quetzales 1926......	100.00
106	10 Quetzales 1926......	225.00
107	20 Quetzales 1926......	275.00

Wartime Issues
Brass

108	1 Centavo 1943-44.......	1.00
109	2 Centavos 1943-44.......	1.25

Silver

110	25 Centavos 1943........	3.00

New Designs
Brass

No. 111   No. 112

111	1 Centavo 1949-54........	.20
112	1 Centavo 1954-58........	.15

		Unc.
113	1 Centavo 1958-64........	.15

GUATEMALA

Silver

No. 114   No. 115

		V. Fine
114	5 Centavos Sm. tree 1949	2.50

		Unc.
115	5 Centavos 1950-59	.40
★117	10 Centavos 1949-59	.60
117a	10 Centavos Larger monolith 1957-58	.60

		Unc.
119	25 Centavos 1950-59	1.50

Later issues in Current Coins of the World.

GUERNSEY

One of the Channel Islands off the coast of France, famous for its cattle. A dependency of the British monarch. Population: 52,000. Capital: *St. Peter Port.*

8 Doubles = 1 Penny

Copper

		Fine
A1	1 Double 1830	1.00
B1	2 Doubles 1858	8.50
C1	4 Doubles 1830-58	1.75

Bronze

		V. Fine
1	1 Double 1868-1911	1.00
2	2 Doubles 1868-1911	2.50
3	4 Doubles 1864-1911	1.50
4	8 Doubles 1864-1911	1.75

Bronze

Obv: Leaf cluster above shield

1a	1 Double 1911-38	.65
2a	2 Doubles 1914-29	2.50
3a	4 Doubles 1914-49	1.00
5	8 Doubles 1914-49	.85

D1	8 Doubles 1834-58	2.75

GUERNSEY

Copper-Nickel

			Unc.
6	4 Doubles 1956-66		1.25
7	8 Doubles 1956-66		.75

			Unc.
8	3 Pence 1956		1.25
8a	3 Pence 1959-66(thicker)		.75

Later issues in Current Coins of the World.

GUINEA—see *Current Coins of the World*

HAITI (République d'Haiti)

Located west of the Dominican Republic on the Caribbean island of Hispaniola, Haiti was originally a prosperous French colony. The lengthy war which gained it independence in 1803 disrupted its agricultural economy to a point from which it has never fully recovered. Coffee is the most important export crop. Most of the inhabitants are descendants of African slaves brought in during the 1700's. Area: 10,714 square miles. Languages: French, Creole. Capital: *Port-au-Prince.*

100 Centimes = 1 Gourde

Bronze

Obv: President Geffrard (1859-67)

			Fine
A1	5 Centimes 1863		2.00
★B1	10 Centimes 1863		1.75
C1	20 Centimes 1863		2.25

Design similar to Nos. 6-9

1	1 Centime 1881	3.50
2	2 Centimes 1881	3.50

			Fine
3	1 Centime 1886-95		2.50
4	2 Centimes 1886-94		2.50

Silver

			V. Fine
6	10 Centimes 1881-94		1.50
7	20 Centimes 1881-95		1.75
8	50 Centimes 1882-95		6.00
9	1 Gourde 1881-95		30.00

HAITI

Insurrection 1889

Copper-Nickel

		V. Fine
A5	5 Centimes 1889	30.00

Bronze

5	1 Gourde ND	200.00

No. 5 is counterstamped B.P. 1G/Gl.H
(Bon pour 1 Gourde/General Hyppolyte.)

Regular Issues
Copper-Nickel

Obv: President Nord Alexis (1902-08)

		Fine
10	5 Centimes 1904-05	.35
11	10 Centimes 1906	.50
12	20 Centimes 1907	.75
13	50 Centimes 1907-08	1.25

14	5 Centimes 1904	3.00

*Obv: President
Estimé (1946-50)*

		V. Fine
15	5 Centimes 1949	.25
16	10 Centimes 1949	.35

Later issues in *Current Coins of the World.*

HAWAII

Became the 50th State in 1959. It was a kingdom from 1791 until 1894 when a republic was proclaimed. The Spanish-American War brought about its annexation to the United States. Mauna Loa, on Hawaii, is the largest active volcano in the world. A great tourist center, Hawaii also is noted for its sugar and pineapple production. Capital: *Honolulu.*

100 Cents = 1 Dollar
Coinage obsolete.

KAMEHAMEHA III
1825-1854

Copper

		V. Fine
1	1 Cent 1847	60.00

HAWAII
KALAKAUA I 1874-1891

Silver

V. Fine

3 ¼ Dollar 1883............12.50
4 ½ Dollar 1883............25.00

V. Fine

5 1 Dollar 1883............90.00

2 1 Dime 1883..............20.00

HEJAZ (AL-HIJAZ)

The Hejaz, meaning "barrier," is the district of the rugged mountain range lying along the northern Red Sea coast of the Arabian peninsula. It contains the Islamic holy cities of Mecca and Medina. In 1916 it gained independence from the Ottoman Empire, but was conquered by Nejd in 1925. The two countries were united in 1932 to form Saudi Arabia. Language: Arabic. Capital: *Mecca.*

40 Para = 1 Ghirsh
20 Ghirsh = 1 Riyal
100 Ghirsh = 1 Dinar

Coinage obsolete.

Note: Because of extensive revisions, new numbers have been assigned in the 11th edition. The original numbers are given in parentheses.

HUSAIN IBN ALI
1916-1924

(Accession Date AH 1334 On Coins)

Nickel or Copper-Nickel

Counterstamp: incuse "al-Hijaz" in Arabic

Fine

1 (—) on Turkish 10 Para.....2.00
2 (—) on Turkish 20 Para.....1.00
★3 (—) on Turkish 40 Para.....1.25

Billon *Good*

4 (—) on Turkish 10 Para
pre-1844................5.00
5 (—) on sim. 20 Para........5.00

Silver *Fine*

8 (—) on Turkish or Egyptian
2 Ghirsh..............10.00
9 (—) on sim. 5 Ghirsh......10.00
10 (—) on sim. 10 Ghirsh......15.00
11 (—) on sim. 20 Ghirsh......25.00
12 (—) on Austria No. 55.....20.00

Copies of the Hejaz counterstamps on some or all of the above silver types are believed to have been produced in recent years.

Regular Issues

Copper

V. Fine

16 (1) ⅛ Ghirsh Yr. 5 (1920)
12-13mm..........15.00
17 (2) ¼ Ghirsh Yr. 5
(16mm)............7.50
★18 (3) ½ Ghirsh Yr. 5
(18-19mm).........7.50
19 (4) 1 Ghirsh Yr. 5
(21-22mm)........10.00

HEJAZ

Silver

V. Fine

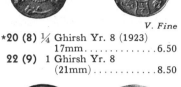

★20 (8) ¼ Ghirsh Yr. 8 (1923)
17mm............6.50
22 (9) 1 Ghirsh Yr. 8
(21mm)...........8.50

23 (10) 5 Ghirsh Yr. 8   *V. Fine*
(24mm)..........25.00
★24 (11) 10 Ghirsh Yr. 8
(28mm).........42.50
25 (12) 20 Ghirsh Yrs. 8-9
(37mm).........40.00

Gold
26 (13) 1 Dinar Yr. 8.......90.00
For later issues see Saudi Arabia.

HONDURAS

A Central American republic bounded on the north by Guatemala and on the south by Nicaragua. Fertile soil, rich forests, and abundant mineral resources have not been developed. Exports mostly to the United States are bananas (65%), coffee, cocoanuts, and hardwoods. Population: 2,600,000. Language: Spanish. Capital: *Tegucigalpa.*

100 Centavos = 1 Peso (1871-1926)
100 Centavos = 1 Lempira (Since 1926)

PROVISIONAL ISSUES
Bronze

Fine
P1 1 Peso 1862..............10.00
P2 2 Pesos 1862.............6.50
P3 4 Pesos 1862.............5.00
P4 8 Pesos 1862.............20.00

REPUBLIC
Copper-Nickel

                   V. Fine
2 ¼ Real 1869-70.............2.25
3 ½ Real 1869-70.............3.50
4 1 Real 1869-70............12.50

Note: Because of extensive catalog revisions, new numbers were assigned in the 7th Edition, beginning with No. 5.

Silver

                   Fine
5 5 Centavos 1871........150.00
6 10 Centavos 1871.........45.00
★7 25 Centavos 1871..........6.00
8 50 Centavos 1871.........10.00

V. Fine
1 ⅛ Real 1869-70.............7.50

HONDURAS

Issues of 1878-1880
(Dies made in U.S.)
Bronze

Fine

9 1 Centavo 1878-80 . . . . 15.00

Silver

10 5 Centavos 1879 . . . . 300.00
11 10 Centavos 1878 . . . . 300.00
12 50 Centavos 1879 . . . . 200.00

New Designs Starting 1881
Bronze

13 ½ Centavo 1881-91 . . . . 20.00

★14 1 Centavo 1881-1907, normal
obverse and reverse 2.00
15 1 Centavo 1890-1908
Normal obv., Rev. altered
from No. 21 . . . . 2.50

16 1 Centavo ND, Normal obv.,
rev. of No. 9 . . . . 125.00

Fine

17 1 Centavo 1890-1908, obv.
of No. 21, rev. altered
from No. 21 . . . . 2.50

18 1 Centavo 1895, obv. of No. 6,
rev. of No. 9 . . . . 125.00

Silver

19 5 Centavos 1884-1902
Obv. like No. 21 . . . . 15.00
★20 5 Centavos 1895-96
Obv. of No. 13 . . . . 6.50

21 10 Centavos 1884-1900 . . . . . . 9.00

22 10 Centavos 1886-95 Obv. of
No. 6, rev. like No. 21 . . 22.50

0.900 Fine
23 25 Centavos 1883-96 . . . . 3.50

HONDURAS

24 50 Centavos 1883-97 . . . . . . 6.50
25 1 Peso Sm. CENTRO AMERICA
on rev. 1881-83 . . . . 25.00
25a 1 Peso "25 G^MOS" above UN
PESO on obv., Lg. CENTRO
AMERICA on rev. 1883-
1914 . . . . 17.50
25b 1 Peso Obv. of No. 25, rev.
of No. 25a 1894-96 . . . . 22.50

0.835 Fine

23a 25 Centavos 1899-1913 . . . . . 4.50
24a 50 Centavos 1908 . . . . 40.00

Gold

V. Fine

26 1 Peso 1871 (Obv. of
1871 silver coins) . . . . . . ——
27 1 Peso 1888-1922 . . . . 225.00
★28 5 Pesos 1888-1913 . . . . . . 650.00
29 10 Pesos 1889 . . . . ——
30 20 Pesos 1888-1908 . . . . ——

Reduced Size Bronze

Fine

31 2 Centavos 1907-08 Rev.
altered from No. 21 . . . . 25.00

32 1 Centavo 1910-11 Obv. of
No. 13, rev. altered from
No. 13 . . . . 17.50

★33 2 Centavos 1910-13 Obv.
of No. 14, rev. altered
from No. 14 . . . . 1.75
36 1 Centavo 1910, Obv. of
No. 13, rev. altered from
No. 19 . . . . 25.00

Obv: pyramid in wreath (die of No. 19)

34 1 Centavo 1910, rev. altered
from No. 13 . . . . 17.50
35 1 Centavo 1910-11, rev.
altered from No. 19 . . . . . . 8.50

Obv: large pyramid of Nos. 13-14

37 1 (Centavo) 1919-20, rev.
altered from No. 13 . . . . 2.00
38 2 (Centavos) 1919-20, rev.
altered from No. 14 . . . . . . 1.75

New Coinage System

Bronze

Unc.

39 1 Centavo 1935-57 15
40 2 Centavos 1939-56 20

Copper-Nickel

41 5 Centavos 1931-56 30
42 10 Centavos 1932-56 50

HONDURAS

Silver

		V. Fine
43	20 Centavos 1931-58	.65
44	50 Centavos 1931-51	1.50
45	1 Lempira 1931-37	2.50

Later issues in Current Coins of the World.

HONG KONG

A British Crown Colony at the mouth of the Canton River, 90 miles south of Canton, China. Often called the "Gateway between East and West," it is an important trans-shipment port and British naval station. In an area of 391 square miles there is a population of 4,000,000. The great increase in population in recent years has been caused by the influx of refugees from Communist China.

100 Cents = 1 Dollar

VICTORIA 1837-1901
Bronze

		V. Fine
1	1 Mil 1863-65, Chinese value 1 Wen	1.50
1a	1 Mil 1866, Chinese value 1 Ch'ien	1.50

2	1 Cent 1863-1901	1.25

Several die varieties exist.

Silver

3	5 Cents 1866-1901	1.50
4	10 Cents 1863-1901	1.75

		V. Fine
5	20 Cents 1866-98	9.00

6	½ Dollar 1866-67	110.00
8	1 Dollar 1866-68	60.00

7	50 Cents 1890-94 (31-32mm)	17.50

HONG KONG

EDWARD VII 1901-1910

Bronze

Rev. Designs Similar to Nos. 2-5, 7

V. Fine

9 1 Cent 1902-05. 60

Silver

10 5 Cents 1903-05. . . . . .1.00
11 10 Cents 1902-05. . . . . .1.50
12 20 Cents 1902-05. . . . . .*Fine* 22.50

13 50 Cents 1902-05. . . . . .15.00

GEORGE V 1910-1936

Bronze

★14 1 Cent 1919-26 28 mm. 50
15 1 Cent 1931-34 22 mm. 35

Copper-Nickel

16 5 Cents 1935. . . . . .3.00
17 10 Cents 1935-36. 35

Silver

18 5 Cents 1932-33 . . . . . . .1.25

GEORGE VI 1936-1952

Nickel

V. Fine

20 5 Cents 1937. 65
21 10 Cents 1937. 60

Larger Head

Bronze

19 1 Cent 1941. . . . .——
Not released into circulation.

Nickel

22 5 Cents 1938-41. 25
23 10 Cents 1938-39. 35

New Legend:
KING GEORGE THE SIXTH

Nickel-Brass

24 5 Cents 1949-50. 15
25 10 Cents 1948-51. 20
26 50 Cents Cop.-Nic. 1951. 50

ELIZABETH II 1952-

Nickel-Brass

Unc.

27 5 Cents 1958-. 15
28 10 Cents 1955-. 20

Copper-Nickel

29 50 Cents 1958-. 50

Later issues in *Current Coins of the World*.

HUNGARY

A republic in Central Europe, formerly part of the Austro-Hungarian Empire. Allied with Germany in World War II, it was taken by Russia in 1945. Declared a republic in 1946, under Communist control industry has been nationalized and collective farming established. Population: 10,400,000. Area: 35,900 square miles. Capital: *Budapest*.

Restrikes of many issues for the period covered in this book have recently been made at the Budapest mint. These reportedly include dates not originally issued and pieces from mis-matched dies.

100 Krajczar (Kreuzer) = 1 Forint (Florin or Gulden) 1857-92
100 Filler = 1 Korona 1892-1921
100 Filler = 1 Pengö 1925-45
100 Filler = 1 Forint 1946-

FERENCZ JÓZSEF I 1848-1916
Issues Under Austro-Hungarian Empire

Copper or Bronze

		Fine
1	1 Krajczar 1868-73	1.00
2	4 Krajczar 1868	3.00

3	⁵⁄₁₀ Krajczar 1882	1.60
4	1 Krajczar 1878-88	1.00
5	1 Krajczar (Diff. Arms) 1891-92	1.50

Billon

Obv: legend ends KIRALYA
Rev: legend VALTO PENZ only

6	10 Krajczar 1868	2.00
8	20 Krajczar 1868	2.00

Obv: as Nos. 6, 8
Rev: MAGYAR KIRALYI added

		Fine
7	10 Krajczár 1868-69	1.50
9	20 Krajczár 1868-69	2.00

Silver

12	1 Forint 1868-69	5.00

Gold

21	1 Dukát 1868-69, rev. Emperor standing	100.00

HUNGARY

Billon

Obv: legend ends KIR.
Rev: as Nos. 6, 8

Fine
10 10 Krajczár 1870-88........2.50
11 20 Krajczár 1870-72........2.00

Silver

13 1 Forint 1870-81 (2 vars.)...4.00

14 1 Forint 1882-90..........4.50

Gold
Rev: as No. 13

Ex. Fine
22 1 Dukát 1877-81........300.00
22a 1 Dukát 1870 (modern
restrike)........ Proof 27.50
17 4 Forint/10 Francs
1870-90..............40.00
18 8 Forint/20 Francs
1870-90..............60.00

Silver

Fine
15 1 Forint 1890-92..........5.00

Gold
Ex. Fine
19 4 Forint/10 Francs
1890-92..............45.00
20 8 Forint/20 Francs
1890-92..............70.00

Reopening of József II Mine at Selmeczbánya

Silver
16 1 Forint 1878.............——

KORONA SYSTEM
1892-1921

Bronze
V. Fine
23 1 Filler 1892-1906.......... .15
24 2 Filler 1892-1915.......... .15

Nickel

25 10 Filler 1892-1909......... .25
27 20 Filler 1892-1914......... .35

HUNGARY

Silver

V. Fine

32 1 Korona 1892-1906
   (large head)............2.00
32a 1 Korona 1912-16
   (small head)...........1.50
33 2 Korona 1912-14........2.50

34 5 Korona 1900-09.........8.50

Gold

Ex. Fine

36 10 Korona 1892-1915....30.00
A36 20 Korona 1892-1916....50.00
B36 20 Korona (Bosnian Arms
   added) 1916..... ...70.00
D36 100 Korona 1907-08.....400.00

Millennium Commemorative
Silver

V. Fine
31 1 Korona 1896............3.00

40th Anniversary of
Franz Josef's Coronation

35 5 Korona 1907............10.00

Gold   *Ex. Fine*
C36 100 Korona 1907........300.00

World War I Issues
Nickel-Brass

26 10 Filler (branches instead
   of wreath) 1915-16....... .40

Iron
Struck under Franz Josef to 1916,
Karl 1916-18, the Red Republic 1918
and Regency 1920-21.

28 2 Filler 1916-18........... .50
29 10 Filler (Similar to No. 26)
   1915-20.................2.00

HUNGARY

V. Fine
30 20 Filler 1916-21 75

REGENCY 1920-1945
Bronze

37 1 Filler 1926-39 30
38 2 Filler 1926-40 30

Copper-Nickel

39 10 Filler 1926-40 30
40 20 Filler 1926-40 45
41 50 Filler 1926-40 60

Silver

42 1 Pengö 1926-39 . . . . .1.75

E.F.
43 2 Pengö 1929-39 . . . . 3.00

COMMEMORATIVE ISSUES
10th Year of Regency

Obv: Admiral Horthy, Regent

Ex. Fine
44 5 Pengö 1930 . . . . 7.00

Tercentenary Founding of Pázmány University

45 2 Pengö 1935 . . . . *V. F.* 6.00

Bicentennial Death of Ferenc Rákóczi

46 2 Pengö 1935 . . . . 6.00

HUNGARY

50th Anniversary
Death of Liszt

WORLD WAR II COINAGE

Iron

Ex. Fine

47 2 Pengö 1936.............6.00

V. Fine

50 2 Fillér 1940,
plain rim.............3.00
★50a 2 Fillér 1940-42,
toothed rim.............50

900th Anniversary
Death of St. Stephan

Zinc

51 2 Fillér 1943-44.............35

48 5 Pengö 1938.............8.00

Iron

Horthy Government
Commemorative

52 10 Fillér 1940-42...........35

Admiral Horthy
49 5 Pengö 1939.............6.50   **53** 20 Fillér 1941-44...........45

HUNGARY

Aluminum

V. Fine
54 1 Pengö 1941-44 35

55 2 Pengö 1941-43 60

75th Birthday, Admiral Horthy

Ex. Fine
57 5 Pengö 1943 . . . . 2.50

PROVISIONAL GOVERNMENT 1944-1946

Aluminum

V. Fine
56 5 Pengö 1945 . . . . 1.50

REPUBLIC 1946-1949
Legends:
MAGYAR ALLAMI VALTOPENZ
OR
MAGYAR KOZTARSASAG

58 2 Fillér Bronze 1946-47 20

59 5 Fillér Alum. 1948-51 35

Aluminum-Bronze

60 10 Fillér 1946-50 30
60a 10 Fillér Aluminum 1950 . . .——

HUNGARY

61 20 Fillér 1946-50.. .... .40

Aluminum

62 50 Fillér 1948............1.00

63 1 Forint 1946-49........... .60

64 2 Forint 1946-47...........1.00

Silver

Unc.

65 5 Forint (Thick) 1946......8.00
66 5 Forint (Thin) 1947.......2.50

COMMEMORATIVE ISSUES

Centenary of 1848 Revolution

Silver

Alexander Petöfi

Unc.

67 5 Forint 1948.............4.00

Stephen Szechenyi

68 10 Forint 1948... ....6.50

Michael Táncsics

69 20 Forint 1948...........10.00

Later issues in *Current Coins of the World.*

ICELAND (Island)

Island in the North Atlantic near the Arctic Circle. Now a republic, it was until 1944 a sovereign state united with Denmark under King Christian X. It is governed by the Althing (Parliament), the oldest parliamentary assembly in the world. Area: 39,758 square miles. Language: Icelandic. Capital: *Reykjavik*.

100 Aurar = 1 Krona

CHRISTIAN X 1912-1944

NOTES:

1. The 1930 commemorative issues (former Nos. 8-10) are considered to be medals by most authorities.

2. Some coins of 1940 and all of 1942 were struck in Great Britain without the customary Copenhagen mint marks.

Bronze

		V. Fine
1	1 Eyrir 1926-42	.35
2	2 Aurar 1926-42	.45
3	5 Aurar 1926-42	.55

Copper-Nickel

4	10 Aurar 1922-40	.75
5	25 Aurar 1922-40	1.00

Aluminum-Bronze

6	1 Krona 1925-40	1.75
7	2 Kronur 1925-40	2.25

World War II Issues

Zinc

		V. Fine
4a	10 Aurar 1942	1.00
5a	25 Aurar 1942	1.00

REPUBLIC 1944-

Bronze

		Unc.
11	1 Eyrir 1946-66	.15
12	5 Aurar 1946-66	.20

Copper-Nickel

13	10 Aurar 1946-69	.20
14	25 Aurar 1946-67	.30

Aluminum-Bronze

15	1 Krona 1946	1.00
16	2 Kronur 1946	1.50

Later issues in Current Coins of the World.

INDIA

South Central Asia, peninsula extending into the Indian Ocean. Formerly under British government, it became a sovereign democratic republic, but remained a member of the Commonwealth of Nations. Under the new constitution education is compulsory and religious freedom has been granted. Area: 1,221,880 square miles. Population: 547,000,000. Exports: tea, jute, cotton, hides, tobacco. Capital: *New Delhi*.

INDIA

3 Pies = 1 Pice (Paisa)
12 Pies = 1 Anna
16 Annas = 1 Rupee
15 Rupees = 1 Mohur (Gold)

Fine

6	½ Pice 1862	.40
7	¼ Anna 1862-76	.30
8	½ Anna 1862, 76	3.00

BRITISH INDIA
VICTORIA 1837-1901

Legend: EAST INDIA COMPANY

For similar copper coinage 1845-1862 see
Straits Settlements.

Silver

Continuous legend on obverse

Fine

1	2 Annas 1841	2.25
2	¼ Rupee 1840	2.50
3	½ Rupee 1840	4.50
4	1 Rupee 1840	6.00

Gold

A4	1 Mohur 1841	*V. F.* 150.00

Divided legend on obverse

Silver

1a	2 Annas 1841	2.25
2a	¼ Rupee 1840	2.25
3a	½ Rupee 1840	4.50
4a	1 Rupee 1840	6.00

Gold

A4a	1 Mohur 1841	*V. F.* 140.00

New Legend: INDIA only
Copper

5	¹⁄₁₂ Anna 1862-76	.25

Silver

9	2 Annas 1862-76	1.35
10	¼ Rupee 1862-76	1.50
11	½ Rupee 1862-76	3.50
12	1 Rupee 1862-76 (Several Varieties of 1862)	5.00

Gold

Thin Face

V. Fine

13	5 Rupees 1870-76	40.00
14	10 Rupees 1870-76	70.00
15	1 Mohur (15 Rupees) 1860-76	120.00

Plump Face

13a	5 Rupees 1870	50.00
14a	10 Rupees 1870	70.00
15a	1 Mohur 1870	120.00

INDIA

New Obverse Legend:
VICTORIA EMPRESS
Designs Sim. to Nos. 5-12, 13a-15a

Copper

		Fine
16	1/12 Anna 1877-1901	.20
17	1/2 Pice 1885-1901	.40
18	1/4 Anna 1877-1901	.30
19	1/2 Anna 1877	3.50

Silver

20	2 Annas 1877-1901	1.35
21	1/4 Rupee 1877-1901	1.50
22	1/2 Rupee 1877-99	3.50
23	1 Rupee 1877-1901	5.00

Gold
V. Fine

24	5 Rupees 1879	55.00
25	10 Rupees 1879	70.00
26	1 Mohur (15 Rupees) 1877-1900	110.00

EDWARD VII 1901-1910

Copper 1903-06, Bronze 1906-10

		Fine
27	1/12 Anna 1903-10	.35
28	1/2 Pice 1903-10	.35
29	1/4 Anna 1903-10	.25

Copper-Nickel

		Fine
30	1 Anna 1907-10	1.25

Silver

31	2 Annas 1903-10	1.00
32	1/4 Rupee 1903-10	1.25
33	1/2 Rupee 1905-10	3.50
34	1 Rupee 1903-10	4.50

GEORGE V 1910-1936

Bronze

		V. Fine
35	1/12 Anna 1911-36	.15
36	1/2 Pice 1911-36	.25
37	1/4 Anna 1911-36	.25

Copper-Nickel

38	1 Anna 1912-36	.35
39	2 Annas 1918-36 (square)	.50

INDIA

GEORGE VI 1936-1947
Small Head

Bronze

V. Fine

40 4 Annas 1919-21...........1.75

V. Fine

47 ¹⁄₁₂ Anna 1938-39..........20
★49 ½ Pice 1938-40...........25
50 ¼ Anna 1938-40..........25

41 8 Annas 1919-20..........5.00

★51 1 Pice 1943 Sm. letters.....75
51a 1 Pice 1943-47 Lg. letters. .15

Silver

Copper-Nickel

42 2 Annas 1911-17...........75
43 ¼ Rupee 1911-36..........1.00
44 ½ Rupee 1911-36..........2.00
45 1 Rupee 1911-22..........4.00

53 1 Anna 1938-40.............25
54 2 Annas 1939...............35

Gold

Silver

55 ¼ Rupee 1939-40..........2.00
56 ½ Rupee 1938-39..........3.00

Large Head
Bronze

46 1 Mohur (15 Rupees)
   1918................100.00
A46 1 Sovereign 1918........65.00

47a ¹⁄₁₂ Anna 1939-42..........25
49a ½ Pice 1942........ *Proof* 6.50
50a ¼ Anna 1940-42..........40

INDIA

Bronze

V. Fine

52 ½ Anna Nic.-Br. 1942-45.. .10
52a ½ Anna Cop.-Nic. 1946-47. .10
53b 1 Anna Cop.-Nic. 1940-47. .15
53a 1 Anna Nic.-Br. 1942-45.. .15

V. Fine

61 1 Pice 1950................ .35
61a 1 Pice (Thin) 1951-55...... .10

Copper-Nickel

54b 2 Annas Cop.-Nic.
1939-47................. .25
54a 2 Annas Nic.-Br. 1942-45.. .25

Silver

62 ½ Anna 1950-55........... .10

55a ¼ Rupee 1939-45......... .60
56a ½ Rupee 1939-45.........1.00
57 1 Rupee 1938-45.........2.25
The above silver coins exist with minor differences of type, alloy and with either safety or reeded edges of varying dates.

63 1 Anna 1950-55............ .30
64 2 Annas 1950-55 (square).... .30

Nickel

Nickel

58 ¼ Rupee 1946-47.......... .50
59 ½ Rupee 1946-47.......... .70
60 1 Rupee 1947.............1.00

65 ¼ Rupee 1950-55 Lg. lions. .20
65a ¼ Rupee 1954-56
Sm. lions.............. .20
66 ½ Rupee 1950-56......... .35
67 1 Rupee 1950-54.........1.00
Later issues in Current Coins of the World.

INDIA—NATIVE STATES

ALWAR

Mangal Singh 1874-1892

Silver

Fine

1 1 Rupee 1788 (error),
1877-82 . . . . 6.00

1a 1 Rupee 1891 . . . . 6.00

BAHAWALPUR

Sadiq Muhammad Khan 1866-1899

Copper

C1 1 Paisa AH 1301-15
(1884-97) 3.00

Silver

D1 1 Rupee AH 1284-85
(1867-68) 19-21mm 7.50

Muhammad Bahawal Khan V 1899-1907

Copper

Fine

E1 1 Paisa AH 1324 (1906) 5.00

Silver

F1 1 Rupee 1323 . . . . 10.00

Sadiq Mohammed V 1907-1947

Bronze

B1 1 Paisa AH 1326-27
(1908-09) inscription 4.50

★A1 1 Paisa AH 1342-43
(1924-25) 15.00

V. Fine

1 1 Paisa AH 1343 (1925) 17.50

INDIA—NATIVE STATES

Silver

Ex. Fine
2 1 Rupee 1343............150.00

Gold

3 1 Ashrafi 1343...........200.00

Copper

V. Fine
★4 ½ Pice 1940.............1.00
 5 ¼ Anna 1940.............1.25

BANSWARA

Lakhsman Singh 1844-1905

Copper

Fine
1 1 Paisa ND.............3.00

Silver

V. Fine
2 ⅛ Rupee ND (10mm)....20.00
3 ¼ Rupee ND (13mm).....15.00
★4 ½ Rupee ND (17mm).....12.50
5 1 Rupee ND (21mm).....17.50

BARODA

Sayaji Rao III 1875-1939

Bronze

Fine
A1 ½ Paisa S. 1948 (1891)....2.00
★B1 1 Paisa S. 1937-49.......3.00
C1 2 Paisa S. 1947-49.......3.75

Silver

D1 ⅛ Rupee AH 1294 (1877)
   10mm..................2.50
E1 ¼ Rupee 1299
   (13mm)...............2.50
★F1 ½ Rupee 1294
   (15-16mm)............3.50
G1 1 Rupee 1294-1300
   (20mm)..............5.00

INDIA—NATIVE STATES

Copper

V. Fine

11　1 Mohur S. 1945-59 . . . . . 175.00

Thick planchet

　　　　　　　　　　　　　　V. Fine
1　1 Pie S. 1944-45 (1887-88) . . . 1.00
2　1 Paisa S.E. 1940-47 65
3　2 Paisa S.E. 1940-47 . . . . 1.00

Thin planchet

1a　1 Pie S. 1949-50 . . . . 1.50
2a　1 Paisa S. 1948-50 75
★3a　2 Paisa S. 1948-50 . . . . 1.25
Nos. 1-3a have several varieties of
wreath and arrangement of legends.

Silver

Designs like Nos. 9-11

5　2 Annas S. 1949 (1892)
　　16mm 5.00
6　¼ Rupee S. 1949 (19mm) . . . 6.00
7　½ Rupee S. 1948-49
　　(24mm) 25.00
8　1 Rupee S. 1948-49
　　(30mm) 10.00

Reduced Size

5a　2 Annas S. 1951-52
　　(1894-95) 14mm 5.00
6a　¼ Rupee S. 1951-52
　　(17mm) 6.00
7a　½ Rupee S. 1951-52
　　(22mm) 10.00
8a　1 Rupee S. 1951-55
　　(28mm) 8.00

Gold

9　⅙ Mohur S. 1943-59
　　(1886-1902) 75.00
10　⅓ Mohur S. 1942 . . . . 95.00

BIKANIR
Ganga Singhji 1887-1942

Copper

　　　　　　　　　　　　　　　　Fine
1　½ Pice 1894 . . . . 6.00
2　¼ Anna 1895 . . . . 5.50

Silver

3　1 Rupee 1892-97 . . . . 6.50

50th Year of Reign
Silver

　　　　　　　　　　　　　　　　Ex. Fine
4　1 Rupee S. 1994 (1937) 7.00

INDIA—NATIVE STATES

Gold

Ex. Fine

5 ½ Mohur S. 1994 . . . . 75.00
★6 1 Mohur S. 1994 . . . . 110.00

BUNDI

Owing to unregulated minting methods coins listed may be found in round, square or irregular shapes.

IN THE NAME OF
QUEEN VICTORIA

Copper

Obv: horizontal English legend

Fine

1 ¼ Paisa S. 1924 . . . . 2.00
★2 ½ Paisa Samvat 1924-46
    (1867-89) 75
3 1 Paisa Samvat 1919-29
    (1862-72) 1.00

Silver

4 ¼ Rupee S. 1915-36
    (1858-79) 4.00
5 ½ Rupee S. 1915-41 . . . . 6.00
★6 1 Rupee Samvat 1915-43 . . . 9.00

Nos. 1-6 have AD dates on obverse and Samvat dates on reverse. Coins with both dates identifiable usually command higher prices.

Obv: katar (dagger) in center

Fine

7 ¼ Rupee S. 1953-55
    (1896-98) 3.00
8 ½ Rupee S. 1949-56
    (1892-99) 5.00
★9 1 Rupee Samvat 1943-57
    (1886-1900) 5.00

Obv: seated figure in center

★10 1 Rupee S. 1958 (1901) 35.00

IN THE NAME OF EDWARD VII

Silver

Obv: seated figure in center

A11 ½ Rupee S. 1958 (1901)
    16mm 25.00
★11 1 Rupee S. 1958-62
    (1901-05) 10.00

Obv: katar (dagger) in center

A12 ¼ Paisa S. 1965 (1908) . . . 7.50

INDIA—NATIVE STATES

Silver

Fine

Obv: AD date in center

12 ¼ Rupee S. 1963-66
(1906-09)............4.00
13 ½ Rupee S. 1964-66......5.00
★14 1 Rupee S. 1963-68
(1906-11).............7.50
A14 1 Rupee (Square) S.
1967-69 ....40.00

IN THE NAME OF GEORGE V

 Copper

Obv: katar (dagger) in center

★15 ¼ Paisa Samvat 1973-86
(1916-29).............2.00

 Silver

★16 ¼ Rupee S. 1972-81
(1915-24).............2.00

★17 ½ Rupee S. 1974-83
(1917-26).............3.00
18 1 Rupee S. 1979-84
(1922-27).............5.00
A18 1 Rupee (Sq.) S. 1974-83
(1917-26)............30.00

Fine
19 ½ Rupee 1925...........35.00
★20 1 Rupee 1925...........35.00

CAMBAY
Ja'afar Ali 1880-1915

Copper

1 1 Paisa S. 1963-68 (1906-11)..3.00

Silver

★2 1 Rupee AH 1317 (1899)...15.00

COOCH BEHAR
Nrpendra Narayana
1863-1911

Gold
Ex. Fine
B1 1 Mohur Yr. 354 (1864)
21mm.................200.00

· 250 ·

INDIA—NATIVE STATES

Jitendra Narayan 1913-1922

Gold

Ex. Fine

1 1 Mohur 402-04 (1912-14)..160.00

DATIA
Govind Singh 1907-1948

Gold

1 ½ Mohur ND.............60.00

DEWAS—Senior Branch
Legend: DEWAS STATE S.B.

Copper

Obv: Bust of Queen Victoria
Rev: Value in wreath

Fine

1 1/12 Anna 1888.............10.00
2 ¼ Anna 1888.............12.50

Vikrama Simha Rao
1937-1948

3 1 Paisa 1944.............40.00

DEWAS—Junior Branch
Legend: DEWAS STATE J.B.

Copper

1 1/12 Anna 1888.............15.00
3 ¼ Anna 1888.............17.50

DHAR
Anand Rao 1857-1898

Copper

Fine

A1 ½ Paisa AH 1289 (1872)
16mm...............7.50
★B1 1 Paisa 1289
(17-20mm)............6.00

V. Fine

1 1/12 Anna 1887...............5.00
2 ½ Pice 1887...............7.50
3 ¼ Anna 1887.............10.00

DUNGARPUR
Lakshman Singh 1918-1948

1 1 Paisa Bronze S. 2001 (1944) 30.00

GWALIOR
Madho Rao II 1886-1925

Copper

Fine

B1 1 Pie S. 1946 (1889)
14mm...............35.00

INDIA—NATIVE STATES

Fine

C1 ½ Pice S. 1946 (20mm)..40.00
★A1 ¼ Anna S. 1945-46
  (25mm)............30.00
D1 ½ Anna S. 1946 (31mm).50.00

★1 ½ Pice S. 1956-58
  (1899-1901).............1.25
 2 ¼ Anna S. 1953-58.........1.00

★3 ¼ Anna S. 1970 (1913)
  thick...................1.25
 4 ¼ Anna S. 1970, 74, thin....1.00

Silver

 5 2 Annas (1911)...........1.50
 6 ¼ Rupee (1911)............2.50
 7 ½ Rupee (1911)............3.50
★8 1 Rupee Yrs. 22-25
  (1886-1910)...............6.50

Gold

*Obv. Bust r., border of
widely spaced radiating lines
Rev. Arms, Supporters*

9 ⅓ Mohur Samvat 1959 *V. Fine*
  (1902)..................90.00

Jivaji III 1925-1948

Copper

Obv: young bust

V. Fine

★10 ¼ Anna S. 1986 (1929),
   thick.................. .60
10a ¼ Anna S. 1986, 99,
   thin..................1.00

Obv: older bust

★11 ¼ Anna S. 1999 (1942)
   22mm................. .30

Brass

12 ½ Anna S. 1999 (19mm)... .35

HYDERABAD

Mir Mahbob Ali Khan II
A.H. 1285-1329 (1869-1911)

First Coinage

Copper or Brass

Fine

1 1 Dub AH 1289-1313
  (1872-95)................ .50

INDIA—NATIVE STATES

Silver

Fine

2 1/16 Rupee 1299-1321 (1880-1903) 7-9mm.....1.00
3 1/8 Rupee 1286-1321 (10-13mm).............1.50
4 1/4 Rupee 1286-1321.......2.50
★5 1/2 Rupee 1286-1317.......3.50
A5 1 Rupee 1286-1318.......4.50

Gold

6 1/16 Ashrafi 1321 (7mm).....17.50
★7 1/8 Ashrafi 1306-21 (10mm).40.00
8 1/4 Ashrafi 1301-21 (14mm).55.00
9 1/2 Ashrafi 1306-19 (17mm).65.00
10 1 Ashrafi 1294-1314 (1877-96) 22mm........80.00

Second Coinage

Other machine-struck silver dated AH 1305-07, and copper dated 1312-16, are believed to be patterns.

Silver

11 1/8 Rupee 1318 (1900) 15mm................15.00
12 1/4 Rupee 1318 (19mm)...17.50
★13 1/2 Rupee 1312-18 (24mm)..............25.00
14 1 Rupee 1312-18 (30mm)..............17.50

Gold

A10 1 Ashrafi 1311 (1893) 24mm...............200.00
A10a 1 Ashrafi 1311 (30mm)............200.00

Third Coinage

Copper

Fine

15 1 Pai 1326-29............ .75
★16 2 Pai 1322-29............ .60
17 1/2 Anna 1324-29 (1906-11).1.00

Silver

18 1/8 Rupee 1323............1.50
19 1/4 Rupee 1323-29.........1.75
★20 1/2 Rupee 1322-29.........3.00
21 1 Rupee 1321-29.........4.50

Gold

V. Fine

22 1/8 Mohur 1325 (1907).....50.00
23 1/4 Mohur 1325, 29........50.00
24 1/2 Mohur 1325-26 (21mm).65.00
25 1 Mohur 1325 (24mm)...100.00

Mir Osman Ali Khan
AH 1329-1367 (1911-1948)

First Coinage

Bronze

26 1 Pai 1338-53........... .75
B27 2 Pai 1329-30, short "Ain" in toughra......3.50
★27 2 Pai 1330-49........... .50
A27 1/2 Anna 1332-48 (1913-29).............1.00

INDIA—NATIVE STATES

Copper-Nickel

V. Fine

28 1 Anna 1338-54 75

29 1 Anna 1356-61 50

Silver

Obv: Partial initial "Ain" in doorway
A30 1 Rupee 1330 (1912) 7.50

Gold

A37 1 Mohur 1330 . . . . 175.00

Silver

Obv: Full initial "Ain" in doorway

30 ⅛ Rupee 1335-58 (1917-39)1.75
★31 ¼ Rupee 1337-58 . . . . .2.25
32 ½ Rupee 1342-54 . . . . .4.50
33 1 Rupee 1330-43 . . . . .4.00

Gold

V. Fine

34 ⅛ Mohur 1337-44 . . . . . . .30.00
35 ¼ Mohur 1337 . . . . .35.00
36 ½ Mohur 1337-53 . . . . . . .50.00
★37 1 Mohur 1331-67 . . . . . .125.00

Second Coinage

Bronze

43 2 Pai 1362-68 15

42 1 Anna 1361-68 20

Silver

38 2 Annas 1362-64
   (1943-45) 15.5mm 50
39 4 Annas 1362-64 (20mm) 75
★40 8 Annas 1363 (24mm) 2.50
41 1 Rupee 1361-65 . . . . .3.50

INDIA—NATIVE STATES

Third Coinage
Nickel

44 2 Annas 1366-68   *V. Fine*
    (1947-49) 15.5mm 25
45 4 Annas 1365-68 (20mm). . . .50
★46 8 Annas 1366 (24mm) 85

All Hyderabad coinage was demonetized April 1, 1955.

INDORE
Shivaji Rao 1886-1903

Copper

                              Fine
3 ½ Paisa Samvat 1944-46
    (1887-89) (21mm.) 20.00
★1 ¼ Anna Samvat 1943-59
    (1886-1902) (25mm.) 75
2 ½ Anna Samvat 1943-59
    (31mm.) 1.00

Silver

4 ⅛ Rupee S. 1947-54
    (1890-97) 10mm 4.00
5 ¼ Rupee S. 1947-54
    (12mm) 4.00
6 ½ Rupee S. 1947-54
    (16mm) 5.00
★7 1 Rupee S. 1947-57
    (22mm) 6.00

A7 1 Rupee S. 1956-58   *V. Fine*
    (1899-1901) 100.00

Yeshwant Rao 1926-48

Copper

★8 ¼ Anna S. 1992 (1935) 60
9 ½ Anna S. 1992 (1935) 1.00

JAIPUR
Madho Singh II 1880-1922

Bronze

                             Fine
★1 1 Paisa Yrs. 4-39
    (1883-1918) 20mm 50
A1 1 Paisa Yrs. 1-37
    (thin, 32-36mm) 4.00

Silver

A2 ⅟₁₆ Rupee Yr. 10 (1890)
    10mm 3.50

INDIA—NATIVE STATES

2 ⅛ Rupee Yrs. 4-29   *Fine*
   (1883-1908) 13mm......2.00
★3 ¼ Rupee Yrs. 1-42
   (16mm)..............2.50
4 ½ Rupee Yrs. 1-30
   (18mm)..............5.00
5 1 Rupee Yrs. 1-42
   (21mm)..............4.00

A5 1 Rupee Yrs. 1-4
   (1880-83) 30-31mm....12.50
★A5a 1 Rupee Yrs. 3-37
   (1882-1916) 36-37mm..12.50

Gold

B5 1 Mohur Yrs. 4-42   *V. Fine*
   (1883-1922) 18mm......90.00

Man Singh II 1922-1949

IN THE NAME OF GEORGE V

Silver

C5 1 Rupee Yr. 1 (22mm).....10.00

IN THE NAME OF GEORGE VI

Bronze

A6 ½ Paisa Yr. 21-23 (1942-44) .75
B6 1 Paisa Yr. 28 (1949)
   Large thin flan........10.00

Brass

           V. Fine
6 1 Anna 1943-44.............. .50

7 1 Anna 1944.............. .50

8 2 Annas Yr. 21 (1942).......2.00

Silver

9 1 Rupee Yrs. 18-28 (1939-49)
   Broad Flan............14.00
9a 1 Rupee (Small Flan)
   Yrs. 17-20 (1938-41).....10.00

Gold

10 1 Mohur Yr. 20 (1941).....75.00

JAORA
Muhammad Ismail 1865-1895

Copper

           Fine
★1 1 Paisa 1893-96...........2.00
2 2 Paisa 1893-94.............4.00

INDIA—NATIVE STATES

JODHPUR
Sardar Singh 1895-1911

IN THE NAME OF VICTORIA

Silver

Fine
A1 ⅛ Rupee (1898-99)........5.00
B1 ¼ Rupee (1898-99)........5.00
C1 ½ Rupee (1898-99)........7.50
D1 1 Rupee (1898-99)........7.00

Gold

F1 ½ Mohur (1898-99).......75.00

IN THE NAME OF EDWARD VII

Bronze

2 ¼ Anna 1901-10...........3.50
★1 ½ Anna 1906..............7.00

Silver

J2 ¼ Rupee S. 1965 (1908)....6.00

Gold

E2 ¼ Mohur 1906 (13mm)...45.00
F2 ½ Mohur 1906 (18mm)...60.00
G2 1 Mohur 1906 (20mm)...80.00

Sumar Singh 1911-1918

IN THE NAME OF EDWARD VII

Gold

K2 ½ Mohur ND (19mm).....——

IN THE NAME OF GEORGE V

Bronze
Fine

D2 ¼ Anna 1911-14...........5.00

Silver

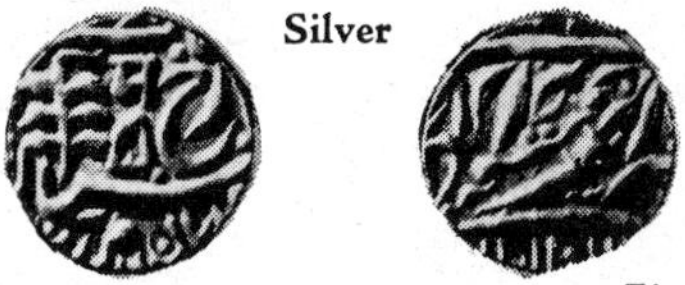

Fine
A2 ⅛ Rupee ND (1911).....6.00
B2 ¼ Rupee ND (1911).....6.00
C2 ½ Rupee ND (1911).....8.00
5 1 Rupee ND (1911).....15.00

Umaid Singh 1918-1947

IN THE NAME OF GEORGE V

Silver

D3 ¼ Rupee ND.............7.50

Gold

G3 ½ Mohur ND............——
H3 1 Mohur ND............——

IN THE NAME OF EDWARD VIII

Bronze

A3 ¼ Anna ND (1936).......4.00

IN THE NAME OF GEORGE VI

Bronze

4 ¼ Anna 1937-39, S. 1996
  (thick, 10 gr.)...........2.00
★3 ¼ Anna S. 2002 (1945)
  thin, 3 gr...............1.00

Gold

7 1 Mohur (1937-39)........130.00

Hanwant Singh 1947
IN THE NAME OF GEORGE VI

Gold
V. Fine
8 1 Mohur ND..............——

JUNAGADH

Mahabat Khan II 1851-1882

Copper

B1 1 Dokdo S. 1935 (1878)....10.00

Silver

C1 1 Kori AH 1292-99/
S. 1932-38 (1875-82)......3.00

Bahadur Khan III 1882-1892

Gold

★1 ½ Kori AH 1309 (1891)...90.00
A1 1 Kori 1309...........120.00

Rasal Khan 1892-1911

Copper

Fine
★2 1 Dokdo ND, S. 1963-67
(1906-10) vars...........1.25
A2 2 Dokda S. 1964 (1907)...15.00

Silver
B2 1 Kori S. 1966 (1909)
15mm.................12.00

Mahabat Khan III 1911-1948
Copper
3 1 Dokdo 1985-90...........2.00

KUTCH
48 Trambiyo = 24 Dokda = 1 Kori

Pragmalji II 1860-1875
Copper
1 1 Trambiyo 1865............2.00

5 1 Trambiyo 1767 (error),
1865-68 (16mm)..........1.50
★6 1 Dokdo 1865-69...........1.50

8 3 Dokda 1868...............3.00

INDIA—NATIVE STATES

		Fine
9	1 Trambiyo 1869	1.50
★10	1 Dokdo 1869-74	1.50
11	1½ Dokdo 1869-75	1.50
12	3 Dokda 1869 (32mm)	3.00

Silver

13	½ Kori 1862-63	2.50
★14	1 Kori 1862-63	2.50

Designs similar to Nos. 36-37

15	2½ Kori 1875	4.50
16	5 Kori 1863-75	6.50

Gold

17	25 Kori 1862-70, sim. to No. 14 (16mm)	50.00
18	50 Kori 1866-74, sim. to No. 36 (24mm)	100.00
19	100 Kori 1866 (29mm)	200.00

Note: Because of extensive revisions, new numbers were assigned in the 10th edition.

Khengarji III 1876-1942
QUEEN VICTORIA
MIGHTY QUEEN
Copper

22 (—)	1 Dokdo 1878	20.00
★23 (A1)	1½ Dokdo 1876-79	2.00

Silver

		Fine
26 (—)	1 Kori 1876	45.00
28 (B1)	5 Kori 1876	25.00

VICTORIA EMPRESS OF INDIA

Copper

★30 (C1)	1 Trambiyo 1881-83	.75

★31	1 Dokdo 1882-99 (2 var.) 21-22mm	1.00
32	1½ Dokda 1882-99 (3 var.) 23-25mm	1.25
33	3 Dokda 1883-99 (2 var.) 33-34mm	2.00

Silver

		V. Fine
★34 (G1)	½ Kori 1898-1900 (13mm)	5.00
35 (H1)	1 Kori 1881-1900 (2 var.) 16.5mm	2.00

★36 (I1)	2½ Kori 1881-99 (3 var.)	3.00

INDIA—NATIVE STATES

V. Fine
37 (J1) 5 Kori 1880-99 (4 var.)..4.50

IN THE NAME OF GEORGE V
First Coinage
Copper

			Fine
46 (3)	1 Trambiyo 1911-20 (16mm)	....	.50
47 (5)	1 Dokdo 1911-20 (21mm)	....	1.00
★48 (7)	1½ Dokda 1926 (23.5mm)	....	1.50
49 (8)	3 Dokda 1926 (33mm)	....	3.00

Silver

V. Fine
★51 (A9) 1 Kori 1913-27......1.75

IN THE NAME OF EDWARD VII

Copper

			Fine
38	**(1)**	1 Trambiyo 1908-10 (16mm)	1.00
★39	**(2)**	1 Dokdo 1909 (20.5mm)	1.25
40	**(—)**	1½ Dokda 1909....	100.00
41	**(B2)**	3 Dokda 1909....	100.00

52 (11) 2½ Kori 1916-26.....2.75
★53 (12) 5 Kori 1913-27.....5.00

Second Coinage
Copper

54 (4) 1 Trambiyo 1928 (16mm) .50

Silver

V. Fine
45 (A2) 5 Kori 1902-09.....135.00

• 260 •

INDIA—NATIVE STATES

V. Fine

55	(6)	1 Dokdo 1928-29 (21mm)	1.00
★56	(A7)	1½ Dokda 1928-32 (23mm)	1.00
57	(A8)	3 Dokda 1928-35 (33mm)	1.00

Silver

58	(9)	½ Kori 1928 (14mm)	1.00
59	(10)	1 Kori 1928-36 (17mm)	1.25
52a	(11)	2½ Kori 1928-35	2.50
53a	(12)	5 Kori 1928-36	4.50

IN THE NAME OF EDWARD VIII
Copper

63 (13)   3 Dokda 1936 .... 7.50

Silver

★65 (14)   1 Kori 1936 .... 2.50
66 (15)   2½ Kori 1936 ...... 22.50
67 (16)   5 Kori 1936 .... 4.50

IN THE NAME OF GEORGE VI
Copper

71 (17)   3 Dokda 1937 .... 2.00

Silver

V. Fine

73	(19)	1 Kori 1937-40	1.00
74	(20)	2½ Kori 1937-39	4.00
75	(21)	5 Kori 1936-41	5.00

Vijayaarijji 1942-1947
IN THE NAME OF GEORGE VI
Copper

76 (22)   1/48 Kori (Trambiyo) 1943-44 .... .25

77	(23)	1/16 Kori 1943-47 (21mm)	.35
★78	(24)	1/8 Kori 1943-44 (23mm)	.40
79	(25)	1/4 Kori 1943-47 (27mm)	.50
80	(26)	½ Kori 1943-46 (36.5mm)	1.00

Silver

★81 (27)   1 Kori 1942-44 .... 1.00
82 (29)   5 Kori 1942 .... 5.00

Madanasinhji 1947
(In his own name)
Copper

83 (30)   1/8 Kori 2004 (1947) 1.00

INDIA—NATIVE STATES

Silver

V. Fine

84 (31) 1 Kori 2004 (1947)...10.00
★85 (32) 5 Kori 2004.......135.00

Fine

5 ½ Paisa S. 1949 (1892),
obv. lion...............4.00
★6 1 Paisa 1949, sim. 4.00

LUNAVADA
Wakhat Singhji 1867-1929

Copper

Fine

1 1 Paisa ND, obv. 2 swords...4.00
2 1 Paisa ND, obv. cannon.....3.50

7 ½ Paisa ND, obv.
hand in square..........3.50
★8 1 Paisa ND, sim. 3.50

Nos. 1-8 are crude and vary greatly in shape
and size. Later coins were usually struck
over earlier types, often causing two or more
designs to show.

3 1 Paisa ND, obv.
lotus blossom............3.00

MEWAR UDAIPUR (Mewar)
Silver
(In Name of "Friend of London")

4 1 Paisa ND, obv. hand......3.50

A2 1/16 Rupee ND (1851-1930)
8-9mm................2.00
B2 ⅛ Rupee ND (11-12mm)..2.00
C2 ¼ Rupee ND (14-15mm)..2.50
D2 ½ Rupee ND (17-18mm)..3.50
★E2 1 Rupee ND (23-24mm)..4.50

INDIA—NATIVE STATES

Gold

F2 1 Mohur ND (23-24mm)..100.00 *V. Fine*

Bhupal Singh 1930-1948

Copper

1 ¼ Anna S. 1999 (1942) ...... .35

2 ½ Anna S. 1999 .... .35

3 1 Anna S. 2000 (1943) .... .50

Silver

4 1 Anna S. 1985 (1928)
    12mm................... .50
5 2 Annas S. 1985 (15mm) .... .75
*6 ¼ Rupee S. 1985 (19mm)...1.00
7 ½ Rupee S. 1985 (24mm)...2.00
8 1 Rupee S. 1985 (30.5mm)..4.00

Former Nos. 9-13 are now thought to be patterns and restrikes.

NAVANAGER
Vibhaji 1852-1894 A.D.
First Coinage

This series was crudely copied from the Gujerati coinage of Muzaffar Shah III (1560-84). Coins bear the frozen date AH 978 (1570), often misread as 1178 or 1278.

Copper

Fine

1 ½ Dokdo AH 978
    (to ca. 1880)........... .50
*2 1 Dokdo 978............. .60
C2 1½ Dokda 978.............1.50

Silver

A4 ½ Kori 978...............1.50
4 1 Kori 978...............1.50

Gold

V. Fine

7 ½ Kori 978................40.00
8 1 Kori 978................50.00

Second Coinage
Copper

Fine

1a ½ Dokdo AH 978
     (ca. 1860-95)......... .75
*2a 1 Dokdo 978........... .75

B2 1 Dokdo S. 1909-17
    (1852-60)..............7.50
*A2 2 Dokda Samvat 1943
    (1886)................10.00

INDIA—NATIVE STATES

Fine
3 3 Dokda S. 1928 (1871)......5.00

A3 3 Dokda S. 1942 (1885)....6.50

Silver

B4 1 Kori S. 1934-36
(1877-79).............3.00

5 2½ Kori S. 1949-50
(1892-93) 19-21mm....15.00
★6 5 Kori S. 1945-50
(22-27mm)............15.00

Jaswant Singh 1894-1907
Bronze

Fine
A9 1½ Dokda S. 1956 (1899) .15.00
9 2 Dokda S. 1956.......15.00

PUDUKOTA
Copper

A1 1 Amman Cash ND
(native issue ca. 1810-90).1.50

Martanda Bhairava 1886-1929
Bronze

1 1 Amman Cash ND *V. Fine*
(1889-1934)..............1.50

RAJKOT
Dharmendra Singhji
1930-1948
Gold

Ex. Fine
1 1 Mohur 1945............125.00

No. 1 was a presentation coin, not issued
to circulation. Silver restrikes exist.

INDIA—NATIVE STATES

RATLAM (Rutlam)
Ranjit Singh 1864-1893

Copper

A1 1 Paisa S. 1928 (1871)..... *Fine* 3.50

B1 1 Paisa 1885...............5.00

1 1 Paisa S. 1947 (1890).......1.00

2 1 Paisa S. 1947 (thin, crude restrike of No. 1)........... .75

REWA (Rewah)
Gulab Singh 1918-1946

Gold

1 1 Mohur S. 1975 (1918) *Ex. Fine*
26mm..................275.00

SAILANA
Jaswant Singh 1895-1919

Copper

1 ¼ Anna 1908 Head of *Fine*
Edward VII...........10.00
★2 ¼ Anna 1912........ *V. F.* 5.00

SIKKIM
Thotab Namgyel 1874-1911

Copper

1 1 Paisa S. 1940-42
(1883-85)...............15.00

TONK
Mohammad Ibrahim Ali Khan
1867-1930

Copper

1 1 Paisa AH 1284-1346
(1867-1928)...............2.00

Silver

C1 ⅛ Rupee AH 1316
(13mm)...............4.00
D1 ¼ Rupee 1316-17 (14mm)..4.00

INDIA—NATIVE STATES

A1 ½ Rupee 1305-09   *Fine*
    (1888-92) 16mm........5.00
★B1 1 Rupee 1288-1348
    (20mm)..............5.00

Mohammed Saadat Ali Khan
1930-1949

Bronze

V. Fine

2 1 Pice 1932/AH 1350
   (26mm, struck 1933-36)...1.25
★3 1 Pice 1932/1350
   (21mm, struck 1943-47)... .75

Silver

4 ⅛ Rupee 1934/AH 1353... ——

TRAVANCORE

16 Cash = 1 Chuckram
4 Chuckram = 1 Fanam
2 Fanam = 1 Anantaraya
52½ Fanam = 1 Pagoda

Dates are expressed in the Malabar Era (ME), which began in AD 824. For AD date, add 824 or 825 to ME date. Example:
    ME 1114 + 824-25 = AD 1938-39

Note: Because of extensive revisions, new numbers were assigned in the 11th edition. The original numbers are given in parentheses.

Martanda Varma II
1847-1860

Copper

★1 (—) 1 Cash ND (1848-60)   *Fine*
       8-10mm............. .75
2 (—) 2 Cash ND (1848-49)
       10-11mm............2.00

Fine
3 (—) 4 Cash ND (13-14mm)...3.00

Gold

Obv: 3-line legend in beaded circle
Rev: blank

V. Fine
4 (—) ¼ Pagoda ND (1850)
       13mm, 0.64 gm. 75.00
5 (—) ½ Pagoda ND (14.5mm,
       1.27 gm.)..........100.00
6 (—) 1 Pagoda ND (17mm,
       2.55 gm.)..........150.00
7 (—) 2 Pagoda ND (20mm,
       5.10 gm.)..........225.00

Rama Varma IV 1860-1880

Copper

Fine
1a (—) 1 Cash ND (1860-85)... .40
No. 1a is a slightly degenerate form of No. 1, often with no features on face or body.

Silver

Obv: leaf sprays at sides
8 (A6) 1 Chuckram ND
       (1860-1901)...........50

9 (—) 1 Velli Fanam ND
      (1860-61)............3.00

INDIA—NATIVE STATES

Fine

10 (—) 1 Velli Fanam ND
(1864) 2.50

Gold

Obv: leaf sprays at sides

11 (—) 1 Anantaraya ND   *V. Fine*
(1860-90) 7.00

Obv: similar to No. 10
Rev: similar to Nos. 29-34

16 (—) 1 Pagoda 1877
(17mm) 150.00
17 (—) 2 Pagoda 1877
(19mm) 200.00

Rama Varma V 1880-1885

Note: Nos. 1a, 8 and 11 were continued through this reign.

Silver

18 (—) 1 Viraraya Fanam ND
(1881) 2.75

Gold

19 (—) 1 Viraraya Fanam ND
(1881) 7.50

V. Fine

20 (—) ½ Sovereign 1881/
ME 1057 (20mm) 350.00
★21 (—) 1 Sovereign 1881/
1057 (22mm) 450.00

Nos. 20-21 are presentation coins struck to the British gold standard.

Rama Varma VI 1885-1924

First Coinage

Note: Nos. 8 and 11 were continued into this reign.

Copper

Fine

1b (2) 1 Cash ND (1885-95) 30

No. 1b is a yet more degenerate version of No. 1.

22 (—) ¼ Chuckram ND
(1888-89) 13mm 3.00
★23 (—) ½ Chuckram ND
(17-20mm) 3.50

Gold

V. Fine

24 (A5) 1 Kali Fanam ND
(1890-95) 7.50

INDIA—NATIVE STATES

Second Coinage
Bronze

V. Fine

35 (9) ¼ Rupee AD 1889,
ME 1087-1106
(1907-30)...........5.00
36 (10) ½ Rupee 1889,
ME 1086-1107......7.50

Fine

29 (1) CASH 1 ND (1901)......7.50
30 (3) CASH FOUR ND........1.50
★31 (4) CASH EIGHT ND
(1901-03).............2.50
32 (5) CHUCKRAM ONE ND....3.00

Bala Rama Varma II
1924-1949

Bronze

41 (11) 1 Cash ND (1938-45)... .20

V. Fine

30a (3) FOUR CASH ND
(1924-30)..............1.25
31a (4) EIGHT CASH ND......1.75
32a (5) ONE CHUCKRAM ND....2.50

Silver

42 (12) 4 Cash ND............ .30
43 (13) 8 Cash ND............ .35

33 (6) CH(uckram)S 2
ND (1901)...........3.00
33a (6) 2 CHS. ND (1928).....2.50
34 (7) ONE FANAM
ND (1889)...........5.00
★34a (8) FANAM ONE ND (1911),
ME 1087-1106
(1912-30).............1.50

44 (14, 15) 1 Chuckram
ME 1114 (1938),
ND (1939-45).... .75

The undated variety of No. 34a has edge
either plain or reeded.

INDIA—NATIVE STATES

Silver

V. Fine

45 (16) 1 Fanam ME 1112
(1936)............1.75
★45a (16) 1 Fanam 1116-21,
modified dies.......1.25

46 (17) ¼ Rupee ME 1112 ..3.00
★46a (17) ¼ Rupee 1116-21,
modified dies.....3.00
47 (18) ½ Rupee 1112......7.00
47a (18) "Chitra" ½ Rupee
1114, reeded edge....6.00
47b (19) "Chitra" ½ Rupee
1116-21, security
edge...............3.75

INDO-CHINA (See French Indo-China)
INDONESIA

A group of 3,000 islands lying along the Equator southeast of Asia, formerly known as East Indies. Owned by the Netherlands before World War II, it was occupied by the Japanese. Except for Netherlands New Guinea, the area was proclaimed a republic Aug. 17, 1945. Population: 120,000,000. Most of the population is engaged in agriculture. Capital: *Jakarta*.

100 Sen = 1 Rupiah

Aluminum

Unc.
1 1 Sen 1952.................. .60
2 5 Sen 1951-54 .... .60

3 10 Sen 1951-54............. .35
4 25 Sen 1952............... .35

Unc.
3a 10 Sen 1957 (English inscription
INDONESIA over Eagle). .75
6 25 Sen 1955-57............. .35

Copper-Nickel

5 50 Sen 1952................. .35
5a 50 Sen 1955-57 (Malayan word
behind head omitted)..... .25

Aluminum

7 50 Sen 1958-61............... .25
Later issues in *Current Coins of the World.*

IRAN (See Persia)

IRAQ

Western Asia, bounded by Turkey, Iran, Syria, Jordan, Kuwait and Saudi Arabia; its only seacoast on the Persian Gulf. Extending along the Tigris and Euphrates valleys, it encompasses the area of the oldest world civilization known. In modern times it has been held by Turkey, been a British mandate under the League of Nations, and became a sovereign state in 1932. It is one of the great oil-producing countries of the world. Capital: *Baghdad*.

50 Fils = 1 Dirham
200 Fils = 1 Riyal
1000 Fils = 1 Dinar (Pound)

FAISAL I 1921-1933

Bronze

V. Fine
*1   1 Fils 1931-33 75
2   2 Fils 1931-33 . . . . 1.25

Nickel

3   4 Fils 1931-33 (Scalloped) . . 1.25
4   10 Fils 1931-33 (Scalloped) . . 1.75

Silver

5   20 Fils 1931-33 . . . . 2.00
Fine
*6   50 Fils 1931-33 . . . . 3.50
7   1 Riyal 1932 . . . . 15.00

GHAZI I 1933-1939

Bronze

V. Fine
8   1 Fils 1936-38 40

No. 8 dated 1938 was struck to 1952.

Nickel

Fine
*9   4 Fils Nic. 1938-39 . . . . . . 1.25
9a   4 Fils Cop.-Nic. 1938 40
9b   4 Fils Bronze 1938 40
10   10 Fils Nic. 1937-38 . . . . . . 2.00
10a 10 Fils Cop.-Nic. 1938 75
10b 10 Fils Bronze 1938 60

Silver

V. Fine
11   20 Fils 1938 . . . . 1.50
*12 50 Fils 1937-38 . . . . 3.00

FAISAL II 1939-1958

Bronze

Fine
13   4 Fils 1943 . . . . 2.00
*14 10 Fils 1943 . . . . 2.50

IRAQ

Silver

V. Fine

★15 1 Fils 1953 20
16 2 Fils 1953 85

Copper-Nickel

V. Fine

19   20 Fils 1953 . . . . 35.00
20   50 Fils 1953 . . . . 35.00
★21 100 Fils 1953 . . . . 5.00

Redesigned Reverse,
Slightly Reduced Size

22   20 Fils 1955 . . . . 1.75
23   50 Fils 1955 . . . . 3.00

17   4 Fils 1953 (Scalloped) 35
★18 10 Fils 1953 50

Later issues in *Current Coins of the World.*

IRELAND (Eire)

Formerly a part of the United Kingdom but became a self-governing Dominion of the British Commonwealth in 1922. Adopted a Republican form of government in 1949. Capital: *Dublin.* Area: 27,137 square miles. Population: 3,000,000. Languages: English and Gaelic.

  4 Farthings = 1 Penny
 12 Pence = 1 Shilling
  2 Shillings = 1 Florin
  5 Shillings = 1 Crown
 20 Shillings = 1 Pound

Gaelic Legend:
SAORSTAT EIREANN

Bronze

V.F.

2 ½ Penny 1928-37 . . . . 1.00

V. Fine

1 1 Farthing 1928-37 . . . . 1.25

3 1 Penny 1928-37 . . . . 1.00

· 271 ·

IRELAND

Nickel

V. Fine
4 3 Pence 1928-35............1.25

V. Fine
8 ½ Crown 1928-37...........7.00
New Legend: EIRE only
Designs similar to Nos. 1-8

5 6 Pence 1928-35............1.75

Silver

6 1 Shilling 1928-37..........3.00

		Unc.
	Bronze	
9	1 Farthing 1939-66.......	.35
10	½ Penny 1939-67.........	.20
11	1 Penny 1940-68.........	.30
	Nickel	V. Fine
12	3 Pence 1939-40.........	1.50
13	6 Pence 1939-40.........	2.25
	Silver	
14	1 Shilling 1939-42.......	3.00
15	1 Florin 1939-43........	4.50
★16	½ Crown 1939-43........	5.50
	Copper-Nickel	Unc.
12a	3 Pence 1942-68..........	.35
13a	6 Pence 1942-68..........	.50
14a	1 Shilling 1951-68........	.65
15a	1 Florin 1951-68.........	1.50
16a	½ Crown 1951-67.......	2.00

7 1 Florin 1928-37............5.00

Later issues in *Current Coins of the World.*

ISRAEL
(Medinat Israel)

Middle East, bordering the Mediterranean Sea. A new republic created in 1948. With the Nazi persecution of Jews during World War II, a great exodus began toward Palestine, which is now part of Israel. The largest export crop is citrus fruits, but a gradual increase in manufactured commodities is seen. Area: 7,993 square miles. Population: 3,300,000. Language: Hebrew. Capital: *Jerusalem.*

1000 Mils = 1 Pound   1000 Pruta = 1 Pound   100 Agora = 1 Pound

ISRAEL
HEBREW DATES ON ISRAEL COINS
Regular Issues

Hebrew Date on Coin	A.D. Date	Hebrew Date in Arabic Numerals	Appears on Catalog Numbers
תש"ח	1948	5708	1
התש"ט	1949	5709	{1, 2, 3, 4, 6, 8, 10, 12, 13, 14
התשי"ב	1952	5712	5
התשי"ד	1954	5714	7, 8, 8a, 9, 11
התשט"ו	1955	5715	10
תשי"ז	1957	5717	5a, 5b

Aluminum

V. Fine
1 25 Mils 1948-49 . . . . 12.50

New Coinage System

Unc.
2 1 Pruta 1949 . . . . 1.50

Bronze

Unc.
3 5 Pruta 1949 . . . . 2.00

4 10 Pruta 1949 . . . . 1.75

Aluminum

5 10 Pruta 1952 . . . . 1.00
5a 10 Pruta 1957 (Round) 1.00
Anodized Aluminum
5b 10 Pruta 1957 (Round) 1.00

ISRAEL

Unc.
*6 25 Pruta Cop.-Nic. 1949 . . . . 1.75
7 25 Pruta Nickel-Clad Steel
   1954 (Smooth Edge) 2.50

8 50 Pruta Cop.-Nic. 1949-54
  (Reeded Edge) 3.00
8a 50 Pruta Cop.-Nic. 1954
  (Smooth Edge) 3.50
9 50 Pruta Nickel-Clad Steel
  1954 (Smooth Edge) 3.00

10 100 Pruta Cop.-Nic.
   1949-55 . . . . 3.25
*11 100 Pruta Nickel-Clad Steel
   1954 (Smooth Edge,
   Reduced Size) 3.00

Copper-Nickel

12 250 Pruta 1949 . . . . 3.00
Silver
13 250 Pruta 1949 . . . . 11.00

Unc.
14 500 Pruta 1949 . . . . 22.50

Tenth Anniversary
of Republic

Silver

16 5 Pounds 1958 . . . . 27.50

Law Is Light (Chanuka)

Copper-Nickel

17 1 Pound 1958 . . . . 12.50

Later issues in Current Coins of the World.

ITALY (Italia)

The modern state of Italy did not develop until 1860. Though a kingdom under Victor Emanuel, during the 1920's the country was completely controlled by the Fascisti under Mussolini. After the death of Mussolini and the abdication of the king following Italy's defeat in World War II, the country became a republic (1946). Population: 53,800,000. Capital: *Rome*.

100 Centesimi = 1 Lira

VITTORIO EMANUELE II
1861-1878

Commemorating Accession to Throne of Unified Italy

Dated MARZO 1861
(Florence Mint)

Silver

Regular Issues

Copper

		Fine
6	1 Centesimo 1861-67	.60
7	2 Centesimi 1861-67	.85
8	5 Centesimi 1861-67	1.00
9	10 Centesimi 1862-67	1.75

Silver

Arms on Reverse

10	20 Centesimi 1863	——
11	50 Centesimi 1861-63	7.00
12	1 Lira 1861-67	2.00
13	2 Lire 1861-63	5.00
★14	5 Lire 1861-78	10.00

V. Fine

5 5 Lire 1861 .... 800.00

ITALY

Value in Center on Reverse

Fine

15 20 Centesimi 1863-67 . . . . . . 2.50
16 50 Centesimi 1863-67 . . . . . . 3.00
17 1 Lira 1863 . . . . 3.50
18 2 Lire 1863 . . . . 5.00

Gold

V. Fine

A18 5 Lire 1863-65 . . . . . . 100.00
B18 10 Lire 1861-65 . . . . 45.00
19 20 Lire 1861-78 . . . . 60.00
20 50 Lire 1864 . . . . —
21 100 Lire 1864-78 . . . . —

UMBERTO I 1878-1900

Copper

Fine

22 1 Centesimo 1895-1900 . . . . . 1.00
23 2 Centesimi 1895-1900 . . . . . 1.00
24 5 Centesimi 1895-96 . . . . 8.00
25 10 Centesimi 1893-94 . . . . 1.25

Copper-Nickel

Fine

26 20 Centesimi 1894-95 . . . . . . 1.00

Silver

27 50 Centesimi 1889-92 . . . . . . 45.00
28 1 Lira 1883-1900 . . . . 2.00
29 2 Lire 1881-99 . . . . 3.00
30 5 Lire 1878-79 . . . . 20.00

Gold

V. Fine

32 20 Lire 1879-97 . . . . 55.00
33 50 Lire 1884-91 . . . . —
34 100 Lire 1880-91 . . . . —

VITTORIO EMANUELE III
1900-1946
First Coinage

Bronze

Fine

35 1 Centesimo 1902-08 . . . . 1.50
36 2 Centesimi 1903-08 . . . . 1.50

ITALY

Note: Because of extensive catalog revisions to Italy, new numbers were assigned in the 8th edition.

Nickel

V. Fine

37 25 Centesimi 1902-03......14.00

Silver

Fine

38 1 Lira 1901-07.............4.00
39 2 Lire 1901-07.............15.00
40 5 Lire 1901..............——

Gold
Head Left, Rev. Crowned Eagle

V. Fine
41 20 Lire 1902-10..........300.00
(Dates after 1905 not for circulation.)

42 100 Lire 1903-05..........——

Second Coinage

Bronze

43 1 Centesimo 1908-18......1.50
44 2 Centesimi 1908-17......1.50
45 5 Centesimi 1908-18......2.00
46 10 Centesimi 1908.........——

Nickel

V. F.
47 20 Centesimi 1908-35.......25
(Dates after 1922 not for circulation.)

Silver

48 1 Lira 1908-13.............2.50
49 2 Lire 1908-12.............7.50

50 1 Lira 1915-17.............3.00
51 2 Lire 1914-17.............5.00
52 5 Lire 191.4.......*Ex. F.* 1200.00

Gold

Ex. Fine
53 10 Lire 1910-27..........900.00
54 20 Lire 1910-27..........600.00

ITALY

55 50 Lire 1910-27 . . . . 700.00
56 100 Lire 1910-27 . . . .———

(Dates after 1912 of Nos. 53-56 not for circulation.)

50th Anniversary of Kingdom
(Nos. 57-60)
Bronze

V. Fine
57 10 Centesimi 1911 . . . . 4.00

Silver

Ex. Fine
58 2 Lire 1911 . . . . 17.50
59 5 Lire 1911 . . . . 400.00

Gold

60 50 Lire 1911 . . . . 350.00

Third Coinage
Bronze

V. Fine
61 5 Centesimi 1919-37 20

62 10 Centesimi 1919-37 20

Copper-Nickel

63 20 Centesimi 1918-20, over-struck on No. 26 35

Nickel

64 50 Centesimi 1919-28,
plain edge 50
64a 50 Centesimi 1919-35,
reeded edge 50

(Dates after 1925 of Nos. 64-64a not for circulation.)

ITALY

V. Fine

65 1 Lira 1922-35 . . . . 1.00
(Dates after 1928 not for circulation.)

66 2 Lire 1923-35 . . . . 1.50
(Dates after 1927 not for circulation.)

V. Fine

69 20 Lire 1927-34 . . . . 50.00
(Dates after 1928 not for circulation.)

Silver

67 5 Lire 1926-35 . . . . 1.50
(Dates after 1930 not for circulation.)

Gold

Ex. Fine

70 50 Lire 1931-33 . . . . 250.00

68 10 Lire 1926-34 . . . . 10.00
(Dates after 1930 not for circulation.)

71 100 Lire 1931-33 . . . . 325.00

ITALY

First Anniversary of Fascist Government 1922-1923

Gold

Ex. Fine

72 20 Lire 1923............350.00
73 100 Lire 1923..........1000.00

Dual Commemorative —

25th Anniversary of Reign and 10th Anniversary of Italy's Entry into World War I

74 100 Lire 1925.............——

Fourth Coinage
Title: RE E IMPERATORE
Bronze

V. F.

77 5 Centesimi 1936-39........ .30

78 10 Centesimi 1936-39....... .40

Nickel

79 20 Centesimi 1936-38......30.00

80 50 Centesimi 1936-38......20.00

10th Anniversary Ending of World War I
Silver

75 20 Lire 1928.............*Ex. Fine* 65.00

ITALY

Silver

V. Fine

81 1 Lira 1936-38............16.00

V. Fine

89 5 Lire 1936-41............15.00
(Dates after 1937 not for circulation.)

90 10 Lire 1936-41............15.00
(Dates after 1936 not for circulation.)

82 2 Lire 1936-38............16.00
(Dates after 1936 of Nos. 79-82 not
for circulation.)

Aluminum-Bronze

77a 5 Centesimi 1939-43......15
78a 10 Centesimi 1939-43......20

Stainless Steel

79a 20 Centesimi 1939-43......15
80a 50 Centesimi 1939-43......25
81a 1 Lira 1939-43............35

82a 2 Lire 1939-43............50

Two different alloys were used for Nos. 79a-
82a: "Niox" (non-magnetic) in 1939 and
part of 1940, and "Acmonital" (magnetic)
in the balance of 1940 through 1943.

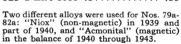
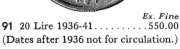

Ex. Fine

91 20 Lire 1936-41..........550.00
(Dates after 1936 not for circulation.)

ITALY

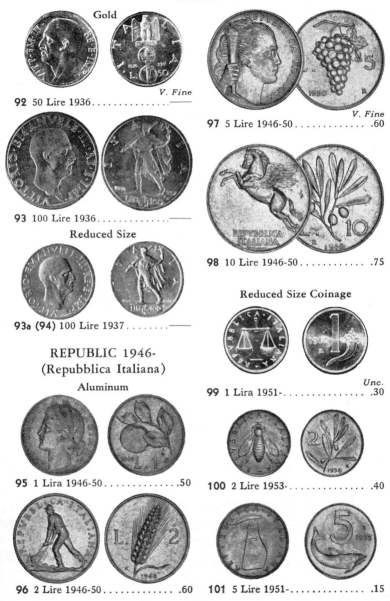

Gold

92 50 Lire 1936 . . . . ——

V. Fine

93 100 Lire 1936 . . . . ——

Reduced Size

93a (94) 100 Lire 1937 . . . . ——

REPUBLIC 1946-
(Repubblica Italiana)

Aluminum

95 1 Lira 1946-50 50

96 2 Lire 1946-50 60

V. Fine

97 5 Lire 1946-50 60

98 10 Lire 1946-50 75

Reduced Size Coinage

Unc.

99 1 Lira 1951- 30

100 2 Lire 1953- 40

101 5 Lire 1951- 15

ITALY

102 10 Lire 1951-.............*Unc.* .20

104 100 Lire 1955-............*Unc.* .70

A102 20 Lire Alum.-Br.
1957-59............1.00

Stainless Steel

Silver

(Date on edge)

105 500 Lire 1958-............3.50

Later issues in *Current Coins of the World.*

103 50 Lire 1954-.............40

ITALIAN SOMALILAND (Somalia Italiana)

The southeastern coast of the Somali region, on the eastern "horn" of Africa, became an Italian colony in the late 1800's. It came under British administration during World War II, but was returned to Italy under U.N. trusteeship in 1950 with ten years to prepare for independence. In 1960 Italian and British Somaliland joined to form the independent Somali Republic. Most of the native population were nomadic herdsmen; Italian colonists practiced agriculture. Languages: Somali, Arabic, Italian. Capital: *Mogadiscio* (Mogadishu).

100 Bese = 1 Rupia   100 Centesimi = 1 Lira
Coinage obsolete.

VITTORIO EMANUELE III 1900-1946

Bronze
Fine
1 1 Besa 1909-21.. 12.50
2 2 Bese 1909-24.. 15.00
3 4 Bese 1909-24.. 20.00

ITALIAN SOMALILAND

Silver

		V. Fine
4	¼ Rupia 1910-13	27.50
5	½ Rupia 1910-19	40.00
6	1 Rupia 1910-21	60.00

New Coinage System

7	5 Lire 1925	65.00
8	10 Lire 1925	95.00

For later issues see Somalia.

JAMAICA

Former colony of the British West Indies in the Caribbean Sea south of Cuba. Achieved national independence and membership in the British Commonwealth in 1962. Winter tourist resort for Americans. Exports: sugar, coffee, bananas, rum. Capital: *Kingston*.

4 Farthings = 1 Penny

VICTORIA 1837-1901
Copper-Nickel

		Fine
1	1 Farthing 1880-1900	1.50
2	½ Penny 1869-1900	1.75
3	1 Penny 1869-1900	2.50
A3	1½ Pence 1838-62 Silver (See Ceylon No. 3)	4.00

EDWARD VII
1901-1910

Copper-Nickel

Horizontal Shading in Arms

4	1 Farthing 1902-03	3.50
5	½ Penny 1902-04	5.50
6	1 Penny 1902-04	4.50

JAMAICA

GEORGE VI 1936-1952
Nickel-Brass

Vertical Shading in Arms

		Fine
13	1 Farthing 1937	1.50
14	½ Penny 1937	1.75
15	1 Penny 1937	2.00

		Fine
7	1 Farthing 1904-10	1.75
8	½ Penny 1904-10	2.00
9	1 Penny 1904-10	3.00

Larger Head   *V. Fine*

		V. Fine
16	1 Farthing 1938-47	.35
17	½ Penny 1938-47	.50
18	1 Penny 1938-47	.75

New Legend:
KING GEORGE THE SIXTH

19	1 Farthing 1950-52	.20
20	½ Penny 1950-52	.25
21	1 Penny 1950-52	.40

GEORGE V 1910-1936

Copper-Nickel

ELIZABETH II 1952-
Nickel-Brass

		V. Fine
10	1 Farthing 1914-34	1.50
11	½ Penny 1914-28	1.50
12	1 Penny 1914-28	2.00

		Unc.
22	½ Penny 1955-63	.15
23	1 Penny 1953-63	.25

Later issues in *Current Coins of the World.*

JAPAN
(Nippon)

Islands in the North Pacific Ocean off the coast of China. After its defeat in World War II, Japan's area was reduced to four main islands, a fifth being returned to it in 1953. Total area is now 142,644 square miles. Important industries are agriculture, the making of silk and steel manufacture. Language: Japanese. Capital: *Tokyo.*

10 Rin = 1 Sen
100 Sen = 1 Yen

JAPAN

MEIJI REIGN
1868-1912 (Years 1 to 45)
Reign Symbols 治 明 on coins

First Coinage
Silver

V. Fine

1	5 Sen Yrs. 3-4 (1870-71)	.50.00
2	10 Sen Yr. 3	8.50
★3	20 Sen Yrs. 3-4	8.50
4	50 Sen Yrs. 3-4 (32mm.)	17.50
4a	50 Sen Yr. 4 (30.5mm.)	35.00
5	1 Yen Yr. 3	120.00

6 5 Sen Yr. 4 . . . . 20.00

Gold

9	1 Yen Yr. 4	300.00
10	2 Yen Yr. 3	450.00
★11	5 Yen Yrs. 3-4	600.00
12	10 Yen Yr. 4	1500.00
13	20 Yen Yr. 3	——

Second Coinage
Copper

15 1 Rin Yrs. 6-17 (1873-84) . . . 2.00

Fine

16	½ Sen Yrs. 6-21	1.50
★17	1 Sen Yrs. 6-21	.75
18	2 Sen Yrs. 6-17	1.00

Bronze

20 1 Sen Yrs. 31-35
(1898-1902) 2.50

Copper-Nickel

19 5 Sen Yrs. 22-30 (1889-97) . . . 1.25

21 5 Sen Yrs. 30-38
(1897-1905) 2.50

JAPAN

Silver

V. Fine

22	5 Sen Yrs. 6-13	
	(1873-80)............3.00	
23	10 Sen Yrs. 6-39........2.00	
★24	20 Sen Yrs. 6-38........2.50	
25	50 Sen Yrs. 6-38........5.00	
A25	1 Yen Yrs. 7-45.......20.00	

Gold
Reduced size

9a	1 Yen Yrs. 7-13.......600.00	
10a	2 Yen Yrs. 7-13......... ——	
11a	5 Yen Yrs. 5-30.......500.00	

Same size, smaller design

12a	10 Yen Yrs. 9-13.........——	
13a	20 Yen Yrs. 9-13.........——	

Third Coinage

Silver

29	10 Sen Yrs. 40-45 (1907-12)	1.50
★30	20 Sen Yrs. 39-44........2.00	
31	50 Sen Yrs. 39-45........3.50	

Gold

32	5 Yen Yrs. 30-45	
	(1897-1912).........400.00	
★33	10 Yen Yrs. 30-43.......450.00	
34	20 Yen Yrs. 30-45......750.00	

Trade Coins
Silver

14 Trade Dollar Yrs. 8-10　　*V. Fine*
(1875-77)..............450.00

An expanding trade forced Japan to call in the old one yen pieces (Nos. 5 and A25), counterstamp them with a Japanese character "gin" (meaning "silver") in a small circle and circulate them principally in Taiwan (Formosa).

28	"Gin" stamp (1897) on
	No. 5.................150.00
★28a	"Gin" on No. A25
	dated Yrs. 7-30........15.00
28b	"Gin" on No. 14......400.00

TAISHO REIGN
1912-1926 (Years 1 to 15)
Reign Symbols 正大 on coins

First Coinage

Like nos. 20, A25 and 29-34 except for symbols of Taisho Reign.
Bronze
35 1 Sen Yrs. 2-4 (1913-15)....1.25

JAPAN

Silver

		V. Fine
36	10 Sen Yrs. 1-6 (1912-17)	2.00
37	50 Sen Yrs. 1-6	4.00
38	1 Yen Yr. 3 (1914)	17.50

Gold

39	5 Yen Yrs. 2, 13	550.00
40	20 Yen Yrs. 1-9	850.00

Second Coinage
Bronze

41 5 Rin Yrs. 5-8 (1916-19) 1.50

42 1 Sen Yrs. 5-13 (1916-24) 30

Copper-Nickel

43 5 Sen Yrs. 6-9 (1917-20)
20mm 3.00
★44 5 Sen Yrs. 9-12 (1920-23)
18.5mm 35

45 10 Sen Yrs. 9-15 (1920-26) . . .50

Silver

V. Fine

46 50 Sen Yrs. 11-15 (1922-26) . 1.50

SHOWA REIGN 1926-
Reign Symbols 和昭 on coins

First Coinage

Like nos. 32-34, 39-42, and 44-46 except for symbols of Showa Reign.

Bronze

47 1 Sen Yrs. 2-13 (1927-38) . . .35

Copper-Nickel

48 5 Sen Yr. 7 (1932) 2.50
49 10 Sen Yrs. 2-7 75

Silver

50 50 Sen Yrs. 3-13 . . . . 1.50

Gold

51 5 Yen Yr. 5 (1930) . . . . ——
52 20 Yen Yrs. 5-7 . . . . ——

Second Coinage
Nickel

53 5 Sen Yrs. 8-12 (1933-37) 50

54 10 Sen Yrs. 8-12 50

JAPAN

Bronze

55 1 Sen Yr. 13 (1938) 50

Aluminum

56 1 Sen Yrs. 13-15 (1938-40) 20

Aluminum-Bronze

57 5 Sen Yrs. 13-15 30

58 10 Sen Yrs. 13-15 35

WORLD WAR II ISSUES
Aluminum

59 1 Sen Yrs. 16-18
   (1941-43) 20
59a 1 Sen Yr. 18 thinner 20

V. Fine

60 5 Sen Yrs. 15-16
   (1940-41) 25
60a 5 Sen Yrs. 16-18 thinner 25

61 10 Sen Yrs. 15-16
   (1940-41) 35
61a 10 Sen Yrs. 16-18 thinner 35

Tin

62 1 Sen Yrs. 19-20 (1944-45) 20

63 5 Sen Yr. 19 50

64 10 Sen Yr. 19 50

JAPAN

V. Fine

65 5 Sen Yrs. 20-21 (1945-46)... .50

Aluminum

68 10 Sen Yrs. 20-21 .... .35

POSTWAR ISSUES

Brass

67 50 Sen Yrs. 21-22 (1946-47).. .75

69 50 Sen Yrs. 22-23 (1947-48).. .20

Henceforth numerals in Japanese read from left to right.

70 1 Yen Yrs. 23-25 (1948-50).. .25

V. Fine

71 5 Yen Yrs. 23-24 (1948-49)..1.25

★72 5 Yen Yrs. 24-33 (1949-58)
    Script-style characters... .10

72a 5 Yen Yr. 34- (1959-)   *Unc.*
    Block-style characters... .15

Bronze

73 10 Yen Reeded Edge   *V. Fine*
    Yrs. 26-33 (1951-58).... .10

73a 10 Yen Plain Edge   *Unc.*
    Yr. 34- (1959-)......... .20

Aluminum

74 1 Yen Yr. 30- (1955-)....... .10

JAPAN

Pure Nickel

Silver

75 50 Yen Yrs. 30-33 (1955-58) *Unc.* 1.50

77 100 Yen Yrs. 32-33 *Unc.*
(1957-58)............2.00

Later issues in Current Coins of the World.

JERSEY

One of the Channel Islands belonging to Britain off the northwest coast of France. It has a Lieutenant-Governor appointed by the Crown, but is not bound by Acts of Parliament unless named in the legislation. Area: 45 square miles.

Coinage 1841-1966 in fractional parts of a shilling.

VICTORIA 1837-1901

Copper

Fine
1 $1/52$ Shilling 1841.........27.50
★2 $1/26$ Shilling 1841-61........2.50
3 $1/13$ Shilling 1841-61........3.00

Bronze

4 $1/26$ Shilling 1866-71..........2.00
5 $1/13$ Shilling 1866-71..........2.00

New System

Fine
6 $1/48$ Shilling 1877..........22.50
7 $1/24$ Shilling 1877-94..........1.25
8 $1/12$ Shilling 1877-94..........1.50

EDWARD VII 1901-1910

9 $1/24$ Shilling 1909..........2.75
10 $1/12$ Shilling 1909..........3.00

JERSEY

GEORGE V 1910-1936

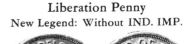

		V. Fine
11	1/24 Shilling 1911-23	3.50
12	1/12 Shilling 1911-23	2.25

19 1/12 Shilling 1945   *Unc.*
    (struck 1949-52) 35

ELIZABETH II 1952-
Bronze

13	1/24 Shilling 1923-26	2.50
14	1/12 Shilling 1923-26	2.25

20 1/12 Shilling 1945 Liberation
    reverse (struck 1954) 50

New Legend:
BAILIWICK OF JERSEY
Bronze

15	1/24 Shilling 1931-35	2.00
16	1/12 Shilling 1931-35	1.25

21 1/12 Shilling 1957-64 50

Nickel-Brass

GEORGE VI 1936-1952

22 1/4 Shilling 1957-60 50

17	1/24 Shilling 1937-47	1.00
18	1/12 Shilling 1937-47	.75

Later issues in Current Coins of the World.

JORDAN (Hashemite Kingdom of the Jordan)

An independent Kingdom in the Middle East, bounded by Israel, Syria, Iraq and Saudi Arabia. The population is mostly Moslem, and one-third of the 2,400,000 total are refugees resulting from the division of Palestine. Area: 37,500 square miles. Export: raw phosphate. Language: Arabic. Capital: *Amman*.

1000 Fils = 1 Dinar (Pound)

ABDULLA IBN AL HUSSEIN
1946-1951

Legend:
KINGDOM OF THE JORDAN

Bronze

Copper-Nickel

		V. Fine
5	20 Fils 1949	.50
6	50 Fils 1949	.80
7	100 Fils 1949	1.35

HUSSEIN I 1952-
New Legend:
KINGDOM OF JORDAN

	Bronze	Unc.
8	1 Fils 1955-65	.35
9	5 Fils 1955-67	.40
10	10 Fils 1955-67	.50

		V. Fine
1	1 "Fil" 1949 (error)	1.00
2	1 Fils 1949	.25
★3	5 Fils 1949	.30
4	10 Fils 1949	.40

	Copper-Nickel	
A10	20 Fils 1964-65	3.50
11	50 Fils 1955-65	1.00
12	100 Fils 1955-65	2.00

Later issues in Current Coins of the World.

KATANGA—see *Current Coins of the World*

KIAO CHAU (Kiautschou) German Possession in China

Formerly a German leased territory on the Shantung peninsula in eastern China; now a district of China. Capital: *Tsingtao*.

100 Cents = 1 Dollar
Coinage obsolete.

Copper-Nickel

		V. Fine
1	5 Cents 1909	10.00
2	10 Cents 1909	12.50

KOREA (Chosŭn)

Peninsula in northeastern Asia extending toward southern tip of Japan. One of the world's oldest nations. During the latter part of the 19th century Korea became a pawn between China, Russia and Japan. Finally, in 1910 Japan annexed the country, holding it until 1945. Independent since World War II, the country has been divided into two zones, North and South Korea, as a result of the war of 1950-53. Capitals: *Seoul* (South), *Pyongyang* (North).

KOREA

1000 Mun = 1 Warn before 1892
100 Fun = 1 Yang 1892-1902
5 Yang = 1 Whan 1892-1902
100 Chon = 1 Won 1902-1910

New System 1892

100 Fun = 1 Yang

Brass

V. Fine

4 1 Fun Yrs. 501-05
(1892-96) 3.50

Copper

5 5 Fun Yrs. 501-05 . . . . .1.50

Copper-Nickel

6 ¼ Yang Yrs. 501-05 . . . . . . .1.25

Silver

7 1 Yang Yrs. 501-02 . . . . .6.50
8 5 Yang Yr. 501 . . . . .200.00
9 1 Whan Yr. 502 . . . .——

EMPEROR KOJONG
1864-1907

Struck Coinage

For earlier coinage of this reign see Mandel,
Cast Coinage of Korea and Craig, *Coins
of the World 1750-1850.*

Brass

V. Fine

A1 5 Mun ND (1890) . . . .——

Dates of Nos. 1-9 are figured from
the beginning of Korea's Yi Dynasty
in 1392 A.D. Nos. 1-3 were actually
struck in 1891.

Copper

1 5 Mun Yr. 497 (1888) 25.00
2 10 Mun Yr. 497 . . . . .25.00

Silver

3 1 Warn Yr. 497 . . . .——
Some authorities claim no. 3 is a pattern.

KUANG MU REIGN
1897-1907 (Years 1 to 11)

Reign symbols 武光 on coins

(Title assumed by Emperor Kojong
in 1897.)

First Coinage

Like Nos. 5-7 except for symbols of
Kuang Mu Reign.

Copper

A10 5 Fun Yrs. 2-6
(1898-1902) 1.50

KOREA

Copper-Nickel

V. Fine

B10 ¼ Yang Yrs. 1-5
(1897-1901)............1.50

Silver

C10 1 Yang Yr. 2 (1898)......5.00

RUSSIAN INFLUENCE
New Denominations
100 Chon = 1 Won

Bronze

10 1 Chon Yr. 6 (1902)......600.00

Copper-Nickel

11 5 Chon Yr. 6............500.00

Silver

12 ½ Won Yr. 5 (1901).....700.00

KUANG MU
COINAGE RESUMED
Second Coinage
Bronze

13 ½ Chon Yr. 10 (1906)......2.00
14 1 Chon Yrs. 9-10..........1.75

Copper-Nickel

V. Fine

15 5 Chon Yrs. 9-11..........2.50

Silver

16 10 Chon Yr. 10............4.00
17 20 Chon Yrs. 9-10.........6.50
18 ½ Won Yrs. 9-10........12.50

Gold

★20 10 Won Yr. 10...........——
21 20 Won Yr. 10...........——

Third Coinage

Bronze

B22 1 Chon Yr. 11 (1907)......1.50

KOREA

Silver

Bronze

V. Fine

C22 10 Chon Yr. 11 (Thin)....3.00
D22 20 Chon Yr. 11..........5.00
E22 ½ Won Yr. 11..........15.00

V Fine

22 ½ Chon Yrs. 1-4 (1907-10)..1.50
23 1 Chon Yrs. 1-4..........1.00

Silver

25 10 Chon Yrs. 2-4..........3.50
26 20 Chon Yrs. 2-4..........4.50
27 ½ Won Yrs. 2-3..........15.00

YUNG HI REIGN

1907-1910 (Years 1 to 4)

Reign Symbols 첼 熙 on coins

Like Nos. B22-E22 except for symbols of Yung Hi Reign.

Gold

19 5 Won Yr. 2.............——

Other gold dates and denominations are known, but are thought to be patterns.

Later issues in Current Coins of the World.

KUWAIT — see *Current Coins of the World*

LAOS

One of the three former French Indo-Chinese States. Bounded by Communist China, Vietnam, Cambodia, Thailand and Burma. Became an independent sovereign state July 19, 1949. Area: 91,000 square miles. Population: 3,000,000. Capital: *Vientiane*.

100 Centimes = 1 Kip

Aluminum

Unc.

1 10 Centimes 1952............ .30

Unc.

2 20 Centimes 1952............ .40

LAOS

Unc.

3 50 Centimes 1952............1.25

LATVIA (Latvijas Republika)

On the Baltic Sea between Lithuania and Estonia. A Russian province until 1918, it became an independent republic until 1940 when Russia incorporated it into the U.S.S.R. (Latvian S.S.R.). The United States has not recognized its return to Russian territory. Capital: *Riga*. Area: 25,305 square miles.

100 Santimu = 1 Lats
Coinage obsolete.

Bronze

V. Fine
6 50 Santimu 1922............4.50

V. Fine
1 1 Santims 1922-35..........2.00
2 2 Santimi 1922-32..........2.50
3 5 Santimi 1922.............2.75

Silver

Nickel

4 10 Santimu 1922...........2.50
5 20 Santimu 1922...........2.75

7 1 Lats 1924................3.00
8 2 Lati 1925-26.............4.50

LATVIA

Bronze

		V. Fine
10	1 Santims 1937-39	2.25
11	2 Santimi 1937 (19mm.)	30.00
11a	2 Santimi 1939 (19.5mm)	2.50

V. Fine
9 5 Lati 1929-32 . . . . 13.00

LEBANON (Grand Liban, République Libanaise)

A republic on the east coast of the Mediterranean, 120 miles long and about 30 miles wide, bordering Israel on the north. Under French Mandate from 1920 until 1944 when France withdrew. Languages: Arabic and French. Capital: *Beirut*.

100 Piastres = 1 Lira (Pound)

Aluminum-Bronze

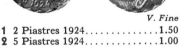

V. Fine
1	2 Piastres 1924	1.50
2	5 Piastres 1924	1.00

Copper-Nickel   *V. Fine*
5 ½ Piastre 1934-36 60

6 1 Piastre 1925-36 50

Silver

3	2 Piastres 1925	2.50
4	5 Piastres 1925-40	.60

8	10 Piastres 1929	3.00
9	25 Piastres 1929-36	3.00
10	50 Piastres 1929-36	5.00

LEBANON

Zinc

V. Fine

5a ½ Piastre 1941 50
6a 1 Piastre 1940 65

Aluminum-Bronze

7 2½ Piastres 1940 50

WORLD WAR II PROVISIONAL ISSUES
Brass

11 ½ Piastre ND 1.50

12 1 Piastre ND 1.50
Aluminum
13 2½ Piastres ND 1.50

POSTWAR ISSUES
Aluminum

14 5 Piastres 1952 85

V. Fine
15 10 Piastres 1952 . . . . .1.25

Aluminum-Bronze

Unc.
16 25 Piastres 1952-61 75

Silver

17 50 Piastres 1952 . . . . .1.75

Aluminum-Bronze

18 1 Piastre 1955 10

19 2½ Piastres 1955 15

LEBANON

Aluminum

Unc.

20 5 Piastres 1954. 50

Unc.

23 10 Piastres 1955. 75

Aluminum-Bronze

21 10 Piastres 1955. . . . . .1.00

Copper-Nickel

24 10 Piastres 1961. 40

Later issues in *Current Coins of the World.*

22 5 Piastres 1955-61. 20

LIBERIA

An independent republic founded 1847 on the southwest coast of Africa. From its rich tropical forests comes 10% of United States' rubber imports. It also produces iron ore, rated as the purest now mined. Area: 43,000 square miles. Capital: *Monrovia.*

100 Cents = 1 Dollar

Regular Issues

Copper

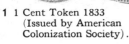

1 1 Cent Token 1833   *Fine*
    (Issued by American
    Colonization Society). 8.50

Fine

2 1 Cent 1847-62. . . . . .5.00

3 2 Cents 1847-62. . . . . .5.00

LIBERIA

Bronze

V. Fine

11 2 Cents 1937.............1.00

Copper-Nickel

Unc.

9a ½ Cent 1941............. .25
10a 1 Cent 1941........ V. F. 1.00
11a 2 Cents 1941.............1.00

Fine

4 1 Cent 1896-1906...........3.50
5 2 Cents 1896-1906..........4.50

Silver

12 1 Cent Br. 1960-........... .15
13 5 Cents Cop.-Nic. 1960-..... .35

6 10 Cents 1896-1906..........3.50
7 25 Cents 1896-1906..........5.00
8 50 Cents 1896-1906..........9.00

Silver

Brass

14 10 Cents 1960-61........... .75
15 25 Cents 1960-61..:.........1.50
16 50 Cents 1960-61..........3.50
17 1 Dollar 1961-62..........7.50

Later issues in Current Coins of the World.

Unc.

9 ½ Cent 1937.............. .50
10 1 Cent 1937.......... V. F. .75

LIBYA

Libya was formed as a constitutional monarchy in 1951 from former Italian-occupied territories in northern Africa. The king was deposed in 1969 and the country was declared a republic. Much of the land is desert but vast oil fields are now being developed. Language: Arabic. Capital: *Beida.*

10 Milliemes = 1 Piastre
100 Piastres = 1 Pound

LIBYA

IDRIS I
1951-1969

Bronze

1 1 Millieme 1952 20

		Unc.
2	2 Milliemes 1952	.30
★3	5 Milliemes 1952	.50

Copper-Nickel

		Unc.
4	1 Piastre 1952	.75
★5	2 Piastres 1952	1.25

Later issues in Current Coins of the World.

LIECHTENSTEIN
(Fürstentum Liechtenstein)

A principality between Austria and Switzerland with an area of 62 square miles. Tied to the Austrian monetary system until the end of World War I, to the Swiss thereafter. Population 17,800. Capital: *Vaduz.*

$1\frac{1}{2}$ Florins = 1 Vereinsthaler 1857-68 (see AUSTRIA)
100 Heller = 1 Krone 1892-1923
100 Rappen = 1 Frank 1924 on

PRINCE JOHN II
1858-1929

Silver
V. Fine
1 1 Thaler 1862 . . 500.00

Modern restrikes of No. 1 have letter M above date.

Values in Terms of "Kronen" (Vienna Mint)

V. Fine
2 1 Krone 1900-1915 . . . . 12.50
3 2 Kronen 1912-15 . . 15.00
4 5 Kronen 1900-1915 . . . 100.00

LIECHTENSTEIN

Gold
V. Fine

5 10 Kronen 1900.........1500.00
6 20 Kronen 1898.........2000.00

No. 5 dated 1898 is thought to be a pattern.

Values in Terms
of "Franken"
(Berne Mint)

Silver
7 ½ Frank *E. F.*
   1924 . . 30.00
8 1 Frank
   1924 . . 30.00
9 2 Franken
   1924 . . 35.00
10 5 Franken
   1924 . 150.00

PRINCE FRANZ I 1929-1938

Gold
Unc.

11 10 Franken 1930.........650.00
12 20 Franken 1930.........800.00

PRINCE FRANZ JOSEF II 1938-

Gold
Unc.

13 10 Franken 1946.........130.00
14 20 Franken 1946.........200.00

Commemorative Franz Josef II
and Princess Gina

Gold
Unc.

15 25 Franken 1956......130.00
16 50 Franken 1956......200.00
←**17** 100 Franken 1952.....1000.00

Later issues in *Current Coins of the World.*

LITHUANIA
(Lietuva)

A Baltic state between Latvia and Poland. It was incorporated in the U.S.S.R. in 1940 and has changed from an agricultural nation to a highly industrialized one. Capital: *Kaunas.*

100 Centu = 1 Litas
Coinage obsolete.

Aluminum-Bronze

			V. Fine
1	1 Centas 1925		2.00
2	5 Centai 1925		2.25

			V. Fine
10	2 Centai 1936		3.50
11	5 Centai 1936		4.00

3	10 Centu 1925	2.50
4	20 Centu 1925	2.75
5	50 Centu 1925	4.50

Silver

Silver

12	5 Litai 1936	7.50

6	1 Litas 1925	3.00
7	2 Litu 1925	5.00
8	5 Litai 1925	12.50

Bronze

13	10 Litu 1936	20.00

9	1 Centas 1936	3.00

LITHUANIA

20th Anniversary of Independence

V. Fine

14 10 Litu 1938...30.00

Other coins dated 1938 are patterns.

Obv: President Smetona

LUNDY

These "unlawful coins" have created considerable interest among collectors and for that reason have been included in this volume. Martin Coles Harman, a London businessman, purchased Lundy Island off the coast of England, in 1925, for approximately $25,000. He issued the coins shown below in 1929 and was fined by Britain in April, 1930, for issuing unauthorized coins. They were struck in Birmingham, England. The Puffin, a sea bird, is shown on the coins; Harman's portrait appears on the obverse of each piece. The coins circulated briefly but had no exchange value in terms of other currencies

Lettered Edge:
LUNDY LIGHTS AND LEADS

Bronze

Unc.

1 ½ Puffin 1929..............5.00
2 1 Puffin 1929..............7.50

Later issues in *Current Coins of the World.*

LUXEMBOURG (Letzeburg)

A Grand Duchy, 55 miles long by 35 miles wide, surrounded by Germany, Belgium, and France. Although primarily an agricultural country, it has a large output of iron and steel. Language: Mosel-frankisch. Capital: *Luxembourg*.

100 Centimes = 1 Frang (Franc)

General Coinage

Bronze

Zinc

Fine

1 2½ Centimes 1854-1908......1.75
2 5 Centimes 1854-70........1.50
3 10 Centimes 1854-70........1.75

Fine

9 5 Centimes 1915...........1.50
10 10 Centimes 1915..........1.75
11 25 Centimes 1916..........2.35

LUXEMBOURG

Iron

Copper-Nickel

Fine

12 5 Centimes 1918-22.......3.00
13 10 Centimes 1918-23.......3.50
14 25 Centimes 1919-22.......6.00

Issues with Royal Portraits or Monograms

There were no portrait or monogram issues for William III of the Netherlands (1849-1890), nor for Marie Adelaide (1912-1919).

ADOLPHE 1890-1905
Copper-Nickel

5 5 Centimes 1901............ .35
6 10 Centimes 1901............ .50

WILLIAM IV 1905-1912

8 5 Centimes 1908............1.00

CHARLOTTE 1919-1964
Copper-Nickel

V. Fine

18 5 Centimes 1924.......... .35
19 10 Centimes 1924.......... .50

Nickel
20 1 Franc 1924-35........... .50
21 2 Francs 1924............3.00

V. Fine

22 25 Centimes 1927.......... .75

Silver

23 5 Francs 1929............3.50
24 10 Francs 1929............5.00

Bronze

25 5 Centimes 1930.......... .20
26 10 Centimes 1930.......... .30

27 25 Centimes 1930......... .40

Copper-Nickel
27a 25 Centimes 1938......... .65

LUXEMBOURG

Nickel

V. Fine

28 50 Centimes 1930 75

Unc.

32 1 Franc Cop.-Nic. (Size reduced to 21 mm.) 1952 75
32a 1 Franc Same — Name
Lowered 1953-64 25

New Spelling: LETZEBURG

Various Metals

29 1 Frang Cop.-Nic. 1939 75

600th Anniversary
John the Blind 1946

Silver

33 20 Francs 1946 . . . . .4.00
34 50 Francs 1946 . . . . .6.00
35 100 Francs 1946 . . . . .15.00

No. 35 without designer's name on
obverse was restruck in 1964.

30 25 Centimes Br. 1946-47 15

Unc.

30a 25 Centimes Alum. 1954- 10

Copper-Nickel

V. Fine

36 5 Frang 1949 75

V. Fine

31 1 Franc Cop.-Nic. 1946-47 35

Later issues in *Current Coins of the World.*

MACAU (Macao)

Part of an island at the mouth of the Canton River in China covering six square miles. The trade is mostly transit. It is a Portuguese overseas province.

100 Avos = 1 Pataca

Bronze

Copper-Nickel

V. Fine

1 5 Avos 1952 30

Unc.

3 50 Avos 1952 . . . . .1.25

Silver

Unc.

2 10 Avos 1952 75

4 1 Pataca 1952 . . . . .2.50
5 5 Patacas 1952 . . . . .5.00

Later issues in Current Coins of the World.

MADAGASCAR

The world's fifth largest island lying off the southeast coast of Africa, it became a French protectorate in 1890. In 1960 it gained independence and, as the Malagasy Republic, remains a member of the French Community. Main industries are agriculture and cattle-raising. Area: 228,000 square miles. Capital: *Tananarive*.

100 Centimes = 1 Franc

World War II Issue
Bronze

Postwar Issues
Aluminum

V. F.

1 50 Centimes 1943 . . . . .2.50
2 1 Franc 1943 . . . . .5.00

Unc.

3 1 Franc 1948, 58 40
4 2 Francs 1948 60
5 5 Francs 1953 85

Aluminum-Bronze
6 10 Francs 1953 . . . . .1.00
←**7** 20 Francs 1953 . . . . .1.50

Later issues in Current Coins of the World.

MALAYA

A peninsula extending out into the South China Sea from the southeast tip of Asia. Formerly a federation of states under British suzerainty, it became an independent elective kingdom within the Commonwealth on August 31, 1957. Its chief products are rubber and tin. Capital: *Kuala Lumpur.*

100 Cents = 1 Dollar

For earlier issues see STRAITS SETTLEMENTS.

GEORGE VI 1936-1952

Bronze

V. Fine
1 ½ Cent 1940................ .50
2 1 Cent 1939-41............. .35

2a (6) 1 Cent 1943-45
       (reduced size)........ .25

Silver

V. Fine
3 5 Cents 1939-45............ .60
4 10 Cents 1939-45........... .80
5 20 Cents 1939-45...........1.50

New Legend:
KING GEORGE THE SIXTH

Copper-Nickel

7 5 Cents 1948-50............ .20
8 10 Cents 1948-50........... .30
9 20 Cents 1948-50........... .60

MALAYA AND BRITISH BORNEO

Issues for Malaya, Singapore, Sarawak, Brunei and British North Borneo. Area: 129,500 square miles.

100 Cents = 1 Dollar

ELIZABETH II 1952-1963

Bronze
Unc.
A1 1 Cent 1956-61............ .20

Copper-Nickel
1 5 Cents 1953-61............ .20
2 10 Cents 1953-61........... .25
3 20 Cents 1954-61........... .40
4 50 Cents 1954-61........... .85

Later issues in Current Coins of the World.

MALDIVE ISLANDS

Coral atolls southwest of Ceylon. Formerly a dependency of Ceylon, it was later a British Protected State. Became fully independent July 26, 1965. Chief export: fish. Population: 110,000. Capital: *Malé*.

100 Lari = 1 Rupee

IBRAHIM NUR-ED-DIN
1882-1900
Copper

			Fine
A1	1 Larin AH 1300, 11 (1882, 93)		2.00

MOHAMMAD IMAD-ED-DIN 1900-1904
Copper

		Fine
*1	1 Larin A.H. 1318-19 (1900-01)	1.50
1a	1 Larin Brass A.H. 1318-19	7.50
2	2 Lari A.H. 1319 13mm	1.75
2a	2 Lari Brass A.H. 1319 13mm	10.00
3	4 Lari A.H. 1320 17mm	2.00
3a	4 Lari Brass A.H. 1320 17mm	12.50

Nos. 3 and 3a Reeded or Plain Edge.

MOHAMMAD SHAMS-ED-DIN 1904-1935
Copper

		Fine
5	1 Larin A.H. 1331 (1913)	2.00

6	4 Lari A.H. 1331	3.00

Later issues in *Current Coins of the World*.

MALI — see *Current Coins of the World*

MALTA

A pair of islands south of Sicily in the Mediterranean Sea, Malta was a British colony from 1814 until gaining independence in 1964. Its economy derived chiefly from its use as the base of British naval operations in the Mediterranean. Area: 121 square miles. Languages: Maltese, English. Population: 325,000. Capital: *Valletta*.

One-third farthing pieces, called "Granos" (Grains), were struck especially for Malta beginning in 1827. English coins were also used.

VICTORIA 1837-1901
Copper

Bronze

		V. Fine
1	⅓ Farthing 1844	15.00

		V. Fine
2	⅓ Farthing 1866-85	5.00

MALTA

EDWARD VII 1901-1910

Ex. Fine
3 ⅓ Farthing 1902............4.50

GEORGE V 1910-1936

Ex. Fine
4 ⅓ Farthing 1913............4.50

Later issues in Current Coins of the World.

MANCHUKUO

After the Japanese invasion of 1931, Manchuria became an independent nation controlled by the Japanese. It was renamed Manchukuo. After the close of the war in 1945 the area was returned to China. The puppet emperor under the assumed name of Kang Teh was previously the last emperor of China (Pu-Yi, or Hsuan T'ung, 1909-11.) Rich soil and large mineral deposits make this territory an important possession. Capital: *Hsinking.*

10 Li (Cash) = 1 Fen
10 Fen = 1 Chio
Coinage obsolete.

TA-TUNG REIGN
1932-1934 (Years 1 to 3)
Reign Symbols 同 大 on coins

KANG TEH REIGN
1934-1945 (Years 1 to 12)
Reign Symbols 德 康 on coins

First Coinage

Like Nos. 1-4 except for symbols of Kang Teh Reign.

Bronze

V. Fine
1 5 Li Yrs. 2-3 (1933-34).....10.00
★2 1 Fen Yrs. 2-3.............2.00

Copper-Nickel

3 5 Fen Yrs. 2-3.............1.00
★4 1 Chio Yrs. 2-3............1.50

Bronze

V. Fine
★5 5 Li Yrs. 1-6 (1934-39).....10.00
6 1 Fen Yrs. 1-6.............2.00

Copper-Nickel

7 5 Fen Yrs. 1-6.............1.00
★8 1 Chio Yrs. 1-6............1.25

MANCHUKUO

Second Coinage

Aluminum

Copper-Nickel

V. Fine

10 1 Chio Yr. 7 (1940)........1.50

V. Fine

9 1 Fen Yrs. 6-10 (1939-43)....1.00

11 5 Fen Yrs. 7-10 (1940-43)...1.50

Third Coinage

Aluminum

13 1 Fen Yrs. 10-11
(1943-44)..............1.25
A13 5 Fen Yrs. 10-11........1.00
14 10 Fen Yr. 10...........1.25

Red Fiber

13a 1 Fen Yr. 12 (1945).....5.00
A13a 5 Fen Yr. 11............3.50

12 10 Fen Yrs. 7-9 (1940-42)...1.50

MARTINIQUE

An island in the West Indies, it has been a French possession since 1635. Principal exports are sugar cane, cocoa, pineapples, and bananas. Area: 380 square miles. Capital: *Fort-de-France.*

100 Centimes = 1 Franc

Coinage obsolete.

Copper-Nickel

Fine

1 50 Centimes 1897, 1922..... 4.00
2 1 Franc 1897, 1922........ 6.00

MAURITIUS

Island in the Indian Ocean formerly under British rule, became independent March 12, 1968. Languages: English, French, Hindustani. Area: 720 square miles. Chief export: sugar. Capital: *Port Louis.*

100 Cents = 1 Rupee

VICTORIA 1837-1901

Bronze

		Fine
1	1 Cent 1877-97	5.00
2	2 Cents 1877-97	5.00
3	5 Cents 1877-97	5.50

Silver

4	10 Cents 1877-97	6.50
5	20 Cents 1877-99	7.00

Silver

		V. Fine
9	¼ Rupee 1934-36	4.50

Rev: like No. 21

10	½ Rupee 1934	7.50

11	1 Rupee 1934	10.00

GEORGE VI 1936-1952

Bronze

12	1 Cent 1943-47	1.25
13	2 Cents 1943-47	1.25
14	5 Cents 1942-45	1.00

GEORGE V 1910-1936

Bronze

		V. Fine
6	1 Cent 1911-24	3.00
7	2 Cents 1911-24	3.50
8	5 Cents 1917-24	4.00

MAURITIUS

Copper-Nickel

V. Fine

21 ½ Rupee 1950-51 . . . . 1.00
22 1 Rupee 1950-51 . . . . 1.75

V. Fine
15 10 Cents 1947 75

ELIZABETH II 1952-

Silver
Reverse designs like Nos. 9-11

16 ¼ Rupee 1938-46 . . . . 4.00
17 ½ Rupee 1946 . . . . 10.00
18 1 Rupee 1938 . . . . 12.50

Bronze

New Legend:
KING GEORGE THE SIXTH

Unc.
25 1 Cent 1953- 20
26 2 Cents 1953- 25
27 5 Cents 1956- 35

Bronze
23 1 Cent 1949-52 35
24 2 Cents 1949-52 45

Copper-Nickel
28 10 Cents 1954- 50
29 1 Rupee 1956- 1.50
30 ¼ Rupee 1960- 50

Copper-Nickel
19 10 Cents 1952 (Scalloped) 75
20 ¼ Rupee 1950-51 75

Later issues in *Current Coins of the World.*

MEXICO
(República Mexicana, Estados Unidos Mexicanos)

A Federal Republic to the south of the United States. Since its independence from Spain in the early 1800's, Mexico has been torn by many revolutions and civil wars, but in the last 50 years has made great progress. Tourist trade has become an important industry. Its principal products include cotton, coffee, shrimp, cattle, lead and petroleum. Two-thirds of its exports are made to the United States. Area: 758,259 square miles. Population: 53,500,000. Capital: *Mexico City.*

8 Reales = 1 Peso
16 Reales = 1 Escudo
100 Centavos = 1 Peso

REPUBLICA MEXICANA
1823-1905

Fourteen mints coined silver and gold 1823-1905. Certain issues are much more rare than the values indicated for a common date and mint. For a detailed listing see Buttrey and Hubbard, *A Guide Book of Mexican Coins.*

Copper
Designs like No. S12

Fine
S9 ⅛ Real 1829 (27mm) . . . . . ——
S10 ¼ Real 1829 (33mm) 11.50

MEXICO

		Fine
S22	1 Real 1825-69	2.25
S23	2 Reales 1825-72	3.00
S24	4 Reales 1825-69	5.50
S25	8 Reales 1824-69	7.00

Hand on Book

Gold		*V. Fine*
S26	½ Escudo 1825-69	37.50
S27	1 Escudo 1825-70	50.00
S28	2 Escudos 1825-70	80.00
S29	4 Escudos 1825-69	250.00
S30	8 Escudos 1823 (Hooked-neck Eagle)	2500.00
S31	8 Escudos 1825-73	225.00

		Fine
S11	⅟₁₆ Real 1831-33	7.00
SA11	⅛ Real 1829-35 (21mm)	2.00
S12	¼ Real 1829-37 (27mm)	1.65

EMPEROR MAXIMILIAN
1864-1867
Legend: IMPERIO MEXICANO

Copper		*Fine*
S32	1 Centavo 1864	17.50

Silver		
S33	5 Centavos 1864-66 (Eagle)	12.50
S34	10 Centavos 1864-66 (Eagle)	8.00
S35	50 Centavos 1866 (Hd.)	25.00
		V. Fine
S36	1 Peso 1866-67	27.50

Gold		
S37	20 Pesos 1866	500.00

S14	⅛ Real 1841-61	2.25

Silver
Obv: "Hooked-neck" eagle

S16	½ Real 1824	20.00
S17	1 Real 1824	——
S18	2 Reales 1824	18.00
S19	8 Reales 1823-25	45.00

S20	¼ Real 1842-63	4.00

REPUBLIC 1863-1905
Copper

Obv: Upright eagle

S21	½ Real 1825-69	2.25

		Fine
S15	1 Centavo 1863	5.50

MEXICO

1 1 Centavo 1869-97 (Eagle). *Fine* .90

Silver

Fine
7 5 Centavos 1867-69........20.00
8 10 Centavos 1867-69........14.00

2 1 Centavo 1898 (Different
    Eagle)................3.50

9 5 Centavos 1863-70......22.50
10 10 Centavos 1863-70......22.50

3 1 Centavo 1899-1905 (Reduced
    Size)....................75

11 5 Centavos 1869-97........ .50
12 10 Centavos 1869-97........ .75

Copper-Nickel

13 25 Centavos 1869-92........1.50
14 50 Centavos 1869-95........2.50
15 1 Peso 1869-73...........7.50

V. Fine
4 1 Centavo 1882-83........... .45
5 2 Centavos 1882-83.......... .55
6 5 Centavos 1882-83.......... .45

V. Fine
16 5 Centavos 1898-1905...... .85
17 10 Centavos 1898-1905......1.15
18 20 Centavos 1898-1905......3.50

MEXICO

ESTADOS UNIDOS MEXICANOS 1905-

Bronze

V. Fine

27 1 Centavo 1905-49 10
28 1 Centavo 1915 (16 mm.) 9.00
29 2 Centavos 1905-41
    (25 mm.) 50

V. Fine
19 8 Reales 1869-97 . . . . 7.50

30 2 Centavos 1915 (20 mm.) . . 4.00

Nickel

Fine
31 5 Centavos 1905-14 40

20 1 Peso 1898-1909 . . . . 6.50

Bronze

Gold

21   1 Peso 1870-1905 . . . . . . 80.00
22 2½ Pesos 1870-93 . . . . . . 210.00

32   5 Centavos 1914-35 40
33 10 Centavos 1919-35 . . . . 3.00
34 20 Centavos 1920, 35 . . . . . . 5.00

Copper-Nickel

23   5 Pesos 1870-1905 . . . . . 210.00
★24 10 Pesos 1870-1905 . . . . . 250.00
25 20 Pesos 1870-1905 . . . . . 325.00

V. Fine
35   5 Centavos 1936-42 50
36 10 Centavos 1936-46 25

MEXICO

Bronze

V. Fine

37 5 Centavos 1942-55......... .15

38 20 Centavos 1943-55 .... .15

Silver

39 10 Centavos 1905-14........ .75
40 20 Centavos 1905-14........1.35
41 50 Centavos 1905-18........2.25

42 1 Peso 1910-14............12.50

Reduced Size .800 Fine
No fineness shown (Type of Nos. 47-50)

Fine

43 10 Centavos 1919..........4.00
44 20 Centavos 1919.........15.00
45 50 Centavos 1918-19........2.00
46 1 Peso 1918-19............3.50

0.720 Fine   *V. Fine*

47 10 Centavos 1925-35........ .30
48 20 Centavos 1920-43........ .45
49 50 Centavos 1919-45.......1.00
50 1 Peso 1920-45............2.00

Independence Centennial

.900 Fine

51 2 Pesos 1921.............15.00

52 50 Centavos 1935 Base Silver .75

MEXICO

Unc.
53 1 Peso 1947-49 . . . . 1.00

Independence Centennial

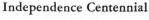

Unc.
60 50 Pesos 1921-47 . . . . 235.00
60a (50 Pesos) 1943, no
value shown 250.00

Decree of December 29, 1949

Brass

61 1 Centavo 1950-69 15

Copper-Nickel

Josefa Dominguez

62 5 Centavos 1950 . . . . . . *V. F.* .60

Billon

54 5 Pesos 1947-48 . . . . 5.00

Gold

55   2 Pesos 1919-48 . . . . 10.00
56 2½ Pesos 1918-48 . . . . 12.00
57   5 Pesos 1905-55 . . . . 20.00
58 10 Pesos 1905-59 . . . . 35.00

59 20 Pesos 1917-59 . . . . 100.00

63 25 Centavos 1950-53 35

MEXICO

Cuauhtémoc

Unc.

64 50 Centavos 1950-51 75

Morelos

Hidalgo

Unc.

67 5 Pesos 1951-54 . . . . 5.00

65 1 Peso 1950 . . . . 1.75

Inaugural of
Southeastern Railway

Silver

Hidalgo Commemorative
1753-1953

68 5 Pesos 1953 . . . . 6.00

Later issues in *Current Coins of the World.*

66 5 Pesos 1950 . . . . 20.00

MEXICO

REVOLUTIONARY ISSUES
1913-1917

Note: Because of extensive revisions, new numbers were assigned in the 11th edition. The original numbers are given in parentheses.

STATE OF AGUASCALIENTES

Copper

Obv: Liberty cap

		Fine
R1	1 Centavo 1915	25.00
R2	2 Centavos 1915	55.00

R3 5 Centavos 1915, rev. large 5c 10.00

Rev: similar to Mexico No. 52

R4 5 Centavos 1915 . . . . 15.00
R5 20 Centavos 1915 (vars.) 7.50

Nos. R1, R2, R3 and R5 were also struck in silver for presentation purposes.

STATE OF CHIHUAHUA
I. Hidalgo del Parral, city

Legend:
FUERZAS CONSTITUCIONALISTAS

Copper or Brass

V. Fine

R7 (53) 2 Centavos 1913 . . . . 6.00

Silver

R8 (54) 50 Centavos 1913 . . . . . 15.00

V. Fine

R9 (55) 1 Peso 1913, rev. ball in center . . . 1500.00
★R10 (55) 1 Peso 1913, without ball 85.00

II. Ejército Constitucionalista (Constitutionalist Army)

Copper

R11 (8) 5 Centavos 1914-15 . . . 1.00
R12 (9) 10 Centavos 1914-15 . . . 2.00

Brass

R11a (—) 5 Centavos 1914-15 . . 6.50
R12a (9a) 10 Centavos 1915 . . . . 3.00

The 50 centavos and 1 Peso with obverse as above are considered patterns, as are two types of 5 Centavos with eagle obverse.

MEXICO

REVOLUTIONARY ISSUES

III. Ejército del Norte (Army of the North)

Silver

V. Fine
R16 (11) 1 Peso 1915.........20.00

STATE OF DURANGO

Aluminum

Ex. Fine
R24 (13) 1 Centavo 1914......1.00

Brass
R25 (17) 5 Centavos 1914......1.00

Silver

Legend: MUERA HUERTA ("Death to Huerta")

	Copper	Fine
R17 (14)	1 Centavo 1914.......	2.00
R18 (14)	I Centavo 1914.......	7.50
R19 (16)	5 Centavos 1914, ESTADO DE-.........	2.75
R20 (16)	5 Centavos 1914, E. DE-.............	2.75
R21 (15)	V Centavos 1914......	6.00

Obv: 3 stars at bottom

R22 (14) 1 Centavo 1914......10.00

Brass
R17a (14) 1 Centavo 1914.....15.00
R18a (14) I Centavo 1914.....15.00
R20a (16) 5 Centavos 1914....25.00

Lead
R17b (14) 1 Centavo 1914....10.00
R18b (14) I Centavo 1914.....15.00
R20b (16) 5 Centavos 1914....——
R21b (15) V Centavos 1914....——
R22b (14) 1 Centavo 1914.....——

Rev: 6 stars around lower border
Crude lettering both sides
R26 (12) 1 Peso 1914..........——

Rev: without stars
★R27 (12) 1 Peso 1914.......100.00

Gold
R28 (—) 20 Pesos 1914, as No. R26...........——

No. R28 also exists in silver and copper. Some authorities consider it a fantasy produced in the 1920's.

STATE OF GUERRERO

Mint towns and mint marks on coins:

ATLIXTAC

CACALOTEPEC

CAMPO MO(rado), COMO, C.M.

SURIANA

TAXCO, T̊

G, GO, GRO, G.R.O. = Guerrero

Copper

Obv: similar to No. R32c
Rev: similar to Mexico No. 32

		Fine
R29 (A17)	2 Centavos 1915....	——
R30 (B17)	3 Centavos 1915....	——
R31 (18)	5 Centavos 1915 C.M.	15.00
R31a (18)	5 Centavos 1915 TAXCO GRO	15.00
R31b (18)	5 Centavos 1915 GRO	——

R32 (19)	10 Centavos 1915 C.M.GRO	20.00
R32a (19)	10 Centavos 1915 TAXCO GRO	15.00
R32b (19)	10 Centavos 1915 GRO	3.50
R32c (19)	10 Centavos 1915 ATLIXTAC GRO	3.50
R33 (20)	20 Centavos 1915 C.M.GRO	15.00
R33b (20)	20 Centavos 1915 GRO	100.00
R34 (21)	50 Centavos 1915 C.M.GRO (vars.)	10.00

Obv: similar to No. R32c
Rev: date on radiant sun

R35 (21)	50 Centavos 1915 TAXCO/GRO	40.00

Obv: eagle, EDO. DE GRO.
Rev: similar to No. R32c

		Fine
R36 (A17)	2 Centavos 1915 T̊	90.00

Type of Mexico No. 32

R37 (18)	5 Centavos 1917 G	75.00

Silver

Types of Mexico Nos. 39-40
Obv. legend:
MEXICO ESTADO (DE)G.R.O.

R38 (—)	10 Centavos 1914, cast.	——
R39 (—)	20 Centavos 1914, cast.	——

Obv: Liberty cap
Crude legends both sides

R40 (A22)	25 Centavos 1915 E.D.G.	——
R41 (—)	50 Centavos 1915 E. de G.	——

Type of No. R35

R35a (22)	50 Centavos 1915 TAXCO/GRO	75.00

R36 (23)	1 Peso 1914-15 GRO	15.00
R36a (23)	1 Peso 1914 COMO GRO	——
R36b (23)	1 Peso 1914 CAMPO MO	40.00
*R36c (23)	1 Peso 1915 TAXCO GRO	17.50

MEXICO
REVOLUTIONARY ISSUES

Rev: radiant sun over mountains

Fine

R37 (24) 2 Pesos 1914-15
GRO 20.00

R37a (24) 2 Pesos 1915
COMO 25.00

R37b (24) 2 Pesos 1915
SURIANA . . . . ——

R38 (25) 2 Pesos 1915
C.M.GRO 20.00

Types of Mexico Nos. 40-41

R39 (A25) 20 Centavos 1917
G . . . . ——

R39a (A25) 20 Centavos 1917
CACALOTEPEC/
GRO . . . . ——

R40 (B25) 50 Centavos 1917
GRO 100.00

Type of Mexico No. 20

R41 (C25) 1 Peso 1917 GO . . . . . ——

STATE OF JALISCO

Copper

R42 (26) 1 Centavo 1915 . . . . . . 12.50
R43 (27) 2 Centavos 1915 . . . . . 10.00
R44 (28) 5 Centavos 1915 . . . . . . 7.50

Obv: state arms

R45 (A28) 10 Centavos 1915 . . ——

STATE OF MEXICO

I. Amecameca, town

Copper or Brass

Obv: incuse eagle
Rev: incuse value

Fine

R47 (A56) 5 Centavos ND . . 125.00
R48 (B56) 10 Centavos ND . . 125.00
R49 (56a) 20 Centavos ND,
Brass (25mm) . . 35.00

R50 (56) 20 Centavos ND
(20mm) 10.00

R51 (57) 25 Centavos ND . . . 15.00
R52 (58) 50 Centavos ND 6.00

II. Tenancingo, town

Copper

R53 (60) 5 Centavos 1915 . . . . . 6.00
R54 (61) 10 Centavos 1916 . . . . 15.00
R55 (62) 20 Centavos 1915 . . . . 35.00

III. Texcoco, town

Reddish Clay

Type similar to Mexico No. 27

R56 (66) 1 Centavo 1915 . . . . . . ——

MEXICO
REVOLUTIONARY ISSUES

IV. Toluca, city

Bronze

Counterstamps on Mexico Nos. 27, 29

                                             Fine
R57 (67) "20 C" in circle on
    1 Centavo 1906..45.00
R58 (68) "40 C" in circle on
    2 Centavos 1906.37.50

Gray Cardboard

R59 (69) 5 Centavos 1915.....25.00

STATE OF MORELOS

Copper

Type similar to No. R69

R60 (30) 10 Centavos ND,
    1915, crude.......——
R62 (29) 2 Centavos 1915..——
R63 (A29) 5 Centavos 1915..——
R64 (30) 10 Centavos 1915..——
R65 (31) 20 Centavos 1915..12.50
R66 (—) 50 Centavos 1915..10.00

R69 (30) 10 Centavos 1916....10.00
R71 (32) 50 Centavos 1916....10.00

Silver

Type similar to No. R36

R72 (A32) 1 Peso 1916........——

STATE OF OAXACA
(Independent State)
Copper

                        V. Fine
R73 (33) 1 Centavo 1915....125.00
*R74 (34) 3 Centavos 1915...100.00
Restrikes or counterfeits of Nos. R73 and
R74 are known.

R75 (35) 1 Centavo 1915......30.00

R76 (36) 3 Centavos 1915,
      lg. flat-top 3.......7.50
R76a (36) 3 Centavos 1915,
      sm. round-top 3...10.00
R77 (38) 5 Centavos 1915.....1.50
R78 (39) 10 Centavos 1915.....2.00
R79 (40) 20 Centavos 1915.....2.50

Silver

R80 (41) 20 Centavos 1915.... ——
R81 (42) 50 Centavos 1915.....6.50
R82 (43) 1 Peso 1915.........5.00

MEXICO
REVOLUTIONARY ISSUES

V. Fine

R83 (44) 2 Pesos 1915........20.00

★R84 (45) 2 Pesos 1915, value
             as numeral......17.50
R84a (46) 2 Pesos 1915, value
             DOS spelled out...17.50

R85 (47) 2 Pesos 1915........25.00
R86 (48) 5 Pesos 1915........50.00

Gold

R87 (49) 5 Pesos 1915.......250.00

V. Fine

R88 (50) 10 Pesos 1915......200.00
R89 (51) 20 Pesos 1915......250.00

R90 (52) 60 Pesos 1916........——
Specimens of No. R90 in copper and silver
are patterns.

STATE OF PUEBLA
I. "Madero Brigade" Coinage

Copper

Fine

R91 (6) X Centavos 1915.....12.50
R92 (7) 20 Centavos 1915......7.50

MEXICO
REVOLUTIONARY ISSUES

II. Tetela del Oro y Ocampo

Copper

Fine

R93 (59) 2 Centavos 1915
(17mm)........7.00
R94 (59) 2 Centavos 1915
(21mm)........ ——
R95 (A59) 5 Centavos 1915.. ——
R96 (B59) 10 Centavos 1915.. ——
R97 (C59) 20 Centavos 1915.. ——

Some authorities feel Nos. R95-97 may be patterns. They also occur in other metals.

STATE OF SINALOA

Cast Silver

Fine

R98 (63) 20 Centavos ND
(1914), copy of
Mexico No. 18..150.00
R99 (64) 50 Centavos ND,
copy of No. 41..150.00
R100 (65) 8 Reales ND,
copy of No. 19...50.00
R101 (65) 1 Peso ND, copy
of No. 20.......50.00

Nos. R98-101 are crudely cast copies of earlier national coinage. Legends, when readable, will show dates of various original coins used to make molds.

MOMBASA

Now a seaport in Kenya. This town came under British administration in 1888. It was their first foothold in the present Kenya.

4 Pice = 1 Anna
16 Annas = 1 Rupee

Coinage obsolete.

Bronze

V. Fine

1 1 Pice (¼ Anna)
1888 (2 Varieties)........2.50

V. Fine

2 2 Annas 1890............11.00
3 ¼ Rupee 1890............12.00
4 ½ Rupee 1890............15.00
5 1 Rupee 1888............20.00

For later issues see East Africa.

MONACO

A small principality on the Mediterranean coast bounded by France, famous for its resort areas and Monte Carlo. Area: Less than one square mile. Population: 24,300.

100 Centimes = 1 Franc

MONACO

CHARLES III 1856-1889

Gold

			V. Fine
A1	20 Francs 1878-79		150.00
B1	100 Francs 1882-86		325.00

ALBERT I 1889-1922

Gold

1 100 Francs 1891-1904......275.00

LOUIS II 1922-1949

Aluminum-Bronze

Within Inner Circle:
REMB. JUSQU'AU
31 X.BRE 1926

(Good Until 31 December 1926)

2	50 Centimes 1924	10.00
3	1 Franc 1924	10.00
4	2 Francs 1924	12.00

No Inscription in Inner Circle

			V. Fine
5	50 Centimes 1926		10.00
6	1 Franc 1926		10.00
★**7**	2 Francs 1926		12.00

8	1 Franc ND (1945)	.70
9	2 Francs ND (1945)	.75

Aluminum

8a	1 Franc ND (1943)	.60
9a	2 Francs ND (1943)	.85

10 5 Francs 1945..............1.00

MONACO

Copper-Nickel

V. Fine

11 10 Francs 1946.............1.25
12 20 Francs 1947.............2.50

Ex. Fine

15 50 Francs 1950...........1.25
16 100 Francs Cop.-Nic. 1950..2.75

RAINIER III 1949-
Aluminum-Bronze

Unc.

13 10 Francs 1950-51...........75
14 20 Francs 1950-51..........1.00

Copper-Nickel

17 100 Francs 1956............1.25

Later issues in Current Coins of the World.

MONGOLIA, Outer
Mongolian People's Republic

In northeastern Asia, bounded on the north by U.S.S.R. A Chinese province until 1911, it patterned its People's Republic after the Soviet's. Principal industry: livestock raising. Area: 626,000 square miles. Population: 1,300,000. Languages: Mongolian and Russian. Capital: *Ulan Bator.*

100 Mongo = 1 Tukhrik   Year 1 = 1911

MONGOLIAN REPUBLIC

Mongolian Script

Copper

V. Fine

1 1 Mongo Yr. 15 (1925)......6.00
★2 2 Mongo Yr. 15 (24mm)....6.00
3 5 Mongo Yr. 15............7.50

MONGOLIA, Outer

Silver
V. Fine

4 10 Mongo Yr. 15 (1925)......5.00
5 15 Mongo Yr. 15 (19mm)....5.00
6 20 Mongo Yr. 15 (22mm)....6.50
7 50 Mongo Yr. 15 (27mm)...10.00
8 1 Tukhrik Yr. 15 (34mm)..17.50

Aluminum-Bronze

★10 1 Mongo Yr. 27 (1937).....3.50
11 2 Mongo (1937) 21 mm.....3.50
12 5 Mongo (1937)..........4.00

Copper-Nickel

★13 10 Mongo Yr. 27 (1937)....3.50
14 15 Mongo (1937) 21 mm....4.50
15 20 Mongo (1937)..........5.50

SOCIALIST MONGOLIA
Russian Script

Aluminum-Bronze

V. Fine

16 1 Mongo Yr. 35 (1945).....5.00
17 2 Mongo Yr. 35...........3.50
18 5 Mongo Yr. 35...........3.50

Copper-Nickel

19 10 Mongo Yr. 35 (1945).....3.00
20 15 Mongo Yr. 35...........3.50
21 20 Mongo Yr. 35...........4.00

Later issues in *Current Coins of the World.*

MONTENEGRO (Crna Gora)

A former kingdom north of Albania, now a part of Yugoslavia. Capital: *Cetinje.*

100 Para = 1 Perper

Coinage obsolete.

NICHOLAS I 1860-1918
As Prince 1860-1910

Bronze

V. Fine

1 1 Para 1906................5.00
2 2 Pare 1906-08............4.50

Nickel

V. Fine

3 10 Para 1906-08.............2.50
4 20 Para 1906-08.............3.50

Silver

5 1 Perper 1909...............7.50
6 2 Perpera 1910.............12.50
7 5 Perpera 1909.............80.00

MONTENEGRO

Gold

Silver

		V. Fine
8	10 Perpera 1910	200.00
9	20 Perpera 1910	250.00
10	100 Perpera 1910	2000.00

As King 1910-1918

Bronze

11	1 Para 1913-14	5.00
12	2 Pare 1913-14	4.00

Nickel

13	10 Para 1913-14	2.50
14	20 Para 1913-14	3.50

		V. Fine
15	1 Perper 1912-14	10.00
16	2 Perpera 1914	12.50
17	5 Perpera 1912-14	90.00

50th Year of Regency

Gold

18	10 Perpera 1910	200.00
← **19**	20 Perpera 1910	250.00
20	100 Perpera 1910	2500.00

MOROCCO

(Empire Chérifien, Maroc)

A monarchy on the northwest coast of Africa. It was formerly a French and Spanish protectorate. From this area all northwest Africa and most of the Spanish peninsula were ruled during the seventh century. Languages: Moorish-Arabic and Berber, French, and Spanish. Population: 15,000,000. Capital: *Rabat.*

50 Mazunas = 1 Dirhem	New Coinage:
10 Dirhems = 1 Rial to 1921	100 Centimes = 1 Franc 1921-59

Nineteenth Century denominations of the Moroccan coinage have been a source of some confusion. The basic unit is designated by the mints of various countries as follows:

> England—Dollars
> France—Piastres
> Germany—Rials

The Moors called them by various names. Those dated before 1320 A.H. (1902) are named from their weights. The largest piece which is dollar-size is valued at 10 dirhems or ounces. The Moors call this 10-Dirhem piece a Mitkal. In 1320 the weight was slightly reduced and the silver coin term changed to rial. The copper coins simply have the figures 1, 2, 5, and 10 which may be called Centimes, Centimos, or Mazunas in Morocco. Since 1920 the coinage has conformed to the French system.

MOROCCO

HASAN I 1873-1894

Bronze

C1   ½ Mazuna AH 1310   *Fine*
      (1893) 15.5mm....... ——

B1   1 Mazuna 1310
      (18.5mm)............

1   2½ Mazunas 1310
      (23.5mm)............ ——

★2   5 Mazunas 1310-11
      (28mm)............30.00

3   10 Mazunas 1310-11
      (34mm)............40.00

Other machine-struck bronze coins dated 1301-09 are now thought to be patterns.

Silver

4   ½ Dirhem A.H. 1299-1314
      (1882-96) 15mm........1.50

★5   1 Dirhem 1299-1314
      (17mm)..............1.75

★6   2½ Dirhems 1299-1314
      (26mm)..............2.00

7   5 Dirhems 1299-1314
      (33mm)..............5.00

8   10 Dirhems 1299........10.00

'ABD AL-AZIZ 1896-1908
First Coinage
Silver

9   ½ Dirhem A.H. 1313-19   *Fine*
      (1896-1901)...........3.00

★10   1 Dirhem 1313-18.......3.50

★11   2½ Dirhems 1313-18......5.00

12   5 Dirhems 1313-18......8.50

13   10 Dirhems 1313....*V. F.* 45.00

Nos. 9-22 have variations in Arabic inscriptions, size of numerals, etc. according to the mints, which were Fez, Birmingham, Berlin and Paris. (Illustration below is 10 Mazunas of Birmingham Mint.)

Second Coinage
Bronze

14   1 Mazuna A.H. 1320-21
      (1901-03).............3.00

15   2 Mazunas 1320-23......2.00

★16   5 Mazunas 1320-22......1.00

17   10 Mazunas 1320-23......1.25

No. 14 dated 1319 is probably a pattern.

MOROCCO

Silver

18 1/20 Rial A.H. 1320-21 *Fine*
  (1902-04) 15mm........1.75
★19 1/10 Rial 1320-21 (16.5mm)..3.00

★20 1/4 Rial 1320-21 (25mm)....2.50
21 1/2 Rial 1320-23 (32mm)....4.00
22 1 Rial 1320-21 (37mm)...10.00

HAFIZ 1908-1912

★23 1/4 Rial A.H. 1329 (1911)...1.75
24 1/2 Rial 1329..............4.50
25 1 Rial 1329..............8.50

YUSUF 1912-1927

Bronze

26 1 Mazuna AH 1330 (1912)..3.50

Fine
27 2 Mazunas 1330..........2.00
★28 5 Mazunas 1330-40
  (1912-22).............. .75
29 10 Mazunas 1330-40.......1.00

Silver

30 1/10 Rial A.H. 1331
  (1913)...............10.00

★31 1/4 Rial 1331..............8.00
32 1/2 Rial 1331-36...........4.00
33 1 Rial 1331-36...........7.50

Second Coinage

(MAROC — EMPIRE CHERIFIEN)

100 Centimes = 1 Franc

Copper-Nickel

V. Fine
34 25 Centimes ND (1921-26) . . .50

MOROCCO

Nickel

V. Fine

35 50 Centimes ND (1921-24).. .60
36 1 Franc ND.............. .75

V. Fine

43 5 Francs A.H. 1365 (1946)... .75

Copper-Nickel

MUHAMMAD BIN YUSUF
A.H. 1345-72 (1927-1953)

(Exiled 1953-55, became King Mohammed V in 1955.)

First Coinage

Silver

44 10 Francs A.H. 1366 (1947). .75
45 20 Francs A.H. 1366.......1.00

Third Coinage

Aluminum

37 5 Francs A.H. 1347-52
   (1929-34).............1.25
38 10 Francs 1347-52.........2.50
39 20 Francs 1347-52.........6.50

Unc.

46 1 Franc 1951.............. .10
47 2 Francs 1951............. .15

Nos. 46-47 were struck through 1967 with
no change of date.

Second Coinage

Aluminum-Bronze

40 50 Centimes 1945.......... .20
41 1 Franc 1945............. .25
42 2 Francs 1945............ .50

48 5 Francs A.H. 1370 (1951)... .20

MOROCCO

Aluminum-Bronze

Silver

Unc.
49 10 Francs A.H. 1371 (1952).. .30
50 20 Francs A.H. 1371........ .50

Unc.
52 100 Francs 1953........... 1.75
53 200 Francs 1953........... 3.25

Later issues in *Current Coins of the World.*

51 50 Francs A.H. 1371........ .75
Nos. 49-51 are still being struck with no
change of date.

MOZAMBIQUE (Moçambique)

Portuguese East Africa. It is a seacoast country of southeast Africa. About
400 square miles of German East Africa was added to it after the First World
War. Area: 297,730 square miles. Population: 6,790,000. Capital: *Lourenço
Marques.*

100 Centavos = 1 Escudo

Counterstamps

Silver

  *Crowned PM
in circle (1889)*

Fine
A1 On India rupee.......... 30.00
B1 On Austria No. 55........ 45.00

*Counterstamp: large PM
in oval (ca. 1889-95)*

C1 On India rupee.......... 25.00
D1 On Austria No. 55....... 40.00

Regular Issues

Bronze

V. Fine
1 10 Centavos 1936........... 1.25
2 20 Centavos 1936........... 1.50

MOZAMBIQUE

Copper-Nickel

V. Fine

3 50 Centavos 1936............1.50
4 1 Escudo 1936..............1.75

Silver

5 2½ Escudos 1935............2.00
6 5 Escudos 1935............2.50
7 10 Escudos 1936............7.50

New Reverse Arms

8 2½ Escudos 1938-51.......3.00
9 5 Escudos 1938-49........4.00
10 10 Escudos 1938..........10.00

Bronze

11 10 Centavos 1942........... .50
12 20 Centavos 1941........... .75
13 50 Centavos 1945..........1.00

V. Fine

14 1 Escudo 1945............1.50
15 20 Centavos 1949-50........ .25

Nickel-Bronze

16 50 Centavos 1950-51........ .60
17 1 Escudo 1950-51.......... .85

Decree of January 21, 1952
COLONIA DE omitted

Bronze

Unc.

18 50 Centavos 1953-57........ .20
19 1 Escudo 1953-65.......... .30

Copper-Nickel

20 2½ Escudos 1952-65........ .40

Silver

21 5 Escudos 1960............1.50
22 10 Escudos 1952-66........2.50
23 20 Escudos 1952-66........4.50

Later issues in Current Coins of the World.

MUSCAT AND OMAN

A sultanate on the southeast coast of the Arabian peninsula, consisting of the Oman district, Dhofar province, and capital city *Masqat (Muscat)*. Independent since 1650, it once owned Zanzibar and other coastal areas of Africa and Asia. Its economy is based on agriculture and nomadic herding, with petroleum becoming important. Area: 82,000 square miles. Language: Arabic.

4 Baizah (Baisa, Pice) = 1 Anna
64 Baizah = 1 India Rupee
200 Baizah = 1 Riyal, Maria Theresia Thaler

FESSUL BIN TURKEE
1888-1913

Copper

Fine
*1 ½₂ Anna A.H. 1311 (1894)..30.00
2 ¼ Anna 1311............15.00

Copper or Brass

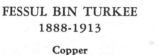

3 ¼ Anna 1312-19 (1895-1902).1.25

Many varieties of No. 3 include size and arrangement of lettering and Arabic inscriptions, omission of wreath, etc. Some are less crude than the example shown.

A3 ¼ Anna 1315............ .75

SA'ID BIN TAIMUR
1932-1970

Copper-Nickel

V. Fine
4 10 Baizah A.H. 1359 (1940)...3.50

5 20 Baizah 1359............5.00
6 50 Baizah 1359............6.50

7 2 Baizah A.H. 1365 (1946). .75

*8 5 Baizah 1365............1.25
10 20 Baizah 1365............2.00

Nos. 4, 5, 6, 11, 12 and 13 used only in Dhufar Province, Oman.

MUSCAT AND OMAN

Silver

11 ½ Dhufari Ryal   *V. Fine*
    AH 1367 (1948)........15.00

Later issues in *Current Coins of the World.*

NEJD (Najd)

Occupying the central desert highlands of the Arabian peninsula, Nejd was first unified as a sultanate in the late 18th century. Torn by strife until the early 1900's, it thereafter became the dominant power in the area. It was proclaimed a kingdom in 1927 and was united with the Hejaz in 1932 to form Saudi Arabia. Language: Arabic. Capital: *ar-Riyad (Riyadh)*.

40 Para = 1 Ghirsh
20 Ghirsh = 1 Riyal

Coinage obsolete.

'ABD AL-AZIZ IBN SA'UD
as Sultan and King of Nejd
1921-1932

Counterstamp:
incuse "Najd" in Arabic

Copies of the Nejd counterstamps on some or all of these silver types are believed to have been produced in recent years.

Billon

		Good
A1 On Turkish 10 Para, pre-1844		5.00
B1 On sim. 20 Para		5.00

Silver

		Fine
1 On Turkish or Egyptian 5 Ghirsh		15.00
2 On sim. 10 Ghirsh		25.00
2a On India Rupee		25.00
3 On sim. 20 Ghirsh		40.00
3a On Austria No. 55		40.00

For later issues see Saudi Arabia.

NEPAL

An independent kingdom in the Himalaya Mountains between India and Tibet, known for its mountains, including Mt. Everest. Languages: Newari (Nepali), Magar, Pahari. Population: 9,380,000. Capital: *Katmandu.*

32 Paisa = 16 Dhyak = 8 Ani = 4 Do-Ani = 2 Suka = 1 Mohar

In the reign of King Prithvi, coin dates are expressed in either the Saka or Samvat era (see page 7 for details), while only Samvat dates are used in later reigns. In the follow-ing listings the term "Saka" is always spelled out in full, and the abbreviation "S." refers only to Samvat dates.

NEPAL

PRITHVI 1881-1911 A.D.

Saka Dates 1803-33
Samvat Dates 1938-68

Copper

Fine

1 ¼ Paisa Saka 1818-19,
   Samvat 1951-64 (14mm) . . 7.50

Type: circular legends

★3 1 Paisa Saka 1810, Samvat
   1945-51 (21-24mm) 1.50

4 2 Paisa S. 1948-50
   (26mm) 2.50

Type: legends in wreaths

A3 1 Paisa S. 1949-64 . . . . .1.50

Type: legends in squares

★B3 1 Paisa S. 1959-68 . . . . .1.25

B4 2 Paisa 1949-50 . . . . .6.00

Ex. Fine

5 ¼ Paisa S. (19)68
   (1911) 16mm 10.00

6 ½ Paisa (19)64, 68
   (19mm) 10.00

★7 1 Paisa 1964, 68 (23mm) . .10.00

8 2 Paisa 1964, 68
   (26.5mm) 10.00

Nos. 5-8 are said to have been issued only
in presentation sets.

 Silver

Rev: incuse mirror image of obverse

V. Fine

A9 ¹⁄₁₂₈ Mohar ND (6mm) . . .10.00

9 ¹⁄₆₄ Mohar ND 7.50

★10 ¹⁄₃₂ Mohar ND (11mm) . . .7.50

11 ¹⁄₁₆ Mohar ND (13mm) . .10.00

12 ⅛ Mohar ND 10.00

★13 ¼ Mohar Saka 1803-27
   (1881-1905) 18mm 3.00

13a ¼ Mohar Saka 1833
   (15.5mm) 3.50

★14 ½ Mohar 1803-29
   (21mm) 2.50

14a ½ Mohar 1833 (19mm) . . .3.00

NEPAL

QUEEN LAKSMI DIVYESWARI (Regent)

Silver

Ex. Fine

A26 ½ Mohar 1971 (1914) 5.00

V. Fine

15 1 Mohar Saka 1803-03
    (26mm, 5.5 grams) 4.00
16 2 Mohar 1804-31 (26mm,
    11 grams, thick) 8.00
★16a 2 Mohar 1832-33 (29mm,
    11 grams) 8.00
17 4 Mohar 1817, 33 (29mm,
    22 grams, thick) 75.00

B26 1 Mohar 1971 . . . . 6.00

Gold

C26 1 Mohar 1971 . . . . 100.00

Gold

Rev: incuse mirror image of obverse

★18 ¹⁄₁₂₈ Mohar ND 20.00
19 ¹⁄₃₂ Mohar ND 20.00
20 ¹⁄₁₆ Mohar ND, (18)33 . . 20.00
21 ⅛ Mohar ND, (18)33 . . . 30.00

TRIVHUVANA, 1st Reign
Samvat 1968-2007 (1911-50)

Copper

Fine

27 1 Paisa 1969-77 (1912-20) . . . 1.50

22 ¼ Mohar 1808-33 . . . . 50.00
23 ½ Mohar 1805-33 . . . . 65.00
24 1 Mohar 1805-33 . . . . . . 100.00
A24 ½ Ashrafi 1805-26
    (6.2 gr.) 125.00
★25 1 Ashrafi 1805-33
    (12.4 gr.) 175.00
26 2 Rupees 1811-33
    (23.2 gr.) 250.00

28 ½ Paisa 1978-85 (1921-28) 10.00
★29 1 Paisa 1975-87 (1918-30) . 2.00
30 2 Paisa 1976-87 . . . . 1.50
31 5 Paisa 1976-88 . . . . 3.00

NEPAL

Silver

Rev: incuse mirror image of obverse
V. Fine

A32 ⅟₁₂₈ Mohar ND 30.00

32 ¼ Mohar 1969-70
(1912-13) 16mm. 1.25
★33 ½ Mohar 1968, 70 . . . . .2.00

Designs similar to Nos. 15-17

34 1 Mohar 1968-71. . . . . .2.50
35 2 Mohar 1968-89 (29mm) . .4.50
36 4 Mohar 1971. . . . . .50.00

Gold

37 ½ Mohar 1969 (1912) 50.00
38 1 Mohar 1969-75. . . . . . . .100.00
39 1 Ashrafi 1969-89
(12.4 gr.). 175.00

Decimal System
Samvat 1989 (1932)

100 Paisa = 1 Rupee

Copper

Rev: Trident in center

40 1 Paisa 1990-97 (1933-40)
23mm. 2.50
★41 2 Paisa 1992. . . . . .5.00
42 5 Paisa 1991-97 (30mm). . . .2.50

Rev: Sword in center

V. Fine

★A41 2 Paisa 1992-97
(27mm). 2.00
A41a 2 Paisa 1992-99
(25mm). 1.25

Reduced Weight Copper

A42 1 Dam 2000, 04
(14mm). 25.00
B42 ½ Paisa 2004 (16mm) . . .25.00
43 1 Paisa 2005 (1948)
20mm. 1.25
★44 2 Paisa 1999-2003
(23mm). 75

Brass

43a 1 Paisa 2000-06. 50
44a 2 Paisa 1999-2010. 75

Copper-Nickel-Zinc

45 5 Paisa 2000-10
(1943-53). 1.00

NEPAL

Silver

V. Fine

A45 ¹⁄₁₆ Rupee (19)96 . . . . 17.50

46 20 Paisa 1989-2004
(1932-47) 1.00

★47 50 Paisa 1989-2005 . . . . 2.00
48 1 Rupee 1989-2005 . . . . . . 3.50

Billon

46a 20 Paisa 2006-10
(1949-53) 75
47a 50 Paisa 2005-10 . . . . 1.25
48a 1 Rupee 2005-11 . . . . 2.50

Gold

50 (B48) ¼ Rupee 1995
(1938) 50.00
51 (C48) ½ Rupee 1995-
2005 . . . . 100.00
52 (D48) 1 Rupee 1995-
2005 . . . . 150.00
53 (E48) 2 Rupees 2005 . . . . . 200.00

Note: Because of extensive catalog
revisions, new numbers have been
assigned in the 10th edition, starting
with No. 50. The original numbers
are given in parentheses.

JNANENDRA
S. 2007 (1950-1951)

Billon

V. Fine

54 (A48) 50 Paisa 2007 . . . . . . ———
★55 (49) 1 Rupee 2007 . . . . . 6.00

TRIVHUVANA, 2nd Reign
S. 2007-2011 (1951-1955)

Nos. 43-45 and 46a-48a were resumed during
this period.

★56 (54) 50 Paisa 2010-11   *Unc.*
(1953-54) 1.75
57 (55) 1 Rupee 2010-11 . . . . 3.50

General Coinage
S. 2010-14 (1953-57)

Nos. 58-65 do not bear the name of the
ruler, and were continued unchanged into
the reign of Mahendra.

Brass

58 (A55) 1 Paisa 2010-12
(18mm) 1.00
★59 (A50) 2 Paisa 2010-11
(21mm) 1.00
59a (56) 2 Paisa 2012-14
(20mm) 35

NEPAL

Unc.
61 (57) 4 Paisa 2012 75

Bronze

62 (50, 58) 5 Paisa 2010-14 50

63 (52, 59) 10 Paisa 2010-12 60

Copper-Nickel

Designs similar to No. 63

Unc.
64 (A52) 20 Paisa 2010-11
(18mm) 3.50
65 (53, 60) 25 Paisa 2010-14
(19mm) 75

MAHENDRA
S. 2012-28 (1955-72)
Copper-Nickel

★82 (A60) 25 Paisa 2015-23
(2 var.) 75
83 (61) 50 Paisa 2011-23
(2 var.) 1.00
84 (62) 1 Rupee 2012-23
(3 var.) 3.00

Gold
85 (—) ⅕ Rupee 2012
(2.33 gr.) 20.00
86 (—) ¼ Rupee 2012
(2.91 gr.) 20.00
87 (E62) ½ Rupee 2012-19 . . . 30.00
88 (F62) 1 Rupee 2012-19 . . . 50.00
89 (G62) 2 Rupees 2012 . . . . . 75.00

Later issues in *Current Coins of the World.*

NETHERLANDS
(Koningrijk der Nederlanden)

A constitutional hereditary monarchy in western Europe between Germany and Belgium. Much of the land is below sea level and a system of dikes has been constructed to reclaim land and control the North Sea. It is the most densely populated country in the world. Over fifty percent of the land is in holdings of 10 acres or less. Most famous exports are cheese and dairy products and tulip bulbs. Land area: 15,800 square miles. Population: 13,300,000. Capital: *Amsterdam.*   100 Cents = 1 Gulden

WILLEM III 1849-1890
Copper
Types of Willem I and Willem II

Fine
1 ½ Cent 1850-77 75
2 1 Cent 1860-77 75

NETHERLANDS

General Bronze Coinage

(Under both William III and Wilhelmina.)

Fine

3 ½ Cent 1878-1906......... .50
4 1 Cent 1877-1907......... .35
★5 2½ Cents 1877-1906........ .50

(Several varieties exist of Nos. 3-5.)

Silver

6 5 Cents 1850-87 ....1.50
7 10 Cents 1849-90.........3.00
8 25 Cents 1849-90........10.00
9 ½ Gulden 1853-68......10.00
10 1 Gulden 1851-66......7.50
★11 2½ Gulden 1850-74......12.50

Gold

V. F.

12 5 Gulden 1850-51.......300.00
13 10 Gulden 1850-51........400.00
14 20 Gulden 1850-53........900.00

V. Fine

A16 10 Gulden 1876-89......50.00
B16 10 Gulden 1875 (Date at
    top of Coat of Arms)..50.00

Trade Coins

Knight Standing, Reverse Plaque

15 1 Ducat 1849-1960......30.00
16 2 Ducats 1854-67........——

WILHELMINA 1890-1948

First Coinage — Child Head

For first bronze issues of Wilhelmina see Nos. 3-5 under William III.

Silver

Fine

20 10 Cents 1892-97...........5.00
21 25 Cents 1892-97...........6.50
22 1 Gulden 1892-97 ....12.50

Gold

V. Fine

28 10 Gulden 1892-97........60.00

NETHERLANDS

Second Coinage
Copper-Nickel

Fine

33 5 Cents 1907-09...........2.00

Young Head
Silver

23 10 Cents 1898-1901.......4.00
23a 10 Cents 1903 (Large Head) 4.00
23b 10 Cents 1904-06 (Small Head,
Legend extends beneath head) 4.50
24 25 Cents 1898-1906.......7.50

25 ½ Gulden 1898........17.50
25a ½ Gulden 1904-09 without
50C below arms......7.50
*26 1 Gulden 1898-1901....15.00
26a 1 Gulden 1904-09 without
100C below arms....12.50
V. Fine
27 2½ Gulden 1898......225.00
Gold

29 10 Gulden 1898.........250.00

Third Coinage
Bronze

E.F.

35 ½ Cent 1909-40..........25
36 1 Cent 1913-41..........25
37 2½ Cents 1912-41..........35
For coins like No. 36 dated 1942-60, see
listings for colonial use following No. 52.

Copper-Nickel

34 5 Cents 1913-40...........50
For similar coin dated 1943, see No. 34a in
listings for colonial use.

Adult Head

Silver   V. Fine
39 10 Cents 1910-25...........1.00
40 25 Cents 1910-25..........2.00

41 ½ Gulden 1910-19.........5.00
42 1 Gulden 1910-17.........6.50

Gold

31 5 Gulden 1912..........100.00
30 10 Gulden 1911-17........ 50.00

NETHERLANDS

Fourth Coinage — Older Head

Silver

Ex. Fine

43 10 Cents 1926-45.......... .25
44 25 Cents 1926-45.......... .35

Nos. 43-44 dated 1941 or 1943 must have a caduceus or acorn mint mark, respectively. For identical 1941-43 coins with palm tree mint mark, see listings for colonial use below.

Reverse design similar to Nos. 41-42

45 ½ Gulden 1921-30 .... *V. F.* 1.25
46 1 Gulden 1922-45 .... 1.50
47 2½ Gulden 1929-40........ 4.50

For 1943 coins like Nos. 46-47, but with palm tree mint mark, see Nos. 46a-47a colonial issues below.

Gold

32 10 Gulden 1925-33 .... 50.00

World War II
Nazi Occupation

Zinc

V. Fine

48 1 Cent 1941-44............. .25

49 2½ Cents 1941-42......... 3.00

50 5 Cents 1941-43............ 1.00

V. Fine

51 10 Cents 1941-43........... .75

52 25 Cents 1941-43........... .75

Netherlands Types for
Colonial Use Only

A. For Surinam and Curacao

Bronze

Unc.

36b 1 Cent 1942, 57-60........ 1.00

Brass

Ex. Fine

36a 1 Cent 1943 (for Surinam only).................... .75

Copper-Nickel-Zinc

34a 5 Cents 1943............. 1.25

Silver
Palm tree mint mark

43a 10 Cents 1941-43.......... .25
44a 25 Cents 1941-43.......... .35

B. For Netherlands East Indies

Silver

46a 1 Gulden 1943.......... 2.00
47a 2½ Gulden 1943......... 5.00

NETHERLANDS

Postwar Issues

Bronze

Ex. Fine
53 1 Cent 1948. 10

54 5 Cents 1948. 20

Nickel

55 10 Cents 1948. 15
56 25 Cents 1948. 25

JULIANA 1948-

Reverse Same as Wilhelmina Issues

Bronze

Unc.
57 1 Cent 1950- 10
58 5 Cents 1950-. 10

Nickel
59 10 Cents 1950- 15
60 25 Cents 1950- 25

Silver

61 1 Gulden 1954-67 . . . . .1.25
62 2½ Gulden 1959-66 . . . . .3.00

Gold Trade Coin — (See Netherlands East Indies No. 16)

Later issues in Current Coins of the World.

NETHERLANDS ANTILLES
(Nederlandse Antillen)

Made up of two groups of islands in the West Indies. Of the total area of 381 square miles, the island of Curacao comprises almost half. Principal industry is oil refining. Population: 207,000. Capital: *Willemstad*.

100 Cents = 1 Gulden

JULIANA 1948-

Bronze

Unc.
1 1 Cent 1952-68. 10

Unc.
2 2½ Cents 1956-65. 15

NETHERLANDS ANTILLES

Copper-Nickel

Unc.
3 (6) 5 Cents 1957-70.......... .25

Silver

4 (2) 1/10 Gulden 1954-70....... .40
5 (3) 1/4 Gulden 1954-70....... .65

Unc.
6 (4) 1 Gulden 1952-70...... 1.50
7 2½ Gulden 1964......... 5.00

Later issues in Current Coins of the World.

NETHERLANDS EAST INDIES
(Nederlandsch Indie)

Now (except for western half of New Guinea) the Republic of Indonesia. Between Asia and Australia, it is composed of about 3,000 islands. After the Japanese occupation in the early 1940's, and subsequent clashes between Netherlands and Indonesian troops, a democracy was formed in 1945. Capital: *Batavia*.

100 Cents = 1 Gulden
Coinage obsolete.

Inscriptions in Malay-Arabic and Javanese

Silver

Fine
4 1/20 Gulden 1854-55.......... 5.00
5 1/10 Gulden 1854-1901 .... 1.50
6 1/4 Gulden 1854-1901 .... 1.00

Copper

Fine
1 ½ Cent 1856-1909.......... .75
2 1 Cent 1855-1912.......... .50
3 2½ Cents 1856-1913......... .75

12 1/10 Gulden 1903-09......... 1.25
13 1/4 Gulden 1903-09......... 1.25

NETHERLANDS EAST INDIES

V. Fine

14 1/10 Gulden 1910-45 25
15 1/4 Gulden 1910-45 (Rims
    flat or raised) 40

Trade Gold Coin

For Netherlands trade ducats, many
of which were used in the Netherlands East Indies, see also Netherlands Nos. 15 and 16.

16 1 Ducat 1849-1960 . . . . .30.00

Copper-Nickel

17 5 Cents 1913-22 75

Bronze

18 1/2 Cent 1914-45 25

        V. Fine

19 1 Cent 1914-29 30
20 2 1/2 Cents 1914-45 35

21 1 Cent 1936-45 20

World War II coins dated 1941-45
were struck in the United States at
Philadelphia, San Francisco and Den-
ver. (P, S or D mint marks and palm.)

1 and 2 1/2 Gulden Netherlands types dated
1943 were made for the East Indies (see
Netherlands Nos. 46a and 47a).

WORLD WAR II
Japanese Occupation Issues

Dated in the Japanese Calendar

Tin Alloy

22 1 Sen 2603-04 (1943-44) 35.00
23 5 Sen 2603 . . . .——

Figure of Native Puppet

24 10 Sen 2603-04 . . . . .25.00

For later issues see INDONESIA.

NEW BRUNSWICK (See Canada)

NEW CALEDONIA
(Nouvelle Caledonie)

An island halfway between Australia and the Fiji Islands. One of the many
French possessions in the South Pacific. Area: 8,548 square miles. Languages:
French and Melanesian dialects. Capital: *Noumea.*

Aluminum

100 Centimes = 1 Franc

		Unc.
1	50 Centimes 1949	.20
2	1 Franc 1949	.35
3	2 Francs 1949	.50
4	5 Francs 1952	1.00

Later issues in *Current Coins of the World.*

NEWFOUNDLAND (See Canada)
NEW GUINEA

Now an Australian territory administered jointly with Papua.

12 Pence = 1 Shilling   20 Shillings = 1 Pound

GEORGE V 1910-1936
Copper-Nickel

		E.F.
1	½ Penny 1929	300.00
2	1 Penny 1929	300.00

		V.F.
3	3 Pence 1935	2.50

4	6 Pence 1935	3.00

Silver

5	1 Shilling 1935-36	1.50

EDWARD VIII 1936
Bronze

		Unc.
6	1 Penny 1936	2.50

GEORGE VI 1936-1952

		Ex. Fine
7	1 Penny 1938-44	2.00

Copper-Nickel

8	3 Pence 1944	2.00
9	6 Pence 1943	3.00

NEW GUINEA

Silver
Ex. Fine
10 1 Shilling 1938-45.........1.50

NEW ZEALAND

Lying east of Australia, New Zealand is two large islands plus many smaller dependencies lying southeast of Australia. It is a self-governing member of the British Commonwealth. Exports: sheep, dairy products. Area: 103,736 square miles. Population: 2,900,000. Capital: *Wellington.*

12 Pence = 1 Shilling
2 Shillings = 1 Florin

5 Shillings = 1 Crown
20 Shillings = 1 Pound

GEORGE V 1910-1936

Silver

V. Fine
1 3 Pence 1933-36............1.00

V. Fine
4 1 Florin 1933-36............3.50

2 6 Pence 1933-36............1.50

3 1 Shilling 1933-35..........2.00

5 ½ Crown 1933-35..........6.00

NEW ZEALAND

Waitangi Treaty

Issued to mark the Silver Jubilee of
King George V.

Unc.
6 1 Crown 1935............850.00

GEORGE VI 1936-1952
Bronze

V.F.
7 ½ Penny 1940-47............25

8 1 Penny 1940-47............35

Silver
Reverse designs same as Nos. 1-5

9 3 Pence 1937-46............75

V. Fine
10 6 Pence 1937-46..........1.25
11 1 Shilling 1937-46.........1.75
12 1 Florin 1937-46..........2.50
13 ½ Crown 1937-46..........3.75

Centennial Half Crown

Ex. Fine
14 ½ Crown 1940........... 22.50

Copper-Nickel
Designs same as Nos. 9-13
V. Fine
15 3 Pence 1947...............75
16 6 Pence 1947..............1.25
17 1 Shilling 1947.............1.75
18 1 Florin 1947..............3.00

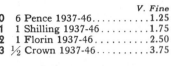

19 ½ Crown 1947.............4.00

NEW ZEALAND

New Legend:
KING GEORGE THE SIXTH

Designs similar to Nos. 7-13

Bronze
		V. Fine
20	½ Penny 1949-52	.40
21	1 Penny 1949-52	.50

Copper-Nickel
22	3 Pence 1948-52	.35
23	6 Pence 1948-52	.75

24	1 Shilling 1948-52	1.25
25	1 Florin 1948-51	1.75
26	½ Crown 1948-51	2.50

Proposed Royal Visit

Silver

		Unc.
27	1 Crown 1949	15.00

ELIZABETH II 1952-

Reverse designs same as Nos. 7-13

Bronze
		Unc.
28	½ Penny 1953-65	.15
29	1 Penny 1953-65	.20

Copper-Nickel
30	3 Pence 1953-65	.20
31	6 Pence 1953-65	.40
32	1 Shilling 1953-65	.75
33	1 Florin 1953-65	1.50
34	½ Crown 1953-65	2.00

35	1 Crown 1953	16.00

Coronation Proof Set of Nos.
28-35 in case 1953 . . . . 85.00

Later issues in Current Coins of the World.

NICARAGUA

Located in the middle of Central America, it is bounded on the north by Honduras, on the south by Costa Rica. Chief products: gold, coffee, cattle, mahogany, bananas, fruit. Area: 57,145 square miles. Population: 2,000,000. Capital: *Managua*.

100 Centavos = 1 Peso (Until 1912)
100 Centavos = 1 Cordoba (1912-)

		Fine
8	10 Centavos 1887	2.00
9	20 Centavos 1887	3.00

Copper-Nickel

		Fine
1	1 Centavo 1878	6.00

| **2** | 5 Centavos 1898 (ESTADO) | 1.00 |

| **3** | 5 Centavos (REPCA) 1899 | 1.00 |

Silver

4	5 Centavos 1880	5.00
5	10 Centavos 1880	4.00
6	20 Centavos 1880	5.00

| **7** | 5 Centavos 1887 | 3.00 |

Bronze

		V. F.
10	½ Centavo 1912-37	.60
11	1 Centavo 1912-40	.40

Copper-Nickel

| **12** | 5 Centavos 1912-40 | .50 |

Silver

13	10 Centavos 1912-36	1.00
14	25 Centavos 1912-36	1.75
15	50 Centavos 1912-29	4.00
16	1 Cordoba 1912	40.00

Copper-Nickel

Edge: lettered BNN

		Unc.
17	5 Centavos 1946-56	.25
18	10 Centavos 1939-56	.35
19	25 Centavos 1939-56	.50
20	50 Centavos 1939-56	.85

NICARAGUA

Brass

Designs Same as Nos. 17-19
Reeded Edge

V. Fine

22 5 Centavos 1943 (21 mm.)..1.00
23 10 Centavos 1943 (24 mm.)..1.50
24 25 Centavos 1943 (27 mm.)..1.75

V. Fine
21 1 Centavo 1943 75

Later issues in *Current Coins of the World.*

NIGERIA—see *Current Coins of the World*
NORTH KOREA—see *Current Coins of the World*
NORTH VIETNAM—see VIETNAM

NORWAY
(Norge)

West section of the Scandinavian peninsula in northern Europe. It is a constitutional hereditary monarchy with legislative power vested in a two-house *Storting* or legislature. It is primarily a maritime nation since less than a third of its land is cultivated. Its merchant marine ranks third in the world. Area: 125,064 square miles. Population: 3,900,000. Capital: *Oslo.*

120 Skilling = 1 Speciedaler (to 1873)
100 Øre = 1 Krone (since 1873)

Note: Because of extensive revisions, new numbers have been assigned in the 11th edition. The original numbers are given in parentheses.

UNION WITH SWEDEN— CARL XV 1859-1872

Copper

Fine
1 ½ Skilling 1863 . . . . .3.50

2 ½ Skilling 1867 . . . . .3.00
3 1 Skilling 1870 . . . . .3.50

Billon

Fine
4 **(8)** 2 Skilling 1870-71 . . . . . . .2.50
5 **(9)** 3 Skilling 1868-69 . . . . . . .4.00
6 (10) 4 Skilling 1871 . . . . .5.00

Silver

7 (4) 12 Skilling 1861-62 . . . .125.00
8 (5) 24 Skilling 1861-62 . . . . .75.00
★9 (6) ½ Speciedaler 1861-62. .85.00
10 (7) 1 Speciedaler 1861-62.150.00

NORWAY

OSCAR II 1872-1905
First Coinage

Billon

Silver

Second Coinage
Transition to Decimal System

Silver

Gold

Third Coinage
Decimal System

Bronze

Silver

NORWAY

Gold

V. Fine

28 (30) 10 Kroner 1877, 1902 . 150.00
29 (31) 20 Kroner 1876-1902 . . 135.00

INDEPENDENT NORWAY—
HAAKON VII 1905-57

First Coinage

Bronze

Fine

30 (32) 1 Øre 1906-07 . . . . 1.50
31 (33) 2 Øre 1906-07 . . . . 1.75
32 (34) 5 Øre 1907 . . . . 2.50

Independence Commemorative

Silver

Ex. Fine

33   (47) 2 Kroner 1906 . . . . . . 22.50
33a (47a) 2 Kroner 1907
       Smaller shield 27.50

"Watch on the Border" Commemorative

Ex. Fine

34 (52) 2 Kroner 1907 . . . . 100.00

Second Coinage

V. Fine

35 1 Øre 1908-52 25
36 2 Øre 1909-52 35
37 5 Øre 1908-52 50

Silver

38 (48) 10 Øre 1909-19 . . . . 1.00

39 (49) 25 Øre 1909-19 . . . . 1.00

40 (50) Øre 1909-19 . . . . 2.00

NORWAY

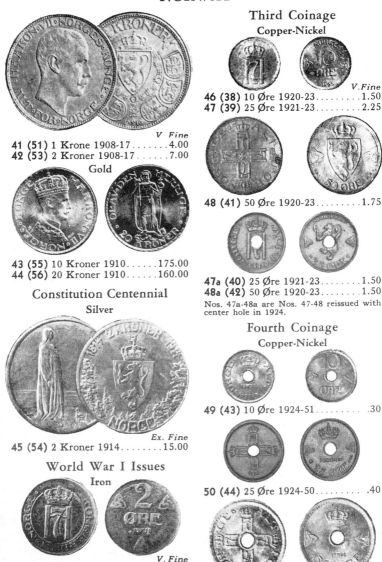

Third Coinage
Copper-Nickel

V.Fine
46 (38) 10 Øre 1920-23 . . . . 1.50
47 (39) 25 Øre 1921-23 . . . . 2.25

V Fine
41 (51) 1 Krone 1908-17 . . . . 4.00
42 (53) 2 Kroner 1908-17 . . . . . . 7.00

Gold

48 (41) 50 Øre 1920-23 . . . . 1.75

43 (55) 10 Kroner 1910 . . . . . 175.00
44 (56) 20 Kroner 1910 . . . . . 160.00

47a (40) 25 Øre 1921-23 . . . . 1.50
48a (42) 50 Øre 1920-23 . . . . 1.50
Nos. 47a-48a are Nos. 47-48 reissued with
center hole in 1924.

Constitution Centennial
Silver

Fourth Coinage
Copper-Nickel

49 (43) 10 Øre 1924-51 30

Ex. Fine
45 (54) 2 Kroner 1914 . . . . 15.00

World War I Issues
Iron

50 (44) 25 Øre 1924-50 40

V. Fine
35a (57) 1 Øre 1918-21 . . . . 2.00
36a (58) 2 Øre 1917-20 . . . . 2.00
37a (59) 5 Øre 1917-20 . . . . 3.50

51 (45) 50 Øre 1926-49 75

NORWAY

V. Fine

52 (46) 1 Krone 1925-51 . . . . . . 1.25

Ex. Fine

50a (67) 25 Øre 1942 . . . . 15.00
51a (68) 50 Øre 1942 . . . . 15.00

World War II Issues
German Occupation
Iron

53 (60) 1 Øre 1941-45 60
54 (61) 2 Øre 1943-45 . . . . 1.00
55 (62) 5 Øre 1941-45 . . . . 1.25

Zinc

56 (63) 10 Øre 1941-45 75
57 (64) 25 Øre 1943-45 . . . . 1.00
58 (65) 50 Øre 1941-45 . . . . 1.75

Government in Exile
(Struck in London)
Nickel-Brass

Ex. Fine

49a (66) 10 Øre 1942 . . . . 15.00

Postwar Issues
Bronze

Unc.

59 (69) 1 Øre 1952-57 10
60 (70) 2 Øre 1952-57 15
61 (71) 5 Øre 1952-57 25

Copper-Nickel

62 (72) 10 Øre 1951-57 25
63 (73) 25 Øre 1952-57 35

64 (74) 50 Øre 1953-57 60
65 (75) 1 Krone 1951-57 . . . . . . 1.00

Later issues in *Current Coins of the World.*

NOVA SCOTIA (See Canada)

PAKISTAN

When India was given independence in 1947, the two predominantly Muslim areas were separated to form the dominion of Pakistan. It became a republic within the British Commonwealth in 1956. The eastern section broke away in late 1971 to form Bangladesh, whereupon West Pakistan left the Commonwealth. The economy is primarily agricultural. Area (to 1971): 365,529 square miles. Languages: Urdu, Bengali. Capital: *Islamabad.*

3 Pies = 1 Pice   4 Pice = 1 Anna   16 Annas = 1 Rupee

PAKISTAN

Bronze

V. Fine

1 1 Pice 1948-52 10

Copper-Nickel

2 ½ Anna 1948-51 15

3 1 Anna 1948-52
   (Crescent Facing Right) 20
3a 1 Anna 1950
   (Crescent Facing Left) 3.00

4 2 Annas 1948-51
   (Crescent Facing Right) 25
4a 2 Annas 1950
   (Crescent Facing Left) 4.00

Nickel

5 ¼ Rupee 1948-51
   (Crescent Facing Right) . . .30

V. Fine

5a ¼ Rupee 1950
   (Crescent Facing Left) . .10.00
6 ½ Rupee 1948-51 60
7 1 Rupee 1948-49 . . . . .1.25

Bronze

Unc.

8 1 Pie 1951-56 10

Nickel-Brass

9 1 Pice 1953-59 15

10 ½ Anna 1953-58 20

Copper-Nickel

11 1 Anna 1953-58 25

12 2 Annas 1953-59 50

Later issues in Current Coins of the World.

PALESTINE

From the earliest times this area has been the bridge between Asia and Africa. The Turks lost it in 1917 during World War I, and in 1920 the League of Nations placed it under British administration. After long and bitter disputes between Jews and Arabs, UNO in 1948 divided the country: ⅘ became the new state of Israel, and the remainder was split between Jordan and Egypt.

1000 Mils = 1 Pound   Coinage obsolete.

Hebrew-English-Arabic Legends

Bronze

		V. F.
1	1 Mil 1927-47	.50
2	2 Mils 1927-47	.75

Bronze   V. Fine

3a	5 Mils 1942-44	2.00
4a	10 Mils 1942-43	4.00
5a	20 Mils 1942-44	6.00

Silver

Copper-Nickel

6	50 Mils 1927-42	4.00

		V. F.
3	5 Mils 1927-47	1.00
4	10 Mils 1927-47	1.50
5	20 Mils 1927-41	4.00

7	100 Mils 1927-42	6.00

PANAMA

The Isthmus of Panama joining Central and South America. It is bisected by the United States Panama Canal Zone. It became an independent nation in 1903. Exports: bananas, pineapple, cocoa, coconuts, sugar. Capital: *Panamá*.

100 Centesimos = 1 Balboa

Copper-Nickel

		V. F.
1	½ Centesimo 1907	.85

V. Fine

2	2½ Centesimos 1907 MEDIOS	1.00
2a	2½ Centesimos 1916 MEDIO	1.00

PANAMA

V. Fine
3 2½ Centesimos 1929........1.00

4 5 Centesimos 1929-32...... .65

Silver

5 2½ Centesimos 1904 (Called
   "Panama Pill")..........9.00
6 5 Centesimos 1904-16......2.50
7 10 Centesimos 1904........4.00
8 25 Centesimos 1904........7.50
9 50 Centesimos 1904-05.....20.00

NEW LAW 1930
Bronze

10 1 Centesimo 1935-37........2.00

*11** 1¼ Centesimos 1940......1.00

Copper-Nickel
V. Fine
12 2½ Centesimos 1940......1.00

Silver

Unc.
13 1/10 Balboa 1930-47, 62..... .75
14 ¼ Balboa 1930-47, 62....1.50
15 ½ Balboa 1930-47, 62....3.00

Because new dies were cut at the
London Mint, design details are more
distinct on 1962 issues (Nos. 13-15).

V. Fine
16 1 Balboa 1931-47..........5.50

50th Anniversary
of the Republic — 1953

(Nos. 17-21)

Bronze

17 1 Centesimo 1953........... .20

PANAMA

Silver

		V. Fine
18	⅒ Balboa 1953	.60
19	¼ Balboa 1953	1.50
20	½ Balboa 1953	2.75
21	1 Balboa 1953 (Reverse	Unc.
	Similar to No. 16)	15.00

Later issues in *Current Coins of the World.*

PARAGUAY

An inland country of South America. Products include oranges, timber, tobacco, beef products, corn, and cotton. Area: 157,000 square miles. Languages: Spanish and Guaraní. Capital: *Asunción.*

100 Centesimos = 1 Peso
100 Centavos = 1 Peso   100 Centimos = 1 Guaraní

Copper

		Fine
1	1/12 Real 1845	7.50

Silver

		V. Fine
5	1 Peso 1889	110.00

Copper-Nickel

2	1 Centesimo 1870	5.00
3	2 Centesimos 1870	4.00
4	4 Centesimos 1870	6.00
4a	4 Centesimos 1870,	
	crude local issue	40.00

6	5 Centavos 1900-03	2.25
7	10 Centavos 1900-03	2.00
8	20 Centavos 1900-03	2.50

PARAGUAY

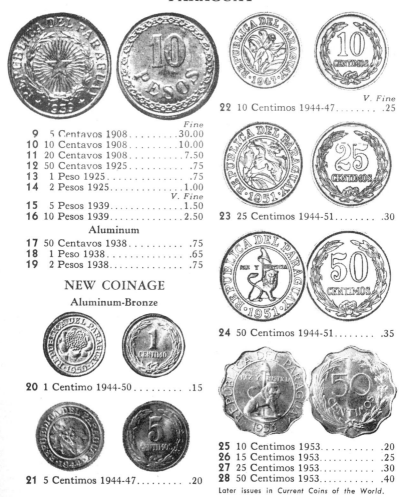

		Fine
9	5 Centavos 1908	30.00
10	10 Centavos 1908	10.00
11	20 Centavos 1908	7.50
12	50 Centavos 1925	.75
13	1 Peso 1925	.75
14	2 Pesos 1925	1.00

		V. Fine
15	5 Pesos 1939	1.50
16	10 Pesos 1939	2.50

Aluminum

17	50 Centavos 1938	.75
18	1 Peso 1938	.65
19	2 Pesos 1938	.75

NEW COINAGE

Aluminum-Bronze

20	1 Centimo 1944-50	.15

21	5 Centimos 1944-47	.20

		V. Fine
22	10 Centimos 1944-47	.25

23	25 Centimos 1944-51	.30

24	50 Centimos 1944-51	.35

25	10 Centimos 1953	.20
26	15 Centimos 1953	.25
27	25 Centimos 1953	.30
28	50 Centimos 1953	.40

Later issues in *Current Coins of the World.*

PERSIA (IRAN)

Between the Tigris and Indus Rivers in southwest Asia. A constitutional monarchy since 1906, it is one of the oldest countries in the world, being mentioned in the Bible as the Land of the Persians. Use of the name *Iran* became widespread in the 1920's. Agriculture is the most important industry, but large oil fields and other mineral wealth ensure a revenue for economic development. Languages: Persian, Arabic, Kurdish. Area: 628,060 square miles. Population: 30,300,000. Capital: *Tehran.*

PERSIA (IRAN)

50 Dinar = 1 Shahi
1000 Dinar = 20 Shahi =
    1 Qiran (Kran)
10 Qiran = 1 Toman (Tuman)

NASIR AL-DIN SHAH
AH 1264-1313 (1848-1896)

Copper

		Fine
1	12 Dinar ND, AH 1301 (1884) 15mm	7.50
2	25 Dinar ND, 1293-1300 (20mm)	1.00
★4	50 Dinar ND, 1293-1305, 1330 (error) 25mm	.75
5	100 Dinar ND, 1297-1307, 1330 (error) 30mm	2.50
4a	1 Shahi ND, 1305 (25mm)	7.50
5a	2 Shahi ND, 1305 (30mm)	15.00

6	200 Dinar 1300-01	17.50

Note: Former Nos. 7 and 8 (copper-nickel 50 and 100 Dinar 1293) are not believed to be regular issues.

New Year Issues

Silver

These pieces, although having monetary value, were primarily exchanged as New Year tokens among friends. Valued at 3 Shahi by weight, they bear only the word "Shahi" and often are known as *shahi sefid* or "white shahi."

V. Fine

7 (A9)	(3 Shahi) 1296, date within wreath (17mm, thin)	3.50
★7a	(3) Shahi ND, 1297-1309, date at bottom	2.50
7b	(3) Shahi 1313, date in lion's legs	3.00

Obv: in name of Nasir
Rev: in name of Sahib al-Zaman

8	(3 Shahi) ND	3.50

Regular Issues

Silver

A. Values in Qiran and Dinar

Obv: 3-line legend
Rev: Date at bottom

		Fine
9	¼ (Qiran) ND, 1296-1309 (1879-92) 15mm	2.00
10	500 Dinar ND, 1296-1311 (18mm)	4.00
★11	1000 Dinar ND, 1296-98 (23mm)	1.50

PERSIA (IRAN)

Fine

12 2000 Dinar 1296-98
(27mm) 2.00
13 5000 Dinar 1296-97
(35mm) 50.00

Obv: 4-line legend
Rev: Date at bottom

★11a 1000 Dinar 1298-1303 . . . . . 2.00
12a 2000 Dinar 1298-1308 . . . . . 3.00

B. Values in Shahi and Qiran

Rev: Date in lion's legs

10b 10 Shahi 1310, 3-line
legend 12.50
★10c 10 Shahi 1310-11, 4-line
legend 10.00
11c 1 Qiran 1310-11 (23mm) . 2.50
12c 2 Qiran 1310-11 (27mm) . 4.00
13c 5 Qiran 1311 . . . . 125.00

C. Qiran-Dinar values resumed

9d ¼ (Qiran) 1311-12
(15mm) 4.00
★10d 500 Dinar 1311-13 . . . . . 10.00
11d 1000 Dinar 1311 (23mm) . . 8.50
12d 2000 Dinar 1311-12
(27mm) 2.50

Largesse Issue

V. Fine

15 1 Toman (10 Qiran)
1301 (1884) 350.00

Some authorities consider No. 15 a medal
rather than a coin.

Commemorating Shah's Return from Europe

A15 500 Dinar 1307 (1889) . . . 25.00

Gold

Obv: as Nos. 18, 20
Rev: as obv. of A15

D15 1 Toman 1307 . . . . —
B15 2 Toman 1307 . . . . —

PERSIA (IRAN)

50 Years of Reign

V. Fine

C15 2000 Dinar 1313.........—

No. C15 may not have been released to circulation, due to the assassination of the Shah. Silver pieces dated 1313 with portrait are medals.

Gold

16 ⅕ Toman A.H. 1292-1305
(1875-88)............10.00
17 ½ Toman.............12.50
★18 1 Toman.............30.00
19 2 Tomans A.H. 1271-1305
(1855-88)............45.00

★20 2 Tomans A.H. 1306-11
(1889-94)............50.00
21 10 Tomans (1878).......300.00

22 2 Tomans A.H. 1305-21
(1888-1903)............45.00

GENERAL COINAGE

Nos. 23-24 were issued without the name of the ruler through successive reigns. They have been combined with former Nos. 42-43 and 62-63.

Copper-Nickel

Fine

23 50 Dinar AH 1318-37
(1900-19) 19mm.......1.00
★24 100 Dinar 1318-37.........1.00

MUZAFFAR AL-DIN SHAH
AH 1314-1324 (1897-1907)

New Year Issues

Silver

*Obv: in name of Muzaffar
Rev: Date in lion's legs*

★25 (3) Shahi ND, 1314-20
(16-17mm, thin)......2.00
25a (3 Shahi) ND, no value
below lion............2.00

*Obv: in name of Muzaffar
Rev: in name of Sahib al-Zaman*

A25 (3 Shahi) ND............2.00

PERSIA (IRAN)

Regular Issues

Some coins in this series are characterized by poor dies, weak strikes, blundered dates and variable date positions.

First Coinage

Silver

Obv: in name of Muzaffar
Rev: Date in lion's legs

		Fine
26	¼ (Qiran) ND, AH 1316-19 (1898-1901) 15mm	2.00
27	500 Dinar ND, 1313-22 (18-19mm)	4.00
A27	1000 Dinar 1313-14, no obv. crown (23mm)	10.00
★A27a	1000 Dinar 1317-22, with obv. crown	10.00
28	2000 Dinar 1313-14, no obv. crown	2.25
28a	2000 Dinar 1314-20, with obv. crown	2.25
28b	2 Qiran 1320-22	3.00

		V. Fine
29	5000 Dinar 1320	6.00

Gold

		V. Fine
★38	½ Toman AH 1324 (1906)	27.50
39	5 Tomans 1317 (1899)	250.00

Second Coinage

Silver

		Fine
30	500 Dinar 1319, 23 (1901, 05)	10.00
31	1000 Dinar 1319, 23	12.50
★32	2000 Dinar 1319, 23	5.00
33	5000 Dinar 1319, 24	100.00

Some authorities feel the pieces dated 1319 may be patterns.

Gold

Bust ¾ Left
Rev. Inscription in Wreath

		V. Fine
34	⅕ Toman AH 1319-24 (1901-06)	10.00

★35	½ Toman 1316-24	17.50
36	1 Toman 1316-22	25.00
37	2 Tomans 1321-22	50.00

PERSIA (IRAN)

Commemorating Royal Birthday
Silver

V. Fine

A40 5000 Dinar 1322 (1904) . 200.00

As no. 33 with inscription added at sides of head.

Gold

40 1 Toman AH 1322 (1904) . 25.00
★41 2 Tomans 1322 . . . . 50.00

MUHAMMAD ALI SHAH
AH 1324-1327 (1907-1909)

New Year Issues

Silver

Obv: in name of Muhammad Ali
Rev: Date in lion's legs

44 (3) Shahi AH 1325-27
(17mm, thin) 3.50

Obv: in name of Muhammad Ali
Rev: in name of Sahib al-Zaman

A44 (3 Shahi) ND 3.00

Obv: Like rev. of No. A44
Rev: Like rev. of No. 44

V. Fine

B44 (3) Shahi 1326 . . . . 3.50

Regular Issues

Former Nos. 42-43 are now combined with Nos. 23-24.

First Coinage
Silver

Obv: in name of Muhammad Ali
Rev: Date in lion's legs

45 ¼ (Qiran) AH 1325- *Fine*
27 (15mm) 5.00
★46 500 Dinar 1325-26
(18mm) 10.00
A47 1000 Dinar 1325-26
(23mm) 35.00
47 2 Qiran 1325-27
(28mm) 3.00

Gold

★56 ½ Toman 1324-25 . . . . . . 15.00
A56 1 Toman 1324 . . . . 35.00

Second Coinage
Silver

48 500 Dinar 1326-27 . . . . 10.00

PERSIA (IRAN)

Fine

★**49** 1000 Dinar 1326-27......17.50
50 2000 Dinar 1326.......350.00
A50 5000 Dinar 1327......175.00

Gold
Bust Facing

51 5 Tomans AH 1324 *V. Fine*
(1906)................250.00

Bust Facing Half Left

52 ⅕ Toman AH 1326 (1908).15.00
53 ½ Toman 1326...... ..25.00
54 1 Toman 1326..........50.00
55 2 Tomans 1326..........100.00

Bust Slightly Left

57 ⅕ Toman AH 1326.......10.00
58 ½ Toman 1326..........17.50
59 1 Toman 1327..........25.00

AHMAD SHAH 1909-1925

Former Nos. 60, 62 and 63 are now combined with Nos. 5, 23 and 24 respectively.
Former No. 61 is probably a medal.

First Coinage
New Year Issue

Silver

Obv: in name of Ahmad
Rev: Date at bottom

64 (3) Shahi AH 1328-30 (1909-
12) 17mm, thin.......1.50
A64 (3) Shahi 1332, date
in legs..............3.50

Regular Issues

Obv: in name of Ahmad
Rev: Date at bottom

65 ¼ (Qiran) 1327-31 (15mm)..1.50

Fine

66 500 Dinar 1327-30
(18mm)............2.25
★**67** 1000 Dinar 1327-30
(23mm)............1.50
68 2 Qiran 1327-29
(28mm)............2.25
68a 2000 Dinar 1330.........2.25

Rev: Date in lion's legs

68b 2000 Dinar 1330-31.......3.00

Gold *V. Fine*

75 ⅕ Toman AH 1329-32
(1911-14).............10.00
76 ½ Toman 1329-32........17.50
77 1 Toman 1329-32........25.00
78 5 Tomans 1332 (Rare)...150.00

Second Coinage
New Year Issues

Mules exist from various dies of Nos. 64,
A70 and B70.

Silver

Obv: in name of Ahmad/date

A70 (3) Shahi 1333-42........1.00

Obv: in name of Sahib al-Zaman
Rev: Date in lion's legs

B70 (3) Shahi ND, 1332-42... 1.00

No. B70 without date cannot be assigned
definitely to this reign.

PERSIA (IRAN)

Regular Issues

Obv: in name of Ahmad
Rev: Date in lion's legs

V. Fine

C70 ¼ (Qiran) AH 1327 (error),
32-43 (1914-25) 1.50

70 500 Dinar 1331-43 . . . . 3.50
★71 1000 Dinar 1331-44 . . . . 1.25
72 2000 Dinar 1330-44 . . . . 2.00
69 5000 Dinar 1331-44 . . . . 8.00

Gold

79 ⅕ Toman 1333-43
(1915-25) 10.00
80 ½ Toman 1332-43 . . . . 17.50
★81 1 Toman 1333-44 . . . . 25.00

Tenth Year Jubilee Issues

Silver

Obv: Inscriptions at sides of head
73 1000 Dinar 1337 (1919) 7.50
★74 2000 Dinar 1337 . . . . 13.50

Gold

Obv: Like No. 69
Rev: Like No. 87

V. Fine

83 10 Tomans AH 1331
(1913) 300.00

Fifth Year Jubilee

Lion Type

82 5 Tomans AH 1332 (1914) . 150.00

Lion on Obv.
Inscription in Field of Rev.

86 5 Tomans AH 1332 (1914) . 150.00

One Toman Size — Twice as Thick

84 2 Tomans AH 1333 (1915) . 100.00

87 5 Tomans AH 1334 (1916) . 175.00

Bust Slightly Left, Lion on Rev.

85 2 Tomans AH 1337 (1919) . . 75.00

PERSIA (IRAN)

Bust Slightly Left

V. Fine

88 5 Tomans AH 1337 (1919).175.00

Same Type as 2 Kran Silver

89 5 Tomans AH 1337 (1919).150.00

Tenth Year Jubilee
Bust on Obv., Lion on Rev.

90 1 Toman AH 1337 (1919)..25.00
91 10 Tomans 1337.........300.00

REZA SHAH PAHLAVI
1925-1941

Solar Year Adopted
S.H. 1304, Started
March 21, 1925

10,000 Dinar = 1 Pahlavi 1926-30

New Year Issue
Gold
Obv: 4-line legend, no wreath
Rev: Date below lion

119 1 Toman SH 1305 (1926)
19mm.................50.00

Regular Issues
First Coinage
Copper-Nickel

95 50 Dinar SH 1305-07
(1926-28)..............75
96 100 Dinar 1305-07.........50

Nos. 95-96 are identical to Nos. 23-24 except for the use of solar dating system.

Silver

Obv: in name of Kingdom of Iran
Rev: Date below lion

100 ¼ (Qiran) SH 1304
(1925) 15mm.......7.50
★**101** 1000 Dinar 1304-05......1.75

V. Fine

102 2000 Dinar 1304-05......2.50
103 5000 Dinar 1304-05.....12.00

Second Coinage
Silver

Obv: in name of Reza
Rev: Date at bottom

105 500 Dinar 1305........25.00
106 1000 Dinar 1305-06......1.75
★**107** 2000 Dinar 1305-06......2.50
108 5000 Dinar 1305-06.....10.00

Gold

No. 116   No. 117

116 1 Pahlavi SH 1305 (1926).20.00
117 2 Pahlavi 1305...........45.00
118 5 Pahlavi 1305..........100.00

Third Coinage
Silver

A109 500 Dinar 1306-08......3.00
109 1000 Dinar 1306-08......1.75
★**110** 2000 Dinar 1306-08......2.50
111 5000 Dinar 1306-08......6.00

PERSIA (IRAN)

Gold

120 1 Pahlavi SH 1306-08 *V. Fine*
  (1927-29)............20.00
★121 2 Pahlavi 1306-08......45.00
122 5 Pahlavi 1306-08.....110.00

Fourth Coinage

5 Dinar = 1 Shahi
100 Dinar = 1 Rial
100 Rial = 1 Pahlavi

Bronze

93 1 Dinar SH 1310 (1931)....1.50
★94 2 Dinar 1310............1.50

Copper-Nickel

97 5 Dinar 1310 (18.5mm)...1.50
★98 10 Dinar 1310 (21mm).....1.50
99 25 Dinar 1310 (24mm).....5.00

Copper

97a 5 Dinar 1314...........7.50
98a 10 Dinar 1314...........3.00
99a 25 Dinar 1314...........7.50
92 10 Shahi (50 Dinar) 1314
  (24.5mm)............2.00

Silver

Obv: Like No. 100
Rev: Date at bottom
104 ¼ (Rial) 1315............ .50

Obv: in name of Reza
  V. Fine
112 ½ Rial 1310-15 (1931-36)
  18mm................ .65
113 1 Rial 1310-13
  (22.5mm)............1.25
★114 2 Rial 1310-13 (26mm)...2.00
115 5 Rial 1310-13 (37mm)...5.00

Gold

★123 ½ Pahlavi 1310-15......30.00
124 1 Pahlavi 1310........150.00

GENERAL COINAGE

Nos. 125-128 were issued without the name
of the ruler through the last years of Reza
Shah and continued into the following reign.
The listings have been combined with former Nos. A129-E129.

Aluminum-Bronze

125 5 Dinar SH 1315-21
  (1936-42) 16mm...... .15
★126 10 Dinar 1315-21 (18mm) .20
127 25 Dinar 1326-29
  (19mm).............1.25
128 50 Dinar 1315-32
  (1936-53) 20mm...... .30
128a 50 Dinar Bronze
  1322 (1943)..........1.00

PERSIA (IRAN)

MOHAMMAD REZA PAHLAVI 1941-

First Coinage

Silver

Obv: in name of Mohammad Reza
Rev: Lion in full wreath

V. Fine

129 1 Rial SH 1322-30
(1943-51) 18mm....... .25
★130 2 Rial 1322-30 (22mm)... .50
131 5 Rial 1322-28 (26mm)...1.25
132 10 Rial 1323-26 (32mm)...2.00

Gold

133 ½ Pahlavi SH 1322-23
(1943-44)............35.00
★134 1 Pahlavi 1322-24......60.00

Obv: Head in high relief

135 ½ Pahlavi SH 1324-30
(1945-51)............35.00
★136 1 Pahlavi 1324-30......60.00

Second Coinage

Aluminum-Bronze

Design like No. 128

Unc.

137 50 Dinar 1333-
(1957-) thin........... .40

Copper-Nickel

Obv: No crown at top
Rev: Lion in small wreath

V. Fine

138 1 Rial (13)31-36
(18.5mm)............. .30
★139 2 Rial 1331-36
(2 vars.) 22.5mm....... .40
140 5 Rial 1331-36 (26mm).... .50

No. 138 uses only the last two digits of the date.

Gold

Obv: Head in lower relief

Unc.

★141 ¼ Pahlavi 1332-35
(14mm)............14.00
141a ¼ Pahlavi 1336-
(16mm)............12.00

★142 ½ Pahlavi SH 1333-....35.00
143 1 Pahlavi 1333-.......60.00
144 2½ Pahlavi 1339-52...120.00
145 5 Pahlavi 1339-52...240.00

Later issues in Current Coins of the World.

PERU

(Republica del Peru, Republica Peruana)

On the west coast of South America, it encompasses some of the highest peaks in the Andes Mountains. Its exports include cotton, petroleum, sugar and copper. Peru, which had been Spain's foremost colony in the new world, won its independence in 1824. Area: 514,059 square miles. Population: 13,-600,000. Languages: Spanish and Indian. Capital: *Lima*.

16 Reales = 1 Escudo (Gold)
10 Centavos = 1 Dinero

100 Centavos = 1 Sol
10 Soles = 1 Libra (Gold Pound)

Note: Because of extensive revisions, new numbers have been assigned in the 11th edition. The original numbers are given in parentheses.

Transition to Decimal System 1858-1863

Silver

		V. Fine
★1 (C135)	½ Real 1858	4.00
2 (C137)	50 Céntimos 1858	10.00

		Fine
3 (14)	½ Real 1859-61	2.50
4 (15)	1 Real 1859-61	6.00
★5 (16)	25 Centavos 1859	20.00
6 (17)	50 Centavos 1858-59	12.50

Gold

		V. Fine
7 (26)	4 Scudos 1863	750.00
8 (27)	8 Scudos 1862-63	300.00

Decimal System 1863- First Coinage

Bronze

Obv: Date at top

		V. Fine
9 (1)	1 Centavo 1863-78, 1919	.50
10 (2)	2 Centavos 1863-95, 1919	.75

The 1863-64 dates of Nos. 9-10, formerly listed as copper-nickel, often have a lighter color due to a small amount of silver in the alloy.

Obv: Date at bottom

★11 (3)	1 Centavo 1901-41, CENTAVO straight	.30
12 (4)	1 Centavo 1909-37, CENTAVO curved	.35
13 (5)	2 Centavos 1916-41	.35

PERU

V. Fine

14 (18) ½ Dinero 1863-1917... .50
15 (19) 1 Dinero 1863-1916... .65
★16 (20) ⅕ Sol 1863-1917......1.00
17 (21) ½ Sol 1864-1917......3.00
18 (22) 1 Sol 1864-1916......6.00

Nos. 14-18 contain many die varieties.

Branch Mints

Fine

14a (18) ½ Dinero 1885
    Cuzco...........75.00
★15a (19) 1 Dinero 1886
    Cuzco...........30.00
16a (20) ⅕ Sol 1885
    Arequipa.......200.00

Gold

V. Fine

★17 (28) 5 Soles 1863........75.00
18 (29) 10 Soles 1863......120.00
19 (30) 20 Soles 1863......325.00

20 (42) ⅕ Libra 1906-.......17.50
21 (43) ½ Libra 1902-.......30.00
★22 (44) 1 Libra 1898-.......55.00

V. Fine

23 (A45) 1 Sol 1910 Silver....20.00
24 (45) 5 Soles 1910 Gold...40.00

Provisional Issues
Copper-Nickel

25 (11) 5 Centavos 1879-80....1.00
26 (12) 10 Centavos 1879-80....1.00
27 (13) 20 Centavos 1879......4.00

Silver

28 (A23) ½ Real 1882
    Ayacucho 250.00
29 (23) 1 Peseta 1880 Lima. 2.00
30 (24) 5 Pesetas 1880
    Lima..........15.00
30a (25) 5 Pesetas 1881-82
    Ayacucho.....100.00

Second Coinage
Copper-Nickel

Dates spelled out in Spanish

31 5 Centavos 1918-41........ .15
32 10 Centavos 1918-41........ .20
33 20 Centavos 1918-41........ .25

PERU

Third Coinage

Silver

V. Fine

34	(40)	½ Sol 1922-35	1.25
35	(A40)	1 Sol 1923 (no fineness)	35.00
36	(41)	1 Sol 1923-35 (5 Décimos fine)	3.50

Gold

37 (46) 50 Soles 1930-68 . . . . . 425.00

Bronze

Thin planchet

11a (6) 1 Centavo 1941-44,   *V. Fine*
CENTAVO straight 50
12a (7) 1 Centavo 1941-49,
CENTAVO curved 15
13a (8) 2 Centavos 1941-49 20

Brass

Dates spelled out in Spanish

31a 5 Centavos 1942-44 . . . . . . .1.00
32a 10 Centavos 1942-44 . . . . . . .1.25
33a 20 Centavos 1942-44 . . . . . . .2.50

Dates in numerals

38 (34) 5 Centavos 1945-51 15
39 (35) 10 Centavos 1945-51 20
40 (36) 20 Centavos 1942-51 25

Unc.

43 (47) ½ Sol 1935-65 20
44 (48) 1 Sol 1943-65 35

Later issues in *Current Coins of the World.*

PHILIPPINES
(Filipinas—Islas Filipinas)

A Spanish colony until 1898, it was bought by the American government following the Spanish-American War. It was invaded by the Japanese in December, 1941. It was recognized as an independent nation on July 4, 1946. Exports: pineapples, sugar, copra, lumber, iron and tobacco. Languages: Pilipino, English, Spanish. Area: 115,758 square miles. Capital: *Quezon City* (Luzon).

100 Céntimos = 1 Peso to 1898
100 Centavos = 1 Peso 1903-1966

ISABEL II 1833-1868

For the 1835 copper issue and provisional counterstamps on silver crowns, see *Craig*.

Silver

Fine

3 10 Céntimos 1864-68........5.00
4 20 Céntimos 1864-68........3.00
5 50 Céntimos 1865-68........4.00

Gold

V. Fine

6 1 Peso 1861-68.............45.00
7 2 Pesos 1861-68............75.00
8 4 Pesos 1861-68...........120.00

ALFONSO XII 1875-1885

Silver

Fine

9 10 Céntimos 1880-85.......1.00
10 20 Céntimos 1880-85.......1.75
11 50 Céntimos 1880-85.......2.50

Gold

12 4 Pesos 1880-85.. *Ex. Fine* 450.00

ALFONSO XIII 1886-1898

Silver

V. Fine

13 1 Peso 1897...............15.00

UNDER SOVEREIGNTY OF THE UNITED STATES

Bronze

14 ½ Centavo 1903-08......... .80
15 1 Centavo 1903-36......... .50

PHILIPPINES

Copper-Nickel

V. Fine

16 5 Centavos 1903-28........ .75
16a 5 Centavos 1918, rev. of
No. 23 (error).........30.00

Reduced Size

17 5 Centavos 1930-35......... .90

Silver

18 10 Centavos 1903-06.......1.25
19 20 Centavos 1903-06.......1.75
20 50 Centavos 1903-06.......5.00
21 1 Peso 1903-06...........7.00

Reduced Size

22 10 Centavos 1907-35....... .80
23 20 Centavos 1907-29.......1.50
23a 20 Centavos 1928, rev. of
No. 16. ....12.50
24 50 Centavos 1907-21.......3.00
25 1 Peso 1907-12...........5.00

Commemorative Issues — Establishment of the Commonwealth 1935

Silver

Obv: Murphy and Quezon

Unc.
26 50 Centavos 1936.........40.00

Obv: Roosevelt and Quezon

Unc.
27 1 Peso 1936..............75.00

Obv: Murphy and Quezon

28 1 Peso 1936..............75.00

Bronze

V. Fine
29 1 Centavo 1937-44.......... .10

Copper-Nickel

30 5 Centavos 1937-41........ .50

PHILIPPINES

Nickel-Silver

	V. Fine
30a 5 Centavos 1944-45	.10

REPUBLIC 1946-
MacArthur Commemoratives
Silver

Silver

	V. Fine
31 10 Centavos 1937-45	.35
32 20 Centavos 1937-45	.65
33 50 Centavos 1944-45	1.50

	Unc.
34 50 Centavos 1947	3.00
35 1 Peso 1947	7.00

Later issues in Current Coins of the World.

POLAND
(Rzeczpospolita Polska)

A Central European republic bordering the Baltic Sea between Russia and Czechoslovakia. Its great deposits of coal and iron have made it valuable conquest for other countries. It has been controlled by Austria, Germany, Prussia, and Russia. It declared its independence after the First World War, but was invaded by Germany and Russia in 1939. In 1945 it ceded about 70,000 square miles in the eastern section to Russia, in return getting some 40,000 square miles of German territory. Capital: *Warszawa* (Warsaw).

100 Fenigow = 1 Marka
100 Groszy = 1 Zloty

OCCUPATION MONEY
World War I

See GERMANY Nos. A18-C18

REGENCY—
Under Germany and Austria
Iron

	V. Fine
4 1 Fenig 1918	7.50
5 5 Fenigow 1917-18	1.00
6 10 Fenigow 1917-18	1.25
7 20 Fenigow 1917-18	1.75

Zinc

	V. Fine
6a 10 Fenigow 1917	25.00
7a 20 Fenigow 1917	25.00

REPUBLIC 1919-

Bronze

8 1 Grosz 1923-39	.15
9 2 Grosze (Yellow Bronze) 1923	1.00
9a 2 Grosze 1923-39	.20
10 5 Groszy (Yellow Bronze) 1923	1.50
10a 5 Groszy 1923-39	.25

POLAND

Nickel

V. Fine

11 10 Groszy 1923 20
12 20 Groszy 1923 30
13 50 Groszy 1923 50

V. Fine

18 5 Zlotych 1928-1932 . . . . . . .15.00

14 1 Zloty 1929 . . . . .1.25

Centennial of 1830 Revolution

Silver

15 1 Zloty 1924-25 . . . . .3.00
16 2 Zlote 1924-25 . . . . .4.00

19 5 Zlotych 1930 . . . . .20.00

17 5 Zlotych 1925 . . . .——
No. 17 not issued to circulation.

20 2 Zlote 1932-34 . . . . .1.00
21 5 Zlotych 1932-1934 . . . . . . .2.00
22 10 Zlotych 1932-1933 . . . . . . .5.00

POLAND

250th Anniversary of Relief of Vienna (Jan Sobieski)

Similar but no Badge under Eagle

V. Fine

27 2 Zlotc 1934-36.... .....2.50
28 5 Zlotych 1934-1938.......2.50
29 10 Zlotych 1934-1939.......5.00

V. Fine

23 10 Zlotych 1933...........10.00

1863 Insurrection (Traugutt)

30 2 Zlote 1936...............3.00
31 5 Ziotych 1936.............6.00

Boleslaus I Commemoratives

Gold

24 10 Zlotych 1933...........10.00

Silver

Rifle Corps August 6, 1914

32 10 Zlotych 1925...........65.00
33 20 Zlotych 1925...........80.00

WORLD WAR II GERMAN OCCUPATION ISSUES

Similar to Nos. 8, 10-12

Zinc

Bust of Pilsudski

25 5 Zlotych 1934............5.50
26 10 Zlotych 1934............9.00

34 1 Grosz 1939.............2.50

POLAND

35 5 Groszy 1939.............3.50

V. Fine
42 10 Groszy Cop.-Nic. 1949... .50
42a 10 Groszy Alum. 1949...... .35

36 10 Groszy 1923............ .25
37 20 Groszy 1923............ .35
(Dated 1923 but Struck 1941-44)

Nickel-Plated Iron
38 50 Groszy 1938............2.00

43 20 Groszy Cop.-Nic. 1949.. .65
43a 20 Groszy Alum. 1949..... .50

POSTWAR ISSUES

Various Metals

44 50 Groszy Cop.-Nic. 1949...1.00
44a 50 Groszy Alum. 1949...... .75

Unc.
39 1 Grosz Alum. 1949........ .15

40 2 Grosze Alum. 1949....... .20
V. Fine
41 5 Groszy Bronze 1949......1.00
41a 5 Groszy Alum. 1949....... .50

45 1 Zloty Cop.-Nic. 1949.....1.25
45a 1 Zloty Alum. 1949........1.00

Later issues in *Current Coins of the World.*

PORTUGAL
(Republica Portuguesa)

Western section of the Iberian Peninsula facing the Atlantic Ocean. A kingdom until 1910 when, following a revolution, a republic was established. Population: 9,000,000. Area: 34,500 square miles. Exports: Cork and wines. Capital: *Lisbon*.

1000 Reis = 1 Milreis to 1910   100 Centavos = 1 Escudo 1912 -

LUIS I 1861-1889

Copper

			Fine
1	3 Reis 1868-75	....	3.50
2	5 Reis 1867-79	....	2.50
3	10 Reis 1867-77	....	3.00
4	20 Reis 1867-74	....	5.00

For other similar copper coins of 1865-1880, see AZORES.

Bronze

			Fine
5	5 Reis 1882-86	....	.60
6	10 Reis 1882-86	....	.75
7	20 Reis 1882-86	....	1.00

Obverse Crown and Date

Silver

8	50 Reis 1862-89	....	1.75

			Fine
9	100 Reis 1864-89	.....	..2.50
10	200 Reis 1862-88 (2 Different Heads)	....	3.50
11	500 Reis 1863-89	....	5.00

Gold

			V. Fine
A12	2000 Reis 1864-66	.....	100.00
12	2000 Reis 1868-88	.....	110.00
A13	5000 Reis 1862-63	....	175.00
13	5000 Reis 1867-89	....	175.00
14	10,000 Reis 1878-89	....	300.00

CARLOS I 1889-1908

Bronze

			Fine
15	5 Reis 1890-1906	....	.40
16	10 Reis 1891-92	....	.60
17	20 Reis 1891-92	....	.85

For bronze coins of 1901 with coat of arms replacing portrait, see AZORES.

PORTUGAL

Copper-Nickel

V. Fine

18 50 Reis 1900 75
19 100 Reis 1900 50

Silver

20 50 Reis 1893 . . . . .3.50

V. Fine

24 1000 Reis 1899 . . . . .20.00

21 100 Reis 1890-98 . . . . .3.00
22 200 Reis 1891-1903 . . . . .2.75

400th Anniversary of Voyages of Discovery 1498-1898

25 200 Reis 1898 . . . . 7.50
26 500 Reis 1898 . . . . .10.00
23 500 Reis 1891-1908 . . . . .4.50   **27** 1000 Reis 1898 . . . . .27.50

PORTUGAL

MANUEL II 1908-1910

Bronze

V. Fine
28 5 Reis 1910................ .75

Silver

29 100 Reis 1909-10.......... 1.50
30 200 Reis 1909............. 2.00
31 500 Reis 1908-09.......... 3.00

COMMEMORATIVE ISSUES
Peninsular War Centennial

32 500 Reis 1910............ 17.50
33 1000 Reis 1910............ 30.00

Marquis de Pombal

V. Fine
34 500 Reis 1910 .... 17.50

REPUBLIC 1910-

World War I Provisional Issue

Iron

35 2 Centavos 1918......... 40.00

Bronze

36 1 Centavo 1917-21 .... .20
37 2 Centavos 1918-21........ .35
38 5 Centavos 1920-22........ .75

PORTUGAL

Bronze

V. Fine
39 5 Centavos 1924-27........ .30
40 10 Centavos 1924-40........ .50
41 20 Centavos 1924-25....... .40

Copper-Nickel

42 4 Centavos 1917-19........1.00
43 10 Centavos 1920-21........ .85
44 20 Centavos 1920-22.......1.00

Aluminum-Bronze

45 50 Centavos 1924-26........1.00
46 1 Escudo 1924-26..........1.25

Commemorating Birth of Republic 5th October 1910

Silver

V. Fine
47 1 Escudo (1914)...........17.50

48 10 Centavos
1915......2.25
49 20 Centavos
1913-16...4.00
50 50 Centavos
1912-16...5.00
51 1 Escudo
1915-16..13.50

PORTUGAL

NEW REGIME 1926-

Nickel-Brass

Unc.
54 50 Centavos 1927-68........ .20
55 1 Escudo 1927-68.......... .35

Battle of Ourique 1139

Silver

V. Fine
56 10 Escudos 1928.......... 12.50

Regular Issues

57 2½ Escudos 1932-51........ 1.00
58 5 Escudos 1932-51........ 1.50
59 10 Escudos 1932-48........ 3.50

Bronze

Unc.
60 X Centavos 1942-69...... .15
61 XX Centavos 1942-69....... .20

Commemorative Issue— 25 Years of Financial Reform

Silver

62 20 Escudos 1953........ 8.50

Regular Issue

Silver

63 10 Escudos 1954-55........ 4.50

Later issues in Current Coins of the World.

PORTUGUESE GUINEA (Guiné)

A Portuguese Overseas Province on the west coast of Africa. Exports: wax, ivory, hides. Area: 13,948 square miles. Population: 550,000. Capital: *Bissau*.
100 Centavos = 1 Escudo

Bronze

		V. Fine
1	5 Centavos 1933	2.00
2	10 Centavos 1933	1.75
3	20 Centavos 1933	1.50

Nickel-Bronze

4	50 Centavos 1933	3.50
5	1 Escudo 1933	2.50

500th Anniversary of Discovery
Bronze

		V.F.
6	50 Centavos 1946	.65
7	1 Escudo 1946	.90

Decree of Dec. 29, 1951
Bronze

		Unc.
8	50 Centavos 1952	.60

Copper-Nickel

		V. Fine
9	2½ Escudos 1952	.60

Silver

10	10 Escudos 1952	1.75
11	20 Escudos 1952	3.50

Later issues in Current Coins of the World.

PORTUGUESE INDIA
(India Portugueza, Estado da India)

Three small areas — Goa, Damão and Diu — on the west coast of India. They contain many salt and manganese mines. India occupied these enclaves in 1962. Capital: *Pangim*.

60 Réis = 1 Tanga (Indian Annà)
16 Tangas = 1 Rupia
Coinage obsolete.

LUIS I 1861-1889

Copper

		Fine
1	3 Réis 1871	6.00
2	5 Réis 1871	6.00
3	10 Réis 1871	7.00

PORTUGUESE INDIA

Fine

16 ⅛ Tanga 1901-03.........1.75
17 ¼ Tanga 1901-03.........1.00
18 ½ Tanga 1901-03.........1.50

Silver

Fine

4 ¼ Tanga/15 Réis 1871......5.50
5 ½ Tanga/30 Réis 1871.....12.50
6 1 Tanga/60 Réis 1871.....25.00

19 1 Rupia 1903-04.......... 7.50

PORTUGUESE REPUBLIC
ISSUES 1910-1961

★7 ⅛ Tanga 1881-86..........2.00
8 ¼ Tanga 1881-86..........2.50

Silver

Silver

11 ⅛ Rupia 1881............5.00
12 ¼ Rupia 1881............6.00
13 ½ Rupia 1881-82........5.00
★14 1 Rupia 1881-82........6.00

CARLOS I 1889-1908

Bronze

20 1 Rupia 1912.............15.00

Bronze

21 1 Tanga 1934............1.50

Copper-Nickel

22 2 Tangas 1934............2.00
★23 4 Tangas 1934............2.25

15 1/12 Tanga 1901-03..........1.75

PORTUGUESE INDIA

Silver

Copper-Nickel

V. Fine
27 ¼ Rupia 1947, 52.........1.00
28 ½ Rupia 1947, 52.........1.25

V. Fine
24 ½ Rupia 1936.............7.50
25 1 Rupia 1935.............7.50

Silver

Bronze

29 1 Rupia 1947.............6.00

26 1 Tanga 1947
(25mm)............. .75

Copper-Nickel

Unc.
29a (33) 1 Rupia 1952....... 5.00

26a (30) 1 Tanga 1952 *Unc.*
(20mm)............. .75

Later issues in Current Coins of the World.

PRINCE EDWARD ISLAND (See Canada)

PUERTO RICO

The farthest east of the Greater Antilles in the Atlantic Ocean. Ceded to the United States after the Spanish-American war, it is a self-governing Commonwealth of the United States. Major industry: sugar cultivation and processing. Area: 3,435 square miles. Capital: *San Juan.*

100 Centavos = 1 Peso
Coinage obsolete.

UNDER SPAIN —
ALFONSO XIII 1886-1898

Silver

V. Fine
2 10 Centavos 1896..........15.00
3 20 Centavos 1895..........15.00
4 40 Centavos 1896..........65.00

V. Fine
1 5 Centavos 1896.............7.50

5 1 Peso 1895..............90.00

REUNION
(Ile de la Reunion)

A French overseas island territory in the Indian Ocean east of Madagascar. Chief exports: sugar, rum, vanilla, spices. Area: 969 square miles. Population: 382,000. Capital: *St. Denis*.

100 Centimes = 1 Franc

Regular Issues

Copper-Nickel

Aluminum

V. Fine

1 50 Centimes 1896 . . . . 10.00
2 1 Franc 1896 . . . . 17.50

Unc.

8 1 Franc 1948-69 25
9 2 Francs 1948-69 35
10 5 Francs 1955 75

Bank Tokens

Aluminum

Aluminum-Bronze

Fine

3 5 Centimes 1920 . . . . 12.50
4 10 Centimes 1920 . . . . 15.00
5 25 Centimes 1920 . . . . 17.50

11 10 Francs 1955-64 . . . . 1.00
12 20 Francs 1955-64 . . . . 1.25

Note: Former Nos. 6 and 7 (50 Centimes and 1 Franc 1941) have been deleted until their existence can be confirmed.

Nickel

13 50 Francs 1962- 1.50
14 100 Francs 1964- 2.00

RHODESIA AND NYASALAND
— see *Current Coins of the World*

ROMANIA

A socialist industrial-agrarian state in southeast Europe, bounded by the Black Sea, Bulgaria, Yugoslavia, Hungary and the U.S.S.R. The nation began in 1859 by the union of Moldavia and Wallachia, and later gained other territory including Transylvania. It became a republic late in 1947. Area: 91,699 square miles. Population: 20,700,000. Language: Romanian. Capital: *Bucureşti* (Bucharest).   100 Bani = 1 Leu

ROMANIA

CAROL I —
as Domnul (Prince) 1866-81
First Coinage
Bronze

		Fine
1	1 Banu 1867	3.00
2	2 Bani 1867	2.50
3	5 Bani 1867	1.50
4	10 Bani 1867	1.25

Gold
Obv: Young head, sideburns

V. Fine

5 (A7) 20 Lei 1868 . . . . 850.00

Second Coinage
Silver

Obv: Young head, short beard

6 1 Leu 1870 . . . . 12.00

Gold

7 (B7) 20 Lei 1870 . . . . 125.00

Third Coinage

Silver

8 50 Bani 1873-76 . . . . 3.00

		Fine
9	1 Leu 1873-76	2.00
10	2 Lei 1872-76	2.50

Fourth Coinage
Rev: ROMANIA above arms

Copper

11 2 Bani 1879-81 75

Silver

13	50 Bani 1881	1.50
14	1 Leu 1881	2.50
15	2 Lei 1881	6.00
16	5 Lei 1880-81 (2 vars.)	12.50

as Rege (King) 1881-1914
New Legend:
REGE replaces DOMNUL

Silver

27 5 Lei 1881, rev. of No. 16
(with **ROMANIA**) 20.00

ROMANIA

Copper

Rev: ROMANIA at top removed

Fine
A17 1 Ban 1888. . . . . ——
17 2 Bani 1882. . . . . 1.00
18 5 Bani 1882-85. 75

No. A17 was not issued to circulation.

Fine
34 5 Bani 1905-06. 20
35 10 Bani 1905-06. 25
36 20 Bani 1905-06. 35

Silver

19 50 Bani 1884-85. . . . . 3.00
20 1 Leu 1884-85. . . . . 2.50
23 5 Lei 1881-85,
   lettered edge. 15.00
23a 5 Lei 1901, reeded edge. . . 20.00

Silver

24 50 Bani 1894-1901. . . . . 2.00
25 1 Leu 1894-1901. . . . . 2.75
26 2 Lei 1894-1901. . . . . 6.00

Gold

28 20 Lei 1883-90. . . . . . . *V. F.* 65.00

Copper
Rev: ROMANIA restored above arms

29 1 Ban 1900. 50
30 2 Bani 1900. 65

Copper-Nickel

31 5 Bani 1900. 35
32 10 Bani 1900. 50
33 20 Bani 1900. . . . . 2.50

40th Anniversary of Reign

Silver

37 1 Leu 1906. . . . . 6.50
38 5 Lei 1906. . . . . 30.00

Gold

V. Fine
39 12½ Lei 1906. . . . . 65.00
40 25 Lei 1906. . . . . 125.00

ROMANIA

V. Fine
41 20 Lei 1906.............95.00
42 100 Lei 1906...........300.00

43 50 Lei 1906.............225.00

Regular Issues
Silver

44 50 Bani 1910-14...........1.00

45 1 Leu 1910-14.............2.00
46 2 Lei 1910-14.............2.75

FERDINAND I 1914-1927
Aluminum

V. Fine
47 25 Bani 1921.............1.00
48 50 Bani 1921.............1.00

Copper-Nickel

49 1 Leu 1924............... : .25
50 2 Lei 1924............... .. .50

Note: Gold 20, 25, 50 and 100 Lei pieces dated 1922 exist, but their status as official issues is in dispute.

MIHAI I
First Reign 1927-1930

Nickel-Brass

55 5 Lei 1930.................1.00

56 20 Lei 1930.................2.50

ROMANIA

CAROL II 1930-1940

Nickel-Brass

Silver

V. Fine

57 1 Leu 1938-41 25

V. Fine

62 100 Lei 1932 .3.50

58 10 Lei 1930 50
59 20 Lei 1930 75

63 250 Lei 1935 . . . . .10.00

Nickel

60 50 Lei 1937-38 . . . . .1.25

64 250 Lei 1939-40 . . . . .5.00

61 100 Lei 1936-38 . . . . .1.50

Commemorative Medals
(Nos. 65-70)
Centennial of Birth of
King Carol I
April 20, 1839

Gold

65 20 Lei 1939 (Arms) 150.00
66 20 Lei 1939 (Eagle) 150.00

ROMANIA

Obv: small head, plain border

		V. Fine
72	20 Lei 1940	150.00
A72	100 Lei 1940	575.00

MIHAI I
Second Reign 1940-1947
Zinc

73 2 Lei 1941 75

74 5 Lei 1942 . . . . .1.00

75 20 Lei 1942-44 . . . . .1.25

Nickel-Clad Steel

76 100 Lei 1943-44 . . . . .1.25

V. Fine

67 100 Lei 1939 . . . . 550.00

68 100 Lei 1939 . . . . 500.00

Tenth Anniversary
Reign of Carol II

Gold

Obv: large head, ornate border

71	20 Lei 1940	160.00
A71	100 Lei 1940	600.00

ROMANIA

Silver

V. Fine
77 200 Lei 1942.............2.25

V. Fine
80 500 Lei 1944.............3.50
Note: The 1944 gold piece (size of 20 Lei No. 71) is considered a commemorative medal.

Second Coinage

Brass

Ex. Fine
78 250 Lei 1941, edge lettered
NIHIL SINE DEO.......5.00
78a 250 Lei 1941, edge lettered
TOTUL PENTRU TARA..15.00

81 200 Lei 1945.............2.50

82 500 Lei 1945.............3.50

Aluminum

79 500 Lei 1941.............10.00

83 500 Lei 1946.............2.00

ROMANIA

Brass

84 2000 Lei 1946.............. *V. Fine* 2.25

85 10,000 Lei 1947............3.00

Silver

86 25,000 Lei 1946............5.00

87 100,000 Lei 1946............8.50

COINAGE REFORM AUGUST 1947

Brass

88 50 Bani 1947 .... *V. Fine* 1.75

89 1 Leu 1947................1.75

Bronze

90 2 Lei 1947.................1.75

Aluminum

91 5 Lei 1947.................1.50

PEOPLE'S REPUBLIC
1947-1965
Aluminum-Bronze

92 1 Leu 1949-51 ....1.50

ROMANIA

V. Fine

93 2 Lei 1950-51 . . . . .1.50

Aluminum

92a 1 Leu 1951-52 . . . . .2.00
93a 2 Lei 1951-52 . . . . .2.00

94 5 Lei 1948-51 . . . . .1.50

95 20 Lei 1951 . . . . .10.00

CURRENCY REVALUATION

Aluminum-Bronze
Unc.

96 1 Ban (No star at top of obv.)
1952 40
97 3 Bani (No star) 1952 60
98 5 Bani (No star) 1952 75

Copper-Nickel

Unc.

99 10 Bani (No star)1952 65
100 25 Bani (No star) 1952 . . . .1.00

Aluminum-Bronze

96a 1 Ban (Star) 1953-54 30
97a 3 Bani (Star) 1953 45
★98a 5 Bani (Star) 1953-57 60

Copper-Nickel

99a 10 Bani (Star, ROMANA)
1954 65
99b 10 Bani (Star, ROMINA)
1955-56 50
100a 25 Bani (Star, ROMANA)
1953-54 . . . . .1.00
100b 25 Bani (Star, ROMINA)
1955 . . . . .1.00

101 50 Bani 1955-56 . . . . .1.50

Later issues in Current Coins of the World.

RWANDA and BURUNDI
— see Current Coins of the World

RUSSIA

The largest country in the world in area, it occupies eastern Europe and northern Asia, about one-sixth of the world's surface. The imperialist Russia of the Czars was destroyed in 1917 by revolution. Population: 249,000,000. Capital: *Moscow.*   100 Kopeks = 1 Rouble

CZARIST EMPIRE — General Coinage

First Coinage

*Obv: 6 coats of arms on wings,
no ribbons from crown*

Copper

		Fine
4	2 Kopeks 1855-59	1.00
*5	3 Kopeks 1855-59	1.25
6	5 Kopeks 1855-59	1.50

Silver

13	5 Kopeks 1855-58	1.50
14	10 Kopeks 1855-58	1.00
15	20 Kopeks 1855-58	1.50

16	25 Kopeks 1855-58	1.75
*17	½ Rouble 1855-58	3.50
18	1 Rouble 1855-58	7.50

Gold

		V. Fine
A26	5 Roubles 1855-58	75.00

Second Coinage

*Obv: 8 coats of arms on wings,
with ribbons from crown*

Copper

		Fine
4a	2 Kopeks 1859-67	1.00
5a	3 Kopeks 1859-67	1.25
6a	5 Kopeks 1859-67	1.75

9	1 Kopek 1867-1916	.35
10	2 Kopeks 1867-1916	.45
11	3 Kopeks 1867-1916	.55
12	5 Kopeks 1867-1916	1.00

RUSSIA

Silver

Edge: engrailed

		Fine
19	5 Kopeks 1859-66	1.00
20	10 Kopeks 1859-66	.50
21	15 Kopeks 1860-66	.65
22	20 Kopeks 1859-66	.75

Edge: reeded

19a	5 Kopeks 1867-1917	.75
20a	10 Kopeks 1867-1917	.50
21a	15 Kopeks 1867-1917	.65
22a	20 Kopeks 1867-1917	.75

23	25 Kopeks 1859-85	2.00
★24	½ Rouble 1859-85	4.00
25	1 Rouble 1859-85	9.00

Gold

		V. Fine
26	3 Roubles 1869-85	160.00
B26	5 Roubles 1859-85	75.00
27	25 Roubles 1876	—

Issues With Royal Portraits or Monograms

ALEXANDER II 1855-1881

Copper

		Fine
1	¼ Kopek 1855-67	2.00
★2	½ Kopek 1855-67	1.50
3	1 Kopek 1855-67 (3 Var.)	.75

| 7 | ¼ Kopek 1867-81 | 1.50 |
| 8 | ½ Kopek 1867-81 | 1.00 |

Memorial to Nicholas I

Silver

Ex. Fine

| 28 | 1 Rouble 1859 | 100.00 |

RUSSIA

ALEXANDER III 1881-1894
Coronation Commemorative
Silver

Ex. Fine

43 1 Rouble 1883 . . . . 45.00

Copper

Fine

29 ¼ Kopek 1881-94 . . . . 1.50
30 ½ Kopek 1881-94 . . . . 1.00

Silver

44 25 Kopeks 1886-94 . . . . . . 12.50
*45 50 Kopeks 1886-94 . . . . 10.00
46 1 Rouble 1886-94 . . . . 15.00

Gold   *V. Fine*

42 5 Roubles 1886-94 . . . . . . 65.00
A42 10 Roubles 1886-94 . . . . . 300.00

NICHOLAS II 1894-1917
Copper

Fine

47 ¼ Kopek 1894-1916 . . . . 1.50
48 ½ Kopek 1894-1916 75

Silver

57 25 Kopeks 1895-1901 . . . . . . 5.00
58 50 Kopeks 1895-1914 . . . . . . 2.50
59 1 Rouble 1895-1915 . . . . 7.00

Coronation Commemorative

Ex. Fine

60 1 Rouble 1896 . . . . 50.00

RUSSIA

In Memory of
Alexander II

Memory of Alexander III

300th Anniversary
Romanoff Regime

Early strikes are in low relief.

Centennial
Defeat of Napoleon

200th Anniversary Battle
of Gangut (Peter I)

RUSSIA

Gold

A61 5 Roubles 1895-96 . . . . . ——
A63 10 Roubles 1895-97 . . . . . ——
A65 25 Roubles 1896, 1908 . . . . ——
This series was for presentation only, not released to circulation.

Reduced Weight Gold

Ex. Fine
62 5 Roubles 1897-1911 . . . . 35.00
★63 7½ Roubles 1897 . . . . . . 100.00

Ex. Fine
64 10 Roubles 1898-1911 . . . 55.00
65 15 Roubles 1897 . . . . . . 120.00
B65 37½ Roubles 1902 . . . . ——

No. B65 was for presentation only.

World War I Issues

Iron

For 1, 2 and 3 Kopeks 1916 (obv. German legend, rev. Russian value in cross) used during German occupation of northwest Russia, see GERMANY Nos. A18-C18.

U.S.S.R.
(Union of Soviet Socialist Republics)

Capital: *Moscow*. A confederacy of Soviet republics in Eastern Europe and Asia. Government resulted from the overthrow of the Czarist regime in 1917.

For Armavir issues, formerly Nos. 71-73, see Russian Caucasia.

First Coinage

Legend: РСФСР

Silver

V. Fine
80 10 Kopeks 1921-23 . . . . 1.00
81 15 Kopeks 1921-23 . . . . 1.50
82 20 Kopeks 1921-23 . . . . 1.50

83 50 Kopeks 1921-22 . . . . 4.00
84 1 Rouble 1921-22 . . . . 10.00

Gold

Ex. Fine
85 10 Roubles (Tchervonetz)
1923 . . . . 300.00

Second Coinage

New Legend: C.C.C.P.

Bronze

V. Fine
75 ½ Kopek 1925-28 . . . . 9.50

RUSSIA—U.S.S.R.

V. Fine

76 1 Kopek 1924-25.........2.50
77 2 Kopeks 1924-25.........3.00
78 3 Kopeks 1924...........3.50
79 5 Kopeks 1924...........5.00

Silver

86 10 Kopeks 1924-31.........60
87 15 Kopeks 1924-31.........60
88 20 Kopeks 1924-31.........75

89 50 Kopeks 1924-27........3.00

90 1 Rouble 1924...........10.00

Third Coinage

Aluminum-Bronze

V. Fine

91 1 Kopek 1926-35...........25
92 2 Kopeks 1926-35..........35
93 3 Kopeks 1926-35..........50
94 5 Kopeks 1926-35........2.00

Copper-Nickel

95 10 Kopeks 1931-34.........50
96 15 Kopeks 1931-34.........50
97 20 Kopeks 1931-34.........60

3 Ribbons ea. Side of Wreath
Aluminum-Bronze

Ribbons signify states within the
Soviet Union.

98 1 Kopek 1935-36.......1.00
99 2 Kopeks 1935-36......1.25
100 3 Kopeks 1935-36......2.00
101 5 Kopeks 1935-36......6.00

RUSSIA—U.S.S.R.

Copper-Nickel

Copper-Nickel

V. Fine

102 10 Kopeks 1935-36........ .75
103 15 Kopeks 1935-36....... 1.00
104 20 Kopeks 1935-36....... 1.25

V. Fine

109 10 Kopeks 1937-1946...... .50
110 15 Kopeks 1937-1946...... .60
111 20 Kopeks 1937-1946...... .75

8 and 7 Ribbons on Wreath

Aluminum-Bronze

5 Ribbons ea. Side of Wreath

Aluminum-Bronze

Unc.

112 1 Kopek 1948-56.......... .20
113 2 Kopeks 1948-56......... .25
114 3 Kopeks 1948-56......... .35
115 5 Kopeks 1948-56.........1.50

Copper-Nickel

105 1 Kopek 1937-1946........ .20
106 2 Kopeks 1937-1946....... .25
107 3 Kopeks 1937-1946....... .35
108 5 Kopeks 1937-1946....... 1.00

116 10 Kopeks 1948-56........ .35
117 15 Kopeks 1948-56........ .45
118 20 Kopeks 1948-56........ .60

Later issues in *Current Coins of the World.*

RUSSIAN CAUCASIA

This mountainous region lies just north of Turkey and Iran, between the Black Sea and the Caspian Sea. Northern Caucasia is separated from Transcaucasia by the Greater Caucasus Mountains.

Copper

CITY OF ARMAVIR

A trade center in northwestern Caucasia, Armavir issued provisional coins and notes after coming under Soviet control early in 1918. The coins listed here formerly appeared as Russia Nos. 72-74.

V. Fine

1 1 Ruble 1918 (24mm)....... 50.00

RUSSIAN CAUCASIA

V. Fine

2 3 Rubles 1918 (28mm)..... 50.00
3 5 Rubles 1918 (32mm)......75.00

Pieces with larger diameters and/or in different metals are now thought to be patterns.

Emir Uzun-Chadji
AH 1338 (1919-20)

Brass

V. Fine

1 2½ Toman................——
2 5 Toman AH 1338........——

3 10 Toman 1338............——

AMIRATE OF DAGHISTAN
(Dagestan)

An Islamic state in North Caucasia, Dagestan came under Russian domination in 1877. It regained independence for a few months during the Russian revolution in 1919-20. Mint town: *Vedeno.*

Copper

3a 10 Toman 1338 (struck over Russia No. 10).....——

RUSSIAN TURKESTAN

The south-central area of Russia, lying north of Iran and Afghanistan, and stretching from Sinkiang in the east to the Caspian Sea in the west. Serving traders and conquerors as the bridge between the Eastern and Western worlds, it was one of the earliest centers of civilization.

Note: Because of extensive catalog revisions, new numbers were assigned in the 10th edition. The original numbers are given in parentheses.

KHANATE OF KHIVA
(Khwarezm)

A former Islamic state between Iran and the Aral Sea. It was independent until becoming a Russian protectorate in 1873, regaining independence in 1918. In 1920 it became the Khwarezm Soviet People's Republic (see below). Capital: *Khiva.*

RUSSIAN TURKESTAN

Sayyid Muhammad Khan
AH 1272-1282 (1856-1865)

Copper
Fine

1 1 Pul AH 1274 (1857)
  15mm.................5.00

Silver

2 1 Tenga 1275-81 (2 vars.)...15.00

Sayyid Muhammad Rahim
AH 1282-1328 (1865-1910)

Copper

3 1 Pul AH 1302-11 (1884-
  93) 17mm.............4.00
4 2½ Tenga 1303 (26mm).....25.00
5 5 Tenga 1303 (30mm).....30.00

Silver

6 1 Tenga 1284-1313
  (1867-95)...............15.00

Gold

7 1 Tilla AH —.............70.00

Sayyid Abdullah Khan
and Djunaid Khan
AH 1337-38 (1918-20)

Copper

8   1 Tenga AH 1337.......50.00
9 2½ Tenga 1337 (21mm)...30.00
10 5 Tenga 1337 (28mm)...40.00

KHWAREZM SOVIET
PEOPLE'S REPUBLIC

The successor to the Khanate of
Khiva was formed by Bolshevik factions early in 1920. Four years later
it was divided between the Uzbek and
Turkmen Soviet Socialist Republics.

Bronze or Brass

Fine

1 20 Rubles AH 1338-39
  (1920-21)..............30.00

2 25 Rubles 1339...........25.00

3 100 Rubles 1339..........25.00

4   500 Rubles 1339 (25mm)..75.00
*4a 500 Rubles 1339-40
  (19mm)............30.00

RUSSIAN TURKESTAN

EMIRATE OF BUKHARA

A former Islamic state situated north of Afghanistan and east of Khiva. Falling under Russian protection in 1868, it was again briefly independent from 1920 to 1924. In the latter year it was divided between the Uzbek, Turkmen and Tadzhik Soviet Socialist Republics. Capital: *Bukhara*.

Sayyid Abdul Ahad
AH 1303-1329 (1885-1911)

Copper
Fine

1 (—) 1 Falus AH 1322, 24 (1904, 06) 15mm 5.00

Silver

2 (A1) 1 Tenga 1304-22 (1886-1904) 2 vars. . . 15.00

Gold

3 (B1) 1 Tilla 1303-28 (21-23mm) 75.00

Alim ibn Sayyid Mir Amin
AH 1329-38 (1911-20)

Bronze

4 (C1) 1 Falus AH 1331-36 (1913-18) 15-16mm, vars. 5.00

5 (—) 4 Falus 1333-34 (15mm) 6.00

A5 (—) 8 Falus 1335 (16mm) 6.00

6 (1a) 1 Tenga 1336 (15mm) . . . 20.00

6a (1) 1 Tenga 1336-37 (17-18mm) 25.00

Bronze or Brass *Fine*

7 (2) 2 Tenga 1337 . . . . 25.00

*8 (3) 3 Tenga 1336-37 . . . . . . 25.00

9 (—) 4 Tenga 1336 (30mm) . . 40.00

10 (4) 5 Tenga 1336-37 (27mm) 35.00

11 (5) 10 Tenga 1337 . . . . 15.00

12 (6) 20 Tenga 1336-37 (Brass or Bronze) . . . 35.00

SAARLAND

An important mining region between France and Germany. Taken from Germany and united economically to France after both World Wars by way of reparation. In 1935, and again in 1957 the inhabitants, mostly German, voted to return to Germany. Capital: *Saarbrucken.*

100 Centimen = 1 Frank
Coinage obsolete.

Aluminum-Bronze

Copper-Nickel

Ex. Fine

1 10 Franken 1954 . . . . .2.50
2 20 Franken 1954 . . . . .3.50
3 50 Franken 1954 . . . . .8.00

Ex. Fine

4 100 Franken 1955 . . . . .6.00

ST. PIERRE AND MIQUELON
(Saint-Pierre et Miquelon)

Barren islands off the southwest coast of Newfoundland belonging to France. Inhabited by fishermen, the only exports are cod and other fish products. Population: 6,000. Capital: *St. Pierre.*

100 Centimes = 1 Franc

Aluminum

Unc.

1 1 Franc 1948 35

Unc.

2 2 Francs 1948 50

ST. THOMAS AND PRINCE ISLANDS
(S. Tomé e Príncipe)

In the gulf of Guinea off the west coast of Africa. The islands form a Portuguese Overseas Province. Products include cacao, coffee, copra and coconuts. Area: 372 square miles. Population: 74,000. Capital: *Sao Tomé.*

100 Centavos = 1 Escudo

ST. THOMAS AND PRINCE ISLANDS

Nickel-Bronze

Silver

		V. Fine
1	10 Centavos 1929	2.00
2	20 Centavos 1929	3.00
3	50 Centavos 1928-29	5.00

		V. Fine
7	2½ Escudos 1939, 48	4.00
8	5 Escudos 1939, 48	5.00
9	10 Escudos 1939	15.00

Copper-Nickel

4 1 Escudo 1939 . . . . 4.50

COLONIA DE Omitted

Copper-Nickel

		Unc.
10	50 Centavos 1951	3.50
11	1 Escudo 1951	4.50

Nickel-Bronze

Silver

12	2½ Escudos 1951	5.00
13	5 Escudos 1951	7.50
14	10 Escudos 1951	7.50

5 50 Centavos 1948 . . . . 4.50
6 1 Escudo 1948 . . . . 3.50

Later issues in Current Coins of the World.

EL SALVADOR

The smallest of the Central American countries. Lying in the tropics, its economy is based on its coffee plantations. 80% of all exports from the country is coffee. Language: Spanish. Area: 8,259 square miles. Population: 3,600,000. Capital: *San Salvador*.

100 Centavos = 1 Peso   100 Centavos = 1 Colon

EL SALVADOR

Copper-Nickel

Head of Morazán

Fine

1 1 Centavo 1889, 1913 . . . . 1.25
2 3 Centavos 1889, 1913 . . . . 2.50

Copper

Ex. Fine

3 1 Centavo 1892-93 . . . . 100.00

Silver

Fine

8 5 Centavos 1892-93 . . . . 5.00
9 10 Centavos 1892 . . . . 32.50
*10 20 Centavos 1892 . . . . 7.50

V. Fine

4 50 Centavos 1892 . . . . 30.00
5 1 Peso 1892 . . . . 100.00

V. Fine

6 50 Centavos 1892-94 . . . . 8.00
7 1 Peso 1892-1911 . . . . 10.00
7a 1 Peso 1904-14
    (Heavier portrait) 10.00

Gold

Ex. Fine

11 2½ Pesos 1892 . . . . ——
12 5 Pesos 1892 . . . . ——
13 10 Pesos 1892 . . . . ——
14 20 Pesos 1892 . . . . ——

Copper

15 ¼ Real 1909 . . . . 35.00

Silver

V. Fine

22 5 Centavos 1911 . . . . 2.00
23 10 Centavos 1911 . . . . 2.25
24 25 Centavos 1911 . . . . 3.25

EL SALVADOR

Legend: with DEL SALVADOR

Copper-Nickel

V. Fine

16 1 Centavo 1915-36 50
17 3 Centavos 1915 . . . . .2.50
18 5 Centavos 1915-25 . . . . .1.00

New Legend:
with DE EL SALVADOR

19 1 Centavo 1940 . . . . .1.50
Unc.
20 5 Centavos 1940- 25
21 10 Centavos 1921- 35

Bronze

19a 1 Centavo 1942- 10

Copper-Nickel-Zinc

20a 5 Centavos 1944-52 50
21a 10 Centavos 1952 50

V. Fine

25 5 Centavos 1914 . . . . .1.25
26 10 Centavos 1914 . . . . .1.75
27 25 Centavos 1914 . . . . .2.25
28 25 Centavos 1943-44
  (Design sim. to No. 21) . .1.00

400th Anniversary of San Salvador

Silver

Ex. Fine

30 1 Colon 1925 . . . . .150.00

Gold

29 20 Colones 1925 . . . .———

Silver

Unc.

31 25 Centavos 1953 60
32 50 Centavos 1953 . . . . .1.10

Later issues in Current Coins of the World.

• 414 •

SAN MARINO

The world's smallest republic, situated in Italy. Area: 24 square miles. Population: 19,000. Products: Cattle and wines.

100 Centesimi = 1 Lira

Copper

Ex. Fine

9 5 Lire 1931-38 . . . . 10.00

Fine

1   5 Centesimi 1864-94 . . . . 3.50
2 10 Centesimi 1875-94 . . . . 4.50

Silver

Ex. Fine

3 50 Centesimi 1898 . . . . 25.00
4   1 Lira 1898, 1906 . . . . 30.00
5   2 Lire 1898, 1906 . . . . 45.00

10 10 Lire 1931-38 . . . . 15.00

6 5 Lire 1898 . . . . 200.00

11   20 Lire (15 gram.) 1931-36 . 100.00
11a 20 Lire (20 gram.)
      1935-38 . . . . 250.00

SAN MARINO

Gold

Ex. Fine
12 10 Lire 1925.............400.00
13 20 Lire 1925.............550.00

Bronze

Ex. Fine
15 10 Centesimi 1935-38.......3.50

14 5 Centesimi 1935-38........2.50   *Later issues in Current Coins of the World.*

SARAWAK

A British Protectorate since 1888 on the northwest coast of Borneo. Sir James Brooke obtained the territory from the Sultan of Brunei in 1841, becoming the "White Rajah."

It was ruled by his descendants until 1946, when it became a British colony. Independence was granted in 1963 and it joined the Federation of Malaysia. Area: 48,000 square miles. Capital: *Kuching.*

100 Cents = 1 Dollar

Coinage obsolete.

J. BROOKE, RAJAH 1841-68
Provisional Issue

Copper or Brass

Fine
1 1 Kapang Sept. 24, 1841.....200.00

Some authorities consider No. 1 a token rather than a coin.

Regular Coinage

Copper

Fine
2 ¼ Cent 1863..............15.00
3 ½ Cent 1863..............10.00
4 1 Cent 1863...............6.00

SARAWAK

C. BROOKE, RAJAH
1868-1917

CHARLES VYNER BROOKE, RAJAH 1917-1946

Copper

		Fine
5	¼ Cent 1870, 96	10.00
6	½ Cent 1870-96	7.50
7	1 Cent 1870-91	2.50

Bronze

		V. Fine
13	½ Cent 1933	1.00
14	1 Cent 1927-41	1.00

Copper

8	1 Cent 1892-97	3.50

Copper-Nickel

15	1 Cent 1920	10.00
16	5 Cents 1920, 27	1.50
17	10 Cents 1920-34	1.50

Silver

		V. Fine
9	5 Cents 1900-15	12.50
10	10 Cents 1900-15	12.50
11	20 Cents 1900-15	15.00
12	50 Cents 1900, 06	30.00

Silver

18	5 Cents 1920	35.00
19	10 Cents 1920	20.00
20	20 Cents 1920, 27	3.50
21	50 Cents 1927	10.00

SAUDI ARABIA

An absolute monarchy covering most of the Arabian Peninsula comprising the former sultanate of Nejd, and Kingdom of Hejaz in western Asia. Mostly desert area, the country is hot and dry. Its greatest wealth is in its oil fields. Population: 5,000,000.   Capital: *Riyadh*.

20 Ghirsh = 1 Riyal   1 Gold Guinea = 40 Riyals, Silver (1959)

'ABD AL-AZIZ IBN SA'UD
1926-1953

Copper

Fine
1 ¼ Ghirsh AH 1343 (1925)...5.00
*2 ½ Ghirsh AH 1343........3.00

These copper coins were struck in occupied Mecca, Hejaz mint in 1925 by Ibn Sa'ud while establishing his dual kingdom.

V. Fine
A3 (4a) ½ Ghirsh Bronze 1344.2.50

Title: King of Hejaz and
Sultan of Nejd

Copper-Nickel

3 ¼ Ghirsh AH 1344 (1926)...1.25
4 ½ Ghirsh 1344.............1.50
*5 1 Ghirsh 1344.............1.25

Title: King of Hejaz, Nejd
and its Dependencies

Copper-Nickel
V. Fine
6 ¼ Ghirsh AH 1346 (1928)....1.00
7 ½ Ghirsh 1346.............1.10
8 1 Ghirsh 1346.............1.25

Modified Dies

6a ¼ Ghirsh AH 1348 (1930)...1.00
7a ½ Ghirsh 1348.............1.10
8a 1 Ghirsh 1348.............1.25

Silver

12 ¼ Riyal AH 1346-48
    (1928-30) 24mm......12.50
13 ½ Riyal 1346-48 (27mm)..15.00
*14 1 Riyal 1346-48 (37mm)..22.50

Title: King of Saudi Arabia

Copper-Nickel

*9 ¼ Ghirsh AH 1356 (1937)
    Plain edge.............75
9a ¼ Ghirsh 1356 Reeded edge .35

SAUDI ARABIA

V. Fine

10 ½ Ghirsh 1356 Plain edge.. .75
10a ½ Ghirsh 1356 Reeded edge .50
11 1 Ghirsh 1356 Plain edge.. .85
11a 1 Ghirsh 1356 Reeded edge .75

Silver

Gold

Unc.
23 1 Guinea AH 1370 (1951)..65.00

SA'UD IBN ABDUL AZIZ
1953-64

18 ¼ Riyal AH 1354 (1935)...1.00
19 ½ Riyal 1354.............1.35
★20 1 Riyal 1354-70.........2.00

Copper-Nickel

Copper-Nickel

A23 1 Ghirsh AH 1376-78
(1957-59)..............20
24 2 Ghirsh AH 1376-79.....30
25 4 Ghirsh AH 1376-78.....50

Silver

A21 ¼, **B21** ½ and **C21** 1 Ghirsh
pieces counterstamped with Arabic
"65" to break money changers' mo-
nopoly on small coins in AH 1365
(1946)......................2.00

Gold

Similar to Nos. 18, 19 and 20
26 ¼ Riyal AH 1374 (1955)....75
27 ½ Riyal AH 1374.........1.40
28 1 Riyal AH 1374.........2.75

Gold

21 (1 Sovereign) ND (1947)
.2354 Troy ounces fine
gold.................——
22 (4 Sovereigns) ND (1945-46)
Gross weight 493.1
grains...............——

Nos. 21-22 were struck at Philadelphia and,
although often considered bullion pieces
only, are said to have circulated briefly.
Counterfeits exist.

29 1 Guinea AH 1377
(1957-58)..............65.00
Later issues in Current Coins of the World.

SERBIA

Now a part of Yugoslavia. For five hundred years Serbia was a vassal principality of Turkey. It gained its freedom in 1878. After the First World War it joined with other Slavic states to form what is now Yugoslavia. Capital: *Belgrade.* 100 Para = 1 Dinar Coinage obsolete.

Note: Because of extensive revisions, new numbers have been assigned in the 11th edition. The original numbers are given in parentheses.

MICHAEL, OBRENOVICH III
1839-42, 1860-68

Bronze

			Fine
1	1 Para 1868		4.50
2	5 Para 1868		5.00
3	10 Para 1868		2.50

MILAN, OBRENOVICH IV
as Prince 1868-82

Silver

Obv: Young head, no moustache

4	(9)	50 Para 1875	3.00
5	(10)	1 Dinar 1875	4.00
6	(11)	2 Dinara 1875	8.00

Bronze

Obv: Older head with moustache

			Fine
7	(4)	5 Para 1879	2.00
8	(5)	10 Para 1879	2.50

Silver

4a	(9)	50 Para 1879	4.50
5a	(10)	1 Dinar 1879	6.00
6a	(11)	2 Dinara 1879	8.50
9	(12)	5 Dinara 1879	30.00

Gold

			V. Fine
10	(13)	20 Dinara 1879	100.00

as King Milan I 1882-89
Gold

11	(14)	10 Dinara 1882	70.00
12	(15)	20 Dinara 1882	120.00

GENERAL COINAGE

Nos. 13-16 were issued without the name of the ruler through successive reigns.

Bronze

13	(18)	2 Pare 1904	2.00

SERBIA

Copper-Nickel

Fine

14 (6) 5 Para 1883-1917......1.00
15 (7) 10 Para 1883-1917......1.25
16 (8) 20 Para 1883-1917......1.50

ALEXANDER I 1889-1902

Silver

17 (16) 1 Dinar 1897..........4.00
18 (17) 2 Dinara 1897.........6.00

PETAR I 1903-1918

Silver

*Obv: Designer's name SCHWARTZ
below neck*

V. Fine

19 (22) 50 Para 1904-15......1.50
20 (23) 1 Dinar 1904-15......2.25
21 (24) 2 Dinara 1904-15.....4.00

Obv: Without name below neck

19a 50 Para 1915.............2.75
20a 1 Dinar 1915.............3.50
21a 2 Dinara 1915............5.50

Centennial First Uprising Against Turks

Fine

22 (25) 5 Dinara 1904.......30.00

WORLD WAR II
German Formed State

Zinc

V. Fine

23 (26) 50 Para 1942..........3.00
24 (27) 1 Dinar 1942.......... .75
25 (28) 2 Dinara 1942........ .85

26 (29) 10 Dinara 1943.......1.75

SEYCHELLES

92 islands in the Indian Ocean near Mauritius. A British possession. Chief products: coconuts, cinnamon, vanilla, tortoise shell. Area: 156 square miles. Population 53,000. Capital: *Victoria*.

100 Cents = 1 Rupee

GEORGE VI 1936-1952

Copper-Nickel

Fine
1 10 Cents 1939-44............1.25

Silver

2 25 Cents 1939-44...........2.00
3 ½ Rupee 1939..............5.00
4 1 Rupee 1939..............5.00

New Legend:
KING GEORGE THE SIXTH

Bronze

V. Fine
5 1 Cent 1948................50
6 2 Cents 1948...............65
7 5 Cents 1948..............1.25

Copper-Nickel

V. Fine
8 10 Cents 1951..............1.00

9 25 Cents 1951..............2.00

ELIZABETH II 1952-

Bronze

Unc.
14 1 Cent 1959-69........... .35
15 2 Cents 1959-69........... .50
16 5 Cents 1964-71........... .85

Nickel-Brass

10 10 Cents 1953-.............. .75

Copper-Nickel

11 25 Cents 1954-.............. .85
12 ½ Rupee 1954-.............1.25
13 1 Rupee 1954-............2.50
Later issues in *Current Coins of the World.*

SIAM (THAILAND)

A constitutional monarchy in southeast Asia, extending down onto the Malay Peninsula. The name was officially changed to Thailand in 1939. Exports: rice, teak, tungsten, rubber and tin. Languages: Thai and Khmer. Area: 200,148 square miles. Population: 37,000,000. Capital: *Bangkok*.

8 Fuang = 1 Tical   64 Att = 1 Tical   100 Satang = 1 Tical (Baht)

Siamese Numerals

Western	1	2	3	4	5	6	7	8	9	0	10
Siamese	๑	๒	๓	๔	๕	๖	๗	๘	๙	๐	๑๐

For details of dating systems see Introduction, page 7.

Modern Coinage of the Bangkok Dynasty

PHRA CHOM KLAO (MONGKUT) 1851-1868

Silver

V. Fine

7	1/16 Tical ND (1860) 13mm	15.00
8	1/8 Tical ND (15mm)	4.50
9	1/4 Tical ND (20mm)	7.50
*10	1/2 Tical ND	25.00
11	1 Tical ND (31mm)	15.00
12	2 Ticals ND (37mm)	200.00
A12	4 Ticals ND, rev. Chinese inscr.	——

Tin Composition

Fine

5	1/16 Fuang ND (1862) 23mm	3.00
*6	1/8 Fuang ND	2.00

Contemporary counterfeits of Nos. 5-6 are common and are usually heavier than originals.

Cast Copper, Thick Flan (3mm)

1	1/4 Fuang ND (1865) 22mm	4.00
2	1/2 Fuang ND (28mm)	6.00

Thin Flan (1.5mm)

3	1/4 Fuang ND (1865)	5.00
4	1/2 Fuang ND	6.00

Gold

13	2 Ticals ND (1863, 95) Like no. 8	125.00

14	4 Ticals ND (1863, 95)	125.00
*15	8 Ticals ND (1863, 95)	200.00

Nos. 13-15 have reeded edges. Similar gold pieces with plain edges are presentation strikings of Nos. 7-A12.

Contemporary counterfeits of Nos. 7-15, A34 and 39 were made primarily to be worn as religious charms.

SIAM

PHRA MAHA CHULALONGKORN
1868-1910

First Coinage
Tin

Fine

16 1/16 Fuang ND (1868) 9.00

Silver

28 1/8 Tical ND (1868) 3.50
★29 1/4 Tical ND 11.50
31 1 Tical ND 5.00

Second Coinage
Copper

17 1/2 Att CS 1236-44
 (1874-82) 75
★18 1 Att 1236-44 . . . . 1.00
19 2 Att 1236-44 . . . . 1.50
20 4 Att 1238 (1876) 7.50

Bronze

Fine

21 1/2 Att CS 1249, RS 109-
 124 (1887-1905) 1.00
22 1 Att CS 1249, RS 109-
 124 . . . . 1.50
★23 2 Att CS 1249, RS 109-
 124 . . . . 2.00

Copper-Nickel

Ex. Fine

24 2½ Satang RS 116 (1897) . . 5.00
25 5 Satang 116 . . . . 7.50
★26 10 Satang 116 . . . . 10.00
27 20 Satang 116 . . . . 12.00

Silver

32 1/8 Tical ND (1876-1902) . . 1.75
33 1/4 Tical ND 4.50
★34 1 Tical ND 3.50
32a 1/8 Tical RS 121-27
 (1902-08) 2.50
33a 1/4 Tical RS 120-27 . . . . . . 4.50
34a 1 Tical RS 120-26 . . . . . . 3.50

SIAM

Gold

Obv: bust to left
Rev: crown and umbrellas

V. Fine

A34 2 Ticals ND (1876)...... 95.00

Third Coinage

Silver

39 1 Tical RS 127 (1908) 100.00

The ¼ and ½ Tical of this design are patterns.

General Coinage

Nos. 35-37 were struck during four reigns without regal identification. Because of consolidation, nos. 40-42, 46-47 and 52-53 have been eliminated.

Bronze

★50 ½ Satang BE 2480 (1937).. .20

35 1 Satang RS 127-30,
BE 2456-80 (1908-37)..... .15

Nickel

V. Fine

36 5 Satang RS 127-31,
BE 2456-80............. .25
37 10 Satang RS 127-31,
BE 2456-80............. .40

VAJIRAVUDH
1910-1925

Silver

43 ¼ Tical BE 2458-68
(1915-25)............. 1.50
★44 ½ Tical 2458-64......... 2.50
★45 1 Tical 2456-61......... 4.50

PRAJADHIPOK 1925-1935

Silver

48 25 Satang BE 2472 (1929).. 4.00
★49 50 Satang 2472........... 5.00

ANANDA MAHIDOL
1935-1946

Beginning with No. 51, coins bear a longer legend because of the change in name from Siam to Thailand.

Bronze

51 1 Satang BE 2482 (1939).... .35

SIAM—THAILAND

V. Fine

★54 1 Satang BE 2484 (1941)... .50

Silver

55 5 Satang 2484 75
56 10 Satang 2484 . . . . 1.00
A56 20 Satang 2485 . . . . 2.50

Tin Alloy

Unc.

57 1 Satang BE 2485 Not holed. .15

No. 57 was restruck for circulation in 1969-1971.

V. Fine

★58 5 Satang 2485 35
59 10 Satang 2485 50

Values and B. E. Dates in "Western" Numerals

60 1 Satang BE 2487 Not holed. .20

61 5 Satang Thick BE 2487-88 (1944-45) 35
61a 5 Satang Thin 2488 40

V. Fine

62 10 Satang Thick 2487 75
62a 10 Satang Thin 2488 75
63 20 Satang 2488 . . . . 1.00

Child Head of Ananda

64 5 Satang BE 2489 (1946) . . 1.50
65 10 Satang 2489 . . . . 2.00
★66 25 Satang 2489 . . . . 5.00
67 50 Satang 2489 . . . . 7.50

Youth Head of Ananda

68 5 Satang 2489 20
69 10 Satang 2489 25
70 25 Satang 2489 35
★71 50 Satang 2489 50

PHUMIPHOL ADULYADET 1946-

Tin

One Medal on Uniform

Unc.

72 5 Satang BE 2493 (1950). .35
73 10 Satang 2493 35

Aluminum-Bronze

72a 5 Satang 2493 25
73a 10 Satang 2493 30
76 25 Satang 2493 50
★77 50 Satang 2493 65

Later issues in *Current Coins of the World.*

SOMALIA

Part of the northeast horn of Africa, this independent republic was set up in July 1960 with the union of the former British Somaliland Protectorate and the former Italian trust territory of Somalia. The largely nomadic population, 2,900,000, is mainly engaged in cattle-raising. Area: 262,000 square miles. Capital: *Mogadiscio*.   100 Centesimi = 1 Somalo

Italian Trust Territory Issues

 Bronze  Billon

Unc.

1 1 Centesimo 1950.......... .40
2 5 Centesimi 1950........... .60
3 10 Centesimi 1950........... .90

Unc.

4 50 Centesimi 1950...........5.50
5 1 Somalo 1950.............4.50

Later issues in *Current Coins of the World.*

SOUTH AFRICAN REPUBLIC
(Zuid Afrikaansche Republiek)

Boer Republic in the Transvaal, now part of the Republic of South Africa. Capital: *Pretoria*.

12 Pence = 1 Shilling   20 Shillings = 1 Pond   Coinage obsolete.

THOMAS FRANCOIS BURGERS
President 1872-1877
Gold

A1 1 Pond 1874
      (Only 837 Struck).......——

PAUL KRUGER
President 1883-1902
Bronze

Fine

1 1 Penny 1892-98........... 3.00

Silver

Fine

2 3 Pence 1892-97.............2.00
3 6 Pence 1892-97.............3.00
4 1 Shilling 1892-97...........3.50

5   2 Shillings 1892-97........4.50
6 2½ Shillings 1892-97........6.00
7   5 Shillings 1892   *V. Fine*
       single shaft on wagon..100.00
7a 5 Shillings 1892
       double shaft on wagon..120.00

SOUTH AFRICA

Gold

8 ½ Pond 1893-97   *V. Fine*
   single shaft on wagon....85.00
8a ½ Pond 1892 double shaft..85.00
9 1 Pond 1893-1900
   single shaft on wagon....90.00
9a 1 Pond 1892 double shaft..90.00

The Veld Pond —
ZAR Monogram

                             V. Fine
10 1 Pond 1902.............500.00

UNION OF SOUTH AFRICA (Zuid-Afrika, Suid-Afrika)

The Union was formed by Britain after the Boer War, May 31, 1910. Settled in the 1800's by the Dutch, the government is still controlled by their descendants (Afrikaaners). The country became a republic and left the Commonwealth in May 1961. Has the world's largest gold and diamond mines. Other exports: coal, asbestos, copper. Area: 472,360 square miles. Population: 22,100,000. Languages: English, Afrikaans. Capital: *Pretoria*.

12 Pence = 1 Shilling
 2 Shillings = 1 Florin
20 Shillings = 1 Pound

GEORGE V 1910-1936
Legend: ZUID-AFRIKA
Bronze

11 ¼ Penny 1923-26   *V. Fine*
   (¼ Penny ¼).........3.50
11a ¼ Penny 1928-31
   (¼ Penny)............3.00

12 ½ Penny 1923-26
   (½ Penny ½).........4.00

12a ½ Penny 1928-31   *V. Fine*
   (½ Penny)............2.75
13 1 Penny 1923-24........4.50
14 1 Penny 1926-30
   ("1" not shown)........2.00

Silver

Value in Closed Wreath

15 3 Pence 1923-25...........3.00
16 6 Pence 1923-24...........4.00

17 3 Pence 1925-30............1.75
18 6 Pence 1925-30............2.00

SOUTH AFRICA

19 1 Shilling 1923-24   *V. Fine*
    (1 Shilling 1)............4.00
19a 1 Shilling 1926-30
    (Shilling)..............4.00

20   1 Florin 1923-30........5.00
21   2½ Shillings 1923-25
    (2½ Shillings 2½).....7.50
21a 2½ Shillings 1926-30
    (2½ Shillings)........7.50

Gold

Same as British Sovereign, But
With Pretoria Mint Mark SA

A21 ½ Sovereign 1923-26....35.00
22   1 Sovereign 1923-32.....65.00

New Spelling: SUID-AFRIKA

Bronze

"D" for Penny

23 ¼ Penny 1931-36.........1.50
24 ½ Penny 1931-36.........1.25
25 1 Penny 1931-36.......... .75

Silver

                      V. Fine
26 3 Pence 1931-36............. .75
27 6 Pence 1931-36............1.50

28   1 Shilling 1931-36.......2.00
29   2 Shillings 1931-36.......3.00
30 2½ Shillings 1931-36........4.00

GEORGE VI 1936-1952

Bronze

31 ¼ Penny 1937-47.......... .35

32 ½ Penny 1937-47.......... .50
33 1 Penny 1937-47.......... .50

SOUTH AFRICA

Silver

V. Fine
34 3 Pence 1937-47............ .35

35 6 Pence 1937-47 .... .50

36 1 Shilling 1937-47......... 1.00

37 2 Shillings 1937-47......... 2.00

38 2½ Shillings 1937-47....... 3.00

Royal Visit Commemorative

Ex. Fine
39 5 Shillings (Crown) 1947..... 7.50

New Legend:
GEORGIUS SEXTUS REX
Reverse:
SOUTH AFRICA—SUID-AFRIKA
Designs similar to Nos. 31-39

Bronze

V. Fine
40 ¼ Penny 1948-50........... .50

41 ½ Penny 1948-52........... .60
42 1 Penny 1948-50........... .75

Silver

43 3 Pence 1948-52......... .65
44 6 Pence 1948-50........ 1.00

SOUTH AFRICA

All Values Abbreviated

Bronze

V. Fine

45   1 Shilling (Value spelled
out) 1948-50. . . . . 2.00

★45a   1 Shilling (Value as 1^S)
1951-52. . . . . 2.50

46   2 Shillings 1948-50. . . . 12.00

47   2½ Shillings (Value spelled
out) 1948-50. . . . . . . 40.00

47a   2½ Shillings (Value as 2½^S)
1951-52. . . . . 3.00

V. Fine

49   ¼ Penny 1951-52. 35
50   1 Penny 1951-52. 50

Silver

51   6 Pence 1951-52. 85

Ex. Fine

48   5 Shillings (Crown) 1948-50. . 5.00

52   2 Shillings (Value as 2^S)
1951-52. . . . . 1.75

Gold

57   ½ Pound 1952. . . . . 35.00

Reverse:
SUID-AFRIKA—SOUTH AFRICA

Beginning in 1951 the following
denominations used the transposed
reverse legend, while the other denominations continued to place the
English name first. The change was
intended to give the Afrikaans language equal stature with the English.

Ex. Fine

53   5 Shillings (Value as 5^S) 1951. 6.00

SOUTH AFRICA

Third Centennial
Founding of Capetown

ELIZABETH II 1952-61
Legend:
SOUTH AFRICA—SUID-AFRIKA
on Nos. 60, 62, 64, 66 and 68.
SUID-AFRIKA—SOUTH AFRICA
on all other numbers 59-70.

Ex. Fine

56 5 Shillings 1952 . . . . 5.00

Gold

58 1 Pound 1952 . . . . 65.00

		Bronze	*Unc.*
59	¼ Penny 1953-60		.50
60	½ Penny 1953-60		.60
61	1 Penny 1953-60		.75

		Silver	
62	3 Pence 1953-60		.50
63	6 Pence 1953-60		.75
64	1 Shilling 1953-60		1.10
65	2 Shillings 1953-60		2.00
66	2½ Shillings 1953-60		3.00
67	5 Shillings 1953-59		8.50

		Gold	
68	½ Pound 1953-60		65.00
69	1 Pound 1953-60		75.00

Later issues in *Current Coins of the World.*

SOUTHERN RHODESIA

From 1953 to 1963 a part of the Central African Federation, in south central Africa. Victoria Falls on the Zambesi River is one of the world's largest waterfalls. Agriculture and mining are important industries. Area: 150,333 square miles. Capital: *Salisbury.*

12 Pence = 1 Shilling   5 Shillings = 1 Crown
2 Shillings = 1 Florin   20 Shillings = 1 Pound

GEORGE V 1910-1936
Copper-Nickel

Silver

V. Fine

3 3 Pence 1932-36 . . . . 1.50

V.F.

1 ½ Penny 1934-36 . . . . 1.00
2 1 Penny 1934-36 . . . . 1.25

4 6 Pence 1932-36 . . . . 2.50

SOUTHERN RHODESIA

V. Fine

5 1 Shilling 1932-36 . . . . 4.50

V. Fine

9a (11) 1 Penny 1942-47 65

6 2 Shillings 1932-36 . . . . 5.50

EMPEROR to right of head
Silver

Rev. designs same as Nos. 3-7

Fine

12	3 Pence 1937	1.25
13	6 Pence 1937	2.00
14	1 Shilling 1937	3.50
15	2 Shillings 1937	4.50
16	½ Crown 1937	7.50

KING EMPEROR to right of head
Rev. designs same as Nos. 3-7

V. Fine

17	3 Pence 1939-46	1.25
18	6 Pence 1939-46	1.50
19	1 Shilling 1939-46	3.00
20	2 Shillings 1939-46	4.00
21	½ Crown 1938-46	6.50

Copper-Nickel

17a	3 Pence 1947	.75
18a	6 Pence 1947	1.00
19a	1 Shilling 1947	1.50
20a	2 Shillings 1947	3.00
21a	½ Crown 1947	4.00

7 ½ Crown 1932-36 . . . . 8.00

GEORGE VI 1936-1952
Copper-Nickel

8	½ Penny 1938-39	1.00
9	1 Penny 1937-42	1.25

Bronze

8a (10) ½ Penny 1942-44 50

New Legend:
KING GEORGE THE SIXTH
Bronze

27	½ Penny 1951-52	.45
28	1 Penny 1949-52	.60

SOUTHERN RHODESIA

Copper-Nickel *V. Fine*
29 3 Pence 1948-52 50
30 6 Pence 1948-52 60
31 1 Shilling 1948-52 . . . . .1.25
32 2 Shillings 1948-52 . . . . .1.75
33 ½ Crown 1948-52 . . . . .2.25

ELIZABETH II 1952-
Commemorating
Birth of Cecil Rhodes
Silver (.500 Fine)

Unc.
34 1 Crown 1953 . . . . 20.00
Proof . . .130.00

Types of George VI
Bronze

Ex. Fine
35 ½ Penny 1954 . . . . .1.50
36 1 Penny 1954 . . . . .2.00

Copper-Nickel

37 2 Shillings 1954 . . . . .7.50
38 ½ Crown 1954 . . . . .6.50

See Rhodesia and Nyasaland for later issues.

SOUTH KOREA— see *Current Coins of the World*

SOUTH VIETNAM

Southern zone of Vietnam established by Geneva accord below the 17th parallel. Formerly a part of French Indo-China. Area: 65,000 square miles. Population: 18,800,000. Capital: *Saigon*.
100 Xu (Su) = 1 Dong

Aluminum

Unc.
1 10 Su 1953 40
2 20 Su 1953 50

Unc.
3 50 Xu 1953 . . . . .1.25
Later issues in Current Coins of the World.

SPAIN (España)

A monarchy covering most of the Iberian Peninsula in southwest Europe. Though Spain has tried twice to become a republic, neither attempt was long-lived. At present, General Franco is government head with the understanding that he has life tenure and may enthrone a king of his choosing as his successor. Primarily an agricultural nation, it exports wines, cork, wheat, olives, fruits, and many other products. Area: 195,504 square miles. Population: 34,400,000. Capital: *Madrid*.

34 Maravedis = 1 Real

ISABEL II 1833-1868

First Coinage

Obv: Legend ends DIOS
Rev: Legend ends INDIAS

Copper

		Fine
1	4 Maravedis 1835-36	7.50
2	8 Maravedis 1835-36	4.50

Silver

5	2 Reales 1836	8.00
★6	4 Reales 1834-36	12.50

		V. Fine
7	20 Reales 1834-36	225.00

Gold
A7 80 Reales 1834-37 .... 120.00

Second Coinage

Obv: Legend ends CONST(ITUCION)
Rev: Legend ends ESPAÑAS

Copper

		Fine
3	1 Maravedi 1842-43	10.00
4	2 Maravedis 1838-58	2.00
★A4	4 Maravedis 1837-55	2.00
B4	8 Maravedis 1837-58	2.50

Cast Bell Metal

B4a 8 Maravedis 1837 Pamplona
(PP mint mark) 100.00

SPAIN

Third Coinage

10 Décimas = 1 Real (1848-55)

Silver

		Fine
8	1 Real 1838-52	4.00
9	2 Reales 1844-51	3.00
10	4 Reales 1837-38,	
	obv. CONSTITUCION	6.00
10a	4 Reales 1837-49,	
	obv. CONST.	5.00
11	10 Reales 1840-45	25.00
12	20 Reales 1837-49	50.00

Gold

		V. Fine
14	80 Reales 1837-38,	
	obv. CONSTITUCION	125.00
14a	80 Reales 1837-49,	
	obv. CONST.	115.00

Cataluña (Catalonia), Province

Barcelona Mint

Copper

Obv: arms of Spain
Rev: arms of Cataluña

		Fine
48	3 Quartos 1836-46	5.00
49	6 Quartos 1836-48	6.00

Silver

50	1 Peseta 1836-37	11.00

Rev: design like Nos. 8-14

		Fine
13	20 Reales 1850	50.00

Copper

15	$\frac{1}{20}$ Real 1852-53	4.00
16	$\frac{1}{10}$ Real 1850-53	3.50
17	$\frac{1}{5}$ Real 1853	4.50
★18	$\frac{1}{2}$ Real 1848-53	3.00

Silver

Rev: arms without pillars

19	1 Real 1852-55	3.50
20	2 Reales 1852-55	4.00
21	4 Reales 1852-55	7.50

SPAIN

Rev: arms flanked by pillars

		Fine
22	10 Reales 1851-55	12.00
23	20 Reales 1850-55	30.00

Gold

		V. Fine
A23	1 Doblón (100 Reales) 1850-51	160.00
B23	100 Reales 1851-55	150.00

Fourth Coinage

100 Centimos = 1 Real (1854-64)

Copper

		Fine
24	5 Centimos (de Real) 1854-64	1.00
25	10 Centimos 1854-64	1.00
26	25 Centimos 1854-64	1.25

Silver

Rev: arms without pillars

27	1 Real 1857-64	3.00
28	2 Reales 1857-64	3.00
29	4 Reales 1856-64	4.50

Rev: arms flanked by pillars

		Fine
30	10 Reales 1857-65	12.00
31	20 Reales 1856-64	25.00

Gold

Rev: oval arms on cartouche

		V. Fine
32	20 Reales 1861-63	110.00
33	40 Reales 1861-63	100.00
35	100 Reales 1856-62	125.00

Rev: mantled arms

A35	40 Reales 1864	100.00
B35	100 Reales 1863-64	125.00

Fifth Coinage

100 Centimos = 1 Escudo (1864-68)

Bronze

		Fine
36	½ Centimo (de Escudo) 1866-68	1.50
37	1 Centimo 1865-68	1.50
★38	2½ Centimos 1865-68	1.50
39	5 Centimos 1865-68	2.00

SPAIN

Silver

		Fine
40	10 Centimos 1865-68	3.50
41	20 Centimos 1865-68	3.00
42	40 Centimos 1864-68	3.50

Rev: arms flanked by pillars

43	1 Escudo 1865-68	12.50
44	2 Escudos 1865-68	30.00

For similar silver coins 1864-68 with values in Céntimos de Peso, see PHILIPPINES.

	Gold	*V. Fine*
45	2 Escudos 1865	110.00
46	4 Escudos 1865-68	60.00
47	10 Escudos 1865-68	125.00

PROVISIONAL ISSUES
1868-1870
Commemorating Battle of
Bridge of Alcolea

Bronze

A50	25 Milesimas de Escudo 1868	35.00

Dates on Spanish Coins

Beginning about 1868 (possibly starting with 1868 dates of Nos. 40-47) most Spanish coins bear two dates. The large, obvious date is the year of authorization, and does not necessarily correspond to the year of coinage. True dates of coinage appear as tiny incuse numerals on the *six-pointed stars* found on most types.

In the following listings the large dates are shown in normal fashion. Coinage dates are indicated by ☆, within parentheses. Coins in this catalog which do not have stars with small incuse dates are Nos. A50-54, 63-67, 69-70, 100-107, 103-106, 109-112.

New Coinage System
100 Céntimos = 1 Peseta 1869-

Bronze

		Fine
51	1 Centimo 1870	.50
52	2 Centimos 1870	.50
53	5 Centimos 1870	.60
54	10 Centimos 1870	.50

Obv. Legend:
GOBIERNO PROVISIONAL

Silver

A55	1 Peseta 1869 (☆69)	3.00

New Obv. Legend: ESPAÑA
Silver

55	20 Centimos 1869-70 (☆69-70)	—
56	50 Centimos 1869-70 (☆69-70)	2.00
58	1 Peseta 1869-70 (☆69-73)	3.00
59	2 Pesetas 1869-70 (☆69-75)	4.00
60	5 Pesetas 1869-70 (☆69-71)	11.00

SPAIN

AMADEO I 1871-1873

Fine
61 5 Pesetas 1871 (☆71-75)....10.00

REPUBLIC 1873-1874
Cartagena Mint
Silver

V. Fine
64 10 Reales (2½ Pesetas)
1873.................85.00
63 5 Pesetas 1873...........40.00
Former No. 62, 2 Pesetas 1873, is thought to be a fantasy struck later for collectors.

CARLOS VII, Pretender
1872-1876, 1885
Bronze

Ex. Fine
66 5 Centimos 1875........10.00
67 10 Centimos 1875........10.00
Silver coins of Carlos VII 1874-85 are fantasies struck later for collectors.

ALFONSO XII 1875-1885
First Coinage
Silver

Obv: legend REY DE ESPAÑA
74 5 Pesetas 1875-76 (☆75-76)..9.00

Second Coinage
Bronze

Fine
69 5 Centimos 1877-79.........75
70 10 Centimos 1877-79.........75

SPAIN

Silver

Obv: legend POR LA G • DE DIOS

Fine

B75 1 Peseta 1876 (☆76)......2.50
75 5 Pesetas 1877-82 (☆77-82).8.50

Gold

V. Fine

77 10 Pesetas 1878-79 (☆78-79,
1961-62)...............50.00
78 25 Pesetas 1876-80 (☆76-80,
1962)................65.00

Third Coinage
Silver

Obv: head with sideburns, moustache

A76 50 Centimos 1880-85   Fine
(☆80-86)............1.25
B76 1 Peseta 1881-85
(☆81-86)............1.75
C76 2 Pesetas 1879-84
(☆79-84)............2.50
76 5 Pesetas 1882-85
(☆82-87)............9.00

Gold

A78 25 Pesetas 1881-85   V. Fine
(☆81-86)..........100.00

ALFONSO XIII 1886-1931

First Coinage
Silver

Fine

79 50 Centimos 1889, 92
(☆89, 92)...............2.00
80 1 Peseta 1889, 91 (☆89, 91).2.50
81 2 Pesetas 1889-92 (☆89-92).3.75
82 5 Pesetas 1888-92 (☆88-92).9.50

Gold

A82 20 Pesetas 1887-90   V. Fine
(☆89-90, 1961-62)....85.00

Second Coinage
Silver

Fine

83 50 Centimos 1894 (☆94).....2.50

SPAIN

Fine

84 1 Peseta 1893-94 (☆93-94)...3.50
85 2 Pesetas 1894 (☆94)......45.00
86 5 Pesetas 1892-94 (☆92-94).12.00

Gold
V. Fine

A86 20 Pesetas 1892 (☆92)..200.00

Third Coinage

Silver

Fine

87 50 Centimos 1896, 1900
    (☆96, 00)..............1.00
88 1 Peseta 1896-1902
    (☆96-02)..............2.50
89 5 Pesetas 1896-99 (☆96-99).8.00

Gold

A89 20 Pesetas 1896, 99   *V. Fine*
    (☆99, 1961-62)......60.00
90 100 Pesetas 1897
    (☆97, 1961-62).....225.00

Fourth Coinage

Bronze

Fine

96 1 Centimo 1906 (☆6).......75
97 2 Centimos 1904-05
    (☆04-05)................60

Silver

92 50 Centimos 1904, 10
    (☆04, 10)..............2.00

Fine

94 1 Peseta 1903-05 (☆03-05)...3.00
95 2 Pesetas 1905 (☆05).......4.50

Gold

V. Fine

91 20 Pesetas 1904 (☆04)....200.00

Fifth Coinage

Bronze

98 1 Centimo 1911-13 (☆1-3)... .75
99 2 Centimos 1911-12
    (☆11-12).................85

Silver

93 50 Centimos 1910 (☆10)....1.75

Sixth Coinage

Nickel-Brass

100 25 Centimos 1925........1.25

Copper-Nickel

101 25 Centimos 1927......... .75

SPAIN

Silver

102 50 Centimos 1926.........2.00

V. Fine

Copper

104 25 Centimos 1938.........1.75

V. Fine

REPUBLIC 1931-1938
(Republica Española)
First Coinage

Nickel-Bronze

107 25 Centimos 1934 .... .75

105 50 Centimos 1937.........1.00

Silver

108 1 Peseta 1933 (☆34).......5.00

Brass

106 1 Peseta 1937............. .50

NATIONALIST
GOVERNMENT 1937-1947

Monarchy declared under regency of Franco, 1947.

Second Coinage

Iron

103 5 Centimos 1937.........1.75

First Coinage

Copper-Nickel

109 25 Centimos 1937......... .50

SPAIN

Aluminum

Nickel

V. Fine

110 5 Centimos 1940-53 20
111 10 Centimos 1940-53 25

Aluminum-Bronze

112 1 Peseta 1944 50

Second Coinage

Copper-Nickel

V. Fine

117 5 Pesetas 1949 (☆49-50) 1.25

Later issues in *Current Coins of the World.*

VISCAYAN REPUBLIC
(Euzkadi)

A province of Spain on the Bay of Biscay, autonomous in 1936-37. Capital and chief port: *Bilbao.*

Nickel

Obv: arrows pointing down
115 50 Centimos 1949 (☆51) . . . 2.00

Obv: arrows pointing up
*116 50 Centimos 1949, 63   *Unc.*
(☆51-65) 20

Ex. Fine

1 1 Peseta 1937 . . . . 2.50

Aluminum-Bronze

V. Fine

113 1 Peseta 1947-63
(☆48-67) 15
114 2½ Pesetas 1953
(☆54-71) 75

2 2 Pesetas 1937 . . . . 2.50

STRAITS SETTLEMENTS

A British Crown Colony until 1946 when it was dissolved to form the Malayan Federation. Its capital and chief port was *Singapore*. Much of United States' tin and rubber was imported from the Straits. Taken by Japan during the Second World War, it was returned to Britain in 1945.

100 Cents = 1 Dollar

VICTORIA 1837-1901

Legend:
EAST INDIA COMPANY

Copper

		Fine
1	¼ Cent 1845	2.00
2	½ Cent 1845	1.25
3	1 Cent 1845	1.00

Legend Changed:
INDIA STRAITS

4	¼ Cent 1862	17.50
5	½ Cent 1862	8.50
6	1 Cent 1862	3.00

New Legend:
STRAITS SETTLEMENTS

Smooth Edge

7	¼ Cent 1872-84	2.25
8	½ Cent 1872-84	1.25
9	1 Cent 1872-86	1.25

Reeded Edge

			Fine
7a	(10)	¼ Cent 1889-1901	1.50
8a	(11)	½ Cent 1889	7.50
9a	(12)	1 Cent 1887-1901	1.00

Silver

13	5 Cents 1871-1901	1.25
14	10 Cents 1871-1901	1.00
15	20 Cents 1871-1901	3.00
16	50 Cents 1886-1901	6.00

EDWARD VII 1901-1910

Rev. design same as Nos. 10-12

Copper

17	¼ Cent 1905-08	2.00
18	½ Cent 1908	2.00
19	1 Cent 1903-08	1.50

Silver

20	5 Cents 1902-10	2.00
21	10 Cents 1902-10	2.50
22	20 Cents 1902-10	3.00
23	50 Cents 1902-05 (31mm)	7.50

STRAITS SETTLEMENTS

24 50 Cents/½ Dollar   *Fine*
1907-08 (28mm)........4.00

                V. Fine
*25 1 Dollar 1903-04 (37mm)...8.00
26 1 Dollar 1907-09 (34mm)...5.00

GEORGE V 1910-1936

Copper

27 ¼ Cent 1916..............1.50
28 ½ Cent 1916..............1.75

Bronze

29 ½ Cent 1932..............50
30 1 Cent 1919-26............35

Copper-Nickel

                V. Fine
31 5 Cents 1920..............2.50

Silver

32 5 Cents 1918-20...........1.50
33 5 Cents (Smaller Head-
Broad Rim) 1926-35......85
34 10 Cents 1916-27...........75
35 20 Cents 1916-35..........1.50
36 50 Cents 1920-21..........2.00

37 1 Dollar 1919-20........10.00

See Malaya for later issues.

THE SUDAN

The Sudan, located along the Nile River in northeastern Africa, is the continent's largest country. First conquered and unified by Egypt in the early 19th century, it revolted in 1881 and issued its first coinage. The country was retaken in 1898 and was made a joint British-Egyptian protectorate. Full independence came in 1956. Primarily an agricultural nation, its main exports are cotton, gum arabic and livestock. Area: 967,500 square miles. Languages: Arabic and native dialects. Capital: *Khartoum.*

40 Para = 1 Ghirsh (Piastre) 1885-98
10 Millim = 1 Ghirsh 1956-

Note: Because of extensive catalog revisions, new numbers were assigned in the 10th edition. The original numbers are given in parentheses.

EL MAHDI 1881-1885

Silver

		Fine
1 (A1)	10 Ghirsh AH 1302 (1885)............	200.00
*2	**(1)** 20 Ghirsh 1302......	125.00

Gold

3 (2) 100 Ghirsh AH 1255, year 2 (1840)........ ——

No. 3 is a crude copy, including date, of Egypt No. 215 in Craig.

KHALIFA ABDULLAH
1885-1898

Copper

4 (3) 10 Para AH 1308 (1891).. ——

Some authorities consider No. 4 a pattern.

Silver or Billon

Borders of double crescents

		Fine
*6 (C3)	5 Ghirsh AH 1304, 11 (1887, 94)......	22.50
7 (D3)	10 Ghirsh 1304......	45.00
8 (E3)	20 Ghirsh 1304, 09....	55.00

Plain borders

9 (A3)	1 Ghirsh 1304, 11..	35.00
10 (B3)	2 Ghirsh 1310-11...	——
*12 (—)	5 Ghirsh 1310....	35.00
13 (—)	10 Ghirsh 1310.....	40.00

THE SUDAN

Copper or Billon

Fine

23 (C3) 5 Ghirsh 1311......——
24 (F3) 20 Ghirsh 1311-12,
        Rev. legend as
        No. 19..........20.00
*25 (F3) 20 Ghirsh 1312, Rev.
        legend as No. 12..20.00

27 (B3) 2 Ghirsh 1311........35.00

Borders of crescents, stars, roses

Fine

16 (—) 2½ Ghirsh AH 1312
         (1895).........40.00
17 (C3) 5 Ghirsh 1311.....35.00
*19 (F3) 20 Ghirsh *1310*-12..25.00

30 (D3) 10 Ghirsh 1310.....45.00
*31 (G3) 20 Ghirsh 1310-15
        Spears on rev. ...17.50
32 (G3) 20 Ghirsh 1312-15
        Spears on obv. 9.50

Borders of crescents only

22 (—) 2½ Ghirsh 1312.......37.50

Later issues in *Current Coins of the World.*

SWEDEN (Sverige)

A constitutional monarchy in the eastern part of the Scandinavian Peninsula of Northern Europe. Its main exports are iron ore and wood products. About one-fifth of the total produce of Sweden is for foreign trade. Area: 173,378 square miles. Population: 8,200,000. Capital: *Stockholm*.

100 Öre = 1 Riksdaler Riksmynt (to 1873)
100 Öre = 1 Krona (since 1873)

CARL XV 1859-1872

Bronze

Fine
1 ½ Öre 1867............... 12.00

2 1 Öre 1860-72............... 2.00
3 2 Öre 1860-72............... 2.50
4 5 Öre 1860-72............... 4.00

Silver

5 10 Öre 1861-71............... 5.00
6 25 Öre 1862-71............... 7.50
7 50 Öre 1862............... ——

V. Fine
8 1 Riksdaler Riksm. 1860-71. 60.00

9 2 Riksdaler Riksm.   V. Fine
    1862-71............... 150.00
10 4 Riksdaler Riksm.
    1861-71............... 100.00

Gold   Ex. Fine

B10 1 Dukat 1860-68....... 350.00

A10 1 Carolin (10 Francs)
    1868-72............... 225.00

OSCAR II 1872-1907

First Coinage

Bronze

Fine
11 1 Öre 1873............... 5.00
12 2 Öre 1873............... 7.50
13 5 Öre 1873............... 12.50

Silver

17 10 Öre 1872-73.......... 20.00
18 1 Riksdaler Riksmynt
    1873............... 150.00

SWEDEN

Second Coinage

Bronze

		Fine
14	1 Öre 1874-77 Sm. letters	3.00
14a	1 Öre 1877-79 Med. letters	5.00
14b	1 Öre 1879-1905 Lg. let.	.75
15	2 Öre 1874-78	1.50
15a	2 Öre 1877-1905	
	Different lettering	.75
16	5 Öre 1874-89	2.00
16a	5 Öre 1889-1905	
	Different lettering	.75

Silver

		Fine
19	10 Öre 1874-76	6.00
20	25 Öre 1874-78	7.50
21	50 Öre 1875-99	5.00

27	10 Öre 1880-1904	1.25

28	25 Öre 1880-1905	1.75

Obv: Legend SVERIGES O. NORGES

		Fine
22	1 Krona 1875-76	4.00
23	2 Kronor 1876-80	10.00

Gold

		Ex. Fine
25	10 Kronor 1873-76	95.00
26	20 Kronor 1873-76	150.00
26c	20 Kronor 1876-77,	
	modified arms	150.00

Silver

Obv: Legend SVERIGES OCH NORGES

		Fine
22a	1 Krona 1877-89	4.00
23a	2 Kronor 1878, 80	20.00

Gold

		Ex. Fine
24	5 Kronor 1881-99	80.00
25a	10 Kronor 1876-95	105.00
26a	20 Kronor 1877-99	125.00

SWEDEN

Silver

Obv: older head

		Fine
29	1 Krona 1890-1904	4.00
30	2 Kronor 1890-1904	10.00

Gold

		Ex. Fine
24a	5 Kronor 1901	80.00

25b	10 Kronor 1901	100.00
26b	20 Kronor 1900-02	165.00

Silver Jubilee 1872-97

Silver

31	2 Kronor 1897	17.50

Third Coinage

Bronze

		Fine
32	1 Öre 1906-07	.75
33	2 Öre 1906-07	1.00
34	5 Öre 1906-07	1.25

Silver

35	10 Öre 1907	3.00
36	25 Öre 1907	4.00
37	50 Öre 1906-07	5.00

38	1 Krona 1906-07	8.00
39	2 Kronor 1906-07	10.00

Commemorating Golden Wedding—Oscar II and Sofia

40	2 Kronor 1907	Ex. Fine 20.00

SWEDEN

GUSTAF V 1907-1950

Regular Issues

Bronze

V. Fine

44 1 Öre 1909-50 15
45 2 Öre 1909-50 25
46 5 Öre 1909-50 40

Silver

47 10 Öre 1909-42 60

48 25 Öre 1910-41 . . . . .1.00
49 50 Öre 1911-39 . . . . .1.50

Nickel-Bronze

55 10 Öre 1920-47 75

56 25 Öre 1921-47 . . . . .1.25
57 50 Öre 1920-47 . . . . .1.50

Silver

V. Fine

50 1 Krona 1910-42 . . . . .2.00
51 2 Kronor 1910-40 . . . . .4.00

Gold

Ex. Fine

62 5 Kronor 1920 . . . . .90.00

63 20 Kronor 1925 . . . . .550.00

WORLD WAR I ISSUES

Design of Nos. 44-46

Iron

V. Fine

52 1 Öre 1917-19 . . . . .2.50
53 2 Öre 1917-19 . . . . .3.50
54 5 Öre 1917-19 . . . . .5.00

SWEDEN

COMMEMORATIVE ISSUES

400th Anniversary of Political Liberty

Silver

Gustaf Vasa

58 2 Kronor 1921 .... *Ex. Fine* 15.00

300th Anniversary Death of Gustaf II Adolf

59 2 Kronor 1932.... *Ex. Fine* 17.50

500th Anniversary of the Riksdag

60 5 Kronor 1935.... *Ex. Fine* 12.50

300th Anniversary of Swedish Settlement in Delaware 1638-1938

61 2 Kronor 1938.... *Ex. Fine* 10.00

SWEDEN

Regular Issues

Silver

		V. Fine
64	10 Öre 1942-50	.40
65	25 Öre 1943-50	.60
66	50 Öre 1943-50	1.00

67	1 Krona 1942-50	1.25
68	2 Kronor 1942-50	2.00

WORLD WAR II ISSUES

Iron

69	1 Öre 1942-50	.35
70	2 Öre 1942-50	.40
71	5 Öre 1942-50	.50

GUSTAF VI ADOLF
1950-1973

Bronze

		Unc.
72	1 Öre 1952-71	.10
73	2 Öre 1952-71	.15
74	5 Öre 1952-71	.20

Silver

		Unc.
75	10 Öre 1952-62	.25

76	25 Öre 1952-61	.50
77	50 Öre 1952-61	.75

78	1 Krona 1952-68	1.00
79	2 Kronor 1952-66	2.50
80	5 Kronor 1954-55	5.00

King's 70th Birthday

81	5 Kronor 1952	50.00

Later issues in Current Coins of the World.

SWITZERLAND

(Helvetia, Confoederatio Helvetica)

A confederated republic bounded by Germany, France, Austria, Liechtenstein and Italy. It forms no military alliances and is not a member of the United Nations. It is noted for its cheese, precision instruments, and wines. Population: 6,300,000. Area: 15,944 square miles (61% of the country is mountainous). Capital: *Berne*.

100 Centimes (Rappen) = 1 Franc

SCHUTZENFEST (SHOOTING FESTIVAL) COINS
(Quantities Minted Shown in Parentheses)

Silver

		Ex. Fine
1-S	Chur 4 Francs 1842 (6000)	500.00
2-S	Glarus 40 Batzen 1847 (3200)	1500.00
3-S	Solothurn "5 Francs 1855" (3000)	1250.00
4-S	Bern 5 Francs 1857 (5195)	200.00
5-S	Zürich 5 Francs 1859 (6000)	175.00
6-S	Nidwalden 5 Francs 1861 (6000)	100.00
7-S	La Chaux-de-Fonds 5 Francs 1863 (6000)	125.00
8-S	Schaffhausen 5 Francs 1865 (10,000)	85.00
9-S	Schwyz 5 Francs 1867 (8000)	110.00
10-S	Zug 5 Francs 1869 (6000)	120.00
11-S	Zürich 5 Francs 1872 (10,000)	70.00
12-S	St. Gallen 5 Francs 1874 (15,000)	70.00
13-S	Lausanne 5 Francs 1876 (20,000)	50.00
14-S	Basel 5 Francs 1879 (30,000)	50.00
15-S	Fribourg 5 Francs 1881 (30,000)	45.00
16-S	Lugano 5 Francs 1883 (30,000)	45.00
17-S	Bern 5 Francs 1885 (25,000)	50.00

Modern Series

44	Fribourg 5 Francs 1934 (40,000)	40.00
45	Fribourg 100 Francs Gold 1934 (2022)	1250.00
47	Lucerne 5 Francs 1939 (40,000)	45.00
48	Lucerne 100 Francs Gold 1939 (6000)	450.00

SWITZERLAND

Regular Issues

Bronze

V. Fine
18 1 Centime 1850-1941 35
19 2 Centimes 1850-1941 65

Zinc

18a 1 Centime 1942-46 . . . . 1.00
19a 2 Centimes 1942-46 . . . . 1.00

Billon

Fine
20 5 Centimes 1850-77 . . . . 6.00
21 10 Centimes 1850-76 . . . . 6.00
22 20 Centimes 1850-59 . . . . 7.50

Copper-Nickel

Unc.
23 5 Centimes 1879- 15
24 10 Centimes 1879- 20
25 20 Centimes 1939- 25

Nickel

V. Fine
23a 5 Centimes 1932-41 20
24a 10 Centimes 1932-39 25
25a 20 Centimes 1881-1938 30

Brass

Fine
23b 5 Centimes 1918 . . . . 7.50
24b 10 Centimes 1918-19 . . . . . . 7.50

Silver

26 ½ Franc 1850-51 . . . . 50.00
27 1 Franc 1850-61 . . . . 45.00
28 2 Francs 1850-63 . . . . 50.00
29 5 Francs 1850-74 . . . . 100.00

Unc.
30 ½ Franc 1875-1967 . . . . 1.00
31 1 Franc 1875-1967 . . . . 1.25
32 2 Francs 1874-1967 . . . . 2.00

V. Fine
33 5 Francs 1888-1916 . . . . 100.00

SWITZERLAND

Obv: Like No. 36

34 5 Fr(ancs) 1922-23 . . . . 50.00 *V. Fine*
35 5 FR(ancs) 1924-28 . . . . . . 60.00

Unc.
41 20 Francs 1897-1935,
    stars on edge 60.00
41a 20 Francs 1947, 49,
    lettered edge 60.00

Ex. Fine
42 10 Francs 1911-22 . . . . 70.00
43 100 Francs 1925 . . . . ——

36 5 Francs (Reduced Size) *Unc.*
    1931-69 . . . . 3.50

COMMEMORATIVE ISSUES
Armament Fund

Gold

40 20 Francs 1883, *Ex. Fine*
     reeded edge 80.00
40a 20 Francs 1886-96,
     lettered edge 75.00

Silver

46 5 Francs 1936 . . . . 20.00

SWITZERLAND

600th Anniversary
Battle of Laupen

49 5 Francs 1939 . . . . *Unc.* 175.00

Zürich Exposition

50 5 Francs 1939 . . . . *Ex. Fine* 40.00

650th Anniversary of
Confederation 1291-1941

51 5 Francs 1941 . . . . 30.00

500th Anniversary Battle of
St. Jakob an der Birs

52 5 Francs 1944 . . . . *Ex. Fine* 30.00

Centennial of
Swiss Confederation

53 5 Francs 1948 . . . . 15.00

Bronze

54 1 Centime 1948- . . . . *Unc.* .10
55 2 Centimes 1948- 15

Later issues in *Current Coins of the World.*

SYRIA

In Western Asia, bordered by Turkey on the north. It was part of the Turkish Empire until 1920 when it was made an independent state under French mandate. In 1944 it was given complete independence and proclaimed a republic. On February 21, 1958 Syria joined Egypt as part of the United Arabic Republic. It broke away and declared itself independent again on September 29, 1961. The principal industries are farming and cattle raising. Area: 72,234 square miles. Languages: Arabic, French. Capital: *Damascus*.

100 Piastres = 1 Lira (Pound)

Copper-Nickel

V. Fine

1 ½ Piastre 1921 75

Aluminum-Bronze

2 2 Piastres 1926 . . . . 3.00
3 5 Piastres 1926-40 50

Various Metals

4 ½ Piastre Nic.-Br. 1935-36 . .65

5 1 Piastre Nic.-Br. 1929-36 . . .50

V. Fine

5a 1 Piastre Zinc 1940 50
6 2½ Piastres Al.-Br. 1940 65

Silver

7 10 Piastres 1929 . . . . 2.75
8 25 Piastres 1929-37 . . . . 2.00
9 50 Piastres 1929-37 . . . . 3.50

World War II Issues

10 1 Piastre ND, Brass 1.50
11 2½ Piastres ND,
      Aluminum 1.50

REPUBLIC 1944-1958

Copper-Nickel

12 2½ Piastres 1948-56 25

SYRIA

13
5 Piastres *V. Fine*
1948-56......30

14
10 Piastres
1948-56.... .40

Silver

V. Fine
17 1 Lira 1950................2.50

Gold

15 25 Piastres 1947............1.25
16 50 Piastres 1947............2.00

*18 ½ Pound 1950...........60.00
19 1 Pound 1950...........90.00
Later issues in Current Coins of the World.

TARIM AND GHURFAH (Cities)

Located in the Hadhramaut in southern part of Arabia (East Aden Protector-ate). This has been a passageway rather than a developed country. Most of the area is desert wadies which in earlier times were used by wandering tribes.
120 Chomsih (Chamsi) = 1 Riyal (Maria Theresia Thaler)
Coinage obsolete.

For TARIM

Copper

Fine
A4 4 Chomsih AH 1270
(1853)................35.00
A5 8 Chomsih 1270........45.00
A6 16 Chomsih 1270........55.00

Fine
A1 1 Chomsih AH 1258
(1842) Thin...........10.00
*A2 3 Chomsih AH 1258
Thick...............12.50

Silver

A3 30 Chomsih AH 1258
Thick...............35.00

Several die varieties exist for Nos.
A1, A2 and A3.

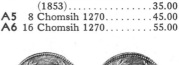

1 6 Chomsih AH 1315
(1897) 11.5mm..........4.00
2 12 Chomsih 1315 (17mm)...5.00
*3 24 Chomsih 1315 (21mm)...8.50

Nos. 1-3 were struck occasionally to 1926.

TARIM AND GHURFAH

For **GHURFAH,** a town in Kathiri State 30 miles southwest of Tarim.

Silver

		Fine
4	4 Chomsih AH 1344 (1926) 11.5mm	27.50
6	8 Chomsih 1344 (14mm)	30.00
8	15 Chomsih 1344 (18mm)	12.50
★10	30 Chomsih 1344 (22mm)	15.00
11	45 Chomsih 1344 (24.5mm)	250.00
12	60 Chomsih 1344 (27.5mm)	60.00

THAILAND (See Siam)

TIBET

Until recent times this country high in the Himalaya and Kunlin Mountains of Central Asia was forbidden country for strangers. It is now under the Chinese Communist government. The average altitude of the country is 16,000 feet. Area: 475,000 square miles. Capital: *Lhasa.*

10 Skar =1 Shokang	10 Sho =1 Srang
15 Skar =1 Tangka	3 Tangka =1 Indian Rupee

Coinage obsolete.

In the Lhasa dialect, *srang* is pronounced *sang;* and *skar* is pronounced *kar* or *karma.*

CHINESE ISSUES
KUANG HSU 1875-1908

Struck in Szechuan Province for Tibet

Silver

		Fine
1	¼ Rupee ND (ca. 1903) 19mm	22.50
2	½ Rupee ND (ca. 1903) 24mm	22.50
★3	1 Rupee ND (ca. 1903-38) Vars.	8.00

HSUAN T'UNG 1908-1911

Copper

		Fine
A4	½ Skar ND (1908) as no. 5	50.00
4	1 Skar ND, sim. (27mm)	40.00

Silver

★5	1 Sho ND (1908)	40.00
6	2 Sho ND (25mm)	50.00

Copper

A7	⅛ Sho Yr. 1 (1909) as no. 9, 22mm	40.00
B7	¼ Sho Yr. 1, as no. 9 (26mm)	40.00

TIBET

Silver

SRANG SYSTEM

First Coinage

Copper

Fine

8 5 Sho Yr. 1 . . . . 150.00
★9 1 Srang Yr. 1
(reeded edge) 175.00

Varieties of no. 9 with plain edge are thought to be counterfeit.

Fine

10 2½ Skar (1909) 22mm . . 150.00
A10 5 Skar (1909) 25mm . . 150.00
11 7½ Skar (1909) 28mm . . 150.00

Silver

12 1 Srang (1909) Plain edge . . 75.00

TANGKA SYSTEM

Silver

A13 1 Tangka (1890-91) 5.00

An earlier issue (1790-94) of this type is listed in Craig as No. 60.

13 1 Tangka ND (ca. 1840-
1925) many vars. 2.00

Nos. 13 and 14 average about 4.4 grams.

Second Coinage

Copper

16 2½ Skar (1913-18) 7.50
★17 5 Skar (1913-18) 4.00

Silver

18 5 Sho (1913-27) as no. 12 . 15.00
A18 1 Srang (1914-19) as no.
12, reeded edge 150.00

14 1 Tangka ND (1909) 5.00
15 2 Tangka ND (1912)
as no. 13; 9.3 grams 75.00

TIBET

Third Coinage

Copper

Fine
A19 2½ Skar (1918-21) 40.00

19 5 Skar (1918-25) 1.50

20 7½ Skar (1918-25) 2.00

21 1 Sho (1918-28) (2 Var.) 1.50

Silver

32 5 Sho ND (ca. 1928-29)
27mm 40.00
32a 5 Sho 1930 (24mm) 50.00

Gold

Ex. Fine
22 20 Srang (1918-21) 300.00

Fourth Coinage

Copper

V. Fine
23 1 Sho (1932-38) 2.00

27 3 Sho (1946) 6.50

Silver

24 1½ Srang (1935-46) 5.00

TIBET

25 3 Srang (1933-34) . . . . *V. Fine* 7.00

26 3 Srang (1935-46) 6.50

Fifth Coinage
Copper

28 5 Sho (1947-50)
Two Suns on Obv 1.75
28a 5 Sho (1949-53)
Moon and Sun on Obv . . . 1.75

Billon

29 10 Srang (1948-49) Two *V. Fine*
Suns on Obv. (2 var.) . . . 6.00
29a 10 Srang (1950-52)
Moon and Sun on Obv . . 6.00

30 10 Srang (1950-51) 6.00

Silver

31 5 Srang ND (ca. 1947-48) . . 6.50
32 5 Srang (1953) 26mm,
sim. to No. 24 . . . . 25.00

TIMOR

An island off the coast of Australia, the eastern part belonging to Portugal, the western to Indonesia. Exports: coffee, sandalwood, copra. Population: 536,000. Area: 7,330 square miles. Capital: *Dili*.
100 Avos = 1 Pataca to 1960

TIMOR

Bronze

Silver

3 50 Avos 1945-51 ...... *V.F.* 15.00

V. Fine

1 10 Avos 1945-51 .... 1.50

Nickel-Bronze

2 20 Avos 1945 .... 10.00 →

Later issues in Current Coins of the World.

TOGO

After World War I the German colony Togoland in West Africa on the Gulf of Guinea was split up and administered for the League of Nations and UNO by Britain and France. The British section is now part of Ghana. The coinage here is that of the French section, which became the independent Republic of Togo in 1960. Area: 20,400 square miles. Capital: *Lomé*.

100 Centimes = 1 Franc

Aluminum-Bronze

Aluminum

Unc.

4 1 Franc 1948 .... 7.50
5 2 Francs 1948 .... 7.50

Fine

1 50 Centimes 1924-26 .... .75
2 1 Franc 1924-25 .... 1.00
3 2 Francs 1924-25 .... 1.50

Aluminum-Bronze

6 5 Francs 1956 (Diff. head) .. 2.50

See French West Africa for Integrated Coinage, 1957

TONKIN

Formerly a state in Indo-China, now a part of Communist North Vietnam. Capital: *Hanoi*.

Coinage obsolete.

Zinc

1 1/600 Piastre 1905 .... *V. Fine* 6.00

Coins less than 1mm thick are counterfeits. Genuine pieces are 1.5mm thick.

TUNISIA (Tunisie)

Formerly a monarchy on the Mediterranean coast of Africa, Tunisia was a French protectorate from 1881 to 1956. An independent kingdom was proclaimed in 1956, but was changed to a republic in 1957. Although the economy is mainly agricultural, mineral ores, petroleum and tourism are significant. Area: 63,378 square miles. Languages: Arabic, French. Capital: *Tunis.*

16 Kharubs = 1 Piastre (Sebili) to 1891
100 Centimes = 1 Franc 1891-1958

Note: Because of extensive catalog revisions, new numbers have been assigned in the 10th edition. The original numbers are given in parentheses.

MUHAMMAD AL-SADIQ
BEY 1859-1882

Under French Protectorate 1881-82

Designs similar to Nos. 5-9

Silver

1	(A1)	8 Kharubs AH 1299 (1882)	——
2	(B1)	1 Piastre 1299	——
3	(C1)	2 Piastres 1299	——

Gold

4	25 Piastres 1298, 1300	——
A4	50 Piastres 1299	——

ALI BEY 1882-1902
First Coinage

Silver

V. Fine

5 (1)	8 Kharubs AH 1301-07 (1884-90) 17.5mm	12.50
6 (2)	1 Piastre 1303-08 (22.5mm)	20.00
★7 (3)	2 Piastres 1307-08 (27mm)	20.00
8 (4)	4 Piastres 1305-08 (31mm)	30.00

Gold

		V. Fine
9	25 Piastres 1300-02	75.00
A10	50 Piastres 1304	——
B10	100 Piastres 1303	——
10	25 Piastres/15 Fr. 1304-08	125.00

Second Coinage

Note: All current silver and gold denominations were coined annually from 1891 to the late 1930's. In years when large quantities were not needed for circulation, limited numbers (20 to 1,000 pieces) of each denomination were struck, probably to be used as gifts by the Bey.

Bronze

Fine

11 (9)	1 Centime 1891	2.50
12 (10)	2 Centimes 1891	2.00
13 (11)	5 Centimes 1891-93	.75
14 (12)	10 Centimes 1891-93	1.00

Silver

15 (13)	50 Centimes 1891-1902	2.00
16 (14)	1 Franc 1891-1902	2.50
17 (15)	2 Francs 1891-1902	3.00

Dates after 1891 of No. 15, and after 1892 of Nos. 16-17, not struck for circulation.

TUNISIA

Gold

Ex. Fine

18 (21) 10 Francs 1891-1902...60.00
19 (22) 20 Francs 1891-1902...60.00

Dates after 1891 of No. 18, and after 1901 of No. 19, not struck for circulation.

MUHAMMAD AL-HADI
BEY 1902-1906

Obv: Name of Bey
Rev. designs like Nos. 13-19

Bronze

Fine

20 (11) 5 Centimes 1903-04....1.00
21 (12) 10 Centimes 1903-04....1.75

Silver

22 (13) 50 Centimes 1903-06...50.00
23 (14) 1 Franc 1903-06......3.00
24 (15) 2 Francs 1903-06......4.00

No. 22, and dates other than 1904 of Nos. 23-24, not for circulation.

Gold

Ex. Fine

25 (21) 10 Francs 1903-06.....70.00
26 (22) 20 Francs 1903-06.....60.00

No. 25, and dates 1905-06 of No. 26, not struck for circulation.

MUHAMMAD AL-NASR
BEY 1906-1922

First Coinage

Obv: Name of Bey
Rev. designs like Nos. 13-19

Bronze

Fine

27 (11) 5 Centimes 1907-17.... .50
28 (12) 10 Centimes 1907-17.... .75

Silver

29 (13) 50 Centimes 1907-21....1.25
30 (14) 1 Franc 1907-21......2.00
31 (15) 2 Francs 1907-21......2.50

Dates after 1917, 1918 and 1916 of Nos. 29, 30 and 31 respectively, not struck for circulation.

Gold
Ex. Fine

32 (21) 10 Francs 1907-21....100.00
33 (22) 20 Francs 1907-21....100.00

Nos. 32 and 33 not struck for circulation.

Second Coinage

Nickel-Bronze

34 (35) 5 Centimes 1918-20
(19mm)........... .35

TUNISIA

34a (38) 5 Centimes 1920   *V. Fine*
        (17mm) 2.00
35 (36) 10 Centimes 1918-20. . . .25
36 (37) 25 Centimes 1918-20. . . .50

GENERAL COINAGE

Issued without name of ruler through successive reigns.

Aluminum-Bronze

37 (32) 50 Centimes 1921-45. 25
38 (33) 1 Franc 1921-45 50
39 (34) 2 Francs 1921-45 75

MUHAMMAD AL-HABIB BEY 1922-1929

Obv: Name of Bey
Rev. designs like Nos. 35, 15-19

Nickel-Bronze

40 (36) 10 Centimes 1926 . . . . . . 2.00

Silver

                             Ex. Fine
41 (13) 50 Centimes 1923-28. . .40.00
42 (14) 1 Franc 1923-28 . . . . .60.00
43 (15) 2 Francs 1923-28 . . . . .75.00
Nos. 41-43 not struck for circulation.

Gold
                      Ex. Fine
44 (21) 10 Francs 1922-28 . . . . .60.00
45 (22) 20 Francs 1922-28 . . . . .65.00

Nos. 44-45 not struck for circulation.

AHMED BEY 1929-1942

Nickel-Bronze

Obv: Name of Bey
Rev. designs like Nos. 34a-36

                             V. Fine
46 (38) 5 Centimes 1931-38. . . .1.00
47 (36) 10 Centimes 1931-38. . . .1.50
48 (37) 25 Centimes 1931-38. . . .2.00

Silver

49 (23) 10 Francs 1930-34 . . . . .25.00
50 (24) 20 Francs 1930-34 . . . . .45.00

51 (26) 5 Francs AH 1353-57
        (1934-38) 1.00
52 (27) 10 Francs AH 1353-57. .2.00
53 (28) 20 Francs AH 1353-57. .7.50

Dates after 1355 of No. 51, and after 1353
of Nos. 52-53, not struck for circulation.

TUNISIA

MUHAMMAD AL-AMIN
BEY 1943-1957

V. Fine

54 (29) 5 Francs 1939 . . . . 2.00
55 (30) 10 Francs 1939 . . . . 4.00
56 (31) 20 Francs 1939 . . . . . . 15.00

Gold

Ex. Fine

57 (25) 100 Francs 1930-37 . . . . 75.00

Dates after 1934 or 1935 of No. 57 not
struck for circulation.

Zinc

V. Fine

58 (41) 10 Centimes 1941-42 . . . . 1.00
59 (43) 20 Centimes 1942 . . . . . . 3.50

Zinc

V. Fine

60 (44) 10 Centimes 1945 . . . . . 40.00
61 (45) 20 Centimes 1945 . . . . . 50.00

Aluminum-Bronze

62 (46) 5 Francs 1946 . . . . 1.25

Copper-Nickel

Ex. Fine

63 (50) 5 Francs 1954-57 20
64 (47) 20 Francs 1950-57 25
65 (48) 50 Francs 1950-57 35
66 (49) 100 Francs 1950-57 . . . . 1.25

Later issues in *Current Coins of the World.*

TURKEY (Türkiye Cumhuriyeti, Ottoman Empire)

A republic in both Europe and Asia, between the Mediterranean and the
Black Seas. The Ottoman Empire was destroyed after World War I and was
reduced in area from 710,224 square miles to 296,500 square miles. The
republic was formed in 1923. The country is the foremost producer of chrome
in the world. Population: 31,100,000. Capital: *Ankara.*

The accession date of the ruler appears in Arabic numerals on the lower
reverse of each coin. The regnal year (year of issue), also in Arabic, is usually
found below the toughra (monogram of ruler).

TURKEY

40 Para = 1 Kuruş (Kurush, Piastre)
100 Kuruş = 1 Lira

ABDUL AZIZ 1861-1876

(Accession Date AH 1277 on Coins)

Copper

Fine

11	5 Piastres Yrs. 1-15	2.50
★12	10 Piastres Yrs. 1-2	25.00
13	20 Piastres Yrs. 1-15	7.50

Gold

V. Fine

16	25 Piastres Yrs. 1-7	20.00
A16	50 Piastres Yrs. 1-9	35.00
★17	100 Piastres Yrs. 1-14	60.00
A17	250 Piastres Yrs. 1-9	120.00
B17	500 Piastres Yrs. 2-13	250.00

Fine

1	5 Para Yr. 1 (1861)	3.00
2	10 Para Yr. 1	1.75
★3	20 Para Yr. 1	2.50

4	5 Para Yr. 4 (1864)	1.00
5	10 Para Yr. 4	1.00
★6	20 Para Yr. 4	1.00
7	40 Para Yr. 4	1.50

Silver

8	20 Para Yrs. 1-7	3.00
9	1 Piastre Yrs. 1-7	2.00
10	2 Piastres Yrs. 1-5	15.00

MURAD V 1876

(Accession Date AH 1293 on Coins)

Designs similar to Nos. 9-17
Obv: No flower at right of toughra

Silver

18	1 Piastre Yr. 1 (1876)	100.00

TURKEY

V. Fine
20 5 Piastres Yr. 1 . . . . 60.00
⋆22 20 Piastres Yr. 1 . . . . 50.00

Gold
A22 25 Piastres Yr. 1 . . . . . . 150.00
B22 50 Piastres Yr. 1 . . . . . 150.00
C22 100 Piastres Yr. 1 . . . . . . 125.00

ABDUL HAMID II
1876-1909

(Accession Date AH 1293 on Coins)

First Coinage
Obv: Flower at right of toughra
Copper

Fine
23 5 Para Yrs. 3-4 50

Silver

26 20 Para Yrs. 1-4 . . . . 25.00

⋆27 1 Piastre Yrs. 1-4 . . . . . . 32.50
28 2 Piastres Yr. 1 . . . . 150.00

Fine
29 5 Piastres Yrs. 1-4 . . . . . . 5.00
⋆30 10 Piastres Yrs. 1-3 . . . . . 12.50
31 20 Piastres Yrs. 1-3 . . . . . 35.00

Gold

V. Fine
A31 25 Piastres Yrs. 3-6 . . . . 30.00
B31 50 Piastres Yrs. 1-6 . . . . 50.00
⋆C31 100 Piastres Yrs. 1-6 . . . . 60.00
D31 250 Piastres Yrs. 1-2 . . . .———
E31 500 Piastres Yrs. 1-2 . . . 250.00

Second Coinage

Obv: "El Ghazi" (the Victorious) at right of toughra
Billon

24 5 Para Yrs. 25-30 50
⋆25 10 Para Yrs. 25-30 25

Silver

⋆F31 20 Para Yr. 8 . . . . 2.50
32 1 Piastre Yrs. 8-34 50
33 2 Piastres Yrs. 8-34 75

TURKEY

Fine

*34 5 Piastres Yrs. 8-34 . . . . . . 1.50
35 10 Piastres Yrs. 12-33 . . . . . 3.50

Gold

V. Fine

36 25 Piastres Yrs. 7-32 . . . . . 20.00
37 50 Piastres Yrs. 7-34 . . . . . 35.00
*38 100 Piastres Yrs. 7-34 . . . . . 60.00
39 250 Piastres Yrs. 7-32 . . . . 150.00
40 500 Piastres Yrs. 7-32 . . . . 250.00

Gold Harem Presentation Pieces (Monnaie De Luxe)

A40 12½ Piastres Yr. 30 . . . . . 25.00
B40 25 Piastres Yrs. 27-30 . 30.00
C40 50 Piastres Yrs. 28-31 . . 45.00
D40 100 Piastres Yrs. 29-33 . 75.00
41 250 Piastres Yrs. 24-33 . 150.00
42 500 Piastres Yrs. 26-33 . 250.00

MOHAMMED RESHAT V
1909-1918

(Accession Date AH 1327 on Coins)

First Coinage

Obv: "Reshat" at right of toughra

Nickel

43 5 Para Yrs. 2-7 . . . . *Fine* .20

Fine

44 10 Para Yrs. 2-7 20
45 20 Para Yrs. 2-6 25
*46 40 Para Yrs. 3-5 30

Silver

47 1 Piastre Yrs. 1-3 . . . . 1.00
*48 2 Piastres Yrs. 1-6 . . . . . . 1.25
49 5 Piastres Yrs. 1-7 . . . . . . 1.50
50 10 Piastres Yrs. 1-7 . . . . . . 7.50

Gold

V. Fine

A51 25 Piastres Yrs. 1-6 . . . . . 20.00
B51 50 Piastres Yrs. 2-5 . . . . . 35.00
C51 100 Piastres Yrs. 1-7 . . . . . 60.00
D51 250 Piastres Yrs. 1-6 . . . . 150.00
E51 500 Piastres Yrs. 1-4 . . . . 250.00

Some gold and silver coins struck in 1910 and 1911 have names of cities visited by Mohammed V. Some are rare. Monnaies De Luxe were also issued during his reign.

Second Coinage

Obv: "El Ghazi" (the Victorious) at right of toughra

Nickel

Fine

43a 5 Para Yr. 7 . . . . 12.50
44a 10 Para Yrs. 7-8 35
46a 40 Para Cop.-Nic. Yrs. 8-9 . .35

Silver

A50 2 Piastres Yrs. 7-9 . . . . . 15.00
B50 5 Piastres Yrs. 7-9 . . . . . . 7.50
C50 10 Piastres Yrs. 7-10 . . . . . 6.00
*51 20 Piastres Yrs. 8-10 . . . . 10.00

TURKEY

Gold

"El Ghazi" at right of Toughra

		V. Fine
53	25 Piastres Yr. 7	20.00
54	50 Piastres Yr. 9	35.00
★55	100 Piastres Yrs. 7-10	60.00
56	250 Piastres Yr. 7	150.00
57	500 Piastres Yr. 10	250.00

MOHAMMED VI
1918-1922

(Accession Date AH 1336
on Coins)
Designs similar to Nos. 43-57

Copper-Nickel

★58	40 Para Yr. 4 (1921)	.50

Silver

59	2 Piastres Yrs. 1-2	40.00
60	5 Piastres Yrs. 1-2	30.00
61	10 Piastres Yrs. 1-2	50.00
62	20 Piastres Yrs. 1-2	45.00

Gold

63	25 Piastres Yrs. 1-2	20.00
64	50 Piastres Yrs. 1, 5	125.00
★65	100 Piastres Yr. 1	60.00
66	250 Piastres Yr. 1	150.00
67	500 Piastres Yrs. 2-3	250.00

**Gold Monnaies De Luxe
Also Struck**

REPUBLIC 1923-
A.H. Dating System

Aluminum-Bronze

68	100 Para AH 1340-41	V. Fine
	(1922-24)	.35
69	5 Piastres 1340-41	.50
70	10 Piastres 1340-41	.65

Nickel

★71	25 Piastres 1341	1.50

Western Dating System

Aluminum-Bronze

68a	100 Para 1926	.35
69a	5 Piastres 1926	.50
70a	10 Piastres 1926	.65

Nickel

71a	25 Piastres 1928	1.50

Gold

72	25 Piastres 1926-28	40.00
73	50 Piastres 1926-28	50.00
74	100 Piastres 1926-29	100.00
★75	250 Piastres 1926-28	200.00
76	500 Piastres 1926-29	300.00

TURKEY

Monnaie De Luxe

V. Fine

77 25 Kuruş 1927-28 (23mm).60.00
78 50 Kuruş 1927-28
    (28mm) 100.00
79 100 Kuruş 1927-28
    (35mm) 150.00
80 250 Kuruş 1927-28
    (45mm) 250.00
81 500 Kuruş 1927-28
    (49mm) 350.00

NEW SYSTEM 1933-

Christian Dates — Western Numerals

100 Kuruş = 1 Lira

Silver

Obv: President Atatürk (1923-38)

82 100 Kuruş 1934 . . . . 8.50

83 25 Kuruş 1935-37 . . . . 5.00
84 50 Kuruş 1935-37 . . . . 5.00

85 1 Lira 1937-39 . . . . 8.50

Obv: President İnönü (1938-50)

V. Fine

86 1 Lira 1940-41 . . . . 10.00

Copper-Nickel

87 1 Kuruş 1935-37 35
88 5 Kuruş 1935-43 40
89 10 Kuruş 1935-40 50

90 1 Kuruş 1938-44 50

91 10 Para Al.-Br. 1940-42 25

92 25 Kuruş Nic.-Br.
    1944-46 40

TURKEY

New Coinage

Brass

Unc.

A92 ½ Kuruş 1948.........70.00
93 1 Kuruş 1947-51........15
94 2½ Kuruş 1948-51.......25

No. A92 was not issued to circulation.

95 5 Kuruş 1949-57..........20
96 10 Kuruş 1949-56..........30
97 25 Kuruş 1948-56..........40

Silver

V. Fine

98 50 Kuruş 1947-48.........1.50
99 1 Lira 1947-48...........2.00

Gold

Rev: President İnönü (1938-50)

Unc.

A99 25 Kuruş Yrs. 20-25
(1943-49) 15mm.....20.00
B99 50 Kuruş Yrs. 20-27
(18mm)............40.00
C99 100 Kuruş Yrs. 20-25
(22mm)............50.00
D99 250 Kuruş Yrs. 20-23
(27mm)............200.00
*E99 500 Kuruş Yrs. 20-24
(35mm)............300.00

Rev: President Atatürk (1923-38)

100 25 Kuruş Yrs. 20-
(1943-).............16.50
101 50 Kuruş Yrs. 20-.......20.00
102 100 Kuruş Yrs. 20-......40.00
103 250 Kuruş Yrs. 20-......100.00
104 500 Kuruş Yrs. 20-......200.00

Gold Monnaies de Luxe with portraits of İnönü and Atatürk were issued in the same denominations, but larger and thinner with ornate borders.

Later issues in Current Coins of the World.

TUVA
(Tannu Tuva People's Republic)

Tuva, located north of Mongolia in central Asia, broke away from the Chinese Empire in 1911 and later became a Russian protectorate. An independent People's Republic was proclaimed in 1921, and the country was annexed by the U.S.S.R. as an autonomous region in 1944. The major occupation is livestock herding, and rich mineral resources are still little exploited. Area: 65,830 square miles. Language: Tuvan. Capital: *Kyzyl*.

100 Kopejek (Kopek) = 1 Aksha

Coinage obsolete.

TUVA

Aluminum-Bronze

Copper-Nickel

Fine

1 1 Kopejek 1934............25.00
2 2 Kopejek 1934............30.00
3 3 Kopejek 1934............25.00
4 5 Kopejek 1934............30.00

Fine

5 10 Kopejek 1934..........30.00
6 15 Kopejek 1934..........30.00
7 20 Kopejek 1934..........30.00

UNITED STATES OF AMERICA

Continental area 2,977,128 square miles. Capital: *Washington, D. C.* The prices shown are for the commonest date and mint. For a detailed catalog of all dates, mint marks and principal varieties of each coin type we recommend *A Guide Book of United States Coins* by R. S. Yeoman, which is revised annually.

10 Cents = 1 Dime
100 Cents = 1 Dollar

Copper-Nickel

Fine

1 1 Cent 1856-58............11.50

Unc.

5 1 Cent 1909-1958........... .10
5a 1 Cent Zinc-coated Steel
   1943.............. *V. Fine* .25

Rev: Laurel wreath

2 1 Cent 1859...............9.00

Unc.

5b 1 Cent 1959-.............. .10

Rev: Oak wreath and shield

3 1 Cent 1860-64.............4.75

Bronze

3a (4) 1 Cent 1864-1909.......1.10

Fine

6 2 Cents 1864-73.............7.50

UNITED STATES OF AMERICA

Copper-Nickel

Fine

7 3 Cents 1865-89 . . . . 5.75

Silver

Obv: no lines around star

8 3 Cents 1851-53 . . . . 11.50

Obv: 3 outlines to star
Rev: olive sprig, arrows added

9 3 Cents 1854-58 . . . . 17.50

Obv: 2 outlines to star
Rev: as No. 9

10 3 Cents 1859-73 . . . . 17.00

Copper-Nickel

Rev: Rays between stars

14 5 Cents 1866-67 . . . . 16.50

Rev: Rays omitted

15 5 Cents 1867-83 . . . . 8.00

Fine

16 5 Cents Liberty Head
Without "CENTS" 1883 . . 3.50

17 5 Cents With "CENTS"
1883-1912 . . . . 2.00

18 5 Cents Buffalo (Bison)
on Mound 1913 . . . . 2.00

V. Fine

19 5 Cents —
Buffalo on
level ground
1913-38 45

Unc.

20 5 Cents Jefferson 1938- 10

20a 5 Cents Silver Alloy
1942-45 . . . . *V. Fine* .60

UNITED STATES OF AMERICA

Silver

Obv: without stars

                    Fine

A11 ½ Dime 1837-38 . . . . 70.00
B11 1 Dime 1837-38 . . . . 80.00

Obv: stars around border

11 ½ Dime 1838-59 . . . . 4.50
21 1 Dime 1838-60 . . . . 6.50

*29 ¼ Dollar 1838-65 . . . . 12.00
37 ½ Dollar 1839-66 . . . . 15.00
45 1 Dollar 1840-65 . . . . 65.00

Obv: arrows at date
Rev: rays around eagle

*30 ¼ Dollar 1853 . . . . 16.00
38 ½ Dollar 1853 . . . . 35.00

Obv: arrows at date
Rev: as Nos. 21, 29

12 ½ Dime 1853-55 . . . . 8.50

                    Fine

22 1 Dime 1853-55 . . . . 7.50
30a ¼ Dollar 1854-55 . . . . 11.00
38a ½ Dollar 1854-55 . . . . 16.00

Obv: legend replaces stars
Rev: modified wreath

13 ½ Dime 1860-73 . . . . 6.00
23 1 Dime 1860-91 . . . . 6.50

Rev: motto on ribbon above eagle

*31 ¼ Dollar 1866-91 . . . . 9.00
39 ½ Dollar 1866-91 . . . . 15.00
46 1 Dollar 1866-73 . . . . 65.00

Obv: arrows at date

24 1 Dime 1873-74 . . . . 25.00
*32 ¼ Dollar 1873-74 . . . . 35.00
40 ½ Dollar 1873-74 . . . . 40.00

28 20 Cents 1875-78 . . . . 50.00

UNITED STATES OF AMERICA

Fine

25 1 Dime 1892-1916.........2.25

V. Fine

26 1 Dime 1916-45.............65

★33 ¼ Dollar 1892-1916.......6.00
41 ½ Dollar 1892-1915.......9.00

★34 ¼ Dollar 1916-17........11.75
35 ¼ Dollar 1917-30,
    modified dies...........4.75

Ex. Fine

47 1 Dollar 1878-1921.........7.00

42 ½ Dollar 1916-47..........3.00

UNITED STATES OF AMERICA

Ex. Fine
48 1 Dollar 1921-35 . . . . 7.00

Obv: President Roosevelt (1933-45)
Unc.
27 1 Dime 1946-64 75

Obv: President Washington (1789-97)
36 ¼ Dollar 1932-64 . . . . .1.75

Obv: Benjamin Franklin
43 ½ Dollar 1948-63 . . . . . . Unc. 3.75

TRADE DOLLAR
Struck for Circulation in the Orient Only

Fine
44 1 Dollar 1873-85 . . . . .50.00

UNITED STATES OF AMERICA

Gold

Obv: Liberty head

Rev: motto above eagle

V. Fine

49 1 Dollar 1849-54 . . . . 110.00

		V. Fine
56	5 Dollars 1866-1908	85.00
★59	10 Dollars 1866-1907	125.00
63	20 Dollars 1866-76, value TWENTY D.	300.00
63a	20 Dollars 1877-1907, TWENTY DOLLARS	275.00

Obv: Indian head

50 1 Dollar 1854-56,
small head 350.00
51 1 Dollar 1856-89,
large head 110.00
★54 3 Dollars 1854-89 . . . . 325.00

★53 2½ Dollars 1908-29 . . . . . . 80.00
57 5 Dollars 1908-29 . . . . . . 90.00

60 10 Dollars 1907-08,
rev. no motto 150.00

52 2½ Dollars 1840-1907 . . . . 60.00
★55 5 Dollars 1839-66 . . . . . . 85.00
58 10 Dollars 1838-66 . . . . . 125.00

61 10 Dollars 1908-33,
rev. with motto 150.00

62 20 Dollars 1850-66 . . . . . . 350.00

UNITED STATES OF AMERICA

Design in low relief

Ex. Fine

65 20 Dollars 1907-08.......325.00

Design in high relief

Ex. Fine

64 20 Dollars MCMVII
(1907).............1700.00

Rev: motto added above sun

66 20 Dollars 1908-32.......325.00

Later issues in Current Coins of the World.

UNITED STATES COMMEMORATIVE COINS

(Prices Are for Uncirculated Specimens and for a Single Coin of Each Type)

		Silver	*Unc.*
C1	1893	Columbian Exposition, Isabella Quarter.............$190.00	
C2	1900	Lafayette Dollar.................................	585.00
C4	1921	Alabama Centennial..........................50¢	200.00
C5	1936	Albany, New York Charter....................50¢	150.00
C6	1937	Battle of Antietam..........................50¢	195.00
C7	1935-39	Arkansas Centennial.........................50¢	37.50
C8	1936-S	San Francisco-Oakland Bay Bridge.............50¢	55.00
C9	1934-38	Daniel Boone Bicentennial....................50¢	45.00
C10	1936	Bridgeport, Conn. Centennial.................50¢	65.00
C11	1925-S	California Diamond Jubilee....................50¢	50.00
C12	1936	Cincinnati Musical Center....................50¢	265.00
C13	1936	Cleveland, Great Lakes Exposition.............50¢	32.50
C14	1936	Columbia, S. C. Sesquicentennial..............50¢	100.00
C16	1892-93	Columbian Exposition.........................50¢	20.00

UNITED STATES OF AMERICA
COMMEMORATIVE COINS

Silver

				Unc.
C17	1935	Connecticut Tercentenary	50¢	$110.00
C18	1936	Delaware Tercentenary	50¢	85.00
C19	1936	Elgin, Illinois Centennial	50¢	75.00
C20	1936	Gettysburg Memorial	50¢	90.00
C22	1922	Grant	50¢	55.00
C23	1928	Hawaiian Sesquicentennial	50¢	900.00
C24	1935	Hudson, N. Y. Sesquicentennial	50¢	550.00
C25	1924	Huguenot — Walloon, Tercentenary	50¢	55.00
C26	1946	Iowa Centennial	50¢	50.00
C27	1925	Lexington-Concord Sesquicentennial	50¢	40.00
C28	1918	Lincoln-Illinois Centennial	50¢	50.00
C29	1936	Long Island Tercentenary	50¢	32.50
C30	1936	Lynchburg, Va. Sesquicentennial	50¢	80.00
C31	1920	Maine Centennial	50¢	67.50
C32	1934	Maryland Tercentenary	50¢	65.00
C34	1921	Missouri	50¢	475.00
C35	1923-S	Monroe Doctrine Centennial	50¢	60.00
C36	1938	New Rochelle, N. Y.	50¢	180.00
C37	1936	Norfolk, Va. Bicentennial	50¢	175.00
C38	1926-39	Oregon Trail Memorial	50¢	40.00
C39	1915-S	Panama-Pacific Exposition	50¢	325.00
C40	1920-21	Pilgrim Tercentenary	50¢	35.00
C42	1936	Providence, R. I. Tercentenary	50¢	45.00
C43	1937	Roanoke Island, N. C., 350th Anniversary	50¢	67.50
C44	1936	Robinson-Arkansas	50¢	65.00
C45	1935-36	San Diego, California Pacific Exposition	50¢	45.00
C46	1926	Sesquicentennial of American Independence	50¢	45.00
C47	1935	Old Spanish Trail	50¢	500.00
C48	1925	Stone Mountain Memorial	50¢	22.00
C49	1934-38	Texas Centennial	50¢	37.50
C50	1925	Fort Vancouver Centennial	50¢	290.00
C51	1927	Vermont Sesquicentennial	50¢	80.00
C52	1946-51	Booker T. Washington Memorial	50¢	7.00
C53	1951-54	Washington-Carver	50¢	6.50
C54	1936	Wisconsin Territorial Centennial	50¢	70.00
C55	1936	York County, Maine Tercentenary	50¢	65.00

Gold

C56	1922	Grant Memorial	$1.00	700.00
C58	1904-05	Lewis and Clark Exposition	1.00	1200.00
C59	1903	Louisiana Purchase-Jefferson	1.00	335.00
C60	1903	Louisiana Purchase-McKinley	1.00	325.00
C61	1916-17	McKinley Memorial	1.00	290.00
C62	1915-S	Panama-Pacific Exposition	1.00	300.00
C63	1915-S	Panama-Pacific Exposition	2.50	1150.00
C64	1915-S	Panama-Pacific Exposition, Round	50.00	14,000.00
C65	1915-S	Panama-Pacific Exposition, Octagonal	50.00	11,500.00
C66	1926	Philadelphia Sesquicentennial	2.50	250.00

URUGUAY
(República Oriental del Uruguay)

The smallest republic in South America. It declared its independence from Brazil in 1825. Largest industry: cattle raising. Area: 72,172 square miles. Population: 3,000,000. Capital: *Montevideo*.

100 Centesimos = 1 Peso

Copper

		Fine
1	5 Centesimos 1840-55	40.00
2	20 Centesimos 1840-55	30.00
3	40 Centesimos 1844	32.50

4	5 Centesimos 1857	4.00
5	20 Centesimos 1857	5.00
6	40 Centesimos 1857	6.50

Montevideo Peso

Silver

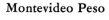

		V. Fine
10	1 Peso 1844	375.00

7	1 Centesimo 1869	2.25
8	2 Centesimos 1869	1.75
9	4 Centesimos 1869	3.50

		Fine
11	10 Centesimos 1877-93	2.00
12	20 Centesimos 1877-93	3.00
13	50 Centesimos 1877-94	6.00
14	1 Peso 1877-95	V. F. 25.00

URUGUAY

Copper-Nickel

V. Fine
15 1 Centesimo 1901-36........ .20
16 2 Centesimos 1901-41....... .25
17 5 Centesimos 1901-41....... .30

Copper
16a 2 Centesimos 1943-51...... .35
17a 5 Centesimos 1944-51...... .50

Silver

Fine
20 20 Centesimos 1920........2.50
22 50 Centesimos 1916-17......4.00
23 1 Peso 1917........ V. F. 17.50

Constitution Centennial Commemoratives
Aluminum-Bronze

18 10 Centesimos 1930........3.00

Silver

21 20 Centesimos 1930........4.00

Gold

24 5 Pesos 1930............150.00

Aluminum-Bronze

V. Fine
19 10 Centesimos 1936........2.00

Silver

25 20 Centesimos 1942........1.00

26 50 Centesimos 1943........1.50

URUGUAY

Copper-Nickel

Unc.

28 1 Centesimo 1953 25
29 2 Centesimos 1953 30
30 5 Centesimos 1953 60
31 10 Centesimos 1953-59 . . . . . .1.00

Silver

32 20 Centesimos 1954 . . . . .1.50

Later issues in Current Coins of the World.

V. Fine
27 1 Peso 1942 . . . . 2.25

VATICAN CITY

(Stato Della Citta del Vaticano)

The Papal States originally covered some 16,000 square miles. In 1871 the territory became part of Italy. Finally in 1929 an independent state of the Vatican City was set up. Its present area is 108.7 acres. The area includes St. Peter's, the Vatican Palace, and the Museum.

100 Centesimi = 1 Lira

POPE PIUS XI 1922-1939

Bronze

Nickel

V. Fine
1 5 Centesimi 1929-38 . . . . .4.00

V. Fine
3 20 Centesimi 1929-37 . . . . .4.00

2 10 Centesimi 1929-38 . . . . .4.00

4 50 Centesimi 1929-37 . . . . .4.50

VATICAN CITY

SEDE VACANTE 1939

Silver

Ex. Fine
20 5 Lire 1939..............16.00
21 10 Lire 1939.............22.50

POPE PIUS XII 1939-58
First Issue — Types of Pius XI

Bronze
22   5 Centesimi 1939-41.......3.00
23 10 Centesimi 1939-41.......3.00

Nickel
24 20 Centesimi 1939..........6.00
25 50 Centesimi 1939..........6.00
26   1 Lira 1939..............8.50
27   2 Lire 1939.............10.00

Stainless Steel
24a 20 Centesimi 1940-41...... .85
25a 50 Centesimi 1940-41......1.00
26a   1 Lira 1940-41..........1.25
27a   2 Lire 1940-41..........1.50

Silver

28   5 Lire 1939-41...........7.50
29 10 Lire 1939-41..........10.00

V. F.
5 1 Lira 1929-37.,............4.00
6 2 Lire 1929-37.............5.00

Silver

7 5 Lire 1929-37.............7.50

8 10 Lire 1929-37...........10.00

Gold

E. F.
9 100 Lire 1929-35........225.00
10 100 Lire (Smaller-5.15 Grams)
　　　1936-37.............185.00

Jubilee Issues 1933
These coins are similar to the 1929-
37 types and are dated "1933-1934."
11　 5 Centesimi.............7.50
12　10 Centesimi.............7.50
13　20 Centesimi.............6.50
14　50 Centesimi.............6.50
15　 1 Lira.................6.00
16　 2 Lire.................7.00
17　 5 Lire.................7.50
18　10 Lire................10.00
19 100 Lire................175.00

VATICAN CITY

Gold

30 100 Lire 1939-41........350.00 *Unc.*

Second Issue

Aluminum-Bronze

31 5 Centesimi 1942-46.......7.50
32 10 Centesimi 1942-46.......7.50

Stainless Steel

33 20 Centesimi 1942-46....... .50
34 50 Centesimi 1942-46....... .65
35 1 Lira 1942-46............ .75
36 2 Lire 1942-46............1.00

Silver

37 5 Lire 1942-46..........5.00
38 10 Lire 1942-46..........7.50
39 100 Lire Gold 1942-49....350.00

Third Issue

Aluminum

Unc.
40 1 Lira 1947-49............1.00
41 2 Lire 1947-49............1.25

42 5 Lire 1947-49...........1.50
43 10 Lire 1947-49...........2.00

Holy Year Commemoratives

Aluminum

44 1 Lira Roman Numerals
MCML (1950)...........1.50

45 2 Lire MCML............ 1.75

VATICAN CITY

Gold

Unc.

46 5 Lire MCML............2.50
47 10 Lire MCML............3.00

Unc.
53 100 Lire 1951-56......800.00
A53 100 Lire 1957-58
    (Papal arms rev.)...250.00

Gold

Stainless Steel

48 100 Lire MCML........225.00

54 50 Lire 1955-58............75
55 100 Lire 1955-58..........1.25

Fourth Issue

Aluminum

Silver

49 1 Lira 1951-58.............25
50 2 Lire 1951-58.............35

Obv. Bust. Rev. Justice Standing
51 5 Lire 1951-58.............50

56 500 Lire 1958............22.50

SEDE VACANTE 1958

52 10 Lire 1951-58...........65
A52 20 Lire 1957-58
    Alum.-Bronze.........1.50

57 500 Lire 1958.............8.50
Later issues in Current Coins of the World.

VENEZUELA

A republic in northern South America. The country is drained by the Orinoco River. Exports: petroleum, coffee, iron. Area: 352,150 square miles. Population: 11,300,000. Capital: *Caracas*.

100 Centavos = 1 Venezolano
10 Reales = 1 Venezolano
100 Centimos = 1 Bolivar

REPUBLICA DE VENEZUELA

Copper

Fine

1 ¼ Centavo 1843, 52
 (19mm)................7.00
2 ½ Centavo 1843, 52
 (24mm)................8.50
3 1 Centavo 1843, 52
 (32mm)...............10.00

Size Reduced

4 ¼ Centavo 1852 (18mm)....15.00
5 ½ Centavo 1852 (22mm)....12.00
6 1 Centavo 1852 (30mm)....15.00

Size Further Reduced

7 1 Centavo 1858-63 (26mm)...6.00

Silver

Fine

8 "1½" (= ½) Real 1858...125.00
9 1 Real 1858..............75.00
10 2 Reales 1858.............75.00
11 5 Reales 1858............175.00

ESTADOS UNIDOS DE VENEZUELA

First Coinage

Copper-Nickel

25 1 Centavo 1876-77.......2.00
26 2½ Centavos 1876-77.......3.50

Silver

Nos. 12-17 bear no denominations, but have their weights stated in grams as shown below. Silver coins are identical to Nos. 20-24, as only the legal names of denominations were changed in 1879.

12 GR.1.250 (5 Centavos)
 1874, 76...............12.50

VENEZUELA

Fine

13 GR.2.500 (10 Centavos)
  1874, 76............17.50
★14 GRAM.5 (20 Centavos)
  1874, 76..........25.00
15 GR.12.500 (50 Centavos)
  1873-76............37.50
16 GRAM.25 (1 Venezolano)
  1876............150.00

Gold

V. Fine

17 GR.8.0645 (5 Venezolanos)
  1875...............250.00

Second Coinage

100 Céntimos = 1 Bolívar

Copper-Nickel

Fine

27 5 Centimos 1896-1938 ... .25
28 12½ Centimos 1896-1938 ... .30

Silver

See note on denominations above No. 12.

19 GR.1.000 (⅕ Bolívar)   Fine
  1879........ ......150.00
★20 GR.1.250 (¼ Bolívar)
  1894-1948...... V. Fine .50

V. Fine

21 GR.2.500 (½ Bolívar)
  1879-1936............ .75
★22 GRAM.5 (1 Bolívar)
  1879-1936..........1.50
23 GRAM.10 (2 Bolívares)
  1879-1936..........2.25
24 GRAM.25 (5 Bolívares)
  1879-1936..........6.00

Gold

31 GR.3.2258 (10 Bolívares)
  1930................45.00
32 GR.6.4516 (20 Bolívares)
  1879-1912.............60.00
33 GR.32.2580 (100 Bolívares)
  1886-89.............300.00

Brass

Obv: modified shield

29 5 Céntimos 1944........2.50
30 12½ Céntimos 1944.......10.00

VENEZUELA

Copper-Nickel

		V. Fine
29a	5 Céntimos 1945-48	.15
30a	12½ Céntimos 1945-48	.25

Silver
Rev: modified arms

21a	GR.2.500 (½ Bolívar)	
	1944-46	.60
★22a	GRAM.5 (1 Bolívar) 1945	1.00
23a	GRAM.10 (2 Bolívares)	
	1945	1.75

Later issues in Current Coins of the World.

VISCAYAN REPUBLIC — see Spain

VIETNAM

Formerly part of French Indochina, Vietnam was formed after World War II of Annam, Tonkin and Cochin China. A provisional communist government was formed in 1945, while a French-sponsored monarchy was established in 1949. After French defeat in 1954 the country was partitioned between the two rival factions. Area: 126,436 square miles. Language: Vietnamese. Capitals: *Hanoi* (communist), *Saigon* (monarchy).

10 Xu = 1 Hao
100 Xu = 1 Dong

Provisional Government
1945-1946

Aluminum

Obv: President Ho Chih Minh
(1945-1969)

V. Fine

3 1 Dong 1946 .... 25.00

Bronze

V. Fine

1 20 Xu 1945 .... 35.00

4 2 Dong 1946 .... 25.00

2 5 Hao 1946 (Value Incused)..7.50
2a 5 Hao 1946 (Value Raised)...7.50

For later issues see North and South Vietnam in *Current Coins of the World*.

· 491 ·

YEMEN
(Mutawakelite Kingdom of Yemen)

Formerly an independent feudal kingdom, it became a republic in 1962. Area: 74,000 square miles, situated in the southwest corner of Arabia. Exports: coffee, cotton, salt, hides. Population: 5,500,000. Capitals: *Taiz* and *San'a*. Maria Theresa Talers are widely used.

2 Halala = 1 Buqsha (Bogach)   40 Buqsha = 1 Imadi, Ahmadi, Riyal
2 Buqsha = 1 Ghirsh (Piastre)   or Maria Theresia Thaler

IMAM YAHYA BIN MOHAMMED HAMID AL-DIN

As Rebel A.H. 1321 (1903-04)

Silver

Fine

A1 1 Ghirsh AH 1321 . . . .———

As Imam and King
A.H. 1322-1367 (1904-48)

Yellow or Red Bronze

1 ½ Halala A.H. 1342 (1923)
(Crescent type) 10.00

1a ½ Halala 1342-46
(Plain type) 8.00

(Several Varieties of Nos. 1-10)

2 1 Halala 1322 (1904) 10.00
★2a 1 Halala 1330-61 . . . . .2.50
3 1 Bogach 1341-67 . . . . .3.00

There are at least 5 distinct varieties of No. 3.

Silver

Fine

4 ⅟₂₀ Imadi A.H. 1337-66 . . . . .3.00
5 ⅟₁₀ Imadi 1337-42 . . . . .5.00
★5a ⅟₁₀ Imadi 1343-66 . . . . .3.50
6 ¼ Imadi 1341-43 . . . . .8.50
7 1 Imadi 1344 . . . . . . *V. F.* 12.00

★10 ¼ Imadi A.H. 1344-66 . . . .4.00
10a ¼ Imadi 1366
(larger inner circle) 6.00

AHMED HAMID AL-DIN
1948-1962

Bronze

11 1 Halala A.H. 1368-86   *V. Fine*
(1949-67) 50
★12 1 Bogach 1368-79 75

YEMEN

Aluminum

Unc.
*11a 1 Halala 1374-78 (1955-59). .75
12a 1 Bogach 1374-77 . . . . 1.00

Silver

V. Fine
13 1/16 Ahmadi A.H. 1367-74
(1948-55) 1.50
*14 1/8 Ahmadi 1367-80 . . . . . . 2.00
14a 1/8 Ahmadi Hexagonal
1368 . . . . 50.00

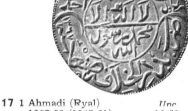

17 1 Ahmadi (Ryal) *Unc.*
1367-80 (1948-61) 12.50

Aluminum

*18 1 Halala ND (1956) 75
19 1 Bogach ND (1956) 1.00
Date 1367 shown on Nos. 18 and 19 is
accession date, not issue date.

Unc.
*15 1/4 Ahmadi A.H. 1367-77 . . 3.00
15a 1/4 Ahmadi 1374
(Larger Inner Circle) . . . 3.00

Gold

G15 1/4 Ahmadi "(1)" . . . . Rare
*G16 1/2 Ahmadi "(2)" . . . . Rare
G17 1 Ahmadi (Ryal) "(5)" . Rare
Later issues in *Current Coins of the World.*

6 1/2 Ahmadi 1367-82 . . . . 5.00

YUGOSLAVIA
(Kraljevina Jugoslavija)

On the east shore of the Adriatic Sea south of Hungary. It was formed after the First World War by uniting to the kingdom of Serbia several Austro-Hungarian provinces plus the erstwhile kingdom of Montenegro. Principal industries are agriculture, cattle raising, and forestry. Area: 98,766 square miles. Languages: Serbo-Croatian, Slovenian, Macedonian. Population: 20,800,000. Capital: *Belgrade*.

100 Para = 1 Dinar

PETAR I 1918-1921
(Hitherto King of Serbia)
Zinc

		V. Fine
1	5 Para 1920	6.50
2	10 Para 1920	1.25

Nickel-Bronze

3	25 Para 1920	1.00

ALEXANDER I 1921-1934
First Coinage
Nickel-Brass

4	50 Para 1925	.50
5	1 Dinar 1925	.75
6	2 Dinara 1925	1.00

Gold

		Unc.
10	20 Dinara 1925	125.00

Second Coinage
Silver

		V. Fine
7	10 Dinara 1931	2.00
8	20 Dinara 1931	5.00
9	50 Dinara 1932	18.50

There are two varieties of No. 9: with and without mint name below truncation of neck.

YUGOSLAVIA

Gold

Ex. Fine

A11 1 Dukat 1931-33........75.00

V. Fine

16 2 Dinara 1938 (Large Crown) .75

12 4 Dukata 1931-32.......300.00

Nos. A11 and 12 have a small official counterstamp on obverse near rim.

PETAR II 1934 1945

Bronze

17 2 Dinara 1938 (Small
Crown)................5.00

Nickel

18 10 Dinara 1938............1.50

V. Fine

13 25 Para 1938.............1.00

Aluminum-Bronze

Silver

14 50 Para 1938.............. .50
15 1 Dinar 1938.............. .60

19 20 Dinara 1938 (Head left)..2.00
20 50 Dinara 1938...........3.50

YUGOSLAVIA

CROATIA — German Formed State

April 1941-November 1944

Zinc

Ex. Fine

1 2 Kune 1941 . . . . 5.00

Other World War II Coins Listed Under Serbia

FEDERATED REPUBLIC
1945-1952

Zinc

V. Fine

21 50 Para 1945 20
22 1 Dinar 1945 30
23 2 Dinara 1945 40

24 5 Dinara 1945 60

Legend: FEDERATIVNA NARODNA REPUBLIKA JUGOSLAVIJA

Aluminum

Unc.

25 50 Para 1953 10
26 1 Dinar 1953 15
27 2 Dinara 1953 20
28 5 Dinara 1953 25

Aluminum-Bronze

29 10 Dinara 1955 25

30 20 Dinara 1955 40

31 50 Dinara 1955 75

Later issues in Current Coins of the World.

ZANZIBAR (Zanjibar)

The Arab sultanate of Zanzibar and Pemba, a group of islands off the east African coast plus a narrow strip of mainland, was a possession of Muscat and Oman until becoming fully independent in the mid-19th century. It enjoyed prosperity as a major Indian Ocean trading center, noted for cloves and other spices, ivory and slaves. In 1890 it became a British protectorate. The Indian rupee and Maria Theresia thaler (ryal) were moneys of account until 1936, when Zanzibar joined the East African currency union. Independence was restored in 1963, and in 1964 Zanzibar united with Tanganyika to form Tanzania. Area: 1,020 square miles. Languages: Swahili, English, Arabic. Capital: *Zanzibar City.*

64 Pysa (Pice) = 1 India Rupee
136 Pysa = 1 Ryal to 1908
100 Cents = 1 Rupee 1908-09
Coinage obsolete.

Sultan Barghash ibn Sa'id
1870-1888

Copper

Fine
1 1 Pysa AII 1299 (1882) 1.25

2 1 Pysa AH 1304 (1887) 2.00

Silver
Ex. Fine
5 1 Ryal 1299 . . . . 250.00 →

Gold

7 5 Ryals 1299 . . . . ——
Other silver and gold coins dated AH 1299 are patterns.

For later issues see East Africa

Sultan Ali bin Hamud
1902-1911
Bronze

Ex. Fine
★8 1 Cent 1908 . . . . 100.00
9 10 Cents 1908 . . . . 150.00

Nickel

10 20 Cents 1908 . . . . 150.00
Nos. 8-10 not released to circulation.

PRECIOUS METAL CONTENT OF WORLD COINAGE

1850-1950

———•◆•———

Compiled by Holland Wallace

Nearly all modern coins are composed of a mixture of two or more metals. This mixture, called an alloy, may be simply the traditional 90% silver and 10% copper, or something as complex as 50% silver, 40% copper, 5% zinc and 5% tin. Usually it is not important to know the exact composition of a coin; therefore, the listings in the body of this catalog indicate only the principal metals used. The heading "silver," for instance, is used for coins containing from 50% to 94½% silver (those with less than 50% silver are termed "billon"), and "gold" is applied to any coin containing enough gold to have a yellow color, from as low as 17½% to as high as 98.6%.

Normally it is only in the case of precious metals that the exact proportions of a coin's alloy become significant to the collector. Such information can be used to determine the genuineness of a given coin, or to compute its intrinsic value based on its bullion content of gold or silver.

A new interest in the bullion value of coins has arisen because of frequent changes in value of gold and silver. The metals have recently been priced at all-time highs, and because of this some coins are now valued more for their metal content than as numismatic items.

Because of today's need for more facts concerning bullion values, this special section has been added to the catalog. In the following tables almost every silver and gold coin of the world from 1850 to 1950 is listed with its gross weight, fineness and net metal content. This content has been calculated both in net grams and ounces troy of pure gold or silver.

To determine the current bullion value of a coin you need only multiply the net ounce troy figure by the daily price quotation for the metal involved. As an example, if the day's fixed price of gold is $160 per ounce, the bullion value of a sovereign is determined by multiplying $160 times .2354 ounce, giving $37.66 as the value of the gold in that coin.

The weights and finenesses in the tables are those specified by law, and do not take into account any tolerances or fluctuations caused by the manufacturing process. Such tolerances range from a fraction of a percent up to many percentage points, depending on the technical ability and the willingness of a country to adhere to its legal standards. Weights shown are, of course, for coins in substantially original condition which have not lost noticeable weight through wear.

In almost every case the weights and finenesses have been taken from official sources such as mint reports and other publications of various governments. Unofficial statistics have been used only where they seem to be highly reliable, and material from supposedly authoritative sources has sometimes been disregarded when it seemed questionable. Figures in italics indicate conflicting information from official sources, or data whose accuracy could not be completely verified. Certain coinages, for the most part those of more irregular manufacture, have been omitted due to lack of any precise official data whatever.

Because of the large volume of statistical material involved in the preparation of these tables, errors are inevitable. Further information that will increase the accuracy of the listings is invited.

Dates	Denomination	Gross Wt., Gms.	Fineness	Silver Content Grams	Ounces
ALBANIA					
1925-37	same as Latin Monetary Union (Franka Ari=Franc)				
1939	same as Italy (Lek =Lire)				
ARGENTINA					
1881 83	10 Centavos	2.5000	.900	2.2500	.0723
	20 Centavos	5.0000	.900	4.5000	.1447
	50 Centavos	12.5000	.900	11.2500	.3617
	1 Peso	25.0000	.900	22.5000	.7234
AUSTRALIA					
1910-45	same as Great Britain 1817-1920				
1946-64	same as Great Britain 1920-46				
AUSTRIA					
1780	MT Thaler	28.0668	.833⅓	23.3890	.7520
1857-68	1 Vereinsthaler	18.5186	.900	16.6667	.5358
	2 Vereinsthaler	37.0371	.900	33.3333	1.0717
1858-67	5 Kreuzer	1.3333	.375	0.5000	.0161
	10 Kreuzer	2.0000	.500	1.0000	.0322
1868-72	10 Kreuzer	1.6667	.400	0.6667	.0214
	20 Kreuzer	2.6667	.500	1.3333	.0429
1857-92	¼ Florin	5.345	.5208	2.7837	.0895
	1 Florin	12.3457	.900	11.1111	.3572
	2 Florin	24.6914	.900	22.2222	.7144
1892-1916	1 Krone	5.0000	.835	4.1750	.1342
	2 Kronen	10.0000	.835	8.3500	.2685
	5 Kronen	24.0000	.900	21.6000	.6944
1924	1 Schilling	7.0000	.800	5.6000	.1800
1925-38	½ Schilling	3.0000	.640	1.9200	.0617
	1 Schilling	6.0000	.640	3.8400	.1235
	2 Schilling	12.0000	.640	7.6800	.2469
	5 Schilling	15.0000	.835	12.5250	.4027
BELGIUM					
1832-65	same as France 1809-66				
1865-1914	see Latin Monetary Union				
1933-35	20 Francs	11.0000	.680	7.4800	.2405
	50 Francs	22.0000	.680	14.9600	.4810
1939-40	50 Francs	20.0000	.835	16.7000	.5369
1948-60	20 Francs	8.0000	.835	6.6800	.2148
	50 Francs	12.5000	.835	10.4375	.3356
	100 Francs	18.0000	.835	15.0300	.4832
BELGIAN CONGO					
1887-96	same as Latin Monetary Union				
BOLIVIA					
1864-71	1/20 Bol/5 Cvos	1.2500	.900	1.1250	.0362
	1/10 Bol/10 Cvos	2.5000	.900	2.2500	.0723
	⅕ Bol/20 Cvos	5.0000	.900	4.5000	.1447
1873-91	½ Bol/50 Cvos	12.5000	.900	11.2500	.3617
1864-79	1 Boliviano	25.0000	.900	22.5000	.7234
1909	20 Centavos	4.0000	.833⅓	3.3333	.1072
	50 Centavos	10.0000	.833⅓	8.3333	.2679
BRAZIL					
1867-69	200 Réis	2.5000	.835	2.0875	.0671
	500 Réis	6.2500	.835	5.2188	.1678
	1000 Réis	12.5000	.835	10.4375	.3356
	2000 Réis	25.0000	.835	20.8750	.6711
1875-1900	400 Réis	5.1000	.916⅔	4.6750	.1503
	500 Réis	6.3750	.916⅔	5.8438	.1879
	1000 Réis	12.7500	.916⅔	11.6875	.3758
	2000 Réis	25.5000	.916⅔	23.3750	.7515
	4000 Réis	51.0000	.916⅔	46.7500	1.5030
1906-13	500 Réis	5.0000	.900	4.5000	.1447
	1000 Réis	10.0000	.900	9.0000	.2894
	2000 Réis	20.0000	.900	18.0000	.5787
1922	2000 Réis	8.0000	.900	7.2000	.2315
1922-35	2000 Réis	8.0000	.500	4.0000	.1286
1936-38	5000 Réis	10.0000	.600	6.0000	.1929
BRITISH GUIANA					
1888-1943	4 Pence	1.8851	.925	1.7437	.0561
1944-45	4 Pence	1.8851	.500	0.9425	.0303

Dates	Denomination	Gross Wt., Gms.	Fineness	Silver Content Grams	Ounces
BRITISH HONDURAS					
1894-1946	same as Canada 1858-1910				
BRITISH NORTH BORNEO					
1929	25 Cents	2.8276	.500	1.4138	.0455
BRITISH WEST AFRICA					
1913-20	same as Great Britain 1817-1920				
BULGARIA					
1882-1916	same as Latin Monetary Union (Stotinki/Leva = Centimes/Francs)				
1930-37	20 Leva	4.0000	.500	2.0000	.0643
	50 Leva	10.0000	.500	5.0000	.1608
	100 Leva	20.0000	.500	10.0000	.3215
CANADA					
1858-1910	5 Cents	1.1620	.925	1.0749	.0346
	10 Cents	2.3240	.925	2.1497	.0691
	20 Cents	4.6480	.925	4.2994	.1382
	25 Cents	5.8100	.925	5.3743	.1728
	50 Cents	11.6200	.925	10.7485	.3456
1910-19	5 Cents	1.1664	.925	1.0789	.0347
	10 Cents	2.3328	.925	2.1578	.0694
	25 Cents	5.8319	.925	5.3945	.1734
	50 Cents	11.6638	.925	10.7890	.3469
1920-67	5 Cents	1.1664	.800	0.9331	.0300
	10 Cents	2.3328	.800	1.8662	.0600
	25 Cents	5.8319	.800	4.6655	.1500
	50 Cents	11.6638	.800	9.3310	.3000
	1 Dollar	23.3276	.800	18.6621	.6000
NEW BRUNSWICK					
1862-64	same as Canada 1858-1910				
NEWFOUNDLAND					
1865-1912	5 Cents	1.1782	.925	1.0898	.0350
	10 Cents	2.3564	.925	2.1797	.0701
	20 Cents	4.7127	.925	4.3592	.1401
	50 Cents	11.7818	.925	10.8982	.3504
1917-44	same as Canada 1910-19				
1945-47	same as Canada 1920-67				
CEYLON					
1892-1917	10 Cents	1.1664	.800	0.9331	.0300
	25 Cents	2.9160	.800	2.3328	.0750
	50 Cents	5.8319	.800	4.6655	.1500
1919-42	10 Cents	1.1664	.550	0.6415	.0206
	25 Cents	2.9160	.550	1.6038	.0516
	50 Cents	5.8319	.550	3.2075	.1031
CHILE					
1852-59	same as Peru 1863-1917 (Décimo/Peso=Dinero/Sol)				
1860-80	½ Décimo	1.1500	.900	1.0350	.0333
	1 Décimo	2.3000	.900	2.0700	.0666
	20 Centavos	4.6000	.900	4.1400	.1331
1879-94	½ Décimo	1.2500	.500	0.6250	.0201
	1 Decimo	2.5000	.500	1.2500	.0402
	20 Centavos	5.0000	.500	2.5000	.0804
1891	20 Centavos	4.0000	.500	2.0000	.0643
	20 Centavos	5.0000	.200	1.0000	.0322
1853-91	50 Centavos	12.5000	.900	11.2500	.3617
	1 Peso	25.0000	.900	22.5000	.7234
1895-97	5 Centavos	1.0000	.835	0.8350	.0268
	10 Centavos	2.0000	.835	1.6700	.0537
	20 Centavos	4.0000	.835	3.3400	.1074
	1 Peso	20.0000	.835	16.7000	.5369
1899-1907	5 Centavos	1.0000	.500	0.5000	.0161
	10 Centavos	2.0000	.500	1.0000	.0322
	20 Centavos	4.0000	.500	2.0000	.0643
	50 Centavos	10.0000	.700	7.0000	.2251
	1 Peso	20.0000	.700	14.0000	.4501
1907-13	5 Centavos	1.0000	.400	0.4000	.0129
	10 Centavos	1.5000	.400	0.6000	.0193
	20 Centavos	3.0000	.400	1.2000	.0386
	40 Centavos	6.0000	.400	2.4000	.0772

Dates	Denomination	Gross Wt., Gms.	Fineness	Silver Content Grams	Ounces
CHILE (cont.)					
	1 Peso	12.0000	.900	10.8000	.3472
1915-19	5 Centavos	1.0000	.450	0.4500	.0145
	10 Centavos	1.5000	.450	0.6750	.0217
	20 Centavos	3.0000	.450	1.3500	.0434
	1 Peso	9.0000	.720	6.4800	.2083
1919-20	same as 1907-13				
1921-27	1 Peso	9.0000	.500	4.5000	.1447
	2 Pesos	18.0000	.500	9.0000	.2894
	5 Pesos	25.0000	.900	22.5000	.7234
1932	1 Peso	6.0000	.400	2.4000	.0772
CHINA					
1932-34	1 Yuan	26.6971	.880	23.4934	.7553
1949	5 Chio	5.0000	.720	3.6000	.1157
COLOMBIA					
1872-86	5 Centavos	1.2500	.666	0.8333	.0268
	10 Centavos	2.5000	.835	2.0875	.0671
	20 Centavos	5.0000	.835	4.1750	.1342
	50 Cs/5 Ds	12.5000	.835	10.4375	.3356
1885-89	10 Centavos	2.5000	.500	1.2500	.0402
	20 Centavos	5.0000	.500	2.5000	.0804
	50 Cs/5 Ds	12.5000	.500	6.2500	.2009
1889-1908	5 Centavos	1.2500	.666	0.8333	.0268
	10 Centavos	2.5000	.666	1.6667	.0536
	20 Centavos	5.0000	.666	3.3333	.1072
	50 Centavos	12.5000	.835	10.4375	.3356
1911-42	5 Centavos	2.5000	.900	2.2500	.0723
	20 Centavos	5.0000	.900	4.5000	.1447
	50 Centavos	12.5000	.900	11.2500	.3617
1945-52	10 Centavos	2.5000	.500	1.2500	.0402
	20 Centavos	5.0000	.500	2.5000	.0804
	50 Centavos	12.5000	.500	6.2500	.2009
1953	20 Centavos	5.0000	.300	1.5000	.0482
1956	1 Peso	25.0000	.900	22.5000	.7234
COMORO ISLANDS					
1890	5 Francs	25.0000	.900	22.5000	.7234
COSTA RICA					
1864-93	5 Centavos	1.2680	.750	0.9510	.0306
	10 Centavos	2.5361	.750	1.9021	.0612
	25 Centavos	6.3402	.750	4.7552	.1529
	50 Centavos	12.6804	.750	9.5103	.3058
1902-14	5 Centavos	1.0000	.900	0.9000	.0289
	10 Centavos	2.0000	.900	1.8000	.0579
	50 Centavos	10.0000	.900	9.0000	.2894
1917-24	10 Centavos	2.0000	.500	1.0000	.0322
	25 Centavos	3.4500	.650	2.2425	.0721
	50 Centavos	10.0000	.500	5.0000	.1608
CRETE					
1901	same as Latin Monetary Union				
	(Lepta/Drachmai = Centimes/Francs)				
CUBA					
1915-53	20 Centavos	5.0000	.900	4.5000	.1447
	40 Centavos	10.0000	.900	9.0000	.2894
	other values; same as United States				
	(Centavos/Pesos = Cents/Dollars)				
CURAÇAO					
1900-48	same as Netherlands				
CYPRUS					
1901-40	3 Piastres	1.8851	.925	1.7437	.0561
	4½ Piastres	2.8276	.925	2.6155	.0841
	9 Piastres	5.6552	.925	5.2311	.1682
	18 Piastres	11.3104	.925	10.4621	.3364
	45 Piastres	28.2759	.925	26.1552	.8409
CZECHOSLOVAKIA					
1928-37	5 Korun	7.0000	.500	3.5000	.1125
	10 Korun	10.0000	.700	7.0000	.2251
	20 Korun	12.0000	.700	8.4000	.2701
1939-44	10 Korun	7.0000	.500	3.5000	.1125

Dates	Denomination	Gross Wt., Gms.	Fineness	Silver Content Grams	Ounces
	20 Korun	15.0000	.500	7.5000	.2411
	50 Korun	16.5000	.700	11.5500	.3713
1947-51	50 Korun	10.0000	.500	5.0000	.1608
	100 Korun	14.0000	.500	7.0000	.2251
DANISH WEST INDIES					
1859-79	3 Cents	1.0440	.625	0.6525	.0210
	5 Cents	1.7400	.625	1.0875	.0350
	10 Cents	3.4800	.625	2.1750	.0699
	20 Cents	6.9600	.625	4.3500	.1399
1905-07	50 Bit/10 Cents	2.5000	.800	2.0000	.0643
	1 Fr/20 Cents	5.0000	.800	4.0000	.1286
	2 Fr/40 Cents	10.0000	.800	8.0000	.2572
DANZIG					
1923-27	½ Gulden	2.5000	.750	1.8750	.0603
	1 Gulden	5.0000	.750	3.7500	.1206
	2 Gulden	10.0000	.750	7.5000	.2411
	5 Gulden	25.0000	.750	18.7500	.6028
1932	2 Gulden	10.0000	.500	5.0000	.1608
	5 Gulden	15.0000	.500	7.5000	.2411
DENMARK					
1874-1958	see Scandinavian Monetary Union				
DOMINICAN REPUBLIC					
1891	same as Latin Monetary Union				
	(Centésimos/Francos = Centimes/Francs)				
1897	10 Centavos	2.5000	.350	0.8750	.0281
	20 Centavos	5.0000	.350	1.7500	.0563
	½ Peso	12.5000	.350	4.3750	.1407
	1 Peso	25.0000	.350	8.7500	.2813
1937-61	same as United States				
	(Centavos/Pesos = Cents/Dollars)				
1944	5 Centavos	5.0000	.350	1.7500	.0563
EAST AFRICA					
1906-19	same as Ceylon 1892-1917				
1920	25 Cents	2.9160	.500	1.4580	.0469
	50 Cents	5.8319	.500	2.9160	.0937
	1 Florin	11.6638	.500	5.8319	.1875
1921-46	50 Cents	3.8879	.250	0.9720	.0312
	1 Shilling	7.7759	.250	1.9440	.0625
ECUADOR					
1884-1916	same as Peru 1863-1917				
	(Décimos/Sucres = Dineros/Soles)				
1928-44	50 Centavos	2.5000	.720	1.800	.0579
	1 Sucre	5.0000	.720	3.6000	.1157
	2 Sucres	10.0000	.720	7.2000	.2315
	5 Sucres	25.0000	.720	18.0000	.5787
EGYPT					
1885-1942	1 Ghirsh	1.4000	.833⅓	1.1667	.0375
	2 Ghirsh	2.8000	.833⅓	2.3333	.0750
	5 Ghirsh	7.0000	.833⅓	5.8333	.1875
	10 Ghirsh	14.0000	.833⅓	11.6667	.3751
	20 Ghirsh	28.0000	.833⅓	23.3333	.7502
1944	2 Ghirsh	2.8000	.500	1.4000	.0450
ERITREA					
1890-96	50 Centesimi	2.5000	.835	2.0875	.0671
	1 Lira	5.0000	.835	4.1750	.1342
	2 Lire	10.0000	.835	8.3500	.2685
	5 Lire	28.1250	.800	22.5000	.7234
1918	1 Tallero	28.0668	.835	23.4358	.7535
ESTONIA					
1930-33	1 Kroon	6.0000	.500	3.0000	.0965
	2 Krooni	12.0000	.500	6.0000	.1929
ETHIOPIA					
1897-1903	1 Gersh	1.4038	.835	1.1721	.0377
	⅛ Talari	3.5094	.835	2.9303	.0942
	¼ Talari	7.0188	.835	5.8607	.1884
	½ Talari	14.0375	.835	11.7213	.3768
	1 Talari	28.0750	.835	23.4426	.7537
1944	50 Cents	7.0307	.800	5.6246	.1808
	50 Cents	7.0307	.700	4.9215	.1582

PRECIOUS METAL CONTENT — SILVER

Dates	Denomination	Gross Wt., Gms.	Fineness	Silver Content Grams	Ounces
FIJI					
1934-45	same as Great Britain 1920-46				
1942-43	6 Pence	2.8276	.900	2.5448	.0818
	1 Shilling	5.6552	.900	5.0897	.1636
	1 Florin	11.3104	.900	10.1794	.3273
FINLAND					
1864-1917	25 Penniä	1.2747	.750	0.9560	.0307
	50 Penniä	2.5494	.750	1.9121	.0615
	1 Markka	5.1828	.868	4.4987	.1446
	2 Markkaa	10.3657	.868	8.9974	.2893
1951-52	500 Markkaa	12.0000	.500	6.0000	.1929
FRANCE					
1803-66	20 Centimes	1.0000	.900	0.9000	.0289
	25 Cmes/¼ Franc	1.2500	.900	1.1250	.0362
	50 Cmes/½ Franc	2.5000	.900	2.2500	.0723
	1 Franc	5.0000	.900	4.5000	.1447
	2 Francs	10.0000	.900	9.0000	.2894
	5 Francs	25.0000	.900	22.5000	.7234
1866-1920	see Latin Monetary Union				
1929-39	10 Francs	10.0000	.680	6.8000	.2186
	20 Francs	20.0000	.680	13.6000	.4372
FRENCH COCHIN CHINA					
1879-85	10 Centimes	2.7216	.900	2.4494	.0787
	20 Centimes	5.4431	.900	4.8988	.1575
	50 Centimes	13.6078	.900	12.2470	.3937
	1 Piastre	27.2156	.900	24.4940	.7875
FRENCH INDO-CHINA					
1885-95	same as French Cochin China				
1895-96	10 Centimes	2.7000	.900	2.4300	.0781
	20 Centimes	5.4000	.900	4.8600	.1562
1898-1919	10 Centimes	2.7000	.835	2.2545	.0725
	20 Centimes	5.4000	.835	4.5090	.1450
1920	10 Centimes	3.0000	.400	1.2000	.0386
	20 Centimes	6.0000	.400	2.4000	.0772
1921-37	10 Centimes	2.7000	.680	1.8360	.0590
	20 Centimes	5.4000	.680	3.6720	.1181
1896-1936	50 Centimes	13.5000	.900	12.1500	.3906
1895-1928	1 Piastre	27.0000	.900	24.3000	.7812
1931	1 Piastre	20.0000	.900	18.0000	.5787
GERMAN STATES					
1874-1918	2 Mark	11.1111	.900	10.0000	.3215
	3 Mark	16.6666	.900	15.0000	.4823
	5 Mark	27.7777	.900	25.0000	.8038
GERMANY					
1873-1919	20 Pfennig	1.1111	.900	1.0000	.0322
	50 Pf/½ Mark	2.7777	.900	2.5000	.0804
	1 Mark	5.5555	.900	5.0000	.1608
1924-33	1 Mark	5.0000	.500	2.5000	.0804
	2 Mark	10.0000	.500	5.0000	.1608
	3 Mark	15.0000	.500	7.5000	.2411
	5 Mark	25.0000	.500	12.5000	.4019
1933-39	2 Mark	8.0000	.625	5.0000	.1608
	5 Mark	13.8888	.900	12.5000	.4019
GERMAN EAST AFRICA					
1890-1914	same as India 1835-1939 (Rupie = Rupee)				
GERMAN NEW GUINEA					
1894	same as Germany and German States 1873-1919				
GREAT BRITAIN					
1817-1920	3 Pence	1.4138	.925	1.3078	.0420
	4 Pence	1.8851	.925	1.7437	.0561
	6 Pence	2.8276	.925	2.6155	.0841
	1 Shilling	5.6552	.925	5.2311	.1682
	1 Florin	11.3104	.925	10.4621	.3364
	½ Crown	14.1380	.925	13.0777	.4204
	2 Florin	22.6207	.925	20.9241	.6727
	1 Crown	28.2759	.925	26.1552	.8409
1895-1935	Trade Dollar	26.9568	.900	24.2611	.7800
1920-46	3 Pence	1.4138	.500	0.7069	.0227
	6 Pence	2.8276	.500	1.4138	.0455
	1 Shilling	5.6552	.500	2.8276	.0909
	2 Sh/Florin	11.3104	.500	5.6552	.1818
	½ Crown	14.1380	.500	7.0690	.2273
	1 Crown	28.2759	.500	14.1380	.4545
GREECE					
1868-1911	see Latin Monetary Union				
	(Lepta/Drachmai = Centimes/Francs)				
1930	10 Drachmai	7.0000	.500	3.5000	.1125
	20 Drachmai	11.3333	.500	5.6667	.1822
GUATEMALA					
1881-99	2 Rs/25 Cvos	6.2500	.835	5.2188	.1678
1869-97	1 Peso	25.0000	.900	22.5000	.7234
1925-64	5 Centavos	1.6667	.720	1.2000	.0386
	10 Centavos	3.3333	.720	2.4000	.0772
	¼ Q/25 Cvos	8.3333	.720	6.0000	.1929
1925	½ Quetzal	16.6667	.720	12.0000	.3858
	1 Quetzal	33.3333	.720	24.0000	.7716
1962-63	50 Centavos	11.9444	.720	8.6000	.2765
HAITI					
1881-95	same as Venezuela 1873-76				
	(Centimes/Gourdes = Centavos/Venezolanos)				
HAWAII					
1883	same as United States 1873-1964				
HONDURAS					
1931-58	20 Centavos	2.5000	.900	2.2500	.0723
	50 Centavos	6.2500	.900	5.6250	.1808
	1 Lempira	12.5000	.900	11.2500	.3617
HONG KONG					
1863-1933	5 Cents	1.3577	.800	1.0862	.0349
	10 Cents	2.7154	.800	2.1723	.0698
	20 Cents	5.4308	.800	4.3446	.1397
1866-68	½ Dollar	13.4784	.900	12.1306	.3900
	1 Dollar	26.9568	.900	24.2611	.7800
1890-1905	50 Cents	13.5769	.800	10.8615	.3492
HUNGARY					
1868-92	same as Austria 1868-92				
	(Krajczar/Forint Kreuzer/Florin)				
1892-1916	same as Austria 1892-1916 (Korona = Krone)				
1926-39	1 Pengö	5.0000	.640	3.2000	.1029
	2 Pengö	10.0000	.640	6.4000	.2058
	5 Pengö	25.0000	.640	16.0000	.5144
1946	5 Forint	20.0000	.833	16.6600	.5356
1947-48	5 Forint	12.0000	.500	6.0000	.1929
	10 Forint	20.0000	.500	10.0000	.3215
	20 Forint	28.0000	.500	14.0000	.4501
INDIA					
1841-1917	2 Annas	1.4580	.916⅔	1.3365	.0430
1835-1943	¼ Rupee	2.9160	.916⅔	2.6730	.0859
1835-1940	½ Rupee	5.8319	.916⅔	5.3459	.1719
1835-1939	1 Rupee	11.6638	.916⅔	10.6918	.3437
1943-45	¼ Rupee	2.9160	.500	1.4580	.0469
1941-45	½ Rupee	5.8319	.500	2.9160	.0937
1940-45	1 Rupee	11.6638	.500	5.8319	.1875
IRAQ					
1931-53	20 Fils	3.6000	.500	1.8000	.0579
	50 Fils	9.0000	.500	4.5000	.1447
	1 Riyal	20.0000	.900	18.0000	.5787
IRELAND					
1928-43	1 Shilling	5.6552	.750	4.2414	.1364
	1 Florin	11.3104	.750	8.4828	.2727
	½ Crown	14.1380	.750	10.6035	.3409
ITALY					
1863-1917	see Latin Monetary Union				
	(Centesimi/Lire = Centimes/Francs)				
1926-41	5 Lire	5.0000	.835	4.1750	.1342
	10 Lire	10.0000	.835	8.3500	.2685
1927-34	20 Lire	15.0000	.800	12.0000	.3858

Dates	Denomination	Gross Wt., Gms.	Fine-ness	Silver Content Grams	Silver Content Ounces
ITALY (Cont.)					
1928	20 Lire commem.	20.0000	.600	12.0000	.3858
1936-41	20 Lire	20.0000	.800	16.0000	.5144
ITALIAN SOMALILAND					
1910-21	same as India 1835-1939 (Rupia = Rupee)				
1925	5 Lire	6.0000	.835	5.0100	.1611
	10 Lire	12.0000	.835	10.0200	.3221
JAPAN					
1870-71	5 Sen	1.2500	.800	1.0000	.0322
	10 Sen	2.5000	.800	2.0000	.0643
	20 Sen	5.0000	.800	4.0000	.1286
	50 Sen	12.5000	.800	10.0000	.3215
1873-1906	5 Sen	1.3479	.800	1.0783	.0347
	10 Sen	2.6957	.800	2.1566	.0693
	20 Sen	5.3914	.800	4.3131	.1387
	50 Sen	13.4785	.800	10.7828	.3467
1870-1914	1 Yen	26.9568	.900	24.2611	.7800
	Trade Dollar	27.2156	.900	24.4940	.7875
1906-17	10 Sen	2.2500	.720	1.6200	.0521
	20 Sen	4.0500	.800	3.2400	.1042
	50 Sen	10.1250	.800	8.1000	.2604
1922-38	50 Sen	4.9500	.720	3.5640	.1146
KOREA					
1892-93	same as Japan 1873-1906 (5 Yang = 1 Yen)				
1901-06	same as Japan 1873-1906				
1907-10	same as Japan 1906-1917	(Chon/Won = Sen/Yen)			
LATIN MONETARY UNION					

The Latin Monetary Union was formed by treaties standard-izing the silver and gold currencies of France, Italy, Belgium, Switzerland and Greece. Derived from the French coinage system established in 1803, the Union was formed in 1865 and dissolved in 1926. Many other countries, although not Union members, struck coinage to these standards.

Dates	Denomination	Gross Wt., Gms.	Fine-ness	Silver Content Grams	Silver Content Ounces
1865-1926	20 Centimes	1.0000	.835	0.8350	.0268
	50 Cmes/½ Franc	2.5000	.835	2.0875	.0671
	1 Franc	5.0000	.835	4.1750	.1342
	2 Francs	10.0000	.835	8.3500	.2685
	5 Francs	25.0000	.900	22.5000	.7234
LATVIA					
1924-32	1 Lats	5.0000	.835	4.1750	.1342
	2 Lati	10.0000	.835	8.3500	.2685
	5 Lati	25.0000	.835	20.8750	.6711
LEBANON					
1929-52	same as Syria 1929-59				
LITHUANIA					
1925	1 Litas	2.7000	.500	1.3500	.0434
	2 Litu	5.4000	.500	2.7000	.0868
	5 Litai	13.5000	.500	6.7500	.2170
1936-38	5 Litai	9.0000	.750	6.7500	.2170
	10 Litu	18.0000	.750	13.5000	.4340
LUXEMBOURG					
1929	5 Francs	8.0000	.625	5.0000	.1608
	10 Francs	13.3000	.750	9.9750	.3207
1946	20 Francs	8.5000	.835	7.0975	.2282
	50 Francs	12.5000	.835	10.4375	.3356
	100 Francs	25.0000	.835	20.8750	.6711
MALAYA					
1939-41	5 Cents	1.3577	.750	1.0183	.0327
	10 Cents	2.7154	.750	2.0365	.0655
	20 Cents	5.4308	.750	4.0731	.1310
1943-45	5 Cents	1.3577	.500	0.6788	.0218
	10 Cents	2.7154	.500	1.3577	.0437
	20 Cents	5.4308	.500	2.7154	.0873
MEXICO					
1822-69	¼ Real	0.8460	.9027	0.7637	.0246
	½ Real	1.6921	.9027	1.5275	.0491
	1 Real	3.3841	.9027	3.0548	.0982
1863-1905	5 Centavos	1.3537	.9027	1.2220	.0393
	10 Centavos	2.7073	.9027	2.4439	.0786

Dates	Denomination	Gross Wt., Gms.	Fine-ness	Silver Content Grams	Silver Content Ounces
	20 Centavos	5.4146	.9027	4.8878	.1571
1822-1905	2 R/25 Cvos.	6.7683	.9027	6.1097	.1964
	4 R/50 Cvos.	13.5365	.9027	12.2194	.3929
1822-1914	8 R/1 Peso	27.0730	.9027	24.4388	.7857
1905-18	10 Centavos	2.5000	.800	2.0000	.0643
	20 Centavos	5.0000	.800	4.0000	.1286
	50 Centavos	12.5000	.800	10.0000	.3215
1918-19	10 Centavos	1.8125	.800	1.4500	.0466
	20 Centavos	3.6250	.800	2.9000	.0932
	50 Centavos	9.0625	.800	7.2500	.2331
	1 Peso	18.1250	.800	14.5000	.4662
1919-45	10 Centavos	1.6667	.720	1.2000	.0386
	20 Centavos	3.3333	.720	2.4000	.0772
	50 Centavos	8.3333	.720	6.0000	.1929
	1 Peso	16.6667	.720	12.0000	.3858
	2 Pesos	26.6667	.900	24.0000	.7716
1935	50 Centavos	7.9733	.420	3.3488	.1077
1947-49	1 Peso	14.0000	.500	7.0000	.2251
	5 Pesos	30.0000	.900	27.0000	.8681
	Troy Ounce	33.6250	.925	31.1031	1.0000
MOMBASA					
1888-90	same as India 1835-1939				
MONGOLIA					
1925	same as Russia (Mongo/Tukhrik = Kopek/Ruble)				
MONTENEGRO					
1909-14	same as Austria 1892-1916 (Perpera = Kronen)				
MOROCCO					
1882-1901	½ Dirhem	1.4558	.835	1.2156	.0391
	1 Dirhem	2.9116	.835	2.4312	.0782
	2½ Dirhem	7.2790	.835	6.0780	.1954
	5 Dirhem	14.5580	.835	12.1559	.3908
	10 Dirhem	29.1160	.900	26.2044	.8425
1902-18	1/20 Rial	1.2500	.835	1.0438	.0336
	1/10 Rial	2.5000	.835	2.0875	.0671
	¼ Rial	6.2500	.835	5.2188	.1678
	½ Rial	12.5000	.835	10.4375	.3356
	1 Rial	25.0000	.900	22.5000	.7234
1929-34	5 Francs	5.0000	.680	3.4000	.1093
	10 Francs	10.0000	.680	6.8000	.2186
	20 Francs	20.0000	.680	13.6000	.4372
MOZAMBIQUE					
1935-51	same as Portugal				
NETHERLANDS					
1848-1945	5 Cents	0.6850	.640	0.4384	.0141
	10 Cents	1.4000	.640	0.8960	.0288
	25 Cents	3.5750	.640	2.2880	.0736
1840-1919	½ Gulden	5.0000	.945	4.7250	.1519
	1 Gulden	10.0000	.945	9.4500	.3038
	2½ Gulden	25.0000	.945	23.6250	.7595
1921-45	½ Gulden	5.0000	.720	3.6000	.1157
	1 Gulden	10.0000	.720	7.2000	.2315
	2½ Gulden	25.0000	.720	18.0000	.5787
NETHERLANDS INDIES					
1854-1945	1/20 Gulden	0.6100	.720	0.4392	.0141
	1/10 Gulden	1.2500	.720	0.9000	.0289
	¼ Gulden	3.1800	.720	2.2896	.0736
NEW GUINEA					
1935-45	1 Shilling	5.38	.925	4.98	.16
NEW ZEALAND					
1933-49	same as Great Britain 1920-46				
NICARAGUA					
1880-1936	5 Centavos	1.2500	.800	1.0000	.0322
	10 Centavos	2.5000	.800	2.0000	.0643
	20 Centavos	5.0000	.800	4.0000	.1286
	25 Centavos	6.2500	.800	5.0000	.1608
	50 Centavos	12.5000	.800	10.0000	.3215
	1 Córdoba	25.0000	.900	22.5000	.7234

PRECIOUS METAL CONTENT — SILVER

Dates	Denomination	Gross Wt., Gms.	Fineness	Silver Content Grams	Ounces
NORWAY					
1874-1919	see Scandinavian Monetary Union				
PALESTINE					
1927-42	50 Mils	5.8319	.720	4.1990	.1350
	100 Mils	11.6638	.720	8.3979	.2700
PANAMA					
1904-16	2½ Centésimos	1.2500	.900	1.1250	.0362
	5 Centésimos	2.5000	.900	2.2500	.0723
	10 Centésimos	5.0000	.900	4.5000	.1447
	25 Centésimos	12.5000	.900	11.2500	.3617
	50 Centésimos	25.0000	.900	22.5000	.7234
1930-62	same as United States				
PARAGUAY					
1889	1 Peso	25.0000	.900	22.5000	.7234
PERSIA					
1878-1929	(3) Shahi	0.6908	.900	0.6217	.0200
	¼ Qiran	1.1513	.900	1.0362	.0333
	500 Dinar	2.3025	.900	2.0723	.0666
	1000 Dinar	4.6050	.900	4.1445	.1332
	2000 Dinar	9.2100	.900	8.2890	.2665
	5000 Dinar	23.0251	.900	20.7226	.6662
	1 Toman	46.0501	.900	41.4451	1.3325
1931-36	¼ Rial	1.2500	.828	1.0350	.0333
	½ Rial	2.5000	.828	2.0700	.0666
	1 Rial	5.0000	.828	4.1400	.1331
	2 Rial	10.0000	.828	8.2800	.2662
	5 Rial	25.0000	.828	20.7000	.6655
1943-51	1 Rial	1.6000	.600	0.9600	.0309
	2 Rial	3.2000	.600	1.9200	.0617
	5 Rial	8.0000	.600	4.8000	.1543
	10 Rial	16.0000	.600	9.6000	.3086
PERU					
1863-1917	½ Dinero	1.2500	.900	1.1250	.0362
	1 Dinero	2.5000	.900	2.2500	.0723
	⅕ Sol	5.0000	.900	4.5000	.1447
	½ Sol	12.5000	.900	11.2500	.3617
	1 Sol	25.0000	.900	22.5000	.7234
1880-82	½ Real	1.2500	.900	1.1250	.0362
	1 Peseta	5.0000	.900	4.5000	.1447
	5 Pesetas	25.0000	.900	22.5000	.7234
1922-35	½ Sol	12.5000	.500	6.2500	.2009
	1 Sol	25.0000	.500	12.5000	.4019
PHILIPPINES					
1864-80	10 Céntimos	2.5960	.900	2.3364	.0751
	20 Céntimos	5.1920	.900	4.6728	.1502
	50 Céntimos	12.9800	.900	11.6820	.3756
1881-97	10 Céntimos	2.5960	.835	2.1677	.0697
	20 Céntimos	5.1920	.835	4.3353	.1394
	50 Céntimos	12.9800	.835	10.8383	.3485
	1 Peso	25.0000	.900	22.5000	.7234
1903-06	10 Centavos	2.6924	.900	2.4232	.0779
	20 Centavos	5.3849	.900	4.8464	.1558
	50 Centavos	13.4784	.900	12.1306	.3900
	1 Peso	26.9568	.900	24.2611	.7800
1907-47	10 Centavos	2.0000	.750	1.5000	.0482
	20 Centavos	4.0000	.750	3.0000	.0965
	50 Centavos	10.0000	.750	7.5000	.2411
	1 Peso	20.0000	.800	16.0000	.5144
POLAND					
1924-25	1 Zloty	5.0000	.750	3.7500	.1206
	2 Zlote	10.0000	.750	7.5000	.2411
	5 Zlotych	25.0000	.900	22.5000	.7234
1928-32	5 Zlotych	13.0000	.750	9.7500	.3135
1932-39	2 Zlote	4.4000	.750	3.3000	.1061
	5 Zlotych	8.8000	.750	6.6000	.2122
	10 Zlotych	22.0000	.750	16.5000	.5305
PORTUGAL					
1854-1903	50 Réis	1.2500	.916⅔	1.1458	.0368
	100 Réis	2.5000	.916⅔	2.2917	.0737
	200 Réis	5.0000	.916⅔	4.5833	.1474
1908-09	100 Réis	2.5000	.835	2.0875	.0671
	200 Réis	5.0000	.835	4.1750	.1342
1854-1910	500 Réis	12.5000	.916⅔	11.4583	.3684
	1000 Réis	25.0000	.916⅔	22.9167	.7368
1912-16	10 Centavos	2.5000	.835	2.0875	.0671
	20 Centavos	5.0000	.835	4.1750	.1342
	50 Centavos	12.5000	.835	10.4375	.3356
	1 Escudo	25.0000	.835	20.8750	.6711
1932-60	2½ Escudos	3.5000	.650	2.2750	.0731
	5 Escudos	7.0000	.650	4.5500	.1463
1928-48	10 Escudos	12.5000	.835	10.4375	.3356
PORTUGUESE INDIA					
1881-1936	same as India (Rupia = Rupee)				
PUERTO RICO					
1895-96	5 Centavos	1.2500	.835	1.0438	.0336
	10 Centavos	2.5000	.835	2.0875	.0671
	20 Centavos	5.0000	.835	4.1750	.1342
	40 Centavos	10.0000	.835	8.3500	.2685
	1 Peso	25.0000	.900	22.5000	.7234
ROMANIA					
1870-1914	same as Latin Monetary Union (Bani/Lei = Centimes/Francs)				
1932-35	100 Lei	14.0000	.500	7.0000	.2251
	250 Lei	13.5000	.750	10.1250	.3255
RUSSIA					
1813-60	5 Kopek	1.0366	.868	0.8998	.0289
	10 Kopek	2.0732	.868	1.7995	.0579
	20 Kopek	4.1463	.868	3.5990	.1157
1860-66	5 Kopek	1.0366	.750	0.7775	.0250
	10 Kopek	2.0732	.750	1.5549	.0500
	15 Kopek	3.1097	.750	2.3323	.0750
	20 Kopek	4.1463	.750	3.1097	.1000
1867-1931	5 Kopek	0.8998	.500	0.4499	.0145
	10 Kopek	1.7996	.500	0.8998	.0289
	15 Kopek	2.6994	.500	1.3497	.0434
	20 Kopek	3.5992	.500	1.7996	.0579
1801-85	25 Kopek	5.1879	.868	4.4988	.1446
	50 Kopek	10.3658	.868	8.9975	.2893
	1 Ruble	20.7316	.868	17.9950	.5785
1886-1931	25 Kopek	4.9987	.900	4.4988	.1446
	50 Kopek	9.9979	.900	8.9981	.2893
	1 Ruble	19.9957	.900	17.9961	.5786
ST. THOMAS & PRINCE					
1939-51	2½ Escudos	3.5000	.650	2.2750	.0731
	5 Escudos	7.0000	.650	4.5500	.1463
1939	10 Escudos	12.5000	.835	10.4375	.3356
1951	10 Escudos	12.5000	.720	9.0000	.2894
EL SALVADOR					
1892-1914	5 Centavos	1.2500	.835	1.0438	.0336
	10 Centavos	2.5000	.835	2.0875	.0671
	20 Centavos	5.0000	.835	4.1750	.1342
	25 Centavos	6.2500	.835	5.2188	.1678
	50 Centavos	12.5000	.900	11.2500	.3617
	1 Peso	25.0000	.900	22.5000	.7234
1943-44	25 Centavos	7.5000	.900	6.7500	.2170
SAN MARINO					
1898-1906	same as Latin Monetary Union (Centesimi/Lire = Centimes/Francs)				
1931-38	5 Lire	5.0000	.835	4.1750	.1342
	10 Lire	10.0000	.835	8.3500	.2685
	20 Lire	15.0000	.800	12.0000	.3858
	20 Lire	20.0000	.600	12.0000	.3858
SAUDI ARABIA					
1935-55	same as India 1835-1939 (Riyal = Rupee)				
SCANDINAVIAN MONETARY UNION					
This union was formed by treaties between Denmark, Sweden					

PRECIOUS METAL CONTENT — SILVER

Dates	Denomination	Gross Wt., Gms.	Fine-ness	Silver Content Grams	Ounces

SCANDINAVIAN MONETARY UNION (Cont.)

and Norway to standardize their monetary systems. Although never formally terminated, it was gradually abandoned following World War I. The only issues on this standard after World War II were Danish 2 Kroner commemoratives to 1958.

Dates	Denomination	Gross Wt., Gms.	Fine-ness	Silver Content Grams	Ounces
1874-1958	10 Øre, Öre	1.4500	.400	0.5800	.0186
	25 Øre, Öre	2.4200	.600	1.4520	.0467
	50 Øre, Öre	5.0000	.600	3.0000	.0965
	1 Krone, Krona	7.5000	.800	6.0000	.1929
	2 Kroner, Kronor	15.0000	.800	12.0000	.3858

SERBIA

1875-1915 same as Latin Monetary Union
(Para/Dinara = Centimes/Francs)

SEYCHELLES

1939-44 same as India 1940-45

SIAM

Dates	Denomination	Gross Wt., Gms.	Fine-ness	Silver Content Grams	Ounces
1908-25	¼ Baht	3.7500	.800	3.0000	.0965
	½ Baht	7.5000	.800	6.0000	.1929
	1 Baht	15.0000	.900	13.5000	.4340
1929	25 Satang	3.7500	.650	2.4375	.0784
	50 Satang	7.5000	.650	4.8750	.1567
1941	5 Satang	1.5000	.650	0.9750	.0313
	10 Satang	2.5000	.650	1.6250	.0522
	20 Satang	3.0000	.650	1.9500	.0627

SOUTH AFRICA

Dates	Denomination	Gross Wt., Gms.	Fine-ness	Silver Content Grams	Ounces
1923-51	3 Pence	1.4138	.800	1.1310	.0364
	6 Pence	2.8276	.800	2.2621	.0727
	1 Shilling	5.6552	.800	4.5241	.1454
	2 Sh/Florin	11.3104	.800	9.0483	.2909
	2½ Shillings	14.1380	.800	11.3104	.3636
	5 Shillings	28.2759	.800	22.6207	.7273
1951-60	same as Great Britain 1920-46				
	(5 Shillings = 1 Crown)				

SOUTHERN RHODESIA

1932-42 same as Great Britain 1817-1920
1944-46 same as Great Britain 1920-46

SPAIN

Dates	Denomination	Gross Wt., Gms.	Fine-ness	Silver Content Grams	Ounces
1850-65	1 Real	1.3146	.900	1.1831	.0380
	2 Reales	2.6291	.900	2.3662	.0761
	4 Reales	5.2582	.900	4.7324	.1521
	10 Reales	13.1455	.900	11.8310	.3804
	20 Reales	26.2910	.900	23.6619	.7607
1864-68	10 Céntimos	1.2980	.810	1.0514	.0338
	20 Céntimos	2.5960	.810	2.1028	.0676
	40 Céntimos	5.1920	.810	4.2055	.1352
	1 Escudo	12.9800	.900	11.6820	.3756
	2 Escudos	25.9600	.900	23.3640	.7512
1869-1934	same as Latin Monetary Union				
	(Céntimos/Pesetas = Centimes/Francs)				

STRAITS SETTLEMENTS

1871-1905 same as Hong Kong

Dates	Denomination	Gross Wt., Gms.	Fine-ness	Silver Content Grams	Ounces
1907-17	5 Cents	1.3577	.600	0.8146	.0262
	10 Cents	2.7154	.600	1.6292	.0524
	20 Cents	5.4308	.600	3.2585	.1048
	50 Cents	10.1088	.900	9.0979	.2925
	1 Dollar	20.2176	.900	18.1958	.5850
1918-21	5 Cents	1.3577	.400	0.5431	.0175
	10 Cents	2.7154	.400	1.0862	.0349
	20 Cents	5.4308	.400	2.1723	.0698
	50 Cents	8.4240	.500	4.2120	.1354
	1 Dollar	16.8480	.500	8.4240	.2708
1926-35	same as 1907-17				

SWEDEN

1874-1942 see Scandinavian Monetary Union

Dates	Denomination	Gross Wt., Gms.	Fine-ness	Silver Content Grams	Ounces
1935	5 Kronor	25.0000	.900	22.5000	.7234
1942-68	10 Öre	1.4400	.400	0.5760	.0185
	25 Öre	2.3200	.400	0.9280	.0298
	50 Öre	4.8000	.400	1.9200	.0617

Dates	Denomination	Gross Wt., Gms.	Fine-ness	Silver Content Grams	Ounces
	1 Krona	7.0000	.400	2.8000	.0900
	2 Kronor	14.0000	.400	5.6000	.1800

SWITZERLAND

1850-51 ½, 1, 2 Francs; same as France 1803-66

Dates	Denomination	Gross Wt., Gms.	Fine-ness	Silver Content Grams	Ounces
1857-63	1 Franc	5.0000	.800	4.0000	.1286
	2 Francs	10.0000	.800	8.0000	.2572
1874-1967	½, 1, 2 Francs				
1850-1928	5 Francs	see Latin Monetary Union			
1931-69	5 Francs	15.0000	.835	12.5250	.4027

SYRIA

Dates	Denomination	Gross Wt., Gms.	Fine-ness	Silver Content Grams	Ounces
1929-37	10 Piastres	2.0000	.680	1.3600	.0437
	25 Piastres	5.0000	.680	3.4000	.1093
	50 Piastres	10.0000	.680	6.8000	.2186
1947-59	25 Piastres	2.5000	.600	1.5000	.0482
	50 Piastres	5.0000	.600	3.0000	.0965
	1 Lira	10.0000	.680	6.8000	.2186

TARIM & GHURFAH

Dates	Denomination	Gross Wt., Gms.	Fine-ness	Silver Content Grams	Ounces
1897	6 Chamsi	0.8500	.900	0.7650	.0246
	12 Chamsi	1.5500	.900	1.3950	.0448
	24 Chamsi	3.1000	.900	2.7900	.0897
1926	4 Chamsi	0.5660	.900	0.5094	.0164
	8 Chamsi	1.0333	.900	0.9300	.0299
	15 Chamsi	1.9375	.900	1.7438	.0561
	30 Chamsi	3.8750	.900	3.4875	.1121
	45 Chamsi	5.8125	.900	5.2313	.1682
	60 Chamsi	7.7500	.900	6.9750	.2242

TIMOR

Dates	Denomination	Gross Wt., Gms.	Fine-ness	Silver Content Grams	Ounces
1945-51	50 Avos	3.5000	.650	2.2750	.0731

TUNISIA

1891-1928 same as Latin Monetary Union

Dates	Denomination	Gross Wt., Gms.	Fine-ness	Silver Content Grams	Ounces
1930-39	5 Francs	5.0000	.680	3.4000	.1093
	10 Francs	10.0000	.680	6.8000	.2186
	20 Francs	20.0000	.680	13.6000	.4372

TURKEY

Dates	Denomination	Gross Wt., Gms.	Fine-ness	Silver Content Grams	Ounces
1844-1919	20 Para	0.6013	.830	0.4991	.0160
	1 Kuruş	1.2027	.830	0.9982	.0321
	2 Kuruş	2.4055	.830	1.9966	.0642
	5 Kuruş	6.0130	.830	4.9908	.1605
	10 Kuruş	12.0270	.830	9.9824	.3209
	20 Kuruş	24.0550	.830	19.9657	.6419
1899-1904	5 Para	1.0023	.100	0.1002	.0032
	10 Para	2.0046	.100	0.2005	.0064
1934-41	25 Kuruş	3.0000	.830	2.4900	.0801
	50 Kuruş	6.0000	.830	4.9800	.1601
	100 Kuruş/1 Lira	12.0000	.830	9.9600	.3202
1947-48	50 Kuruş	4.0000	.600	2.4000	.0772
	1 Lira	7.5000	.600	4.5000	.1447

UNITED STATES OF AMERICA

Dates	Denomination	Gross Wt., Gms.	Fine-ness	Silver Content Grams	Ounces
1851-53	3 Cents	0.8019	.750	0.6014	.0193
1853-73	3 Cents	0.7465	.900	0.6719	.0216
	½ Dime	1.2442	.900	1.1197	.0360
	1 Dime	2.4883	.900	2.2395	.0720
	¼ Dollar	6.2208	.900	5.5987	.1800
	½ Dollar	12.4416	.900	11.1974	.3600
1873-1964	1 Dime	2.5000	.900	2.2500	.0723
	20 Cents	5.0000	.900	4.5000	.1447
	¼ Dollar	6.2500	.900	5.6250	.1808
	½ Dollar	12.5000	.900	11.2500	.3617
1840-1935	1 Dollar	26.7296	.900	24.0566	.7734
1873-85	Trade Dollar	27.2156	.900	24.4940	.7875
1942-45	5 Cents	5.0000	.350	1.7500	.0563

URUGUAY

1877-1917 same as Argentina (Centésimos = Centavos)

Dates	Denomination	Gross Wt., Gms.	Fine-ness	Silver Content Grams	Ounces
1920-30	20 Centésimos	5.0000	.800	4.0000	.1286
1942-54	20 Centésimos	2.0000	.720	2.1600	.0694
	50 Centésimos	7.0000	.720	5.0400	.1620
	1 Peso	9.0000	.720	6.4800	.2083

Dates	Denomination	Gross Wt., Gms.	Fineness	Silver Content Grams	Silver Content Ounces
VATICAN					
1929-46	same as Italy 1926-41				
VENEZUELA					
1858	½ Real	1.1500	.900	1.0350	.0333
	1 Real	2.3000	.900	2.0700	.0666
	2 Reales	4.6000	.900	4.1400	.1331
	5 Reales	11.5000	.900	10.3500	.3328
1873-1965	⅕ Bolívar	1.0000	.835	0.8350	.0268
	5 Cvos/¼ Bol	1.2500	.835	1.0438	.0336
	10 Cvos/½ Bol	2.5000	.835	2.0875	.0671
	20 Cvos/1 Bol	5.0000	.835	4.1750	.1342
	2 Bolívares	10.0000	.835	8.3500	.2685
	50 Centavos	12.5000	.835	10.4375	.3356
	1 Ven/5 Bol	25.0000	.900	22.5000	.7234
YUGOSLAVIA					
1931-32	10 Dinara	7.0000	.500	3.5000	.1125
	20 Dinara	14.0000	.500	7.0000	.2251
	50 Dinara	22.0000	.750	16.5000	.5305
1938	20 Dinara	9.0000	.750	6.7500	.2170
	50 Dinara	15.0000	.750	11.2500	.3617
ZANZIBAR					
1882	same as United States 1873-85 (Ryal = Trade Dollar)				

GOLD

Dates	Denomination	Gross Wt., Gms.	Fineness	Gold Content Grams	Gold Content Ounces
ALBANIA					
1926-38	same as Latin Monetary Union (Franka Ari = Franc)				
ARGENTINA					
1881-96	½ Argentino	4.0322	.900	3.6290	.1167
	1 Argentino	8.0645	.900	7.2581	.2333
AUSTRALIA					
1852-1931	same as Great Britain				
AUSTRIA					
1857-1915	1 Dukat	3.4909	.9861	3.4424	.1107
	4 Dukaten	13.9636	.9861	13.7695	.4427
1858-66	½ Krone	5.5555	.900	5.0000	.1608
	1 Krone	11.1111	.900	10.0000	.3215
1870-92	4 Fl/10 Fr	3.2258	.900	2.9032	.0933
	8 Fl/20 Fr	6.4516	.900	5.8064	.1867
1892-1924	10 Kronen	3.3875	.900	3.0488	.0980
	20 Kronen	6.7751	.900	6.0976	.1960
	100 Kronen	33.8753	.900	30.4878	.9802
1926-38	25 Schilling	5.8811	.900	5.2930	.1702
	100 Schilling	23.5245	.900	21.1721	.6807
BELGIUM					
1848-1914	see Latin Monetary Union				
BRAZIL					
1849-1922	5000 Réis	4.4822	.916⅔	4.1087	.1321
	10000 Réis	8.9645	.916⅔	8.2175	.2642
	20000 Réis	17.9290	.916⅔	16.4349	.5284
BULGARIA					
1894-1912	same as Latin Monetary Union				
CANADA					
1908-19	1 Sovereign: same as Great Britain				
1912-14	5, 10 Dollars: same as United States				
NEWFOUNDLAND					
1865-88	2 Dollars	3.3284	.916⅔	3.0510	.0981
CHILE					
1851-92	1 Peso	1.5253	.900	1.3728	.0441
	2 Pesos	3.0506	.900	2.7455	.0883
	5 Pesos	7.6265	.900	6.8639	.2207
	10 Pesos	15.2530	.900	13.7277	.4413
1895-1917	5 Pesos	2.9955	.916⅔	2.7459	.0883
	10 Pesos	5.9910	.916⅔	5.4918	.1766
	20 Pesos	11.9821	.916⅔	10.9836	.3531

Dates	Denomination	Gross Wt., Gms.	Fineness	Gold Content Grams	Gold Content Ounces
1926-*62*	20 Pesos	4.0679	.900	3.6611	.1177
	50 Pesos	10.1698	.900	9.1528	.2943
	100 Pesos	20.3397	.900	18.3057	.5885
COLOMBIA					
1856-78	same as Latin Monetary Union (1 Peso = 5 Francs)				
1885	5 Pesos	8.0645	.666	5.3763	.1728
1913-30	same as Great Britain (5 Pesos = 1 Sovereign)				
COSTA RICA					
1864-76	1 Peso	*1.4677*	.875	*1.2843*	*.0413*
	2 Pesos	*2.9355*	.875	*2.5685*	*.0826*
	5 Pesos	*7.3387*	.875	*6.4213*	*.2064*
	10 Pesos	*14.6774*	.875	*12.8427*	*.4129*
1873	5 Pesos	8.0645	.900	7.2581	.2333
	20 Pesos	32.2581	.900	29.0323	.9334
1897-1928	2 Colones	1.5560	.900	1.4004	.0450
	5 Colones	3.8900	.900	3.5010	.1126
	10 Colones	7.7800	.900	7.0020	.2251
	20 Colones	15.5600	.900	14.0040	.4502
CUBA					
1915-16	2 Pesos	3.3436	.900	3.0092	.0967
	4 Pesos	6.6872	.900	6.0185	.1935
	Other values: same as United States (Pesos = Dollars)				
CZECHOSLOVAKIA					
1923-51	1 Dukat	3.4909	.9861	3.4424	.1107
	2 Dukaty	6.9818	.9861	6.8848	.2213
	5 Dukatu	17.4545	.9861	17.2119	.5534
	10 Dukatu	34.9089	.9861	34.4237	1.1067
DANISH WEST INDIES					
1904-05	same as Latin Monetary Union (1 Daler = 5 Francs)				
DANZIG					
1923-30	same as Great Britain (25 Gulden = 1 Sovereign)				
DENMARK					
1873-1931	see Scandinavian Monetary Union				
ECUADOR					
1899-1900	10 Sucres	8.1360	.900	7.3224	.2354
1928	1 Cóndor	8.3592	.900	7.5233	.2419
EGYPT					
18*35*-1960	5 Ghirsh	0.4250	.900	0.3825	.0123
	10 Ghirsh	0.8500	.900	0.7650	.0246
	20 Ghirsh	1.7000	.900	1.5300	.0492
	25 Ghirsh	2.1250	.900	1.9125	.0615
	50 Gh/½ Lira	4.2500	.900	3.8250	.1230
	100 Gh/1 Lira	8.5000	.900	7.6500	.2459
	500 Gh/5 Lira	42.5000	.900	38.2500	1.2297
FINLAND					
1878-1913	same as Latin Monetary Union (Markkaa = Francs)				
1926	100 Markkaa	4.2105	.900	3.7895	.1218
	200 Markkaa	8.4211	.900	7.5789	.2437
FRANCE					
1803-1914	see Latin Monetary Union				
1929-36	100 Francs	6.5500	.900	5.8950	.1895
GERMANY					
1871-1915	5 Mark	1.9913	.900	1.7922	.0576
	10 Mark	3.9825	.900	3.5843	.1152
	20 Mark	7.9650	.900	7.1685	.2305
GERMAN EAST AFRICA					
1916	15 Rupien	7.1680	.750	5.3760	.1728
GERMAN NEW GUINEA					
1895	same as Germany				
GREAT BRITAIN					
1817-1968	½ Sovereign	3.9940	.916⅔	3.6612	.1177
	1 Sovereign	7.9881	.916⅔	7.3224	.2354
	2 Pounds	15.9761	.916⅔	14.6448	.4708
	5 Pounds	39.9403	.916⅔	36.6119	1.1771
GREECE					
1876-*1967*	see Latin Monetary Union (Drachmai = Francs)				

Dates	Denomination	Gross Wt., Gms.	Fine-ness	Gold Content Grams	Ounces

GUATEMALA

1869-78 same as Latin Monetary Union (1 Peso = 5 Francs)
1926 same as United States (Quetzales = Dollars)

HONDURAS

1871-1922 same as Latin Monetary Union (1 Peso = 5 Francs)

HUNGARY

1870-1916 same as Austria
(Dukát/Forint/Korona = Dukat/Florin/Krone)

INDIA

1835-1918	5 Rupees	3.8879	.916⅔	3.5639	.1146
	10 Rupees	7.7759	.916⅔	7.1279	.2292
	15 R/1 Mohur	11.6638	.916⅔	10.6918	.3437
	2 Mohur	23.3276	.916⅔	21.3836	.6875
1918	1 Sovereign; same as Great Britain				

ITALY

1861-1927 see Latin Monetary Union (Lire = Francs)

1931-36	50 Lire	4.3995	.900	3.9596	.1273
	100 Lire	8.7990	.900	7.9191	.2546
1937	100 Lire	5.1966	.900	4.6769	.1504

JAPAN

1870-97	1 Yen	1.6667	.900	1.5000	.0482
	2 Yen	3.3333	.900	3.0000	.0965
	5 Yen	8.3333	.900	7.5000	.2411
	10 Yen	16.6667	.900	15.0000	.4823
	20 Yen	33.3333	.900	30.0000	.9645
1897-1932	5 Yen	4.1667	.900	3.7500	.1206
	10 Yen	8.3333	.900	7.5000	.2411
	20 Yen	16.6667	.900	15.0000	.4823

KOREA

1906-10 same as Japan 1897-1932 (Won = Yen)

LATIN MONETARY UNION

This Union (see silver section for explanation) struck denominations as listed below for 1865-1926, though some countries struck coins of identical standards both earlier and later. Other denominations shown below were struck prior to the Union or by nonmember states; these values have proportional weights, however, and are included here for ease of reference.

1865-1926	5 Francs	1.6129	.900	1.4516	.0467
	10 Francs	3.2258	.900	2.9032	.0933
	20 Francs	6.4516	.900	5.8064	.1867
	50 Francs	16.1290	.900	14.5161	.4667
	100 Francs	32.2581	.900	29.0323	.9334
Other:	12½ Francs	4.0323	.900	3.6291	.1167
	25 Francs	8.0645	.900	7.2581	.2333
	40 Francs	12.9032	.900	11.6129	.3734

LIECHTENSTEIN

1898-1900 same as Austria 1892-1924
1930-52 same as Latin Monetary Union (Franken = Francs)

MEXICO

1822-73	½ Escudo	1.6921	.875	1.4805	.0476
	1 Escudo	3.3841	.875	2.9611	.0952
	2 Escudos	6.7683	.875	5.9222	.1904
	4 Escudos	13.5365	.875	11.8444	.3808
	8 Escudos	27.0730	.875	23.6889	.7616
1870-1905	1 Peso	1.6921	.875	1.4805	.0476
	2½ Pesos	4.2301	.875	3.7014	.1190
	5 Pesos	8.4602	.875	7.4027	.2380
	10 Pesos	16.9205	.875	14.8054	.4760
	20 Pesos	33.8410	.875	29.6109	.9520
1905-59	2 Pesos	1.6667	.900	1.5000	.0482
	2½ Pesos	2.0833	.900	1.8750	.0603
	5 Pesos	4.1667	.900	3.7500	.1206
	10 Pesos	8.3333	.900	7.5000	.2411
	20 Pesos	16.6667	.900	15.0000	.4823
	50 Pesos	41.6667	.900	37.5000	1.2056

MONACO

1878-1904 same as Latin Monetary Union

MONTENEGRO

1910 same as Austria 1892-1924 (Perpera = Kronen)

NETHERLANDS

1817-1960	1 Dukaat	3.4940	.983	3.4346	.1104
	2 Dukaat	6.9880	.983	6.8692	.2208
1819-53	5 Gulden	3.3645	.900	3.0281	.0974
	10 Gulden	6.7290	.900	6.0561	.1947
	20 Gulden	13.4580	.900	12.1122	.3894
1875-1933	5 Gulden	3.3600	.900	3.0240	.0972
	10 Gulden	6.7200	.900	6.0480	.1944

NORWAY

1874-1910 see Scandinavian Monetary Union

PERSIA

1879-1926	⅕ Toman	0.5749	.900	0.5174	.0166
	½ Toman	1.4372	.900	1.2935	.0416
	1 Toman	2.8744	.900	2.5870	.0832
	2 Toman	5.7488	.900	5.1739	.1663
	5 Toman	14.3720	.900	12.9348	.4159
	10 Toman	28.7440	.900	25.8696	.8317
1926-29	1 Pahlavi	1.9180	.900	1.7262	.0555
	2 Pahlavi	3.8360	.900	3.4524	.1110
	5 Pahlavi	9.5900	.900	8.6310	.2775
1931-	¼ Pahlavi	2.0340	.900	1.8306	.0589
	½ Pahlavi	4.0680	.900	3.6612	.1177
	1 Pahlavi	8.1360	.900	7.3224	.2354
	2½ Pahlavi	20.3400	.900	18.3060	.5885
	5 Pahlavi	40.6799	.900	36.6119	1.1771

PERU

1863	same as Latin Monetary Union (1 Sol = 5 Francs)				
1898-	⅕ Libra	1.5976	.916⅔	1.4645	.0471
	½ Libra	3.9940	.916⅔	3.6612	.1177
	1 Libra	7.9881	.916⅔	7.3224	.2354
1930-	50 Soles	33.4363	.900	30.0926	.9675
1950-	5 Soles	2.3404	.900	2.1064	.0677
	10 Soles	4.6807	.900	4.2126	.1354
	20 Soles	9.3614	.900	8.4253	.2709
	50 Soles	23.4036	.900	21.0632	.6772
	100 Soles	46.8071	.900	42.1264	1.3544

PHILIPPINES

1861-85	1 Peso	1.6915	.875	1.4801	.0476
	2 Pesos	3.3830	.875	2.9602	.0952
	4 Pesos	6.7661	.875	5.9203	.1903

POLAND

1925 same as Latin Monetary Union (Zlotych = Francs)

PORTUGAL

1855-89	1000 Réis	1.7735	.916⅔	1.6257	.0523
	2000 Réis	3.5470	.916⅔	3.2514	.1045
	5000 Réis	8.8675	.916⅔	8.1285	.2613
	10000 Réis	17.7350	.916⅔	16.2571	.5227

ROMANIA

1868-1940 same as Latin Monetary Union (Lei = Francs)

RUSSIA

1817-85	3 Ruble	3.9264	.916⅔	3.5992	.1157
	5 Ruble	6.5440	.916⅔	5.9987	.1929
	25 Ruble	32.7200	.916⅔	29.9933	.9643
1886-97	5 Ruble	6.4519	.900	5.8067	.1867
	10 Ruble	12.9039	.900	11.6135	.3734
1896-1908	25 Ruble	32.2595	.900	29.0336	.9334
1897-1923	5 Ruble	4.3012	.900	3.8711	.1245
	7½ Ruble	6.4518	.900	5.8066	.1867
	10 Ruble	8.6024	.900	7.7422	.2489
	15 Ruble	12.9036	.900	11.6132	.3734
	37½ Ruble	32.2590	.900	29.0331	.9334

EL SALVADOR

1892 same as Latin Monetary Union (1 Peso = 5 Francs)

SAN MARINO

1925 same as Latin Monetary Union (Lire = Francs)

SAUDI ARABIA

1945-47	1 Sovereign	7.9881	.916⅔	7.3224	.2354
	4 Sovereigns	31.9522	.916⅔	29.2895	.9417

Dates	Denomination	Gross Wt., Gms.	Fine- ness	Gold Content Grams	Ounces
SCANDINAVIAN MONETARY UNION					
The unified currencies of Denmark, Sweden and Norway. See silver section for explanation.					
1873-1931	5 Kronor	2.2402	.900	2.0162	.0648
	10 Kroner/Kronor..	4.4803	.900	4.0323	.1296
	20 Kroner/Kronor..	8.9606	.900	8.0645	.2593
SERBIA					
1879-82	same as Latin Monetary Union (Dinara = Francs)				
SOUTH AFRICA					
1874-	same as Great Britain				
	(Sovereign = Pond, Pound, Rand)				
SPAIN					
1850-64	20 Reales	*1.6674*	.900	*1.5007*	*.0482*
	40 Reales	*3.3349*	.900	*3.0014*	*.0965*
	100 Rs/1 Doblón...	*8.3371*	.900	7.5034	.2412
1865-68	2 Escudos	1.6774	.900	1.5097	.0485
	4 Escudos	3.3548	.900	3.0193	.0971
	10 Escudos	8.3870	.900	7.5483	.2427
1876-1904	same as Latin Monetary Union (Pesetas = Francs)				
SWITZERLAND					
1883-1949	10, 20 Francs	see Latin Monetary Union			
1925	100 Francs				
1934	100 Francs	*25.9000*	.900	23.3100	.7494
1939	100 Francs	*17.5000*	.900	15.7500	.5064
SYRIA					
1950	½ Lira	3.3793	.900	3.0414	.0978
	1 Lira	6.7586	.900	6.0827	.1956
TUNISIA					
1856-91	5 Sebili	*0.9840*	.900	*0.8856*	*.0285*
	10 Sebili	*1.9680*	.900	*1.7712*	*.0569*
	25 S/15 Francs...	*4.9200*	.900	*4.4280*	*.1424*
	50 Sebili	*9.8400*	.900	*8.8560*	*.2847*
	100 Sebili	*19.6800*	.900	17.7120	.5694
1891-1928	same as Latin Monetary Union				
1930-37	same as France 1929-36				

Dates	Denomination	Gross Wt., Gms.	Fine- ness	Gold Content Grams	Ounces
TURKEY					
1844-1919	25 Kuruş	1.8041	.916⅔	1.6538	.0532
	50 Kuruş	3.6083	.916⅔	3.3076	.1063
	100 Kuruş	7.2166	.916⅔	6.6152	.2127
	250 Kuruş	18.0414	.916⅔	16.5380	.5317
	500 Kuruş	36.0828	.916⅔	33.0759	1.0634
1925-	regular issues; same as 1844-1919				
	"de Luxe:"				
	25 Kuruş	1.7540	.916⅔	1.6078	.0517
	50 Kuruş	3.5080	.916⅔	3.2157	.1034
	100 Kuruş	7.0160	.916⅔	6.4313	.2068
	250 Kuruş	17.5400	.916⅔	16.0783	.5169
	500 Kuruş	35.0800	.916⅔	32.1567	1.0338
UNITED STATES OF AMERICA					
1837-1933	1 Dollar	1.6718	.900	1.5046	.0484
	2½ Dollars	4.1795	.900	3.7616	.1209
	3 Dollars	5.0154	.900	4.5139	.1451
	5 Dollars	8.3591	.900	7.5232	.2419
	10 Dollars	16.7181	.900	15.0463	.4837
	20 Dollars	33.4363	.900	30.0926	.9675
	50 Dollars	83.5906	.900	75.2316	2.4187
URUGUAY					
1930	5 Pesos	8.4850	.916⅔	7.7779	.2501
VATICAN					
1929-35	same as Italy 1931-36				
1936-59	same as Italy 1937				
VENEZUELA					
1875	same as Latin Monetary Union				
	(5 Venezolanos = 25 Francs)				
1879-1930	same as Latin Monetary Union (Bolívares = Francs)				
YUGOSLAVIA					
1925	same as Latin Monetary Union (Dinara = Francs)				
1931-33	same as Austria 1857-1915				
ZANZIBAR					
1882	same as United States (Ryals = Dollars)				

ALPHABETICAL INDEX OF
WORLD COIN DENOMINATIONS

ABBASI — Afghanistan
AFGHANI — Afghanistan
AHMADI — Yemen
AMANI — Afghanistan
AMMAN CASH — Pudukota
ANNA—Burma, India, India Native States, Mombasa, Muscat & Oman, Pakistan
ARGENTINO — Argentina
ASHRAFI — Bahawalpur, Hyderabad
ATT — Siam (Thailand)
AURAR — Iceland (see EYRIR)
AVO — Timor

BAHT — Siam (Thailand)
BAIZAH — Muscat and Oman
BALBOA — Panama
BAN (Banu, Bani) — Romania
BELGA — Belgium
BER — Ethiopia
BESA (Bese) — Ethiopia, Italian Somaliland
BIT — Danish West Indies
BOGACH — Yemen
BOLIVAR — Venezuela
BOLIVIANO — Bolivia

CANDAREEN — China
CAROLIN — Sweden
CASH — China, Pudukota, Travancore
CEN — China

CENT — British Honduras, British North Borneo, Canada, Ceylon, China, Curaçao, Danish West Indies, East Africa, Ethiopia, Hawaii, Hong Kong, Kiao Chau, Liberia, Malaya, Mauritius, Netherlands, Netherlands East Indies, Newfoundland, Nova Scotia, Prince Edward Island, Sarawak, Seychelles, Straits Settlements, Surinam, United States, Zanzibar
CENTAS (Centu, Centai) — Lithuania
CENTAVO — Angola, Argentina, Bolivia, Brazil, Cape Verde, Chile, Colombia, Costa Rica, Cuba, Dominican Republic, Ecuador, Guatemala, Honduras, Mexico, Mozambique, Nicaragua, Paraguay, Peru, Philippines, Portugal, Portuguese Guinea, Puerto Rico, St. Thomas & Prince, Salvador, Venezuela
CENTECIMO — Bolivia
CENTESIMO (Centesimi) — Eritrea, Italy, San Marino, Vatican City
—— **(Centesimos)** — Dominican Republic, Panama, Paraguay, Uruguay
CENTIME — Belgian Congo, Belgium, Cambodia, Cameroon, Comoro Islands, France, French Cochin China, French Equatorial Africa, French Indo-China, French Oceania, French West Africa,

WORLD COIN DENOMINATIONS

Guadeloupe, Haiti, Luxembourg, Madagascar, Martinique, Monaco, Morocco, New Caledonia, Reunion, Switzerland, Togo, Tunisia

CENTIMO — Costa Rica, Guatemala, Paraguay, Philippines, Spain, Venezuela

CH'IEN — China

CHIO — China, Manchukuo

CHOMSIH — Mukalla, Quaiti, Tarim & Ghurfah

CHON — Korea

CHRISTIAN d'OR — Denmark

CHUCKRAM — Travancore

COLON (Colones) — Costa Rica, Salvador

CONDOR — Chile, Ecuador

CORDOBA — Nicaragua

CROWN — Australia, Great Britain, Ireland, New Zealand, Southern Rhodesia

CRUZEIRO — Brazil

DALA — Hawaii

DALER — Danish West Indies

DECIMA — Spain

DECIMO — Chile, Colombia, Ecuador

DHYAK — Nepal

DIME — Hawaii, United States

DINAR — Afghanistan, Hejaz, Persia

—— (Dinara) — Serbia, Yugoslavia

DINERO — Peru

DIRHAM — Iraq, Morocco

DOKDO (Dokda) — Junagadh, Kutch, Navanager

DOLLAR — Canada, China, Great Britain, Hawaii, Hong Kong, Newfoundland, Straits Settlements, United States

DONG — North Vietnam

DOUBLE — Guernsey

DRACHMA (Drachmai) — Crete, Greece

DUB — Hyderabad

DUKAT — Sweden

DUKAT (Dukata) — Yugoslavia

DUKAT (Dukaten) — Austria, Hungary

DUKAAT — Netherlands

EAGLE — United States

ESCUDO — Angola, Cape Verde, Chile, Costa Rica, Ecuador, Mexico, Mozambique, Portugal, Portuguese Guinea, St. Thomas & Prince, Spain

EYRIR (Aurar) — Iceland

FALUS — Bukhara

FANAM — Travancore

FARTHING — Ceylon, Great Britain, Ireland, Jamaica, Malta

FEN — China, Chinese Turkestan, Manchukuo

FENIG (Fenigow) — Poland

FILLER — Hungary

FILS — Iraq, Jordan

FLORIN — Australia, Austria, East Africa, Fiji, Great Britain, Ireland, New Zealand, South Africa

FORINT — Hungary

FRANC — Algeria, Austria, Belgian Congo, Belgium, Cambodia, Cameroon, Comoro Islands, Danish West Indies, Ecuador, France, French Equatorial Africa, French Oceania, French Somaliland, French West Africa, Guadeloupe, Hungary, Luxembourg, Madagascar, Martinique, Monaco, Morocco, New Caledonia, Reunion, St. Pierre and Miquelon, Sweden, Switzerland, Togo, Tunisia

FRANCO — Dominican Republic

FRANG — Luxembourg

FRANK (Franken) — Belgium, Liechtenstein, Switzerland

FRANKA ARI — Albania

FUANG — Siam (Thailand)

FUN — Korea

GERSH — Ethiopia

GHIRSH — Egypt, Hejaz, Nejd, Saudi Arabia, Sudan

GOURDE — Haiti

GROAT — Great Britain

GROSCHEN — Austria

GROSZ (Grosze, Groszy) — Poland

GUERCHE — Egypt

GULDEN — Curaçao, Danzig, Netherlands, Netherlands East Indies

HABIBI — Afghanistan

HALALA — Yemen

HALER (Halierov, Halere, Haleru) — Bohemia-Moravia, Czechoslovakia, Slovakia

HAO — China, North Vietnam

HELLER — Austria, German East Africa

HSIEN — China

IMADI — Yemen

JINIA (=Guinea) — Egypt, Saudi Arabia

KAPANG — Sarawak

KHARUB — Tunisia

KOPEJEK — Tuva

KOPEK — Germany, Russia

KORI — Junagadh, Kutch

KORONA — Hungary

KORUNA (Koruny, Korun) — Bohemia-Moravia, Czechoslovakia, Slovakia

KRAJCZAR — Hungary

KRAN — see QIRAN

KREUZER — Austria

KRONA (Kronor) — Sweden

KRONA (Kronur) — Iceland

KRONE (Kronen) — Austria, Liechtenstein

KRONE (Kroner) — Denmark, Greenland, Norway

KROON (Krooni) — Estonia

KUNA (Kune) — Croatia

KURUŞ — Turkey

LARIN (Lari) — Maldive Islands

LATS (Lati) — Latvia

LEI — Romania (see LEU)

LEK (Leku, Lekë) — Albania

LEMPIRA — Honduras

LEPTON (Lepta) — Crete, Greece

LEU (Lei) — Romania

LEV (Leva) — Bulgaria

LI —China, Chinese Turkestan, Manchukuo

LIANG — China, Chinese Turkestan

LIBRA — Peru

LIRA (Lire) — Eritrea, Italian Somaliland, Italy, San Marino, Syria, Turkey, Vatican City

LITAS (Litu, Litai) — Lithuania

MACE — China, Chinese Turkestan

MACUTA — Angola

MARAVEDIS (Maravedi) — Spain

MARK — Estonia, Germany, German New Guinea

MARKKA (Markkaa) — Finland

MATONA — Ethiopia

MAZUNA — Morocco

MEI — China

MELGAREJO — Bolivia

WORLD COIN DENOMINATIONS

MIL — Hong Kong, Israel, Palestine
MILESIMA — Spain
MILLIEME — Egypt
MILREIS (1000 Reis) — Brazil, Portugal
MISCAL — Chinese Turkestan
MOHAR — Nepal
MOHUR — India, India Native States
MONGO — Mongolia
MUN — Korea

ONZA — Costa Rica
ØRE — Denmark, Faeroe Islands, Greenland, Norway
ÖRE — Sweden

PAHLAVI — Persia
PAI — Hyderabad
PAISA (Paise) — Afghanistan, India Native States, Nepal
PARA — Egypt, Hejaz, Sudan, Turkey
—— (Pare) — Montenegro, Serbia, Yugoslavia
PATACA — Timor
PENCE — see PENNY
PENGÖ — Hungary
PENNI (Penniä) — Finland
PENNY (Pence) — Australia, British Guiana, British West Africa, Ceylon, Fiji, Great Britain, Ireland, Jamaica, New Brunswick, New Guinea, New Zealand, Nova Scotia, South Africa, Southern Rhodesia
PERPER (Perpera) — Montenegro
PESA — German East Africa
PESETA — Peru, Puerto Rico, Spain, Viscayan Republic
PESSA — Lahej
PESO — Argentina, Bolivia, Cambodia, Chile, Colombia, Costa Rica, Cuba, Dominican Republic, Guatemala, Honduras, Mexico, Paraguay, Philippines, Puerto Rico, Salvador, Uruguay
PFENNIG — Danzig, German New Guinea, Germany
PIASTRE — Cambodia, Cyprus, Egypt, French Cochin China, French Indo-China, Lebanon, Sudan, Syria, Tonkin, Tunisia, Turkey
PICE — Bhutan, East Africa, India, India Native States, Mombasa, Pakistan
PIE — Baroda
POND — South African Republic
POUND — Great Britain, South Africa
PRUTA (Prutot) — Israel
PUFFIN — Lundy
PUL — Afghanistan, Khiva
PYSA — Zanzibar

QINDAR ARI — Albania
QINDAR LEKU — Albania
QIRAN — Afghanistan, Persia
QUARTO — Catalonia (Spain)
QUETZAL — Guatemala

RAPPEN — Switzerland
REAAL — Curaçao
REAL (Reales) — Chile, Colombia, Dominican Republic, Ecuador, Guatemala, Honduras, Mexico, Paraguay, Peru, Salvador, Spain, Venezuela
REICHSMARK — Germany
REICHSPFENNIG — Germany
REIS — Azores, Brazil, Portugal, Portuguese India
RENTENPFENNIG — Germany
RIAL — Morocco, Persia

RIGSDALER — Denmark
RIKSDALER — Sweden
RIN — Japan
RIYAL — Saudi Arabia
RUBLE — Armavir, Khiva, Khwarezm, Russia
RUPEE — Afghanistan, Bhutan, Burma, India, India Native States, Mauritius, Mombasa, Nepal, Pakistan, Seychelles, Tibet
RUPIA — Italian Somaliland, Portuguese India
RUPIE (Rupien) — German East Africa
RYAL — Hejaz, Iraq, Muscat and Oman, Nejd, Zanzibar

SANAR — Afghanistan
SANTIMS (Santimi, Santimu) — Latvia
SAPEQUE — Annam, French Cochin China, French Indo-China
SATANG — Siam (Thailand)
SCHILLING — Austria
SCUDO — Bolivia, Peru
SEN — China, Japan, Netherlands East Indies
SENT (Senti) — Estonia
SHAHI — Afghanistan, Persia
SHILLING — Australia, British West Africa, Cyprus, East Africa, Fiji, Great Britain, Ireland, Jersey, New Guinea, New Zealand, South Africa, Southern Rhodesia
SHO — Tibet
SKARUNG (Skar) — Tibet
SKILLING — Denmark, Norway
SOL (Soles) — Peru
SOVEREIGN — Australia, Canada, Great Britain, India, South Africa
SPECIEDALER — Norway
SRANG — Tibet
STOTINKA (Stotinki) — Bulgaria
STUIVER — Curaçao
SUCRE — Ecuador
SUELDO — Bolivia

TAEL — China, Chinese Turkestan
TALARI — Ethiopia
TALLERO — Eritrea
TANGA — Portuguese India
TANGKA — Tibet
TENGA — Bukhara, Khiva
THALER (or Taler) — Austria, Liechtenstein
TICAL — Thailand (Siam)
TILLA — Afghanistan, Bukhara
TOMAN — Daghistan, Persia
TRADE DOLLAR — Japan, United States
TRAMBIYA — Kutch
TUKHRIK — Mongolia

VENEZOLANO — Venezuela
VEREINSTHALER — Austria, Liechtenstein

WARK — Ethiopia
WARN — Korea
WEN — China, Chinese Turkestan
WHAN — Korea
WON — Korea

XU — North Vietnam

YANG — Korea
YEN — Japan
YUAN — China

ZLOTY (Zlote, Zlotych) — Poland

INDEX

INDEX

INDEX